Christianity and Education in Modern China

Christianity and Education in Modern China

Edited by
Wong Man Kong and George Kam Wah Mak

Hong Kong University Press
The University of Hong Kong
Pok Fu Lam Road
Hong Kong
https://hkupress.hku.hk

© 2025 Hong Kong University Press

ISBN 978-988-8842-99-5 (*Hardback*)

All rights reserved. No portion of this publication may be reproduced or transmitted in any form or by any means, electronic or mechanical, including photocopying, recording, or any information storage or retrieval system, without prior permission in writing from the publisher.

British Library Cataloguing-in-Publication Data
A catalogue record for this book is available from the British Library.

Digitally printed

Contents

List of Figures and Tables   vii
Acknowledgments   viii
Introduction   1
    WONG Man Kong and George Kam Wah MAK

Part One: The Contexts

1. Everything Is My Concern: Characterizing Modern Chinese Education   17
   Thomas H. C. LEE
2. The Crisis of Mission Education in Republican China, 1922–1929: The Case of Harold Henry Rowley   34
   Brian STANLEY

Part Two: Christian Educators

3. "Going Forth to Teach, We Shall Have Learnt": F. S. Drake at Shantung Christian University/Cheeloo University and His Embrace of Chinese Culture   53
   Wai Luen KWOK
4. Christianity and Medical Education in China in the Second World War: Gordon King and His Wartime Adventures and the Interconnectedness between China and Hong Kong   75
   WONG Man Kong
5. Christian Efforts in Mass Education of Republican China: Zhang Xueyan and Xie Songgao's Christian Literary Work as Examples   90
   CHEN Jianming
6. An Unfulfilled Ideal: Zhu Jingnong's Educational Ideas and Practices   112
   Jiafeng LIU

Part Three: New Initiatives

7. A Project of National Transformation in China: Yu Rizhang's Promotion of Social Education — 145
   Peter Chen-main WANG

8. A Protestant Response to the Drive for Mass Literacy in Early Republican China: The Phonetic Promotion Committee and Its Work, 1918–1922 — 168
   George Kam Wah MAK

9. A College Student's Rural Journey: Early Sociology and Anthropology in China Seen through Fieldwork on Sichuan's Secret Society — 195
   Di WANG

Part Four: The Legacies

10. Extracting the Essence of Sino-Western Interaction: Insights from the Educational Endeavors of Chinese Christian Colleges — 227
    MA Min

11. A Competitive Advantage in Higher Education: The Practice and Realization of Whole-Person Education at Chung Yuan Christian University — 249
    Leah Yiya LEE

12. Developing the Whole Person: Revisiting the History and Mission of Christian Higher Education in Asia — 266
    Wai Ching Angela WONG

List of Contributors — 287

Index — 290

List of Figures and Tables

Figures

Figure 2.1: H. H. Rowley, British Baptist missionary at Shantung Christian University, 1922–1929 ... 40

Figure 4.1: Gordon King and his colleagues from the Shanghai Medical College, Koloshan (Geleshan 歌樂山), Sichuan Province ... 85

Tables

Table 6.1: The structures of the manuscript and the Commercial Press edition of *Seven Lectures on Modern Educational Thoughts* ... 126

Table 7.1: Programs of the Chinese YMCA Lecture Department, October 1915–September 1916 ... 155

Table 8.1: Members of the Phonetic Promotion Committee (PPC) as the China Continuation Committee's (CCC) Special Committee (1918–1922) ... 178

Acknowledgments

Each author has included specific acknowledgments in his or her own chapter. We, as the editors of this volume, would like to express our heartfelt gratitude to Tin Ka Ping Foundation for its financial support to the publication of this volume, the Centre for Sino-Christian Studies of the Hong Kong Baptist University for administrative support, Wu Hui Ascar and Vivian Ko for producing the draft translations of Chapters 5, 6, and 10 (Chapter 5: Wu and Ko; Chapters 6 and 10: Wu), and Alex Lun Ching Ngan for copyediting the manuscripts and preparing the index of this volume.

We are also deeply thankful to Dr. Kenneth Yung at Hong Kong University Press for his patience and guidance. The constructive feedback of the anonymous reviewers on the manuscripts of this volume is truly appreciated.

Last but not least, we wish to thank the United Board for Christian Higher Education in Asia for permission to reproduce the photo entitled "Faculty group in 1920" in its archives as the cover image of this volume.

Wong Man Kong and George Kam Wah Mak

Introduction

Wong Man Kong and George Kam Wah Mak

Challenges from Western imperialism since the nineteenth century have caused changes in the meanings of higher education in Asia, leading to a stronger orientation towards a Westernized approach to scholarship and education. This Westernized approach could be characterized as one promoting secularization of public-funded education while allowing religion to be taught at private schools.[1] However, the waves of decolonization and independence movements in the region demanded that universities and colleges should provide an education compatible with the cause of defining a national identity, which usually warranted some degree of identification with the traditional values, history, and culture of their countries.[2] We may say that in modern times, religious faith and values—traditional and modern alike—coexisted, perhaps paradoxically, along with secularism in the development of higher education in Asia. As part of Asia, China witnessed similar trends in its education development. While Christian missionaries were among those who introduced Western education systems to China, their religion had a mixed reception in the country during the late Qing and Republican periods. It is worth asking under such a circumstance why and how Christianity could still be a relevant factor in the modernization of Chinese education.

---

1. "Editorial," *Chinese Recorder* 61, no. 9 (September 1930): 543.
2. Wang Gungwu, "Universities in Transition in Asia," in *Bind us in Time: Nation and Civilisation in Asia* (Singapore: Times Academic Press, 2002), 286–302. He at first articulated his views in the 1960s and 1970s about the circumstances from which Asian higher education had developed its own salient features. See his "University in Relationship to Traditional Culture," in *Asian Workshop on Higher Education: Addresses, Lectures, Reports and Working Papers*, ed. Li Choh-ming (Hong Kong: Chinese University of Hong Kong, 1969), 21–32; "The University and the Community," in *Proceedings of the Second Asian Workshop on Higher Education*, ed. Rayson Huang (Singapore: McGraw-Hill Far Eastern Publishers Ltd and Association of Southeast Asian Institutions of Higher Education, 1971), 17–29.

Christian roles in the history of modern Chinese education have captured the ongoing attention from scholars of mission studies, Christianity in China and modern Chinese history since the second half of the twentieth century. Nonetheless, in reviewing the historiography of this field of study, one finds that the religion's involvement in the higher education sector has been the most studied aspect. Thanks to the vision of the United Board for Christian Colleges in China (subsequently known as the United Board for Christian Higher Education in Asia), a set of histories of individual Protestant colleges in pre-1950 China was produced during the third quarter of the century; the first book was published in 1954 and the last in 1974.[3] Upon the Chinese government's ordering of the reorganization of China's higher education sector, all Christian colleges left China for good. The United Board invited some education missionaries who had held leading positions at these colleges to write their institutional histories. K. C. Liu (Liu Guangjing 劉廣京) perceptively saw the historical significance of this set of the colleges' histories, as revealed in his review essay in *The Journal of Asian Studies* published in 1960. He asserted that these volumes offered evidence that "the Christian colleges played a vital part in the development of the missionary movement in China and in Chinese cultural change in general."[4] However, neither this set of history books nor Liu's review elicited any positive response in mainland China at that time. Instead, the official line was a categorical refusal of anything positive from missionaries who were considered the running dogs of Western imperialism.[5]

In the English-speaking world, Jessie Lutz wrote the first landmark study of the history of Christian colleges in China. What attracted her most was that Christian education in China enabled the admirable qualities to be passed on among teachers and subsequently down to the next generations—the students and alumni. This was her motivation to complete a doctoral thesis entitled "The Role of the Christian Colleges in Modern China before 1928." She remarked,

---

3. The United Board for Christian Colleges in China published seven institutional history books during the 1950s: R. Scott, *Fukien Christian University: A Historical Sketch* (1954); M. Lamberton, *St. John's University, Shanghai, 1879–1951* (1955); C. H. Corbett, *Shantung Christian University* (1955); C. B. Day, *Hangchow University, a Brief History* (1955); W. B. Nance, *Soochow University* (1956); M. S. C. Thurston and R. M. Chester, *Ginling College* (1956); L. E. Wallace, *Hwa Nan College: The Woman's College of South China* (1956). The United Board for Christian Higher Education in Asia published three more institutional history books: D. E. Edwards, *Yenching University* (1959); J. L. Coe, *Huachung University* (1962); L. C. Walmsley, *West China Union University* (1974). It is noteworthy that *History of the University of Shanghai* by J. B. Hipps was published in 1964 not by the United Board but the university's board of founders.
4. Kwang-Ching Liu, "Early Christian Colleges in China," *Journal of Asian Studies* 20, no. 1 (1960): 78.
5. For details, see Wong Man Kong, "History Matters: Christian Studies in China since 1949," *Monumenta Serica* 58, no. 1 (2010): 335–56.

Three Christian ideals which for me make it superior to other religions are the concepts of love and forgiveness, charity, and respect for the dignity of the individual. The Christian colleges exemplified these virtues. Though alumni memoirs do not always mention specific Christian doctrines, they reveal cherished memories of devout and dedicated Christian teachers. The personal attention given to individual students and the teachers' readiness to help them shine through.[6]

Her dissertation ends at the point in history where "most missionaries at the Christian colleges passed administrative control to their Chinese colleagues." She thus considered it to be only half completed. She extended the scope to include "the story in 1928 at the zenith of nationalism in China and its impact on the colleges and carried it to 1950."[7] Her book is now considered to be a definitive piece of scholarship on the history of Chinese Christian colleges. Subsequently, a few more historical works were published on different Christian colleges, with Yenching University being the most popular choice.[8]

The 1980s saw the beginning of a change in historiography. Zhang Kaiyuan 章開沅 was instrumental in creating a paradigm shift in the historical study of Christian colleges in China among scholars in mainland China. It began in 1985 when James T. C. Liu (Liu Zijian 劉子健) visited China and convinced Zhang to take the lead. Also from Princeton University, Arthur Waldron visited China to carry on the preparation work in 1987.[9] The first international symposium on the history of Christian colleges in China took place in 1989, out of which Zhang Kaiyuan and Arthur Waldron edited a volume entitled *Zhong xi wenhua yu jiaohui daxue* 中西文化與教會大學 (*Christian Universities and Chinese-Western Cultures*), which was

---

6. Wong Man Kong, "An Interview with Jessie Gregory Lutz: Historian of Chinese Christianity," *International Bulletin of Missionary Research* 30, no. 1 (2006): 38.
7. Wong, "An Interview with Lutz," 39.
8. See Philip West, *Yenching University and Sino-Western Relations, 1916–1952* (Cambridge, MA: Harvard University Press, 1976). Monographs on Yenching's individual staff members include Susan Egan Chan, *A Latterday Confucian: Reminiscences of William Hung, (1893–1980)* (Cambridge, MA: Harvard University Press, 1987); Shaw Yu-ming, *An American Missionary in China: John Leighton Stuart and Chinese-American Relations* (Cambridge, MA: Council on East Asian Studies, Harvard University, 1992), and Chu Sin-Jan, *Wu Leichuan: A Confucian-Christian in Republican China.* (New York: Peter Lang, 1995). There are also edited volumes that focus on Yenching, for example Arthur Lewis Rosenbaum, ed., *New Perspectives on Yenching University, 1916–1952: A Liberal Education for a New China* (Chicago: Imprint Publications, 2012). Historical works on the other Christian colleges include Dong Wong, *Managing God's Higher Learning: U.S.-China Cultural Encounter and Canton Christian College (Lingnan University), 1888–1952* (Lanham: Lexington Books, 2008); Pang Shuk Man [Peng Shumin 彭淑敏], *Minguo Fujian Xiehe Daxue zhi yanjiu: yi shizi he caiwu weili (1916–1949)* 民國福建協和大學之研究：以師資和財務為例 (1916–1949) (New Taipei: Taiwan Christian Literature Council, 2013).
9. Zhang Kaiyuan, *Chuanbo yu zhigen: Jidujiao yu Zhong xi wenhua jiaoliu lunji* 傳播與植根：基督教與中西文化交流論集 (Guangzhou: Guangdong renmin chubanshe 廣東人民出版社, 2005), 20.

published in 1991.[10] This book symbolizes the departure of the previous official rhetoric of Christianity as an instrument of Western imperialism. It offers a mix of perspectives, considering such significant factors as historiography, nationalism, wars, senior administrators, and academics, and many other topics.

Subsequently, Zhang edited similar volumes to provide the necessary momentum,[11] and he co-edited with Ma Min 馬敏 a book series called "Zhongguo jiaohui daxue shi yanjiu 中國教會大學史研究" (Studies in the History of Christian Universities in China), which included the Chinese translations of the institutional histories of the Christian colleges that the United Board produced and several original historical monographs. Examples of the translations include Ma Min's translation of John L. Coe's *Huachung University* and Jiafeng Liu's (Liu Jiafeng 劉家峰) translation of Clarence Burton Day's *Hangchow University: A Brief History*.[12] Examples of the monographs include Xu Yihua 徐以驊 investigation of the religious curriculum at St. John's University and Shi Jinghuan's 史靜寰 study of Calvin Wilson Mateer and John Leighton Stuart's activities as missionary educators.[13] Apart from editing scholarly volumes, Zhang charted out new frontiers in the field. A student at the University of Nanking, one of the Christian colleges in Republican China, Zhang had personal knowledge of his mentor M. Searle Bates, an education missionary teaching at the university who witnessed the Nanjing Massacre.[14] From Bates and his associates, Zhang at first identified numerous historical sources written by missionaries to reveal the massacre's salient features.[15] He then expanded his scope of research into missionaries' papers for further studies in the history of Christian higher education and other related topics.[16]

Peter Tze Ming Ng (Wu Ziming 吳梓明), a Hong Kong scholar joining this journey of historical revisionism, deserves a special mention. He was one of the

---

10. Zhang Kaiyuan and Arthur Waldron, eds., *Zhong xi wenhua yu jiaohui daxue: shou jie Zhongguo jiaohui daxue shi xueshu yantaohui lunwenji* 中西文化與教會大學：首屆中國教會大學史學術研討會論文集 (Wuhan: Hubei jiaoyu chubanshe 湖北教育出版社, 1991).
11. For example, Zhang Kaiyuan, ed., *Wenhua chuanbo yu jiaohui daxue* 文化傳播與教會大學 (Hankou: Hubei jiaoyu chubanshe, 1996).
12. John L. Coe, *Huazhong Daxue* 華中大學, trans. Ma Min (Zhuhai Shi: Zhuhai chubanshe 珠海出版社, 1999); Clarence Burton Day, *Zhijiang Daxue* 之江大學, trans. Liu Jiafeng (Zhuhai Shi: Zhuhai chubanshe, 1999).
13. Xu Yihua, *Jiaoyu yu zongjiao: zuo wei chuanjiao meijie de Sheng Yuehan Daxue* 教育與宗教：作為傳教媒介的聖約翰大學 (Zhuhai Shi: Zhuhai chubanshe, 1999); Shi Jinghuan, *Di Kaowen yu Situ Leideng: Xifang Xinjiao chuanjiaoshi zai Hua jiaoyu huodong yanjiu* 狄考文與司徒雷登：西方新教傳教士在華教育活動研究 (Zhuhai Shi: Zhuhai chubanshe, 1999).
14. Zhang, *Chuanbo yu zhigen*, 37–63.
15. Zhang Kaiyuan, *Tianli nan rong: Meiguo chuanjiaoshi yan zhong de Nanjing datusha (1937–1938)* 天理難容：美國傳教士眼中的南京大屠殺 (1937–1938) (Nanjing: Nanjing Daxue chubanshe 南京大學出版社, 1999).
16. Zhang Kaiyuan, *Meiguo chuanjiaoshi de riji yu shuxin* 美國傳教士的日記與書信 (Nanjing: Jiangsu renmin chubanshe 江蘇人民出版社, 2005).

participants in the 1989 conference. Carrying on the spirit of the conference, Ng kept a robust connection with scholars in mainland China while producing several entrepreneurial deliverables. Between the 1990s and 2000s, Ng edited a conference proceeding and a series of ground-breaking monographs,[17] completed a cataloguing project for historical archives of Christian colleges in China,[18] and published one single-authored and one co-authored books.[19]

In Taiwan, Lin Zhiping 林治平 organized a conference to discuss the role of Christian colleges in the modernization of China in 1991, echoing his longtime scholarly interest in Christianity's role in the Chinese search for modernization since the late imperial era. He invited leading historians in the field to discuss their findings and senior administrators of the Christian colleges in Taiwan and Hong Kong to examine the educational ideals of their institutions through their history, which resulted in a conference proceeding offering invaluable insights into issues confronting the management of Christian education in Chinese social contexts from the past and present perspectives.[20]

Peter Chen-main Wang (Wang Chengmian 王成勉), another eminent historian of Chinese Christianity in Taiwan, is noteworthy for his efforts to promote research on Christian elementary and secondary education in modern China. With the encouragement of K. C. Liu, Wang organized a conference entitled "Setting the Roots Right: Christian Education in China and Taiwan" in 2006. This conference represented a breakthrough in scholarship on the history of the Christian involvement in modern Chinese education, because the conference participants, instead of

---

17. Wu Ziming, ed., *Zhongguo jiaohui daxue lishi wenxian yantaohui lunwenji* 中國教會大學歷史文獻研討會論文集 (Hong Kong: Chinese University Press, 1995). The series edited by Ng is known as "Christian education and Chinese society," published by Fujian jiaoyu chubanshi 福建教育出版社. The series include Huang Xinxian 黃新憲, *Jidujiao jiaoyu yu Zhongguo shehui bianqian* 基督教教育與中國社會變遷 (1996); Wu Ziming and Tao Feiya 陶飛亞, *Jidujiao daxue yu guoxue yanjiu* 基督教大學與國學研究 (1998); Shi Jinghuan and Wang Lixin 王立新, *Jidujiao jiaoyu yu Zhongguo zhishi fenzi* 基督教教育與中國知識分子 (1998); Xu Yihua, *Jiaohui daxue yu shenxue jiaoyu* 教會大學與神學教育 (1999); Wu Ziming, *Jidujiao daxue Huaren xiaozhang yanjiu* 基督教大學華人校長研究 (1999); Zhu Feng 朱峰, *Jidujiao yu jindai Zhongguo nüzi gaodeng jiaoyu: Jinling nü da yu Huanan nü da bijiao yanjiu* 基督教與近代中國女子高等教育：金陵女大與華南女大比較研究 (2002); Liu Jiafeng and Liu Tianlu 劉天路, *Kang Ri zhanzheng shiqi de Jidujiao daxue* 抗日戰爭時期的基督教大學 (2003).
18. For details, see Peter Tze Ming Ng (Wu Ziming 吳梓明), "Historical Archives in Chinese Christian Colleges from before 1949," *International Bulletin of Missionary Research* 20, no. 3 (July 1996): 106–8.
19. Peter Tze Ming Ng, Xu Yihua, Shi Jinghuan, and Leung Yuen Sang, *Changing Paradigms of Christian Higher Education in China, 1888–1950* (New York: E. Mellen Press, 2002); Wu Ziming, *Jiduzongjiao yu Zhonguo daxue jiaoyu* 基督宗教與中國大學教育 (Beijing: Zhongguo shehui kexue chubanshe 中國社會科學出版社, 2003).
20. Lin Zhiping, ed., *Zhongguo Jidujiao daxue lunwenji* 中國基督教大學論文集 (Taipei: Cosmic Light Media Center, 1992).

focusing on Christian higher education, explored the religion's roles in primary and secondary education in mainland China, Taiwan, and Hong Kong, a hitherto largely neglected theme in the field that had attracted only a few scholars.[21] The conference proceeding, edited by Wang, comprises nineteen research articles that explored the history of Christian elementary and secondary schools in modern Chinese societies from various approaches and perspectives, such as pedagogical materials, biographical studies, institutional history, intellectual history, and regional studies.[22] In the proceeding's opening chapter, Lutz indicated that the history and influence of Christian primary and secondary schools in modern China is a fruitful subject for study, considering that

> In 1925, the number of students in Christian higher primary and middle schools was over fifty thousand, while that claimed for the Christian colleges was less than four thousand. Unlike the colleges, which were concentrated in major cities and treaty ports, the secondary schools could be also found in county seats and market towns throughout China. They were more pervasive and drew from a broader clientele than the colleges.[23]

Several books on Christian primary and secondary education in pre-1949 China were subsequently published, which indicated the increasing attention to this area. They include the conference proceeding *Jidujiao yu Zhongguo jindai zhongdeng jiaoyu* 基督教與中國近代中等教育 (Christianity and Secondary Education in Modern China), edited by Yin Wenjuan 尹文涓,[24] studies of Longheu Girls' School in Bao'an 寶安 and St. Hilda's School for Girls in Wuchang 武昌,[25] and Bai Limin's 白莉民 monograph on the Chinese Christian educator Wang Hengtong 王亨統.[26]

If one would identify the United Board as a key mover behind the earliest historical studies in Christian education in modern China and K. C. Liu as a pioneering voice stressing the importance of these studies, one could then argue that the history of the Christian involvement in modern Chinese education has become a legitimate

---

21. In addition to Judith Liu and Donald P. Kelly's article on St. Hilda's School for Girls in Wuchang 武昌 (1996) and Heidi A. Ross's article on McTyeire School in Shanghai (2001), only three monographs published between 1995 and 1999 were cited by Wang in the preface to the conference proceeding. Wang Chengmian, ed., *Jiang gen zha hao: Jidu zongjiao zai Hua jiaoyu de jiantao* 將根紮好：基督宗教在華教育的檢討 (Taipei: Liming wenhua shiye 黎明文化事業, 2007), vii.
22. Wang, ed., *Jiang gen zha hao*.
23. Wang, ed., *Jiang gen zha hao*, 2.
24. Yin Wenjuan, ed., *Jidujiao yu Zhongguo jindai zhongdeng jiaoyu* 基督教與中國近代中等教育 (Shanghai: Shanghai renmin chubanshe 上海人民出版社, 2007).
25. Tang Dongmei 唐冬眉 and Wang Yanxia 王豔霞, *Qianzhen Nüxiao* 虔貞女校 (Guangzhou: Huacheng chubanshe 花城出版社, 2015); Judith Liu, *Foreign Exchange: Counterculture Behind the Walls of St. Hilda's School for Girls, 1929–1937* (Bethlehem: Lehigh University Press, 2011).
26. Bai Limin, *Fusion of East and West: Children, Education, and a New China, 1902–1915* (Leiden: Brill, 2019).

area of study, since it is deemed as a valid lens to reveal the inner workings of new initiatives by educators and students, institutions and sponsoring bodies, as well as values and ideals in the development of curriculum and extra-curricular activities, in modern Chinese societies. Nevertheless, it has been fifteen years since the publication of Daniel H. Bays and Ellen Widmer's edited volume, *China's Christian Colleges: Cross-cultural Connections, 1900–1950*, which represents the results of the latest collaborative effort in the area.[27] This suggests that it is time to revisit Christianity's roles in the development of Chinese modern education, particularly expanding the scope of research beyond formal education.

The present volume originates from the conference "Modern Education in China and Its Impacts: A Historical and Philosophical Investigation," held at the Hong Kong Baptist University in December 2018, co-organized by the university's Centre for Sino-Christian Studies and Department of Religion and Philosophy and sponsored by Tin Ka Ping Foundation. It needs to be stressed that this volume is more than a conference proceeding, since, while including selected papers presented at the conference (i.e., those by Thomas H. C. Lee [Li Hongqi 李弘祺], Brian Stanley, Chen Jianming 陳建明, Jiafeng Liu, Di Wang [Wang Di 王笛], and Ma Min), it has been enriched by new chapters written respectively by Wai Luen Kwok (Guo Weilian 郭偉聯), Wong Man Kong (Huang Wenjiang 黃文江), Peter Chen-main Wang, George Kam Wah Mak (Mai Jinhua 麥金華), Leah Yiya Lee (Li Yiya 李宜涯), and Wai Ching Angela Wong (Huang Huizhen 黃慧貞). Drawing together twelve archive-based studies and interpretive works on salient features of the multifaceted Christian roles in the modern history of education in China, the volume aims to update our understanding of Christianity as a driving force in the development of modern Chinese education by offering original and new insights into the Christian involvement in issues concerning education in modern China, including localization of curriculum, non-formal education, the linkage between education and nation-building, and the advocacy and practice of whole-person education. Moreover, thanks to the background and academic expertise of its contributors, who include scholars of World Christianity, Chinese education, and Chinese Christianity from the United Kingdom, the United States, mainland China, Hong Kong, Macau, and Taiwan, the volume strikes a balance between the Western missionary and Chinese Christian perspectives in telling the story of how Christianity contributed to the development of modern Chinese education, which is rare in existing English-language scholarship on the topic. It is hoped that the volume will provide refreshing perspectives for future research into related subjects.

---

27. Daniel H. Bays and Ellen Widmer, eds., *China's Christian Colleges: Cross-cultural Connections, 1900–1950* (Stanford: Stanford University Press, 2009).

The two chapters in section (1) "The Contexts," offer historical contexts for many if not all chapters that follow. In "Everything is My Concern: Characterizing Modern Chinese Education," Thomas H. C. Lee argues that in China, the notion that all men were equal in terms of ability to understand moral teaching and to internalize it had by the eighteenth century already expanded also to mean that all political and social affairs are every man's responsibility or concern. However, the arrival of Western influences, including the one of Christian missionaries, strengthened the Chinese people's realization that the world of knowledge was broad, and its values diversified and competing. This contributed to the rise of modern Chinese education that is best characterized as "everything is my concern," which according to Lee, means "a broadened world of knowledge and its multifaceted prongs that must be dealt with ... Everything now became relevant, meaningful, and threatening."

Brian Stanley's "The Crisis of Mission Education in Republican China, 1922–1929" presents a discussion of the nature and goals of education in relation to systems of value, particularly the religious and moral systems of value that Protestant missions sought to disseminate through Christian schools, colleges and universities in Republican China. Although the attempt by Christian missions to impose on pupils compulsory attendance at services of Christian worship and lessons of religious education appeared to the Nationalist government as an infringement of national sovereignty and a form of indoctrination, Stanley notes that the Nationalists imposed on educational institutions their own form of compulsory veneration of Sun Yat-sen and his Three Principles of the People. In his chapter, Stanley finds that it is difficult to differentiate authentic education from indoctrination.

With the historical contexts properly addressed, the ensuing two sections offer fresh views on Christian educators and new initiatives. The four chapters in section (2) "Christian Educators," address the life and thoughts of a hitherto under-researched group of education missionaries and Chinese Christian educators, shedding light on how their views on education and educational efforts were informed by as well as responding to their social, cultural and political contexts. Focusing on the life and times of Frederick Seguier Drake at Cheeloo University, Wai Luen Kwok's "'Going Forth to Teach, We Shall Have Learnt': F. S. Drake at Shantung Christian University/Cheeloo University and His Embrace of Chinese Culture" discusses how Chinese culture attracted this education missionary and changed his course of service, showing that the cultural exchange of Christian universities in China is not unidirectional, but rather reciprocal. After his years of service in China and his study of Chinese culture, Drake considered that the Neo-Confucian teaching is a religion much akin to Christianity. He also believed that the Western World could be corrected and saved by the Chinese culture. Gordon King, who also taught at the same university, is the subject of Wong Man Kong's "Christianity and Medical Education in China in the Second World War: Gordon King and His Wartime Adventures and the Interconnectedness between China and Hong Kong." Using relevant archival materials of the Baptist Missionary Society, Wong looks at the twists and turns that Gordon King went through in his involvement of medical education at Cheeloo and subsequently at the University of Hong Kong. Special attention is given to how King contributed to the continuation of studies of the University of Hong Kong's medical students in China after the Japanese occupation of Hong Kong and its significance to the city's social developments in the following decade.

Republican Chinese Christian educators are the subject of the other two chapters in section (2). Chen Jianming's "Christian Efforts in Mass Education of Republican China: Zhang Xueyan and Xie Songgao's Christian Literary Work as Examples" studies the educational careers of Zhang Xueyan 張雪岩 and Xie Songgao 謝頌羔, both being champions of mass education movement in modern China, focusing on the literary outputs published by Zhang under *Tianjia banyuebao* 田家半月報 (*The Christian Farmer*) and Xie's works by the Christian Literature Society for China. Chen argues that both Zhang and Xie believed that mass education was the first step to saving the nation. They advocated integrating mass education into social reforms and rural developments, contributing to the modernity projects under the precarious socio-political reality of China. "An Unfulfilled Ideal: Zhu Jingnong's Educational Ideas and Practices" by Liu Jiafeng gives an original account of the educational career of Zhu Jingnong 朱經農 (Chu Ching-nung; King Chu), who studied in the United States and was deeply influenced by Dewey's educational philosophy. A devout Christian, Chu preached the importance of religion in national education, defending the legitimacy of Christian schools during the anti-Christian movement and the movement to restore educational rights in the 1920s. Loyal to Sun Yat-sen, he integrated the educational purposes of the Three Principles of the People with Western educational theories. On the one hand, Chu advocated the independence of university education and the freedom of thought, opposing the interference from the party-state. On the other hand, he engaged in public administration of education in Hunan Province for more than a decade. His public service, however outstanding in many respects, brought regrets to him in his later years, which, according to Liu, was not uncommon among Republican Chinese intellectuals who embraced the idea that "education saves the country."

The new initiatives discussed in the three chapters of section (3) are taking Christian social education to a higher goal of achieving national transformation, promoting the use of the National Phonetic Script to increase popular literacy level, and the application of knowledge of the Western academic disciplines of sociology and anthropology to fieldwork. Peter Chen-main Wang's "A Project of National Transformation in China: Yu Rizhang's Promotion of Social Education" investigates Yu Rizhang's 余日章 (David Z. T. Yui) efforts in social education, exploring the origin of general education in modern China and illustrating a Christian intellectual's response to his changing context. At the beginning of the twentieth century in China, many Christian elites emerged with outstanding achievements in both church and non-church environments. Like many other intellectuals, they were also alarmed by the decline of their country's national power and tried to find a balanced way to save China through their faith and nationalism. Against this background, Yu, a prominent leader of the YMCA in China with a master's degree in education from Harvard University, distinguished himself by presenting a vision for social education and projects to address the evils to restore the prosperity and power of China. Yu and the YMCA addressed China's troubles at their roots in poverty, weakness, and disorder. By cultivating good character, literacy, and citizenship, the YMCA's educational programs made long-lasting contributions to society and the nation.

Based on archival materials about the Phonetic Promotion Committee held by the Burke Library at Union Theological Seminary in New York, George Kam Wah Mak's chapter "A Protestant Response to the Drive for Mass Education in Early Republican China: The Phonetic Promotion Committee and Its Work, 1918–1922" examines the committee's formation and work from its inception to 1922 when it ceased to be the China Continuation Committee's sub-committee. It illustrates that the committee emerged and operated as an organization of what Daniel H. Bays referred to as the Sino-Foreign Protestant Establishment in early Republican China. The committee's work represents an organized effort of mission-related Chinese Protestant churches to tackle mass illiteracy through means including but not limited to developing materials and methods for teaching the National Phonetic Script, arranging training classes for teachers of the phonetic script, and preparing promotional materials to publicize the phonetic script. In doing so, the committee contributed to tackling a nationwide problem which provided the churches with opportunities to work with the Chinese government and play a constructive role in the nation-building of modern China.

Di Wang's "A College Student's Rural Journey: Early Sociology and Anthropology in China Seen through Fieldwork on Sichuan's Secret Society" focuses on the investigators of rural society in the Republican period, specifically research made through fieldwork on the Gowned Brothers (or, Paoge 袍哥) in 1940s Sichuan. It takes up one such investigator, Shen Baoyuan—a student at Yenching University; her youthful work never became published or recognized. In his chapter, Wang explores how the pioneers of Chinese sociology and anthropology, who called themselves "rural activists," tried to understand rural China. He argues that the developments in those fields in China of the 1920s and 1940s made it possible for us today to understand the contemporary rural problems better. Also, playing an essential role in the Rural Reconstruction and Rural Education Movements in Republican China, the investigators showed us how Western sociology and anthropology were localized to answer "Chinese questions" and solve "Chinese problems."

The final section, "The Legacies," consists of three chapters examining the Christian legacies of higher education in mainland China, Taiwan, and Asia, which are related to the history of the United Board. In his chapter "Extracting the Essence of Sino-Western Interaction: Insights from the Educational Endeavors of Chinese Christian Colleges," Ma Min, former president of the Central China Normal University, assesses the historical roles of Christian colleges in modern China. These colleges were an essential part of modern Chinese higher learning. They played a significant role in propagating Western scientific culture, promoting the Sino-Western cultural exchanges, and accelerating the modernization in China. Ma argues that the historical experience of Christian colleges in China could inform the development of higher education in China nowadays and facilitate its modernization from the perspective of educational development and talent cultivation. This includes highlighting the featured and high-quality education, upholding internationalization and Sino-Western integration, emphasizing faculty team building and talent cultivation, and paying attention to institutionalization and creating an open and harmony campus.

Leah Yiya Lee's "A Competitive Advantage in Higher Education: The Practice and Realization of Whole-Person Education at Chung Yuan Christian University" investigates the advocacy and practice of whole-person education at Chung Yuan Christian University, which was established with the support of the United Board in post-war Taiwan. Lee suggests that Chung Yuan's efforts to implement whole-person education, a hallmark of Christian higher education, help explain why the university, despite being a Christian university, survives and becomes so distinguished in Taiwan, a society which has had a low birth rate and witnessed the proliferation of universities since the mid-1990s.

This book concludes with Wai Ching Angela Wong's "Developing the Whole Person: Revisiting the History and Mission of Christian Higher Education in Asia," which explains how the United Board's programs are designed to achieve holistic education in their different forms nowadays, carrying on the spirit of Christian higher education manifested by its work in Republican China. The United Board has a long history of associating Christian colleges in China before 1951, and it has subsequently expanded to work in fifteen countries and areas in Asia, reaching out to more than eighty higher education institutions today. It included "Christian presence" in its mission statement until 2012 and adopted "whole-person education" to reflect its consideration of the increasingly diverse Asian communities. As revealed in Wong's chapter, since 2015 the commitment "to education that develops the whole person—intellectually, spiritually and ethically" has been part of the United Board's mission statement. Whole-person education has since been an inclusive expression to articulate Christian values, permeating and connecting all the United Board's program priorities and initiatives, including institutional capacity and faculty development in peacebuilding, intercultural religious understanding, and gender equality.

Bibliography

Bai, Limin. *Fusion of East and West: Children, Education, and a New China, 1902–1915*. Leiden: Brill, 2019.

Bays, Daniel H., and Ellen Widmer, eds. *China's Christian Colleges: Cross-cultural Connections, 1900–1950*. Stanford, CA: Stanford University Press, 2009.

Chu, Sin-Jan. *Wu Leichuan: A Confucian-Christian in Republican China*. New York: Peter Lang, 1995.

Coe, John L. *Huachung University*. New York: United Board for Christian Higher Education in Asia, 1962.

Coe, John L. *Huazhong Daxue* 華中大學. Translated by Ma Min 馬敏. Zhuhai Shi: Zhuhai chubanshe 珠海出版社, 1999.

Corbett, Charles Hodge. *Shantung Christian University*. New York: United Board for Christian Colleges in China, 1955.

Day, Clarence Burton. *Hangchow University, a Brief History*. New York: United Board for Christian Colleges in China, 1955.

Day, Clarence Burton. *Zhijiang Daxue* 之江大學. Translated by Liu Jiafeng 劉家峰. Zhuhai Shi: Zhuhai chubanshe, 1999.

"Editorial." *Chinese Recorder* 61, no. 9 (September 1930): 543.

Edwards, Dwight Woodbridge. *Yenching University*. New York: United Board for Christian Colleges in China, 1959.

Egan, Susan Chan. *A Latterday Confucian: Reminiscences of William Hung (1893–1980)*. Cambridge, MA: Harvard University Press, 1987.

Hipps, John Burder. *History of the University of Shanghai*. N.p.: Board of Founders of the University of Shanghai, 1964.

Huang, Xinxian 黃新憲. *Jidujiao jiaoyu yu Zhongguo shehui bianqian* 基督教教育與中國社會變遷. Fuzhou: Fujian jiaoyu chubanshe 福建教育出版社, 1996.

Lamberton, Mary. *St. John's University, Shanghai, 1879–1951*. New York: United Board for Christian Colleges in China, 1955.

Lin, Zhiping 林治平, ed. *Zhongguo Jidujiao daxue lunwenji* 中國基督教大學論文集. Taipei: Cosmic Light Media Center, 1992.

Liu, Jiafeng 劉家峰, and Liu Tianlu 劉天路. *Kang Ri zhanzheng shiqi de Jidujiao daxue* 抗日戰爭時期的基督教大學. Fuzhou: Fujian jiaoyu chubanshe, 2003.

Liu, Judith. *Foreign Exchange: Counterculture Behind the Walls of St. Hilda's School for Girls, 1929–1937*. Bethlehem: Lehigh University Press, 2011.

Liu, Judith, and Donald. P. Kelly. "'An Oasis in a Heathen Land': St. Hilda's School for Girls, Wuchang, 1928–1936." In *Christianity in China: From the Eighteenth Century to the Present*, edited by Daniel Bays, 228–42. Stanford, CA: Stanford University Press, 1996.

Liu, Kwang-Ching. "Early Christian Colleges in China." *Journal of Asian Studies* 20, no. 1 (1960): 71–78.

Nance, W. B. *Soochow University*. New York: United Board for Christian Colleges in China, 1956.

Ng, Peter Tze Ming [Wu Ziming 吳梓明]. "Historical Archives in Chinese Christian Colleges from before 1949." *International Bulletin of Missionary Research* 20, no. 3 (July 1996): 106–8.

Ng, Peter Tze Ming, Xu Yihua 徐以驊, Shi Jingghuan 史靜寰, and Leung Yuen Sang [Liang Yuansheng 梁元生]. *Changing Paradigms of Christian Higher Education in China, 1888–1950*. New York: E. Mellen Press, 2002.

Pang, Shuk Man [Peng Shumin 彭淑敏]. *Minguo Fujian Xiehe Daxue zhi yanjiu: yi shizi he caiwu weili (1916–1949)* 民國福建協和大學之研究：以師資和財務為例 (1916–1949). New Taipei: Taiwan Christian Literature Council, 2013.

Rosenbaum, Arthur Lewis, ed. *New Perspectives on Yenching University, 1916–1952: A Liberal Education for a New China*. Chicago: Imprint Publications, 2012.

Ross, Heidi A. "Purposes of Education for the Shanghai McTyeire School for Girls." In *Education, Culture, and Identity in Twentieth-Century China*, edited by Glen Peterson, Ruth Hayhoe, and Yongning Liu, 375–402. Ann Arbor: University of Michigan Press, 2001.

Scott, Roderick. *Fukien Christian University: A Historical Sketch*. New York: United Board for Christian Colleges in China, 1954.

Shaw, Yu-ming. *An American Missionary in China: John Leighton Stuart and Chinese-American Relations*. Cambridge, MA.: Council on East Asian Studies, Harvard University, 1992.

Shi, Jinghuan 史靜寰. *Di Kaowen yu Situ Leideng: Xifang Xinjiao chuanjiaoshi zai Hua jiaoyu huodong yanjiu* 狄考文與司徒雷登：西方新教傳教士在華教育活動研究. Zhuhai Shi: Zhuhai chubanshe, 1999.

Shi, Jinghuan 史靜寰, and Wang Lixin 王立新. *Jidujiao jiaoyu yu Zhongguo zhishi fenzi* 基督教教育與中國知識分子. Fuzhou: Fujian jiaoyu chubanshe, 1998.

Tang, Dongmei 唐冬眉, and Wang Yanxia 王豔霞. *Qianzhen Nüxiao* 虔貞女校. Guangzhou: Huacheng chubanshe 花城出版社, 2015.

Thurston, Matilda S. Calder, and Ruth Miriam Chester. *Ginling College*. New York: United Board for Christian Colleges in China, 1956.

Wang, Chengmian 王成勉, ed. *Jiang gen zha hao: Jidu zongjiao zai Hua jiaoyu de jiantao* 將根紮好：基督宗教在華教育的檢討. Taipei: Liming wenhua shiye 黎明文化事業, 2007.

Wang, Gungwu. "Universities in Transition in Asia." In *Bind Us in Time: Nation and Civilisation in Asia*, 286–302. Singapore: Times Academic Press, 2002.

Wang, Gungwu. "University in Relationship to Traditional Culture." In *Asian Workshop on Higher Education: Addresses, Lectures, Reports and Working Papers*, edited by Li Chohming, 21–32. Hong Kong: Chinese University of Hong Kong, 1969.

Wang, Gungwu. "The University and the Community." In *Proceedings of the Second Asian Workshop on Higher Education*, edited by Rayson Huang, 17–29. Singapore: McGraw-Hill Far Eastern Publishers Ltd and Association of Southeast Asian Institutions of Higher Education, 1971.

Wallace, L. Ethel. *Hwa Nan College: The Woman's College of South China*. New York: United Board for Christian Colleges in China, 1956.

Walmsley, Lewis Calvin. *West China Union University*. New York: United Board for Christian Higher Education in Asia West China Union University, 1974.

West, Philip. *Yenching University and Sino-Western Relations, 1916–1952*. Cambridge, MA: Harvard University Press, 1976.

Wong, Dong. *Managing God's Higher Learning: U.S.-China Cultural Encounter and Canton Christian College (Lingnan University), 1888–1952*. Lanham: Lexington Books, 2008.

Wong, Man Kong. "An Interview with Jessie Gregory Lutz: Historian of Chinese Christianity." *International Bulletin of Missionary Research* 30, no. 1 (2006): 38–41.

Wong, Man Kong. "History Matters: Christian Studies in China since 1949." *Monumenta Serica* 58, no. 1 (2010): 335–56.

Wu, Ziming 吳梓明 [Ng, Peter Tze Ming]. *Jiaoyu yu zongjiao: zuo wei chuanjiao meijie de Sheng Yuehan Daxue* 教育與宗教：作為傳教媒介的聖約翰大學. Zhuhai Shi: Zhuhai chubanshe, 1999.

Wu, Ziming 吳梓明. *Jidujiao daxue Huaren xiaozhang yanjiu* 基督教大學華人校長研究. Fuzhou: Fujian jiaoyu chubanshe, 1999.

Wu, Ziming 吳梓明. *Jiduzongjiao yu Zhonguo daxue jiaoyu* 基督宗教與中國大學教育. Beijing: Zhongguo shehui kexue chubanshe 中國社會科學出版社, 2003.

Wu, Ziming 吳梓明, ed. *Zhongguo jiaohui daxue lishi wenxian yantaohui lunwenji* 中國教會大學歷史文獻研討會論文集. Hong Kong: Chinese University Press, 1995.

Wu, Ziming 吳梓明, and Tao Feiya 陶飛亞. *Jidujiao daxue yu guoxue yanjiu* 基督教大學與國學研究. Fuzhou: Fujian jiaoyu chubanshe, 1998.

Xu, Yihua 徐以驊. *Jiaohui daxue yu shenxue jiaoyu* 教會大學與神學教育. Fuzhou: Fujian jiaoyu chubanshe, 1999.

Yin Wenjuan 尹文娟, ed. *Jidujiao yu Zhongguo jindai zhongdeng jiaoyu* 基督教與中國近代中等教育. Shanghai: Shanghai renmin chubanshe 上海人民出版社, 2007.

Zhang, Kaiyuan 章開沅. *Chuanbo yu zhigen: Jidujiao yu Zhong xi wenhua jiaoliu lunji* 傳播與植根：基督教與中西文化交流論集. Guangzhou: Guangdong renmin chubanshe 廣東人民出版社, 2005.

Zhang, Kaiyuan 章開沅. *Meiguo chuanjiaoshi de riji yu shuxin* 美國傳教士的日記與書信 Nanjing: Jiangsu renmin chubanshe 江蘇人民出版社, 2005.

Zhang, Kaiyuan 章開沅. *Tianli nan rong: Meiguo chuanjiaoshi yan zhong de Nanjing datusha (1937–1938)* 天理難容：美國傳教士眼中的南京大屠殺 (1937–1938). Nanjing: Nanjing Daxue chubanshe 南京大學出版社, 1999.

Zhang, Kaiyuan 章開沅, ed. *Wenhua chuanbo yu jiaohui daxue* 文化傳播與教會大學. Hankou: Hubei jiaoyu chubanshe 湖北教育出版社, 1996.

Zhang, Kaiyuan 章開沅, and Arthur Waldron, eds. *Zhong xi wenhua yu jiaohui daxue: shou jie Zhongguo jiaohui daxue shi xueshu yantaohui lunwenji* 中西文化與教會大學：首屆中國教會大學史學術研討會論文集. Wuhan: Hubei jiaoyu chubanshe, 1991.

Zhu, Feng 朱峰. *Jidujiao yu jindai Zhongguo nüzi gaodeng jiaoyu: Jinling nü da yu Huanan nü da bijiao yanjiu* 基督教與近代中國女子高等教育：金陵女大與華南女大比較研究. Fuzhou: Fujian jiaoyu chubanshe, 2002.

Part One: The Contexts

1
Everything Is My Concern
Characterizing Modern Chinese Education[1]

Thomas H. C. Lee

In my book on traditional Chinese education,[2] I presented some preliminary discussion on the famous saying, "Learning is for one's own self," from Confucius's *Analects*. In the Chinese translation of my book, published in 2012,[3] I decided to use it as the book's subtitle and revised here and there to bring it to relief. For traditional China, I think "learning is for one's own self" was the foundation of the Chinese view of learning, or education. Although it is commonly assumed that the civil service examination system has had the largest influence on traditional Chinese education, it is significant that the content of the examinations was the Confucian classics. The classics, in a broad sense, were considered first as fundamental to the education of a moral human being, and second for a stable and orderly society. By "for one's own self," Confucius meant the cultivation of a person's own moral being, as a contrast to "showing off to others": "Men of antiquity studied to improve themselves; men today study to impress others."[4]

---

1. This is a comprehensive revised translation of my Chinese article, "Zhongguo jiaoyu sixiang de jindai zhuanzhe – jianlun jiaoyu sixiangshi de yanjiu quxiang 中國教育思想的近代轉折：簡論教育思想史的研究趨向" [The modern turn of Chinese educational thought—a brief discussion on the direction of research in educational thought], *Peking University Education Review* 北京大學教育評論 13, no. 4 (2015), 31–64.
2. Thomas H. C. Lee, *Education in Traditional China, a History* (Leiden: Brill, 2000).
3. *Xue yi weiji, Chuantong Zhongguo de jiaoyu* 學以爲己：傳統中國的教育 [Learning for one's self: Education in traditional China] (Hong Kong: The Chinese University of Hong Kong Press, 2012). My choice of this idea was to some extent also a result of Wm Theodore de Bary's influence: *Learning for One's Self: Essays on the Individual in Neo-Confucian Thought* (New York: Columbia University Press, 1991).
4. *Analects*, 14 (*Xianwen* 憲問), 24. The translation is taken from D. C. Lau's *The Analects, Sayings of Confucius* (Hong Kong: Chinese University of Hong Kong Press, 2000).

In early times, Chinese education was conceived as the training and preparation of the young men of the noble class for government service. Confucius talked about how these people, called "gentleman" (*junzi* 君子), should take up the duty of governance, but more importantly, he gave it a new definition: a gentleman is one who is accomplished in moral upbringing. By doing so, Confucius introduced a new way of thinking: that morality, not class, should be the defining character, and the government should be made up of morally qualified individuals. This is a meritocratic idea, and it would henceforth become ingrained in Chinese educational thinking as the foundation of an ideal and stable society; hierarchical, yes, but fair and stable. Confucius also argued that individual moral cultivation and perfection should be the criterion for climbing the social ladder. In his view, learning and education lead to moral betterment, and outstanding moral accomplishment is the qualification for political leadership positions.

In terms of educational institutions and their political and social significance, the more salient features are as follows: First, the government had always established schools, continuing a conviction that it was the responsibility of the government to educate young men to perfect their moral behavior (in Confucian sense) so that they could be chosen to serve in the government, to be the model of the ruled. Second, although it was always clear that moral education should be the core concern of government education, it was also always clear that behind the face of moral education, there was an unspoken desire to acquire offices, and this explains the strength and staying power of the civil service examination system in the Chinese society, which lasted for nearly 1,300 years.

Third, the longevity of the examination system defied the ceaseless criticism for almost the entire time the system was in practice. Fourth, the tradition of academies (*shuyuan* 書院) was considered to be the best manifestation of "learning for one's own self." The institution rose in the mid-Tang times and grew widespread after the Song dynasty. However, the history of the academies—particularly, the eventual "officialization" of the institution—became a parody of the practice of traditional Chinese education, especially the state schools managed by the government.[5] By the early Qing times, almost all academies had become indistinct from normal government schools.

---

5. My article, "Chuantong Zhongguo jiaoyü de tese yü fanxing" 傳統中國教育的特色與反省 [The characters of and reflections on traditional Chinese education], cited in note 1, offers a more general discussion on the salient features of traditional Chinese education. This article is now also included as an appendix to my Chinese revised translation of *Education in Traditional China, a History* cited in note 3. Please see also my "Education in Traditional China," in *The Routledge Encyclopedia of Traditional Chinese Culture*, ed. Chan Sin-wai (London and New York: Routledge, 2020), 253.

Although Confucius is the first person to utter "learning for one's own self," the idea did not immediately inspire Chinese thinkers. From Confucius's times to the ninth century, few thinkers cited it, even though it remained a widely held conviction: a good leader or government official should first and foremost be an educated intellectual with moral rectitude as the core of his learning. By the eleventh century, this saying had come to the forefront and became a widely quoted and cherished maxim that lasted through the later centuries. The person who was most instrumental in bringing it into focus is Zhu Xi 朱熹 (1130–1200). Zhu Xi's influence on Chinese education has been only next to Confucius, and he pointedly called attention to "learning for one's own self" as the best representation of Confucian educational thinking and activities. Among his many works to promote education was the academy education, which became the most influential and long-lasting educational institution in China, well into the twentieth century. The academies were founded to teach Confucian classics, with the singular emphasis on individual moral cultivation. He openly admonished the practice of utilitarian learning for the sole purpose of taking and passing the civil service examinations for admission into the officialdom.

Interestingly, Zhu Xi's educational program was adopted by the Mongols, who were then governing China, and his commentaries on the Four Books classics made the state orthodoxy, used as the standard of the examinations! At the same time, as the reading and learning population grew after the rise of printing technology in the eleventh century, Zhu Xi began to feel the need to provide education to the masses, who might not seek to take the imperial examinations. He and his disciples experimented with and promoted popular education through the compilation of primers and elementary texts, composing proclamations explaining government policies and behavioral standards. These often were directed to commoners (mostly peasants). The elementary readers were above all characterized by the emphasis on a person's moral cultivation, including methods of learning. They were obviously geared to influencing a much wider population than a gentlemen's education. The educational narrative was henceforth no longer limited to those studying to take the examination for entering the officialdom.

In the eleventh century when printing technology was put into broad use, the aim of education began to shift, resulting in a reconsideration of its purpose and justification. The shift in educational focus was inevitable because more and more people became knowledgeable about the multiplicity and complexity of society and social changes. A development suffices to reflect how the narrative of education was now changed, and the entire population was considered as the target of education. Thus, starting in the thirteenth century, some villages or rural communities started to establish schools, sometimes named "community schools" (*shexue* 社學). At this point, there was definitely an increasing awareness that commoners also needed education,[6] and by the early Ming dynasty, the Emperor Taizu 太祖 (r. 1368–1398) decreed that "community schools" should be built all over the nation. The elitist educational ideal of "learning for one's own self" thereafter began to transform into education for the broader commoners. Every person should have access to education.

Philosophically, the thinking brought forth by Wang Shouren 王守仁 (Wang Yangming 王陽明, 1472–1529) represented this transition. It is true that in terms of philosophical outlook, he and Zhu Xi were quite different. However, both were concerned with bringing education to the commoners; Wang Souren provided a carefully articulated philosophical foundation for an egalitarian reading of "learning for one's own self," an effort Zhu Xi did not make in as focused a way. Wang's practice was more down to earth, and his official and educational career was more emphatically focused on carrying out the idea that "learning was for everybody." He was also concentrated on expressing the idea that everybody was equally endowed with the ability to acquire morality and to practice it. True to his teaching, many of his students brought his philosophy into practice. They included such scholars as Wang Gen 王艮 (1483–1541), He Xinyin 何心隱 (1517–1579), and even Luo Rufang 羅汝芳 (1515–1588). In this way, they succeeded, paradoxically, in making commoner and egalitarian education an important responsibility for every educated intellectual. In the words of Wang Gen, the purpose of education is to learn the *dao* 道 of "the daily life of the commoners."[7] Thus, by the sixteenth century, thinking on the purpose of education had gradually moved to focus on commoners' moral upbringing. This philosophy was premised on the equality of human ability, especially in terms of moral potential.

At the time, the activities of the Donglin 東林 Academy in Wuxi 無錫 added to the meaning of education, reflecting that for the commoners. The Donglin intellectuals began to mobilize commoners in all kinds of social associations, lecturing them about the nation's political conditions and malaises. They considered that an educated man's most important duty should be to concern himself with the welfare of all humans "all under heaven." The legendary couplet by its leader, Gu Xiancheng 顧憲成 (1550–1612), has been a perennial reminder of what education for them was all about:

---

6. Luo Dajing 羅大經, *Helin yulu* 鶴林玉露 [Jade dew from the forest of cranes], Ming engraved ed, in *Zhongguo jiben gujiku* 中國基本古籍庫 (Beijing: Airusheng shuzihua jishu yanjiu zhongxin 愛如生數字化技術研究中心, 2009), 7/9b. This is almost the first mentioning of a "shexue" (community school) that I can ascertain. Luo was a disciple of Zhu Xi.

7. Wang Gen repeatedly used this expression in his *Xinzhai Wang Xiansheng yulu* 心齋王先生語錄, Ming ed., in *Zhongguo jiben gujiku* 中國基本古籍庫, 1/4a, passim. It is perhaps useful to point out that the attention to "the ethical principles of daily life" (*renlun riyong* 人倫日用) went back to the Southern Song times, found in the writings of Zhu Xi, Chen Chun 陳淳, and so on.

The sound of wind, the sound of rain, and the sound of reading books, all of them I hear; the affairs of my family, the affairs of my country, and the affairs of all under heaven, all of them are my concern.

Mobilizing thousands of farmers or commoners to attend lectures criticizing the government was almost unprecedented and unheard of before this time.[8] Further, such lecture series were often systematically organized, scheduled over a length of time, and members had to sign up and answer roll calls.[9] In short, things had changed enough that the socio-political activities were now organized with the idea that all men were eligible, and that an intellectual's concern should be with every part of society. The universal and egalitarian principle now became the core ideal of education. The organization of all kinds of intellectual and political associations became widespread,[10] and although organizers were at great risk in such endeavors, they evidently believed that they were upholding the very ideal of education: everybody has a responsibility to receive education, and all affairs in the world should be their concern.

The leading thinkers in the Ming-Qing transition, such as Huang Zongxi 黃宗羲 (1610–1695) and Gu Yanwu 顧炎武 (1613–1682), can be said to be seeking to open a new "private sphere" for Chinese intellectuals.[11] Although philosophically their efforts did not succeed, the attempts reflected the opinion of the time. From the early Qing dynasty, in the late seventeenth century, to the middle of the nineteenth century, significant developments included the following: increasingly,

---

8. Doubts have been raised whether Donglin members were indeed able to mobilize so many people to attend their lectures, as they claimed. The Jesuits, who should have witnessed such activities, did not report them. My answer would be that the Donglin leaders obviously believed that this was what they wished to do, and whether they did succeed in doing so was another issue.
9. And even be examined of their performance in the lecture meetings. See p. 88 of my *Education in Traditional China, a History*. See also my "Chu Hsi, Academies, and the Tradition of Private Chianghsüeh," *Han-hsüeh yan-chiu* 漢學研究 2, no. 1 (1984): 301–29.
10. Ono Kazuko 小野和子, *Minki tōsha kō: Tōrintō to Fukusha* 明季黨社考—東林黨と復社 (Kyoto: Tobosha, 1996); this work is now available in Chinese translation, by Li Qing 李慶, *Mingji dangshe kao* 明季黨社考 (Shanghai: Shanghai guji chubanshe, 2006). Xie Guozhen's 謝國楨 *Ming Qing zhiji dangshe yundong kao* 明清之際黨社運動考 (Beijing: Zhonghua Books, 1983, reprint of 1934 Commercial Press ed.) remains the most comprehensive study. See also Zhu Wenjie 朱文杰, *Donglin dang shihua* 東林黨史話 (Shanghai: East China Normal University Press, 1989) and Wang Fansen 王汎森, "Mingmo Qingchu de renpu yü xingguo hui" 明末清初的人譜與省過會, *Bulletin of the Institute of History and Philology of Academia Sinica* 中央研究院歷史語言研究所集刊 63, no. 3 (1993): 679–712.
11. The seeking for a "private" sphere in the late Ming and early Qing times became a widely discussed topic in the past fifty years or so among historians of China. The leading interpreters on this topic are Mizoguchi Yuzō 溝口雄三, Frederick Wakeman, Huang Kewu 黃克武 and Zhang Zhejia 張哲嘉, and others. See also Chen Ruoshui's 陳弱水 (Chen Jo-shui) recent book on social justice in modern China.

academies were built in urban areas,[12] in contrast to the previous tradition of building them in the countryside, in quiet and isolated forest or mountain areas. This was obviously to allow commoners access to their lectures and related activities, especially in the urban environment. Secondly, the emperors regularly seized on the idea of popular proclamations to preach the state ideology. The tradition began in the fifteenth century, with the Ming founder, Zhu Yuanzhang 朱元璋. He not only issued a monstrous proclamation called *The Grand Pronouncements* (*Dagao* 大誥), but he also issued a simplified *Sacred Edict* (*Shengyu* 聖諭), spelling out the behavioral rules that he wanted the subjects to follow. The latter included the following:

> Be filial to your parents.
> Be respectful to your elders.
> Live in harmony with your neighbors.
> Instruct your sons and grandsons.
> Be content with your calling.
> Do no evil.[13]

What he did was repeated by the early Qing emperors. The Kangxi 康熙 Emperor (r. 1661–1722) issued an expanded *Sixteen Maxims* (*Shengyu shiliu tiao* 聖諭十六條) which, amplified again by Emperor Yongzheng 雍正 (r. 1722–1735) as *Amplified Instructions on the Sacred Edict* (*Shengyu guangxun* 聖諭廣訓), served as the nation's ideology that all people were to follow. They were repeatedly reminded of this in meetings organized by the government, such as in village lectures, village libation ceremonies, and the like.[14]

Another development was the accelerated rise of village and community schools. Not only were local governments much more involved in their building, but the powerful gentry class also became more active than before in the movement, so much so that these schools often were the conservative bastions against modern Western thought and influences in general. Meanwhile, the "village compacts" (*xiangyue* 鄉約) that Wang Shouren had promoted since the mid-sixteenth century now also converged with village schools. Some of these, in Guangdong 廣東 for

---

12. See my article cited in note 9. See also Tilemann Grimm, "Academies and Urban Systems in Kwangtung," in *The City in Late Imperial China*, ed. G. William Skinner (Stanford, CA: Stanford University Press, 1977).
13. For a comprehensive examination of the *Sacred Edict*, see Victor Mair, "Language and Ideology in the Sacred Edict," in *Popular Culture in Late Imperial China*, ed. Andrew J. Nathan, David G. Johnson, and Evelyn Sakakida Rawski (Berkeley: University of California Press, 1985). See also Chen Shilong 陳時龍, "Shengyu de Yanyi: Mingdai shidafu dui Taizu *Liuyu* de quanshi" 聖諭的演繹：明代士大夫對太祖六諭的詮釋, *Journal of Anhui Normal University (Humanities and Social Sciences)* 安徽師範大學學報（人文社會科學版）43, no. 5 (2015), 611–21. The article is also available on http://lishisuo.cass.cn/ddyj/ddyj_msyjs/201603/t20160302_2894759.shtml.
14. See https://en.wikipedia.org/wiki/Sacred_Edict_of_the_Kangxi_Emperor#cite_note-6 for a very useful explanation, including that of "village lectures," one that has been rarely studied.

example, even developed into "public bureaus" (*gongju* 公局), a semi-administrative and semi-judicial institution in the countryside and were the center of state-gentry cooperation in maintaining peace and stability.[15]

The third development is the involvement of students in politics. Zhu Yuanzhang erected the "Horizontal Tablet" (*wobei* 臥碑), laying down detailed regulations on how Imperial University students should conduct themselves in schools, which could generally be summarized as prohibiting students to criticize the government or court politics. The strictures were exceedingly severe, but the semi-official status of an Imperial University student made it almost impossible not to attempt to speak on various political or social issues. By the last half-century of the dynasty (in the early sixteenth century), intellectuals, many identifying themselves as "students of the Imperial University" or "students of the Directorate of National Youth" (both were practically the same thing), began to get involved in various political activities, notably the Donglin movement. This is to say that Zhu Yuanzhang's prohibition was effective most of the time, almost to the end of the Ming. After the Qing dynasty was founded, however, the campuses again returned to normalcy and were forced to remain dormant. There was practically no information that we could find to prove that there was any activism in the university. After the mid-nineteenth century, with the arrival of Western influences, the situation started to change.

Thus, by the mid-nineteenth century, Chinese intellectuals were totally absorbed in the commoners' affairs, especially their moral rectitude, or the ideological control of them. All of these are premised on the belief, now widely held, that all people were equal in their moral potential to become social leaders, or the scholar-officials.[16]

One could well consider that the mid-sixteenth century was a turning point in that the basic meaning of education in China began to shift. It was now recognized that all humans were equal in their potential to learn, and to become morally qualified scholars and officials. At that point, it was thought that educated intellectuals should then take on all political and social affairs as their concerns and responsibilities.

The new thinking did not immediately emerge because of the arrival of Western influences. Rather, it rose from within the Chinese tradition and had begun to

---

15. Many works could be listed here on local political and social control in the Qing dynasty in the nineteenth century. The classic study is Kung-chuan Hsiao, *Rural China: Imperial Control in the Nineteenth Century* (Seattle: University of Washington Press, 1960). See also Qiu Jie 邱捷, "Wanqing Guangdong de "gongju" – shishen kongzhi xiangchun shehui de quanli jiegou" 晚清廣東的"公局" — 士紳控制鄉村基層社會的權力機構, *Journal of Sun Yat-sen University (Social Science Edition)* 中山大學學報（社科版）, no. 4 (2005): 45–51, and Yang Nianqun 楊念群, "Lun shijiu shiji Lingnan xiangyue de junshihua—Zhong Ying chongtu de yige quyuxing jieguo" 論十九世紀嶺南鄉約的軍事化——中英衝突的一個區域性結果, *Studies in Qing History* 清史研究, no. 3 (1993): 114–21.
16. Wang Fansen 王汎森 aptly describes it as "all people of the four classes are eligible for [serving as] scholar-officials." See my article cited in note 5.

inform the Chinese imagination regarding the purpose and practice of education by the seventeenth century. This is, however, the time that Western missionaries began to arrive, but at this stage, their interest in Chinese education was in China's imperial examination system and government school or academy institutions (sometimes referred as "universities"). It was only later that their attention began to shift to the *content* of Chinese religion and education, and how commoners' ideological indoctrination was accomplished.[17]

The Chinese awareness of the impending changes due to Western impact had intensified by the late nineteenth century. Many intellectuals had written about the necessity to reform. Of them, Zhang Zhidong 張之洞 (1837–1909) was the first to look at it from the viewpoint of education, even if by then the Chinese had already failed the Tongzhi 同治 Restoration, and even worse, suffered repeated humiliation in a series of wars against the West, and even against Japan. The Chinese people by and large believed that China should try wholesale reform. Zhang dared to question the usefulness that helped to perpetuate a monolithic state ideology and a monistic model of social hierarchy and mobility (even though in theory, vertical social mobility was open to "all" classes of candidates), specifically, the civil service examination system that was considered to be the prime culprit. Although he would not sacrifice the core position of the Confucian classics in Chinese education, he did see the importance that they be taught not merely to intellectuals but also to all people.[18] Interestingly, Zhang's ideas were widely embraced by Western observers of China, and his book, *Encouraging Learning* (*Quanxue pian* 勸學篇) was quickly translated into English, French, and Japanese.[19] The warm reception abroad reflected a commonly held Western attitude toward Chinese civilization: Chinese ills are best cured by Chinese medicine. However, most Chinese interpreters think that Zhang's approach, "Chinese learning as essence and Western learning as application," was a lukewarm half-concession to the overwhelming threat on China's existence as a

---

17. Please consult note 13 for a brief discussion on the Western translations or studies on China's *Sacred Edicts* and village lectures. William Milne is the first missionary to translate the edicts and publish them in English in 1817.
18. For a study of Zhang Zhidong, see William Ayers, *Chang Chih-tung and the Educational Reform in Modern China* (Cambridge, MA: Harvard University Press, 1971); Daniel Bays, *China Enters the Twentieth Century, Chang Chi-tung and the Issues of a New Age, 1895–1909* (Ann Arbor: University of Michigan Press, 1978). See also Wolfgang Franke, *The Reform and Abolition of the Traditional Chinese Examination System* (Cambridge, MA: Harvard University Press, 1960).
19. As a matter of fact, "encouraging learning" has been a theme for many Chinese authors: Xunzi, Shizi, Lü Buwei (*Lüshi Chunqiu*), Dai Sheng (*Dadai Liji*), etc. have written on it. In 1872–1878, Fukuzawa Yukichi 福澤諭吉, a Japanese thinker, also wrote an important monograph on the topic, *Gakumon no Susume* 学問のすすめ [An encouragement of learning]. It is perhaps not inconceivable that Zhang might have been influenced by Fukuzawa. For a brief discussion on the response to Zhang's *Encouraging Learning* and his "Chinese Learning as Essence and Western Learning as Application" project, see William Ayers's book cited in note 18 above.

nation (civilization). The importance of Zhang's opinion should be understood in the context of the changing *Weltanschauung* of the Chinese intellectuals, pondering the purpose of education. Hailed as "China's only hope" by the English translator,[20] the proposal should be looked upon with favor, if not because there was this misconceived danger of China's impending doom.

Historians of Communist China have argued that "the survival of the Chinese nation" was the sole most important purpose and responsibility of modern Chinese education.[21] This reflects the angst of the time, and many Chinese communists interpreted why there was so much objection to Zhang's famous dictum. For the Western powers, this angst was unfortunate or unnecessary, but for the Chinese at the time, they either felt that Zhang was seeking an impossible synthesis or reconciliation between the traditional and the modern, between China and the rest of the world.

This angst is no longer there for Communist Chinese, and the feeling that there is an urgent need for the program advanced by Zhang has dissipated. "Save the nation from extinction and strive for its survival" no longer seems to describe the character of Chinese education after China was taken over by the communists in 1949.

Nonetheless, the alarm over the position of the Chinese civilization in the modern world continued to concern Chinese thinkers and intellectuals. A corollary of Zhang's proposal to abolish the civil service examinations reflected the realization that Confucian classics, the decreed content of the examinations, obviously could not meet the needs of a modernizing world. Zhang's opinion was quickly accepted and promoted by Chinese intellectuals, even if they continued to hold on to Confucian thinking and ethical teaching as not in disagreement with the other teachings, such as Christianity, that were fundamental to the scientific and technological "application."

Liao Ping 廖平 (1852–1932), himself a Confucian classics scholar, is an example of this opinion. He bravely had this to say:[22]

> Opinions represent various extremes, and there is no need to forcefully reconcile them. Should one classic be the standard for all affairs under Heaven, then there is no need to have "six classics" to exist simultaneously.

---

20. The first English translation came out c. 1900, entitled *China's Only Hope: An Appeal by Her Greatest Viceroy, Chang Chih-tung, with the Sanction of the Present Emperor* (New York: Fleming H. Revell). The translator was Samuel I. Woodbridge.
21. The phrase "save the nation from extinction and strive for its survival" (*jiu wang tu cun* 救亡圖存) first appeared in the mid-seventeenth century, coined by the literatus Qian Qianyi 錢謙益 (1582–1664), but had not been circulated at all until the late Qing dynasty, when it was revived, around 1909, by Lu Shi-huan 路士桓 in one of his memorials to the Xuantong 宣統 Emperor (r. 1908–1911), and by Wang Wusheng 王無生 (1880–1914) in an essay on the social significance of novels (1907). Mao Zedong then put it into wide circulation in many of his speeches and essays.
22. See, for the citation, my "Zhongguo jiaoyü sixiang de jindai zhuanzhe" 中國教育思想的近代轉折, cited in note 1; see p. 60, note 6.

This is quite a pointed refusal of the idea championed by Lu Jiuyuan 陸九淵 (1139–1193) that "This mind-heart (*xin* 心) and this principle (*li* 理) cannot be more than one."[23] The intellectual climate was the context against which the government ordered that the civil service examinations be abolished in 1905.

It is my opinion that "not to seek forceful reconciliation," as quoted above, is in a sense also an admission that the modern world was a diversified one, not only because there are different peoples and ways of life in the world, but they were to be treated as such. Viewed from the angle of education, branches of knowledge are diverse and should be learned—the more the better. As a result, new-style schools mushroomed; many of them taught subjects that did not even exist in traditional Chinese curriculums. Western educators, many of them missionaries, brought in new branches of knowledge. Returned overseas students also began to pay attention to the education of commoners, especially the farmers, teaching them literacy, for example.[24] A lot of primers and elementary readers appeared at the turn of the twentieth century. Most importantly, even the traditional academies were also expanding their teaching curriculum, although nationwide academies were officially closed in 1898, even before the imperial examination system was abolished.

Before we turn to another issue, let me add one additional point: the Western promotion in publications—especially by missionaries—introducing Western and modern knowledge and information. These activities have long been widely studied, and almost need no discussion here. It is, however, important to point out that the missionaries had considered "enlightenment" through introduction of modern knowledge as the true meaning of genuine religious conversion. Proponents of these ideas are represented by such as William Milne (1785–1822), Walter Henry Medhurst (1796–1857), Young John Allen (1836–1907), William Alexander Martin (1827–1916), Timothy Richard (1845–1919), and many others. Their proselytization theology was different from other more fundamentalist missionaries, who were concentrating on "saving the souls" of the Chinese. The difference between the two schools of theology unfortunately grew larger after the rise, in the United States, of fundamentalism around the first decades of the twentieth century.

---

23. *Lu Jiuyuan ji* 陸九淵集 (Beijing: Zhonghua Books, 1980), chapter 12. This sentence in the context of Lu's thought meant that the "mind-heart" was the "principle," but when invoked by Hu Shi 胡適 in 1919–1921, it was used to mean that truth was "the sole principle and mind-heart," and "cannot be two." See Hu Shi, "Qingdai hanxue jia de kexue fangfa" 清代漢學家的科學方法, *Beijing daxue yuekan* 北京大學月刊, no. 5, 7, 9 (1919–1921). This article is also found in his collected papers, *Hushi wencun* 胡適文存.

24. The first missionary university is St. John's University of Shanghai, founded in 1879. For an example of a returned student's popular educational efforts, see Charles W. Hayford, *To the People: James Yen and Village China* (New York: Columbia University Press, 1990). See also Kate Merkel-Hess, *The Rural Modern: Reconstructing the Self and State in Republican China* (Chicago; London: The University of Chicago Press, 2016).

The story of the conflict between the fundamentalists and the so-called "modernists" does not need to concern us here, but by the Second World War, the fundamentalist approach had been severely criticized or condemned, to such an extent that other activities of the more liberal Western missionaries were also rejected, as harmful to the Chinese national feeling. Both in the West (particularly the United States) and in China, Western worldviews and Christianity were now thought of as completely failing to do any good to China and are fundamentally incongruous with the Chinese traditional culture and beliefs.

Chinese communists, looked upon by mid-century American intellectuals as representing the true model of modern secularization, rode on the tide and succeeded in winning the Chinese mind-heart in 1949. They systematically began to purge the Western presence in China. The departure of the Western influences is a sad comment on the struggles in China's search for modernization. The works in the previous century by the liberal Westerners, together with their Chinese compatriots, had introduced a broad vision of education that coincided with the rise in consciousness among Chinese intellectuals on the belief that all things, including those of the outside world, are the concern of every educated person. These works were lost after 1949. Of course, fundamentalist missionaries did not fare better.

By the end of the nineteenth century, education had been understood as something all people should receive, including the hitherto non-educated commoners. Education was no longer a privilege for examination candidates, merely for the acquisition of classic knowledge, as well as their personal moral cultivation. This transformation had in the fifteenth and sixteenth centuries received a significant philosophical justification: the diversity and multiplicity of knowledge as the foundation for a new *Weltanschauung* now replaced the traditional belief in the unity of all values. The arrival of Western missionaries helped to strengthen this new outlook. Their presence is evidence of diversity and multiplicity of the world's societies and branches of knowledge, both human and natural. In short, the parameter of knowledge was widened, and the subsequent sea change went hand in hand with the realization that all humans should receive education. By the end of the nineteenth century, the developments had been all but completed.

There are several consequences of the transformation. The first is student activism, which is no doubt the result of the realization and a consequent sense of urgency by the students about how to build a new, modern nation that could function in the diverse international order. As mentioned previously, Chinese intellectuals now widely held the view that every educated Chinese had a responsibility in the process. From the early Ming times, Imperial University students were assigned to various government jobs, such as land survey and the compilation of the nationwide "Fish-scale Land Registers" (*yü-lin ce* 魚鱗冊), which was a huge project to register the size,[25] shape, and other relevant information of all personally owned lands, fields, fishing ponds, and so on. This was the "concern" the state was instilling in the consciousness of university students. Understandably, it led to the awareness that all national affairs commanded their attention. This kind of awareness reached its height toward the end of the Ming dynasty.

However, throughout the Qing dynasty, the Imperial University ceased to be an active educational institution and was not much more than a place to register examination candidates, many of them who secured their status in the university through purchase. Most university students did not even fulfill residence requirements; they played a very minor, if any, role in the nation's politics through their status as a student. By the late nineteenth century, however, this began to change.

In 1895, the docility ended. It is well known that education in twentieth-century China was marked by repeated student movements, particularly in contrast to the relatively compliant attitude of students in the previous centuries. In 1895, Kang Youwei 康有為 (1858–1927) organized a group of imperial examination candidates to appeal to the then Emperor Guangxu 光緒 to demand reform.[26] This set student movements into motion, even if there were only about eighty signatories, not as many as Kang claimed. In the next few years, a series of similar petitions or protests followed,[27] climaxing in the famous May Fourth Movement of 1919. Subsequent movements were so frequent that it is nearly impossible to list them here.[28]

---

25. There is no in-depth study in English on the "Fish-scale Registers." For a brief discussion, see Denis Twitchett and Frederick W. Mote, ed. *The Cambridge History of China*, vol. 8, pt. 2 (New York: Cambridge University Press, 1998), 443–44.
26. Sang Bing 桑兵, *Wanqing xuetang xuesheng yu shehui bianqian* 晚清學堂學生與社會變遷 (Guilin: Guangxi Normal University Press, 2007). Shang argues that this petition was the beginning of modern Chinese student activism. In a strict sense, Kang and his cohorts were all candidates with preliminary degrees eligible for taking the metropolitan examinations, and were thus not government school students anymore. However, it is "intellectual activism" all the same.
27. For example, in 1905, students in Shanghai joined merchants in an anti-American, anti-imperialist demonstration, against the United States' discriminatory policy against Chinese immigrants. It is interesting to note that mainline American (esp. liberal Protestant) missionaries had stood against the so-called "scientific racists" who advocated for the Chinese Exclusion Act (1882) and National Origins Act (1924), and those involved in organizing the demonstration were likely influenced by the missionaries. See Jennifer C. Snow, *Protestant Missionaries, Asian Immigrants, and Ideologies of Race in America, 1850–1924* (New York: Routledge, 2007).
28. Works on modern China's student movements are plentiful. Tse-tsung Chow's (Zhou Cezong 周策縱) *The May Fourth Movement: Intellectual Revolution in Modern China* (Cambridge, MA: Harvard University Press, 1960) and John Israel's *Student Nationalism in China, 1927–1937* (Stanford, CA: Hoover Institution, 1966) remain the most useful. For June fourth, see Liang Zhang, Andrew J. Nathan, and Perry Link, *The Tiananmen Papers* (New York: Public Affairs, 2008). For a classical study of Republican period's Christian colleges, see Daniel H. Bays and Ellen Widmer, eds., *China's Christian Colleges* (Stanford, CA: Stanford University Press, 2009).

Most of these activities fully demonstrate how concerns of young students (and their teachers) indeed were "to save the nation from extinction and to strive for its survival," but they were possible, more importantly, because of the educational ideal that "everything is my concern."

Another consequence is the awareness that China is one of many nations in the world. This awareness may be traced back to the time when Catholic missionaries first arrived in China in the late sixteenth century. However, recognition that China was no longer a universal state and the center of all under heaven really came only in the late nineteenth century. Chinese students began to go abroad to study and bring back information about other nations. Here are some of the influences returned students brought to the Chinese society. Almost all the presidents of China's modern universities were returned scholars. The most influential undoubtedly was Cai Yuanpei 蔡元培 (1878–1940), who was the fourth president of Peking University after the Republic of China was founded in 1912. He studied in Leipzig, Germany.[29] One of the many things he did was to promote "using aesthetic education to substitute religion." One could conclude by saying that in an interesting twist, the "everything is my concern" was now understood as everything could equally inspire the pursuit for moral accomplishment and true knowledge.

Finally, because of the broadened worldview that added new meanings to the notion of "everything is my concern," one must therefore also refer to the role of foreigners, especially Christian missionaries, considering that they founded most private universities.[30] The modern values of Western capitalist democracy and socialist totalitarian or authoritarian centralism, were now accepted as viable alternatives for China to adopt, thanks to the liberal ideas now filtering into the Chinese thinking arena. The former was often advocated by Western missionaries, especially of the liberal progressive kind, while the latter, the Marxist-Maoist one, was more focused on the mobilization of the Chinese peasants for political action. These alternate ideas had been equally championed for adoption by the Chinese, and this is because the Chinese conviction, now widely held, that "everything is my concern," would allow the thinking that "everything is my acceptable choice." By the post–May Fourth years, the Chinese were open to adopting Western social or

---

29. Nine of the ten presidents before the founding of People's Republic of China had studied abroad. The exception is William Alexander P. Martin (known in Chinese as Ding Weiliang 丁韙良), who was an American. The first president after the Republic was founded is Yan Fu 嚴復 (1854–1921), who studied in England. The second and the third were both returned students from Japan. For a very selective list of university presidents who were returned scholars, see page 62 of my "Zhongguo jiaoyü sixiang de jindai zhuanzhe" cited in note 1.
30. Ruth Hayhoe, *China's Universities, 1895–1995: A Century of Cultural Conflict* (New York: Routledge, 1996). For a very illuminating study of higher education in the first few decades of the twentieth century, please consult Daniel Bays's *A New History of Chinese Christianity* (New York: Wiley, 2011), especially for his discussion on the "Sino-Foreign Protestant Establishment."

political narratives. Social or economic historians may feel that the Chinese had no choice but to accept foreign ideas and adopt their institutions, but without change in commitment to the new educational ideal of "everything is my concern," the new narratives could not have been as influential, much less accepted. Even today, they are still a hard sell to the Chinese people.

Many historians of Chinese education would consider "save the nation from extinction and strive for its survival" as what could best characterize modern Chinese education: the survival of China as a viable nation in the Darwinian world of international power struggles. The danger of possible biological extinction of the Chinese nation was considered by a lot of Chinese as real. But if one sees the enthusiastic reception of Zhang Zhidong's maxim by the foreigners, "Chinese learning as essence and Western learning as application," then one must conclude that their perceived danger was a false one; there was no imminent threat of extinction of the Chinese race, and, by implication, Chinese civilization. But that this should become so well ingrained in the Chinese mind at the time was a result of the broadened horizon of knowledge and of concerns, as argued above. The parameter of things to embrace and knowledge to manage was simply too huge and scary.

In conclusion, "everything is my concern" means a broadened world of knowledge and its multifaceted prongs that must be dealt with. It indeed opened China to modern and challenging ways of life. Everything now became relevant, meaningful, and threatening. However, this is not entirely because of Western (and Japanese) impacts; it had been developing since around the sixteenth century, both philosophically and institutionally. I would even argue that it started in the Ming times, when its founder seized on the significance of commoners' education and began a series of programs to carry out a new kind of education that was directed to the general populace. By the middle of the Ming dynasty (approximately the sixteenth century), philosophers ranging from Wang Shouren to Wang Gen all articulated the educational philosophy that justified the new development. The notion that all men were equal in terms of ability to understand moral teaching and to internalize it had by the eighteenth century expanded also to mean that all political and social affairs are every man's responsibility or concern. This trans-valuation is aptly expressed in the famous couplet, admonishing that everything is the concern of an educated person. The arrival of Western influences strengthened the realization that the world of knowledge was broad, and its values diverse and competing. These developments contributed to the rise of modern Chinese education that is best characterized as "everything is my concern." There is no better way to characterize modern Chinese education than this.

Bibliography

Ayers, William. *Chang Chih-tung and the Educational Reform in Modern China*. Cambridge, MA: Harvard University Press, 1971.

Bays, Daniel. *China Enters the Twentieth Century, Chang Chi-tung and the Issues of a New Age, 1895–1909*. Ann Arbor: University of Michigan Press, 1978.

Bays, Daniel. *A New History of Chinese Christianity*. New York: Wiley, 2011.

Bays, Daniel, and Ellen Widmer, eds. *China's Christian Colleges*. Stanford, CA: Stanford University Press, 2009.

Chen, Shilong 陳時龍. "Shengyu de yanyi: Mingdai shidafu dui Taizu *Liuyu* de quanshi" 聖諭的演繹: 明代士大夫對太祖六諭的詮釋. *Journal of Anhui Normal University (Humanities and Social Sciences)* 安徽師範大學學報（人文社會科學版）43, no. 5 (2015), 611–21.

Chow, Tse-tsung. *The May Fourth Movement: Intellectual Revolution in Modern China*. Cambridge, MA: Harvard University Press, 1960.

De Bary, Wm. Theodore. *Learning for One's Self: Essays on the Individual in Neo-Confucian Thought*. New York: Columbia University Press, 1991.

Franke, Wolfgang. *The Reform and Abolition of the Traditional Chinese Examination System* Cambridge, MA: Harvard University Press, 1960.

Fukuzawa Yukichi 福澤喻吉, *Gakumon no Susume* 学問のすすめ [An encouragement of learning]. 1872.

Grimm, Tilemann. "Academies and Urban Systems in Kwangtung." In *The City in Late Imperial China*, edited by. G. William Skinner. Stanford, CA: Stanford University Press, 1977.

Hayhoe, Ruth. *China's Universities, 1895–1995: A Century of Cultural Conflict*. New York: Routledge, 1996.

Hayford, Charles W. *To the People: James Yen and Village China*. New York: Columbia University Press, 1990.

Hsiao, Kung-chuan. *Rural China: Imperial Control in the Nineteenth Century*. Seattle: University of Washington Press, 1960.

Israel, John. *Student Nationalism in China, 1927–1937*. Stanford, CA: Hoover Institution, 1966.

Hu, Shi 胡適. *Hushi wencun* 胡適文存, edited by Pan Guangzhe. Taipei: Institute of Modern History, Academia Sinica, 2019.

Hu, Shi 胡適. "Qingdai hanxue jia de kexue fangfa" 清代漢學家的科學方法. *Beijing Daxue yuekan* 北京大學月刊, no. 5, 7, 9 (1919–1921).

Lau, D. C. *The Analects, Sayings of Confucius*. Hong Kong: Chinese University of Hong Kong, 2000.

Lee, Thomas H. C. "Chu Hsi, Academies, and the Tradition of Private Chiang-hsüeh." *Han-hsüeh yan-chiu* 漢學研究 2, no. 1 (1984): 301–29.

Lee, Thomas H. C. "Education in Traditional China." In *The Routledge Encyclopedia of Traditional Chinese Culture*, edited by Chan Sin-wai. London and New York: Routledge, 2020.

Lee, Thomas H. C. *Education in Traditional China, a History*. Leiden: Brill, 2000.

Lee, Thomas H. C. *Xue yi weiji: Chuantong Zhongguo de jiaoyu* 學以爲己：傳統中國的教育 [Learning for one's self, education in Traditional China]. Hong Kong: The Chinese University of Hong Kong Press, 2012.

Lee, Thomas H. C. "Zhongguo jiaoyu sixiang de jindai zhuanzhe – jianlun jiaoyu sixiangshi de yanjiu quxiang" 中國教育思想的近代轉折——簡論教育思想史的研究趨向 [The modern turn of Chinese educational thought—a brief discussion on the direction of research in educational thought]. *Peking University Education Review* 13, no. 4 (2015), 31–64.

Liang, Zhang, Andrew J. Nathan, and Perry Link. *The Tiananmen Papers*. New York: Public Affairs, 2008.

Lu, Jiuyuan 陸九淵. *Lu Jiuyuan ji* 陸九淵集. Beijing: Zhonghua Books, 1980.

Luo, Dajing 羅大經. *Helin yulu* 鶴林玉露 [Jade dew from the forest of cranes]. Ming engraved edition. In *Zhongguo jiben gujiku* 中國基本古籍庫. Beijing: Airusheng shuzihua jishu yanjiu zhongxin 愛如生數字化技術研究中心, 2009.

Mair, Victor. "Language and Ideology in the Sacred Edict." In *Popular Culture in Late Imperial China*, edited by Andrew J. Nathan, David G. Johnson, and Evelyn Sakakida Rawski. Berkeley: University of California Press, 1985.

Merkel-Hess, Kate. *The Rural Modern: Reconstructing the Self and State in Republican China*. Chicago; London: The University of Chicago Press, 2016.

Ono Kazuko 小野和子. *Minki tōsha kō: Tōrintō to Fukusha* 明季黨社考—東林黨と復社. Kyoto: Tobosha, 1996.

Ono Kazuko 小野和子. *Mingji dangshe kao* 明季黨社考. Translated by Li Qing 李慶. Shanghai: Shanghai guji chubanshe, 2006).

Qiu, Jie 邱捷. "Wanqing Guangdong de "gongju" – shishen kongzhi xiangchun shehui de quanli jiegou" 晚清廣東的"公局"——士紳控制鄉村基層社會的權力機構. *Journal of Sun Yat-sen University (Social Science Edition)* 中山大學學報（社科版）, no. 4 (2005): 45–51.

Sang, Bing 桑兵. *Wanqing xuetang xuesheng yu shehui bianqian* 晚清學堂學生與社會變遷. Guilin: Guangxi Normal University Press, 2007.

Snow, Jennifer C. *Protestant Missionaries, Asian Immigrants, and Ideologies of Race in America, 1850–1924*. New York: Routledge, 2007.

Twitchett, Denis and Frederick W. Mote, ed. *The Cambridge History of China*. Vol. 8, *The Ming Dynasty, 1368–1644, Part 2*. New York: Cambridge University Press, 1998.

Wang, Fansen 王汎森. "Mingmo Qingchu de renpu yü xingguo hui" 明末清初的人譜與省過會. *Bulletin of the Institute of History and Philology of Academia Sinica* 中央研究院歷史語言研究所集刊 63, no. 3 (1993): 679–712.

Wang, Gen 王艮. *Chongke Xinzhai Wang Xiansheng yulu* 重刻心齋王先生語錄. Ming ed. In *Zhongguo jiben gujiku* 中國基本古籍庫. Beijing: Airusheng shuzihua jishu yanjiu zhongxin, 2009.

Wikipedia. "Sacred Edict of the Kangxi Emperor." Last modified August 31, 2023. https://en.wikipedia.org/wiki/Sacred_Edict_of_the_Kangxi_Emperor.

Xie, Guozhen 謝國楨. *Ming Qing zhiji dangshe yundong kao* 明清之際黨社運動考. Shanghai: Commercial Press, 1934; reprint, Beijing: Zhonghua, 1983.

Yang, Nianqun 楊念群. "Lun shijiu shiji Lingnan xiangyue de junshihua—Zhong Ying chongtu de yige quyuxing jieguo" 論十九世紀嶺南鄉約的軍事化——中英衝突的一個區域性結果. *Studies in Qing History* 清史研究, no. 3 (1993): 114–21.

Zhang, Zhidong. *China's Only Hope: An Appeal by Her Greatest Viceroy, Chang Chih-tung, with the Sanction of the Present Emperor.* Translated by Samuel I. Woodbridge. New York: Fleming H. Revell, 1900.

Zhu, Wenjie 朱文杰. *Donglin dang shihua* 東林黨史話. Shanghai: East China Normal University Press, 1989.

2

The Crisis of Mission Education in Republican China, 1922–1929

The Case of Harold Henry Rowley

Brian Stanley

The Aims of Education

Education and public benefit

There is general agreement that education is a self-evident good. Whether the provider of education is the government of a nation state or a private and voluntary body, it is universally accepted that to supply educational services is a public benefit. Hence in Britain, private or independent schools—which the British perversely insist on calling "public schools"—are given charitable status, which brings substantial tax advantages. The determination of charitable status depends on it being proven that the body seeking charitable status exists for the public benefit. But how, precisely, is public benefit to be measured? Does public benefit mean the transparent good of the society or nation as a whole, or simply that certain more limited communities—or even individuals—within society are deriving benefit from the educational services supplied? What if the education being supplied is, on account of its manifestly superior quality, often purchased by the consumer at considerable financial cost, giving some individuals a demonstrable advantage over other individuals? Is that still "public benefit"?

It thus becomes imperative that we persist in our inquiry into the public value of education by asking three further questions that may help us to define more exactly what education is actually intended to achieve.

First, who is responsible for measuring the public benefit accruing from education? If we say, as most modern societies have done, that the state is responsible for measuring whether those who offer educational services are in fact serving the public benefit, there is a sinister potential that education becomes valued, not for its own sake, but as a means toward a short-term political end as defined by the government of the day. This is a danger of which many of us involved in the delivery of education, especially higher education today, have become keenly aware. The frequent implication is that what universities are chiefly intended to do is to improve the capacity of the nation to create wealth by the imparting of measurable skills in money-making. I for one, and many of my colleagues, are not happy with that definition of the goals of higher education. For one thing, it is self-evidently not the case, if I may use myself as an illustration, that teaching students about the history of non-Western Christianity or the history of the Western missionary movement, as I do, is going to enhance their skills for the commercial economy or maximize their earning potential. My students do not become rich, and neither do they, unless I am much mistaken, expect to do so! Hence the question of who should do the measuring leads necessarily to a second and third question.

Education, virtue, and wisdom

The second question is, therefore, whether education is primarily about the impartation of knowledge, skills, and competencies, or whether it is additionally, or even alternatively, about the formation of whole and well-balanced persons, not simply in the areas of intellect, but also in what may be termed "virtue," or moral capacity and character. Both Western and Chinese educational theorists of a previous age have subscribed to the latter view. The great humanist scholars of the European Renaissance such as Erasmus held that "the educated person would be a morally good person, and that only such education as made a person more upright was worthy of the name."[1] In the same way, a cardinal principle of the Scottish Enlightenment held that education was indeed intended to be useful to society, but its usefulness lay precisely in the fact that it formed habits of virtue, character, and wisdom.[2] Similarly, in classical Confucian thought, the reason that education is so important for the welfare of the state as a whole is that it shapes individuals in patterns of moral uprightness: the benefit accruing to society is proportionate to the effectiveness of the educational process in forming the moral character of individual persons.[3] Most of us who work in the humanities in modern universities would wish to endorse these traditional affirmations from both Western and Chinese traditions

---

1. Euan Cameron, "The Power of the Word: Renaissance and Reformation," in *Early Modern Europe: An Oxford History*, ed. Euan Cameron (Oxford: Oxford University Press, 2001), 72.
2. On education in the Scottish Enlightenment see David Allan, *Virtue, Learning and the Scottish Enlightenment: Ideas of Scholarship in Early Modern History* (Edinburgh: Edinburgh University Press, 1993).
3. Thomas H. C. Lee, *Education in Traditional China: A History*, in vol. 13 of *Handbook of Oriental Studies. Section 4 China* (Leiden: E. J. Brill, 2000), 9–16.

that the formation of persons is ultimately more important than the mere transfer of factual knowledge or wealth-creating skills. Hence, we cannot avoid the conclusion that education involves the quest to encourage students to espouse certain values; values that we believe will not simply be empirically useful, but also sound and wholesome values for living—in other words, values that we wish to affirm as true. That observation then leads us to the third and potentially most difficult question of all.

Value-driven education or brainwashing?

If education is more than just the mere instilling of knowledge and competencies; if in fact it has something to do with teachers commending, and themselves embodying, the espousal of values that are good and true, then where does the boundary fall between true education and indoctrination or brainwashing? What I term value-driven education you may choose to call indoctrination. In denying the validity of my curriculum of education, shaped as it is by my values, you may offer an alternative curriculum, shaped by a quite different set of values. I, in turn, may then object that what you are offering is not genuine education, but rather indoctrination.

Nationalist Demands for Registration of Mission Schools in Republican China

This extended theoretical discussion may seem to be a digression, but it is in fact a necessary introduction to the main concern of this chapter, namely the debates provoked by Christian schools and colleges in Republican China in the 1920s. The escalation of anti-foreign sentiment from 1922, and the working alliance between the Nationalist Guomindang (GMD) government and the embryonic Chinese Communist Party, gave rise to increasingly numerous and vocal demands by Chinese students for the "restoration of educational rights."[4] The government responded by applying pressure on the Christian schools and colleges run by Western Protestant missions to abandon their original insistence on their students attending compulsory acts of religious education or worship. This is mainly, but not entirely, a Protestant story: Catholics in China were slow to invest in higher education; until 1927 there was only one Catholic university in China: l'Université l'Aurore in Shanghai, founded by French Jesuits in 1903. The Jesuit order also established an institution of higher technical education, L'Institut des Hautes Études Industrielles et Commerciales in 1923 in Tientsin (Tianjin). A second Catholic university was

---

4. Jessie G. Lutz, "Chinese Nationalism and the Anti-Christian Campaigns of the 1920s," *Modern Asian Studies* 10, no. 3 (1976): 396–97, 401.

established in 1927, when the Fu Jen Academy in Peking, founded by American Benedictines in 1925, became Fu Jen University, widely known as the Catholic University of Peking (Beijing).[5]

The stakes for the missions were high: those Christian institutions that refused to comply would be denied government registration, and without state registration the schools and colleges would cease to exert any appeal to prospective students, and hence would wither and die. Despite the obstinate resistance of some missionaries, by the end of the decade, almost all the missions had accepted the government's demands, making attendance at prayers or lessons of Christian instruction purely voluntary. The story might therefore appear to be a straightforward one of a system of public education triumphing over a network of private and religiously motivated indoctrination. After all, the missions were in China above all to forward their objective of seeking converts to Christianity, and their massive investment in education was quite avowedly shaped by their overall conversionist goal. Surely proselytism is contrary to any authentic idea of education? However, in the remainder of this chapter, I argue that the issues were in fact more complex. Those who opposed or deplored the abandonment of compulsory religious worship or instruction cannot all be dismissed as mere bigots—they were contending for a particular vision of value-driven education. Moreover, the Nationalist state was itself committed to using the schools for political purposes that were at least as open to the charge of indoctrination as were the missions.

The attack on "foreign" religion

The first point to note about the "Restore Educational Rights" campaign is that the most pointed accusation against the Christian schools and colleges was not that they were religious in purpose, but rather that the religion that they represented was irredeemably foreign in character. It is true that the "Restore Educational Rights" movement followed hard on the heels of the Anti-Christian Federation formed in Shanghai in August 1924, which was itself an outgrowth of the Great Federation of Anti-Religionists that attacked all religious ideologies, including Confucianism, as unscientific and pre-modern.[6] But the central charge leveled by organizations such as the Young China Association and the Anti-Christian Student Federation

---

5. K. S. Latourette, *A History of Christian Missions in China* (London: SPCK, 1929), 559, 729–32; Albert Monshan Wu, *From Christ to Confucius: German Missionaries, Chinese Christians and the Globalization of Christianity, 1860–1950* (New Haven, CT: Yale University Press, 2016), 230–33. Fu Jen University was incorporated within Beijing Normal University in 1952, but was re-founded in Taiwan in the early 1960s.
6. Tatsuro Yamamoto and Sumiko Yamamoto, "The Anti-Christian Movement in China, 1922–1927," *Far Eastern Quarterly* 12, no. 2 (February 1953): 133–47.

was that the mission schools were "running dogs of the foreigners." They demanded not simply the abolition of compulsory religious worship and instruction, but the imposition of full Chinese control of the school. Control of public education, they plausibly maintained, was integral to ideas of national sovereignty. A primary aim of education was the instilling of national ideals of citizenship and the cultivation of uniquely Chinese characteristics. Much of the criticism directed at the Christian colleges was that much—though, as we shall observe, not all—of their high-quality education was delivered through the foreign medium of the English language; as such it was culturally alien.[7] Educational institutions that were under foreign control and disseminated an alien culture were an unacceptable anomaly: the mission schools and colleges must be drastically reformed, not simply because they disseminated religion, but above all because they were so foreign in character.[8]

Chinese Christian support for anti-foreignism in education

A second and closely related point to emphasize is that the majority of Chinese Christians involved in the Christian schools and colleges supported the demand for Chinese control and the campaign for the removal of religious compulsion. Compulsion, they tellingly pointed out, was directly contrary to the spirit of Christianity and to the liberal and democratic ideals that the missionaries—most of whom were Americans—so openly professed. More pragmatically, they argued, again with justification, that compliance with the demands of the Nationalist government was essential if Christian educational institutions were to have any future in China.[9] Educated Chinese Christian opinion, therefore, tended to agree that the most pressing question was not whether the education provided by the mission-founded institutions was sufficiently Christian, but rather whether it was sufficiently national. "The unforgivable sins of Christianity in the eyes of most Chinese," writes Jessie Lutz, "were that it was foreign and that it was an obstacle to the building of a powerful and unified China."[10]

---

7. Edward Yihua Xu, "Liberal Arts Education in English and Campus Culture at St John's University," in *China's Christian Colleges: Cross-Cultural Connections, 1900–1950*, ed. Daniel H. Bays and Ellen Widmer (Stanford, CA: Stanford University Press, 2009), 107–24.
8. Jessie G. Lutz, *China and the Christian Colleges 1850–1950* (Ithaca, NY: Cornell University Press, 1971), 240–41, 251–52.
9. Lutz, *China and the Christian Colleges*, 252, 254.
10. Lutz, *China and the Christian Colleges*, 267–68.

Missionary perspectives

In the third place, and at greater length, we turn to the arguments of those missionaries who attempted to defend the continuance of compulsory religious attendance and instruction. Some argued that they were morally bound by the expectations of the Christian public in the West who had donated large sums for the support of Christian education in China on the understanding that it was precisely that—education that was avowedly and consistently Christian. Charitable institutions, they maintained, with a measure of plausibility, had a legal responsibility to disburse their funds in accordance with the intentions of the donors.[11] Less plausibly, they also did their best to turn the argument for ideological freedom on its head by claiming that those who chose to attend, or to send their children to attend, Christian educational institutions, did so in full knowledge of the nature of the option they were selecting. Other choices of equivalent educational standards, they protested, were available (which was sometimes true, but more often not). It was a matter of religious liberty for Christian parents to be allowed to select schools that gave a prominent place to religious instruction.[12] This was a specious argument, for neither the Restore Educational Rights campaigners nor the GMD government denied the right of Christian schools and colleges to offer religious instruction to those who specifically asked for it.

The most serious arguments against capitulation to the terms set by the GMD government as conditions for registration came from the minority of missionaries who reflected at some depth on the nature of the educational process, and on whether institutions that passed under the control of the GMD would be any less free of indoctrination than they had been previously in the days of untrammeled missionary control.

H. H. Rowley of the Baptist Missionary Society

This chapter will now focus on one such British missionary, Harold Henry Rowley (1890–1969). Rowley's church membership was at Melbourne Hall in Leicester, then a Baptist congregation whose previous pastors included such notable conservative evangelical figures as F. B. Meyer and William Young Fullerton, student and biographer of C. H. Spurgeon, and from 1912 to 1927 Home Secretary of the Baptist Missionary Society (BMS). From 1922 to 1929 Rowley taught—it should be noted in Chinese medium rather than English[13]—at Shantung Christian University

---

11. Lutz, *China and the Christian Colleges*, 252–53.
12. Lutz, *China and the Christian Colleges*, 253.
13. G. W. Anderson, "Harold Henry Rowley 1890–1969," in *Proceedings of the British Academy* 56 (London: Oxford University Press, 1972), 310.

(SCU) in Jinan. The roots of this institution go back to a joint initiative in 1904 by the American Presbyterians and Rowley's own mission, the BMS, with other missions subsequently lending their support. Rowley is most widely remembered today not as a missionary to China, but as a distinguished scholar of Semitic languages and Old Testament studies. He taught first from 1930 to 1935 at University College, Cardiff, before being appointed to professorial chairs at the University College of North Wales in Bangor, and finally from 1945 to 1959 at the University of Manchester.[14] As a recipient in 1947 of the highest academic accolade that can be earned by any British academic working in the humanities—a Fellowship of the British Academy—he cannot be written off as a fundamentalist or an unthinking missionary imperialist. Yet his distinguished career as an Old Testament scholar only got under way because in 1929 he finally resigned from the BMS in protest against its eventual capitulation to Nationalist pressure to weaken the Christian character of Shantung Christian University.

Figure 2.1: H. H. Rowley, British Baptist missionary at Shantung Christian University, 1922–1929. Photograph by Walter Stoneman, 1947 © National Portrait Gallery, London.

---

14. See Anderson, "Harold Henry Rowley 1890–1969," 309–19; Ronald E. Clements, "The Biblical Theology of H. H. Rowley, 1890–1969," *Baptist History and Heritage* 38, no. 1 (Winter 2003): 36–63.

Rowley's discontent with developments at Shantung Christian University, 1925–1929

Rowley's growing unhappiness with the tendency of events in China first became apparent in 1925. On May 30, 1925, British police in the Shanghai international settlement shot dead twelve Chinese demonstrators. A wave of anti-foreign demonstrations followed on Chinese university campuses, some of them calling for the murder of foreigners in retaliation. At SCU, the students, many of them Christians, went on strike in the middle of their examinations and joined the protests. The university senate agreed not to penalize the students, rescheduled their examinations, and lent support to the call for an impartial investigation into the Shanghai massacre. Rowley was uneasy. He wrote a paper on "Mission schools and Chinese politics," deploring the fact that most Christian students in mission institutions had fallen in line with the bitter national hatred being expressed by their non-Christian fellows, expressing sentiments that could not be reconciled with the spirit of Jesus. Rowley offered his resignation from the staff, but was persuaded by the dean of the School of Theology to withdraw it after the university senate passed a more reflective resolution on July 29, 1925. This reaffirmed the university's "unswerving loyalty to Jesus Christ," and warned students that the legitimate expression of patriotism could not be permitted to interfere with the educational objectives and best interests of the university.[15]

Rowley's unease did not go away. While on furlough in England in January 1928, he and other colleagues attended a consultation with the foreign secretary of the BMS, C. E. Wilson, to discuss the problems at SCU. One missionary colleague expressed the view that the problems were related to the disjuncture between the missionaries, who were there because they believed they were called by God, and the growing number of Chinese staff, who were "there for the salary." Rowley judged this to be a sweeping generalization, but one carrying "a substantial element of truth."[16] During the year, SCU appointed a new Chinese acting president, Li Tianlu 李天祿. Within a week of his return to Jinan from furlough, Rowley found that the senate, under Li Tianlu's direction, and with the strong support of the students and Chinese staff, had voted to register SCU with the Nationalist government. The price of registration was the removal of any explicit reference to the Christian objectives of the institution from the university's statement of purpose. The revised statement spoke only in general terms of maintaining the "spirit of love, sacrifice, and service"

---

15. H. H. Rowley, "Mission schools and Chinese politics," and Minutes of Special Meeting of the Senate of Shantung Christian University, July 29, 1925, CH/64, Baptist Missionary Society archives (hereafter BMSA); Brian Stanley, *The History of the Baptist Missionary Society 1792–1992* (Edinburgh: T. & T. Clark, 1992), 310.

16. H. H. Rowley to C. E. Wilson, February 17, 1928, BMSA, CH/64.

of its founders. Rowley wrote to C. E. Wilson on November 11: "I wish to state quite clearly that I cannot remain in the University if it registers."[17]

On December 12, the BMS China sub-committee now dropped its earlier opposition to registration and voted in favor of registering the university by a majority of sixteen votes to one, with five abstentions; the one dissentient was Theo Bamber, pastor of Rye Lane Baptist Chapel in Peckham, one of the Society's most theologically conservative supporters. He ominously warned Wilson in a subsequent letter that "those whose hearts were keen on evangelism and not on higher education" would henceforth be all the more inclined to transfer their support from the BMS to the theologically conservative China Inland Mission.[18]

Although as yet unaware of the committee's decision, Rowley's disillusionment deepened on New Year's Day 1929. The letter he wrote the next day to Wilson is worth quoting at length:

> Yesterday, being New Year's Day, was celebrated by the University with a meeting which was announced in the Bulletin as a short, bright service. It was held in the Institute, under the chairmanship of one of the students. It began with the threefold bow to the Nationalist flag, and the Sun Yat Sen Memorial service, during which the whole audience, with the exception of myself, stood with eyes fixed on a picture of Dr Sun, and solemnly repeated the words of his will. This was followed by prayer. Thereafter the chairman announced the purpose of the meeting in a speech which was purely political, and which was punctuated with the concerted shouting of slogans by the meeting at the top of their voices, led by a student with a megaphone. One of the slogans was "Down with Japanese imperialism,"[19] and another was "Put into practice the San Min Chu I" [*san min zhuyi* 三民主義], i.e., the teachings of Sun Yat Sen.... I have already written to you on my attitude to the Memorial service. I know it is possible to explain it as merely a mark of honour to a dead leader. But even if that were so, I cannot see why we, as a University, should feel it necessary to accord that honour, and certainly not in our religious services. We know that the Nationalist Government has ordered that in all Government offices and Yamens this service shall be weekly observed. In the context of that effort to secure for him honours which are at least unique amongst men, the issue should be judged. For myself I have no intention of joining in such a service, and I protest against the University as an institution engaging in it.[20]

Two days later, Rowley received a letter from Wilson informing him of the resolution of the Society in its China sub-committee to support registration of the SCU.

---

17. H. H. Rowley to C. E. Wilson, November 11, 1928, BMSA, CH/64.
18. Theo Bamber to C. E. Wilson, December 20, 1928, BMSA, CH/46.
19. Although Japan had been compelled to return Shandong to China in 1922, it continued to maintain informal economic control of the province.
20. H. H. Rowley to C. E. Wilson, January 2, 1929, BMSA, CH/64.

He penned an immediate reply expressing his "deepest disappointment." "With a heavy heart," he stated that his resignation from the university would now have to be followed by his resignation from the Society, though he left it to the BMS to determine when his resignation would take effect.[21]

Rowley's resignation from the Baptist Missionary Society

On January 7, 1929, Rowley wrote formally to Dr. Li Tianlu, tendering his resignation from the staff of SCU with effect from the end of the current term. He pulled no punches in explaining the grounds of his decision:

> Either this University stands for a definitely and aggressively Christian purpose, or it does not. If it does, then it seems to me to be the only honest thing to say so clearly and unashamedly, when the Government asks us to define our purpose. If it does not, then it ought to, since it is supported with funds subscribed specifically for aggressive Christian work. From this dilemma I cannot escape.[22]

Rowley also wrote again to Wilson the same day, commenting on "the unspeakable tragedy" of his enforced resignation and deploring what he termed the "policy of drift" toward a cumulative acceptance of Nationalist demands.[23] Wilson, for his part, responded to Rowley's letter of resignation with a telegram urging him to suspend his resignation and notifying him that he would travel to China in an endeavor to rescue the situation.[24] Rowley pointedly ignored the request, and on February 10, informed Wilson that he had booked his sea passage home. He accused the Society of inconsistency: it had agreed to register SCU, but at that stage was still resisting registration of its schools, an untenable position that would place students from unregistered Baptist schools applying for places at a now registered university at a grave disadvantage.[25]

Rowley's final and most outspoken letter to Wilson was penned on board the ship *en route* for England on March 26. Again, it is worth citing at some length:

> I have been treated with what is far worse than discourtesy. I was sent back to work in a missionary University, and within three months the Committee had sanctioned such changes in it that it could no longer claim to be a missionary University. It had consented to the elimination of all aggressive Christian purpose from its avowed aim, and the use of a statement of purpose deliberately prepared to

---

21. H. H. Rowley to C. E. Wilson, January 4, 1929, BMSA, CH/64.
22. H. H. Rowley to Dr. Li Tianlu, January 7, 1929, BMSA, CH/64.
23. H. H. Rowley to C. E. Wilson, January 7, 1929, BMSA, CH/64.
24. Telegram from C. E. Wilson to H. H. Rowley, January 1929 [received on January 25], BMSA, CH/64.
25. H. H. Rowley to C. E. Wilson, February 10, 1929, BMSA, CH/64.

satisfy anti-Christians. It had agreed that for the future the University should cease to be under the control of the Home Boards, but should be managed by a Field Board on which foreigners should only exceptionally and by special permission to sit, and by a politically appointed President, who should act under the authority of the Chinese Government. It had agreed that the University, which had hitherto been the organ of the Home Churches for their religious propaganda, should now become the organ of the Chinese Government for its political propaganda. It was not to work in such an institution that I returned.[26]

Wilson still came to China on his special deputation visit, accompanied by a senior member of the BMS Committee, W. Parker Gray. Their visit was dominated by the issue of registration. They found Chinese Christian opinion almost unanimous in favor of registration of all the Society's educational institutions. Chinese Baptists saw no problem about continuing to provide pupils with religious instruction and worship on an entirely voluntary basis. Although the deputation found missionary opinion to be much more mixed, in May 1929 a conference of all BMS missionaries working in the three provinces of Shandong, Shanxi, and Shaanxi agreed to recommend to the BMS Committee that all the Society's middle schools should be registered with government for a trial period of one year. This recommendation was endorsed by the BMS General Committee in October.[27]

In Shandong, events took a further unexpected turn when the provincial education authority declined to register the two BMS high schools in the province on the grounds that religion still appeared on the curriculum, albeit offered on a voluntary basis. Chinese Baptist opinion in Shandong then hardened significantly against registration. In December 1929 the Shantung Baptist Union refused to register their schools, whereupon almost all Baptist schools in the province were shut down by the provincial government. As a result, the flow of Baptist pupils into higher education at SCU was cut off. By early 1934, only 21 out of 575 students at SCU were Baptists; in 1925 no less than one-third had come from Baptist schools. An institution that had been commended to British Baptists as the means of training Chinese Christian leaders for the task of evangelization had been severed from its roots in Baptist church life.[28]

---

26. H. H. Rowley to C. E. Wilson, March 26, 1929, BMSA, CH/64.
27. Stanley, *History of the Baptist Missionary Society*, 313.
28. Stanley, *History of the Baptist Missionary Society*, 313–14.

Competing Types of "Propaganda" and Competing Visions of Citizenship

As for Rowley, he eventually mended his fences with the BMS, serving twice, in 1959–1960 and 1961–1962, as chairman of its General Committee, and once visiting the Belgian Congo on the Society's behalf in the troubled period after Congolese independence.[29] The language he employed in defending his position in 1929 does not endear him to modern ears. In a postcolonial age, most Christians are disinclined to define either Christian mission as a whole or Christian education in particular in terms of the prosecution of "an aggressive Christian purpose"; that sounds too much like proselytism. Neither are they at all comfortable with the language he used of mission as religious "propaganda," a term that has very long antecedents in the history of Catholic missions since 1622. In 1929 it was possible that the term may not yet have been completely suffused by the negative connotations that it began to assume as a result of unprincipled government manipulation of the media during the First World War. Rowley, for one, could use it without any obvious sign of embarrassment. There seems little doubt that he was an argumentative personality who did not react with instinctive sympathy to the genuine concerns of Chinese Christian students about the apparently imperialistic nature of an approach to Christian education that required all pupils to be exposed to Christian teaching.

Nevertheless, Rowley's case does raise in a pointed way the fundamental question with which this chapter began. Where does the boundary fall between true education and indoctrination? Foreign Christians in China eventually had to abandon the attempt to use education to impart specifically Christian teaching and morality, not so much because it was doctrine, but more pointedly because it was perceived as *foreign* doctrine. What filled the vacuum they left behind was not an educational curriculum devoid of doctrinal content, but rather one shaped by what the GMD had originally defined as "instruction in party doctrine" or "party transformation education," and then subsequently redefined as the *san min zhuyi*. Sun Yat-sen's Three Principles of the People—nationalism, the rights of the people (democracy), and the people's livelihood—may seem relatively uncontroversial, but the GMD gave them explicit quasi-theological status as "doctrine" that was essential for national "salvation."[30] Rowley's complaint that political propaganda had simply been substituted for religious propaganda was justified.

Rowley was in a minority in his own society and probably in the Protestant missionary community as a whole. There was no direct correlation between theological

---

29. Anderson, "Harold Henry Rowley 1890–1969," 318.
30. Susan Rigdon, "National Salvation: Teaching Civic Duty in China's Christian Colleges," in Bays and Widmer, *China's Christian Colleges*, 202.

perspective and stances on the registration question. The first Christian university to register with the government was the University of Shanghai for Science and Technology, also a Baptist foundation, but one associated primarily with the Southern Baptist Convention, a constituency that was even more consistently conservative than were English Baptists.[31] Conversely, Rowley's subsequent biblical scholarship suggests someone who had no difficulty combining a traditional commitment to the global mission of the Church with the adoption of higher critical methods.

What was at stake in the argument at Shantung Christian University was a competition between two different visions of citizenship. Rowley's resistance to registration appears to have been shaped by a synthesis between an absolute Christian conviction about the necessity and priority of conversionist mission, and a typically Western liberal educational confidence in the unique capacity of Christianity to promote human welfare and social morality. However, he placed relatively little importance on those ingredients of education that promised the most tangible short-term material benefits to the fragile Chinese nation state. The competing vision offered by the anti-Christian students and the GMD government also drew deeply from Western political notions, but used these to promote a distinctively modern nationalist agenda, while never abandoning entirely classical Confucian assumptions about the role of education in forming a harmonious society.

As the GMD progressively lost its control over China in the face of the Communist advance during the 1930s, and as the Japanese occupation of Manchuria and northeast China from 1931 accentuated the political crisis, the balance of Chinese Nationalist education tipped further and further away from classical Confucian ideals of education in moral character toward an unashamedly utilitarian approach. This privileged scientific and technological education, and is an approach that continued to gather strength in Chinese government policy both before and after 1949. Reforms introduced by the Ministry of Education in 1938 were avowedly intended to achieve a "unification of educational and political aims."[32]

In Taiwan from 1895 to 1945, and in Japanese-occupied China after 1937, Christian schools and colleges had themselves to face the issue of unwelcome religious compulsion deriving from the demands of the Japanese colonial state for the introduction of Shinto shrine ceremonies in honor of the Japanese emperor. The underlying issue was again the use of education to compel students' participation in worship. But here the object of worship was more sinister, namely the imperial head of an invading colonial state, and Christians here found themselves on the side of

---

31. I owe this point to my former PhD student, Dr. Marina Xiaojing Wang of VID Specialized University, Norway.
32. Rigdon, "National Salvation," 205.

voluntary choice, arguing for exemption on grounds of conscience from ceremonies that appeared to verge on the idolatrous.

Conclusion

We might phrase an appropriate conclusion in the following paradoxical terms. On the one hand, public education is simply too strategic for the welfare of any nation for the state to tolerate any foreign elements maintaining significant influence over its delivery and underlying philosophy. Yet, at the same time, education is so important as a channel for the formation and communication of fundamental human values of what is good and true, that to allow the governments of nation states to exercise wholly unfettered and monopolistic control of educational institutions is a perilous pathway for any society to tread.

Rowley's numerous publications in Old Testament studies covered a wide range of themes, most of them apparently unrelated to his years in China. However, they included a volume on *Submission in Suffering and Other Essays in Eastern Thought* (1951),[33] and his Jordan Lectures in Comparative Religion delivered at the School of Oriental and African Studies in London on *Prophecy and Religion in Ancient China and Israel* (1956).[34] They notably also included the divine election of Israel to be a missionary light to the nations, and the missionary message of the Old Testament.[35] Perhaps above all, Rowley's academic writings concentrated on the central place of wisdom in different literary genres in the Hebrew Bible (not simply in the wisdom literature as conventionally defined). His festschrift, presented to him in 1955 by the British Society of Old Testament Study and the Editorial Board of the journal *Vetus Testamentum*, was entitled *Wisdom in Israel and in the Ancient Near East*.[36]

In the Hebraic religious tradition, as in the Confucian one, education is above all about formation in wisdom. Public utility should not eclipse the provision of wisdom; rather, at the most profound level, it derives quite specifically from such provision. The conundrum I have just outlined about the appropriate extent of state involvement in the direction of public education cannot ultimately be resolved, but Christians—and many others—may well wish to argue that the continual tendency

---

33. H. H. Rowley, *Submission in Suffering and Other Essays in Eastern Thought* (Cardiff: University of Wales Press, 1951).
34. H. H. Rowley, *Prophecy and Religion in Ancient China and Israel* (London: The Athlone Press, 1956).
35. H. H. Rowley, *Israel's Mission to the World* (London: Student Christian Movement Press, 1939); Rowley, *The Missionary Message of the Old Testament* (London: Carey Press, 1944); Rowley, *The Biblical Doctrine of Election* (London: Lutterworth Press, 1950).
36. Anderson, "Harold Henry Rowley 1890–1969," 318; M. Noth and D. Winton Thomas, eds., *Wisdom in Israel and in the Ancient Near East: Presented to Harold Henry Rowley by the Society for Old Testament Study in Association with the Editorial Board of Vetus Testamentum, in Celebration of His Sixty-Fifth Birthday, 24 March 1955* (Leiden: E. J. Brill, 1955).

of governments to subordinate a moral and humane vision of education to crudely utilitarian purposes should be subject to periodic challenge.

Bibliography

Allan, David. *Virtue, Learning and the Scottish Enlightenment: Ideas of Scholarship in Early Modern History*. Edinburgh: Edinburgh University Press, 1993.

Anderson, G. W. "Harold Henry Rowley 1890–1969." Vol. 56 of *Proceedings of the British Academy*, 309–19. London: Oxford University Press, 1972.

Baptist Missionary Society archives, Angus Library, Regent's Park College, Oxford, boxes CH/46 and CH/64.

Bays, Daniel H., and Ellen Widmer, eds. *China's Christian Colleges: Cross-Cultural Connections, 1900–1950*. Stanford, CA: Stanford University Press, 2009.

Cameron, Euan. "The Power of the Word: Renaissance and Reformation." In *Early Modern Europe: An Oxford History*, edited by Euan Cameron, 63–101. Oxford: Oxford University Press, 2001.

Clements, Ronald E. "The Biblical Theology of H. H. Rowley, 1890–1969." *Baptist History and Heritage* 38, no. 1 (Winter 2003): 36–63.

Latourette, K. S. *A History of Christian Missions in China*. London: SPCK, 1929.

Lee, Thomas H. C. *Education in Traditional China: A History*. Vol. 13 of *Handbook of Oriental Studies. Section 4 China*. Leiden: E. J. Brill, 2000.

Lutz, Jessie G. *China and the Christian Colleges 1850–1950*. Ithaca, NY, and London: Cornell University Press, 1971.

Lutz, Jessie G. "Chinese Nationalism and the Anti-Christian Campaigns of the 1920s." *Modern Asian Studies* 10, no. 3 (1976): 395–416.

Noth, M., and D. Winton Thomas, eds. *Wisdom in Israel and in the Ancient Near East: Presented to Harold Henry Rowley by the Society for Old Testament Study in Association with the Editorial Board of Vetus Testamentum, in Celebration of his Sixty-Fifth Birthday, 24 March 1955*. Leiden: E. J. Brill, 1955.

Rigdon, Susan. "National Salvation: Teaching Civic Duty in China's Christian Colleges." In Bays and Widmer, *China's Christian Colleges*, 193–217.

Rowley, H. H. *The Biblical Doctrine of Election*. London: Lutterworth Press, 1950.

Rowley, H. H. *Israel's Mission to the World*. London: Student Christian Movement Press, 1939.

Rowley, H. H. *The Missionary Message of the Old Testament*. London: Carey Press, 1944.

Rowley, H. H. *Prophecy and Religion in Ancient China and Israel*. London: The Athlone Press, 1956.

Rowley, H. H. *Submission in Suffering and Other Essays in Eastern Thought*. Cardiff: University of Wales Press, 1951.

Stanley, Brian. *The History of the Baptist Missionary Society 1792–1992*. Edinburgh: T. & T. Clark, 1992.

Wu, Albert Monshan. *From Christ to Confucius: German Missionaries, Chinese Christians and the Globalization of Christianity, 1860–1950*. New Haven, CT: Yale University Press, 2016.

Xu, Edward Yihua. "Liberal Arts Education in English and Campus Culture at St John's University." In Bays and Widmer, *China's Christian Colleges*, 107–24.

Yamamoto, Tatsuro, and Sumiko Yamamoto. "The Anti-Christian Movement in China, 1922–1927." *Far Eastern Quarterly* 12, no. 2 (February 1953): 133–47.

Part Two: Christian Educators

3
"Going Forth to Teach, We Shall Have Learnt"
F. S. Drake at Shantung Christian University/ Cheeloo University and His Embrace of Chinese Culture

Wai Luen Kwok

James Mellon Menzies's research on the Shang dynasty can be considered an outstanding example of sinology at Shantung Christian University/Cheeloo University.[1] However, another sinologist, Frederick Seguier Drake (1892–1974) of Cheeloo, has received relatively little attention. In this chapter, I will show that through Drake's academic experience, we can witness how Chinese culture attracted an education missionary and changed his course of service. The cultural influence of Christian universities in China is not unidirectional but reciprocal.

Frederick Seguier Drake as an Educational Missionary

Frederick Seguier Drake was born in China. His father, Samuel Bingham Drake, joined the Baptist Missionary Society (BMS) as a missionary in Tsowping (Zouping 鄒平), Shantung (Shandong), in 1886.[2] Samuel retired from China in 1910, and Frederick was appointed by the Baptist Missionary Society as a missionary in 1914.[3] He transferred to Shantung Christian University (SCU)/Cheeloo University in 1922, setting up a college of teachers training.[4] However, he was immediately

---
1. Linfu Dong, *Cross Culture and Faith: The Life and Work of James Mellon Menzies* (Toronto: University of Toronto Press, 2005).
2. "Samuel Bingham Drake," Regents Park College, Baptist Missionary Society Archives, Box CH/57, Angus Library, Regent's Park College, Oxford (hereafter cited as BMSA).
3. "Frederick Seguier Drake," Angus Library and Archive, http://theangus.rpc.ox.ac.uk/?candidate=frederick-seguier-drake-2; "Notes on Contributors," *Chinese Recorder* 54, no. 3 (March 1923): 185.
4. C. H. Corbett, *Shantung Christian University (Cheeloo)* (New York: United Board for Christian Education in China, 1955), 160.

recalled to England by BMS to take special studies in education.[5] He resumed his teaching ministry at SCU in late 1924. He served in the School of Arts and Science of the university until 1928. From 1928 to 1929, he transferred to Gotch-Robinson High School (Shoushan Zhongxuexiao 守善中學校) in Qingzhou 青州.[6] In 1930, he was invited to return to the university and teach at the School of Theology.[7] By that time, the School had been formally separated from the university, following the registration requirements of the Nationalist government,[8] but the mission boards still considered it to be an integral part of the University.[9] From the record, we know that Drake was both a faculty member of the School of Theology and the university librarian before the outbreak of the Pacific War in 1941. He was put into a concentration camp for the duration of the war.[10] In 1947, he was named as professor of the School of Theology and the School of Arts of the University.[11] He was appointed by the University of Hong Kong in 1952 as professor of Chinese and the head of the school. In the same year, he applied to retire from BMS.[12] He remained in office as a professor at the university until 1964. He is praised by the School of Chinese as a leader who gathered outstanding scholars and laid a solid academic foundation for the school.[13]

In the early stage of his missionary work, Drake showed a strong passion for education ministry. When he was about to transfer to SCU, he wrote to C. E. Wilson, the general secretary of BMS, and stated that,

> With regard to the work in University; I feel very strongly that the University is the key to our whole work in Shantung. To have already reached the stage when

---

5. "Our Work in China," *Missionary Herald of the Baptist Missionary Society* (hereafter cited as *Missionary Herald*) 105 (1923): 107; "F. S. Drake to C. E. Wilson, July 6, 1924," BMSA, CH/57.
6. "Li Tien-Lu and C. F. Johnson to C. E. Wilson, January 30, 1928," BMSA, CH/33.
7. "Minutes of the Meeting of Board of Directors, Cheeloo University, Tsinan, March 5–7, 1930," 5, BMSA, CH/34; "Shantung Christian University, British Section of the Board of Governors, Minutes of meeting held at 19, Furnival Street, E.C. 4 on Thursday, April 24, 1930," 3, BMSA, CH/34; "Minutes of Meeting, North American Section; Board of Governors, Shantung Christian University, April 25, 1930," 5, BMSA, CH/34.
8. "Benxiao yange shulue" 本校沿革述略 [A brief account of the development of the University], *Qilu daxue fuyuan jinian tekan* 齊魯大學復員紀念特刊 [Special Bulletin for Demobilization of Cheeloo University], December 25, 1946, 2.
9. "Li Tien-Lu to H. H. Weir, December 3, 1929," 6–7, BMSA, CH/34.
10. "Lin Yangshan jiaoshou furen tushuguanchang" 林仰山教授復任圖書館長 [Prof. Drake resumed to be the University Librarian], *Qilu daxue xiaokan* 齊魯大學校刊 [Cheeloo University Bulletin] 64 (1948): 2.
11. "Qilu shenxue jiaoshou Lin Yangshan mushi ming eryue nei laixiao" 齊魯神學教授林仰山牧師明二月內來校 [Rev. Drake, Professor of Cheeloo School of Theology will come to the university in February], *Qilu daxue xiaokan* 62 (1947): 3.
12. "F. S. Drake to V. E. W. Hayward, February 23, 1952," BMSA, CH/57.
13. "School History," School of Chinese, The University of Hong Kong, accessed May 7, 2020, http://web.chinese.hku.hk/main/school-history/.

the Chinese must increase and the Missionary must decrease. But this can only be safely accomplished when all our workers are very much better educated, and men of very much stronger character than at present. From my position here I can see that each year of students graduated in the University has a more fully developed manhood than the year before. Thus It has been strongly borne upon me that the future of our Church, Evangelistic and Educational Work depends upon the work put into the University during the years now upon us. It is this thought which reconciles me to giving up the work in which I am at present engaged. For in going to the University I do not feel that I am leaving the active evangelistic work of the Mission but doing it in another, and perhaps the most permanent, way.[14]

In this letter, we can see that Drake considered his educational mission as "the most permanent" form of "active evangelistic work." Also, we can appreciate that educational mission was for him a means to pave the way for building up Chinese leadership for churches in China.

Drake had already shown enthusiasm for student work when he served in Tsingchowfu (now Qingzhou). In 1919, he started a series of initiatives in student work.[15] His student ministry has been described as "successful"[16] and "very much encouraged."[17] It has been reported that a "marked changed has taken place in the bearing and spirits of the boys."[18] We can see that learning had always been a preparation for evangelism in his thought:

> We found that a lecture, duly announced beforehand, rarely failed to draw an audience: and that besides being in itself a contribution towards the spread of sound, healthy knowledge, so badly needed, it, prepared ground from which an easy and natural transition might be made to the spiritual basis of everything.[19]

Evangelism can also mean an inculturation into Western culture. In September 1923, Drake wrote for the *Missionary Herald* when on the staff of SCU. In the article, he clearly indicated that missionary education institutions are "the keystone" to preparing Chinese Christian leaders and Chinese missionaries for China. He also suggested that in the future, Chinese leaders should have opportunities to study in the West to receive "the best traditions."

> This means that the Chinese leaders are the men of the future. And this in turn means that we cannot make too great an effort to educate, train and equip these

---

14. "F. S. Drake to C. E. Wilson, February 10, 1922," BMSA, CH/57.
15. F. S. Drake, "City Work in Tsingchowfu," *Missionary Herald* 102 (1920): 91–92; Drake, "City Work in Tsingchowfu (continued)," *Missionary Herald* 102 (1920): 113–15.
16. "Our Missions in China," *Missionary Herald* 104 (1922): 88.
17. F. Madeley, "New Methods," *Chinese Recorder* 51, no. 9 (September 1920): 660.
18. "Our Missions in China," 88.
19. Drake, "City Work in Tsingchowfu," 92.

men for their difficult task. This is why the great missionary educational institutions are the keystone of our work there. But more than that is necessary. The best of these men should be brought to England or America, where alone they can imbibe the best traditions, gain the best scholarship, and share in the best Christian fellowship, that we have to give ... Men are not forthcoming in sufficient numbers in the West. But we have them in the East. There we have men of spiritual insight, of moral courage, of intellectual ability. We beg of you to bring some of these men to England, that they may receive the educational advantages that we have enjoyed, and so send Chinese missionaries to the Chinese.[20]

On the surface, Drake's remarks are typical missionary slogans for evangelism. However, with this strong sentiment of evangelism, one may be surprised that he made neither an important contribution to the discipline of education studies or the training of Chinese church leaders, nor to evangelism, but rather to sinology. He was the scholar who discovered the Shang dynasty's deposits at Ta-hsin Chuang (Daxinzhuang 大辛莊), a village in the east of Jinan, in 1936 and described the remains, its bronzes, lithic and bone artifacts, and pottery of the Shang settlement in subsequent publications.[21] The archaeological discovery can be considered as important as the discovery of Yinxu 殷墟. He also contributed to the discovery of the sites at Li-ch'êng (Lizhuang 歷莊) and Wang-Shê-jên Chuang (Wangsherenzhuang 王舍人莊).[22] In addition, he undertook ample research on Chinese philosophy and religion.[23] The missionary Drake, who decided to evangelize and train the Chinese, eventually became absorbed into Chinese history and culture.

In this paper, I would like to trace the course of Drake's journey of learning Chinese culture and argue that the missionary's educational enterprise with the aim of evangelism achieved an unexpected cultural reciprocal influence on missionary work and Western society. In other words, evangelism and Christian education in the Republican period can become a basis for mutual cultural understanding.

Drake's Early Writing on Chinese Culture

Drake's interest in Chinese culture and history can be seen at the early stages of his being an educational missionary. Drake published an article entitled "the Tao Yuan (道院): A New Religious and Spiritualistic Movement" in the March 1923 issue of

---

20. F. S. Drake, "Some Thoughts on China," *Missionary Herald* 105 (1923): 200.
21. F. S. Drake, "Shang Dynasty Find at Ta-hsin Chuang, Shantung," *China Journal* 31, no. 2 (1939): 77–80; F. S. Drake, "Ta-hsin Chuang Again," *China Journal* 33, no. 1 (1940): 8–10.
22. F. S. Drake, "A Shang Dynasty Site at Li-ch'êng (歷城) Wan-Shê-Jên-Chuang (王舍人庄) Shantung," *China Journal* 31, no. 3 (1940): 118–20.
23. A bibliography of Drake's works that I have found is included at the end of the chapter.

the *Chinese Recorder*.²⁴ "Tao Yuan" is a Chinese religious movement that started in the early Republican period. According to Drake, it is

> the worship of the Most Holy Primeval Father (崇奉至聖先天老祖), the Founders of the Five Religions:—Christianity, Mohammedanism, Confucianism, Buddhism, Taoism; and the Gods, the Saints, the Worthies, and Buddhas of the whole world throughout all generations; together with the perception of the "God-given World-Centre True Scripture" as the connecting link between the truths of the Five Religions.²⁵

The movement is a typical Chinese folk religion and includes magic and spirit possession. It commenced with planchette writing (*fuji* 扶乩), a ritual that the Eight Immortals of Taoist mythology used to deliver their messages by a planchette stick on a tray of sand. Hou Hsueh-fang (Hou Xuefang 侯雪舫/Hou Yanshuang 侯延爽), a *jinshi* 進士 of the Qing dynasty and former high-ranking official in the government, who was a Christian, joined the Tao Yuan. Drake reported that Chinese Christians were scared of the movement and worried that it was deceitfully compelling.

> The Chinese Church in Tsinanfu is on the whole scared of the Tao Yuan. Hou Hsueh-fang has fallen away; the planchette is the work of evil spirits; or at any rate the whole business is one gigantic piece of fraud. Some of the leading Christians vow never to cross the threshold of the place. Some of the best educated dare not associate themselves to any great extent with Mr. Hou lest they too should fall away.²⁶

However, Drake did not have such a negative evaluation of Hou. He could see the sincerity of Hou's new religious faith, and he even appreciated Hou's emphasis upon Christ.

> Consequently I see the movement through Mr. Hou's eyes; that is through the eyes of a man who is thoroughly sincere, and who, entering it as a Christian, feels he has in it a deeper, more spiritual form of Christianity than that represented by the Churches; but a man whose mind is a jumble of religious ideas, collected during his passage through many faiths to Christianity, and a man who is credulous to the last degree.

> Many hours have been spent in conversation with Mr. Hou, and it has been possible to form some idea of his point of view, though it is not likely that many of his fellows put the same emphasis upon Christ as he. To him the Tao Yuan is a means for extending the glory of Christ. The ordinary methods of preaching Christ are

---

24. F. S. Drake, "The Tao Yuan (道院): A New Religious and Spiritualistic Movement," *Chinese Recorder* 54, no. 3 (March 1923): 133–44.
25. Drake, "The Tao Yuan," 133.
26. Drake, "The Tao Yuan," 143.

sufficient for the West and for the masses of China, but not for those imbued with the old Chinese culture. In the East many great and noble religions have been first in the field, and Christ must be preached in the terms of those religions ... Here the supercilious is brought face to face with the Unseen World, in a most striking manner. He receives a knock-down blow, and believes.[27]

Furthermore, the religious movement made Drake think that it was an imperative for the missionaries to take "far more earnest study of Chinese religion than most of us have undertaken."[28] In short, he had the desire to evangelize the Chinese, but he found the sincerity of folk religion believers could only be won by missionaries with a well-versed understanding of Chinese religions.

In June 1923 issue of the *Missionary Herald*, Drake commented on the philosophy of Chu Hsi (Zhu Xi 朱熹, 1130–1200). He criticized the Western view of his time on Zhu Xi and the Neo-Confucianism of the Song dynasty as "materialist and atheist" as being "formed after all too superficial acquaintance with Chu Hsi's works."[29] Conversely, he had a very positive assessment:

> So, then, fundamental to Chu Hsi's view of life is the fact that Goodness is the source of all things, a Goodness which is Love in its origin and Righteousness in all its activities, a Goodness which can be focused in the perfect human life.
>
> It is difficult to conceive of so lofty and at the same time so practical a view of life without the implication of God. And in fact Chu Hsi came as near as it is possible to come, without the revelation of God in Christ, to the acknowledgment of God. "These passages," he says, quoting from the Sages, "indicate that there is a Person, as it were, ruling in it all." And again, "That there is a personal Being above us by whose commands these things come to pass, seems to be taught by the 'Odes' and 'Records.' 'The Decree of Heaven' which plays so large a part in Chu Hsi's philosophy, would, with but a slightly richer connotation, be equivalent to the Christian 'Will of God.'"[30]

Again, Drake's claim that Zhu Xi's philosophy was a revelation of God in Christ and "the Decree of Heaven" would be equivalent to the Christian "Will of God" is indeed striking. It showed he had an extremely open mind to Chinese culture. Even without the missionaries, Chinese culture in its history has already shown God revealed in Christ. Indeed, in his article "Some Thoughts on China," Drake suggested that the reasonable, tolerant, and friendly character of Chinese people made Chinese culture a better candidate than the Western "primitive fighting instincts" for

---

27. Drake, "The Tao Yuan," 141–42.
28. Drake, "The Tao Yuan," 144.
29. F. S. Drake, "The Message of a Chinese Philosopher: Dr. Percy Bruce's New Book," *Missionary Herald* 105 (1923): 135.
30. Drake, "The Message of a Chinese Philosopher," 136.

"full perfection" of the Christian life and "a new world order" of the "Law of Love."[31] He even believed that it is God's will that Chinese culture would be the salvation of the Western world.

> For then the purposes of God will have ripened. The wonder of the whole missionary enterprise will have become apparent. Going forth to teach, we shall have learnt; to give, we shall have received; to heal, we shall have been healed. We shall then see clearly that missions were not a benevolent philanthropic undertaking, given patronisingly to an inferior race; but the operation of the wonderful purpose of God, and an essential part of our own salvation as well.[32]

Drake's statement clearly showed that he did not consider Chinese culture to be inferior. He regarded Chinese culture highly and as a means for the salvation of the West. Remember, in the same journal, he urged the Western support of missionary education institutions and for Chinese students to be educated in the West. In other words, his vision of Christian education in China was a grand dream of cultural exchange and mutual fertilization.

Besides his published writing, one can see through Drake's correspondence with the home mission that he was deeply attracted to Chinese culture. In 1927, he was evacuated to Korea because of the unstable situation in Shandong. Even during the evacuation, he was filled with a passion for Chinese culture. He stated, "Being still in the atmosphere of Chinese civilisation, there is encouragement to continue the study of things Chinese—for instance I am reading Chinese philosophy with a good Chinese scholar—an old friend of mine—who happens to be here."[33]

In short, we can find that Drake showed a genuine interest in Chinese culture from an early stage as an educational missionary. Though he emphasized the importance of evangelism, he explicitly stated that Chinese culture is something that missionaries should learn from and that it could even be the salvation of Western culture. The limitation of his writing at this stage is that he could not articulate Chinese culture with depth and breadth.

Comparative Religion and Chinese Culture

In 1934, from Drake's letters and report, we know that he was responsible for teaching comparative religion. In a letter to friends, he explained that teaching comparative religion is essential for the future of Christianity. He asserted that "God works through these other religions as a preparation for a fuller Gospel, that I cannot

---

31. Drake, "Some Thoughts on China," 201–2.
32. Drake, "Some Thoughts on China," 202.
33. "F. S. Drake to C. E. Wilson, May 12, 1927," BMSA, CH/57.

forbear relating it."³⁴ In the annual report of 1933–1934, he reported that the comparative religion course "leads one out into the vast field of Chinese religions that in so many ways gives the foundations of thought and character to the people amongst whom we live."³⁵ We can also see in the report that he had a real interest in Chinese culture. Preparing possible courses that he might take up in the future, he always "put aside some time each day for the study of the Confucian Classics, Buddhist Scriptures and Chinese Dynastic Histories."³⁶

In 1934, Drake wrote an article recording his experience of meeting with the Taoists of Laoshan 崂山.³⁷ He described the monasteries and Buddhist temples in the Laoshan area in detail. At the end of the article, he voiced a wish that Christ would fulfill the needs of the gentle mystic Taoists and help them rid themselves of superstitions.³⁸ In 1935, he wrote another article on Chinese religion, "Religion in a Manchurian City," and published it in the *Chinese Recorder*.³⁹ The article also is a record of his visit to religious sites of Taoism, Buddhism, Confucianism, Islam, Tao Yuan, and Christianity. Drake related that he had seen "a picture of men and women each in their own way, and according to their own best light, seeking to know GOD, and serving their fellow men."⁴⁰ His comments showed that he did not consider religious faiths other than Christianity as "heathen." Conversely, they all have light within them; they all seek to know God and serve other people. In short, all religions have value.

In the fourth annual retreat of interdenominational and international groups at Peitaiho (Beidaihe 北戴河) in August 1935, Drake was invited to speak. He delivered a series of lectures with the general theme of "The Fellowship of the Spirit." One of his sub-topics was "The Spiritual Experience of Other Faiths."⁴¹ The choice of topic revealed that he continued to hold high regard for Chinese religions and cultures.

In 1938, Drake had another opportunity to take a one-year furlough in England. He expressed the wish to prepare himself well for teaching comparative religion, particularly by studying the Syriac language in order to understand Buddhist and

---

34. "F. S. Drake to Friends, June 1934," BMSA, CH/57.
35. F. S. Drake, "Report of Work for the Year 1933–4," 5, BMSA, CH/57.
36. Drake, "Report of Work for the Year 1933–4," 6.
37. F. S. Drake, "The Taoists of Lao-Shan," *Chinese Recorder* 65, no. 4 (April 1934): 238–45; F. S. Drake, "The Taoists of Lao-Shan (continued)," *Chinese Recorder* 65, no. 5 (May 1934): 308–18.
38. Drake, "The Taoists of Lao-Shan (continued)," 318.
39. F. S. Drake, "Religion in a Manchurian City," *Chinese Recorder* 66, no. 2 (February 1935): 104–11; F. S. Drake, "Religion in a Manchurian City (continued)," *Chinese Recorder* 66, no. 3 (March 1935): 161–70.
40. Drake, "Religion in a Manchurian City (continued)," 170.
41. "Peitaiho Conferences," *Chinese Recorder* 66, no. 10 (October 1935): 635.

Nestorian thought.[42] The dean of Theology, C. A. Stanley, also supported his plan.[43] Drake explained that he wanted to be genuinely "conversant" with living religions in China and engage with the original scriptures of the religions.

> I have to teach Comparative Religions up to B.D. standard in a land where they are living religions, and I am not content to teach them out of a small text-book that does not touch reality; in other words I am not willing to teach about religions of which I am not conversant with their scriptures in the originals.[44]

However, when Drake arrived in London, he wrote to Wilson and made a change in his plan of which he noted that "the details may weary you."[45] The "wearying" change is that he wanted to use "all the time" in England to translate ancient Chinese philosophical work with critical notes. He told Wilson that,

> I brought back with me from China—and it was to me the most valuable part of my baggage—a collection of Chinese books and a manuscript upon which I have been working in my spare time during the past three or four years; the manuscript is a translation with critical notes of one of the Chinese philosophers about 300 B.C. who has not yet been translated into any foreign language, and who has his bearing upon my class work. It has already reached more than a thousand pages, and requires two or three hundred more, besides thorough revision of the whole, before it can be made available for use. I had hoped to get this finished soon after arrival in England, and to be able to offer it to a publisher, as a contribution to the study of Chinese thought. However I have not been able to make the progress I had hoped, and I can foresee that it will still demand all the time, and more than all the time, that I can muster in England to finish it. I am particularly desirous of finishing it, because unfinished it is useless, and means so many years thrown away. I am also unwilling to take an uncopied manuscript back to China for fear of its being destroyed.[46]

In this long quotation, we can find that Drake had a great passion for introducing ancient Chinese philosophy to his English readership. At this point, he took one step further. He moved from a Christian teacher of comparative religion and became a transmitter of Chinese culture.

---

42. "F. S. Drake to C. E. Wilson, February 13, 1937," BMSA, CH/57.
43. "Chas. A. Stanley to C. E. Wilson, December 8, 1936," BMSA, CH/57.
44. "F. S. Drake to C. E. Wilson, July 11, 1938," BMSA, CH/57.
45. "F. S. Drake to C. E. Wilson, June 12, 1938," BMSA, CH/57.
46. "F. S. Drake to C. E. Wilson, June 12, 1938."

"The Contribution of Chinese Religious Thought"

In the September and October 1941 issues of the *Chinese Recorder*, Drake published an article entitled "The Contribution of Chinese Religious Thought."[47] To a certain extent, we can treat it as a full development of his article from 1923. Through this work, one can see that the educational missionary in China eventually became a missionary of Chinese culture and religion to the West.

Drake reminded readers that we must not think of religion merely as a religious system, but rather as the "life of the people," "quality," and "value."[48] He explicitly commended Chinese thought as making a "contribution to the solution of the present world problem, and to the creation of a new world."[49] He criticized the Western view of life as "partial" and "distorted." He believed that "Without the help of another race . . . we cannot get a correct view of life as a whole."[50] His early theme of the salvation of the West by Chinese culture appeared again in this work. However, after Drake's over eighteen years of study, we can have a clear picture of how he understood Chinese culture. For him, cultures are "grounds" for "the good seed of the Word" of the Gospel.[51] In other words, cultures are vessels for the Christian faith. Different cultures will produce different fruits of Christianity. In his opinion, the Chinese culture is a "good ground in which that seed can bear fruit, not choked by the thorns and the weeds of the West."[52] His statement showed that he treated cultures equally and recognized the limitations of Western culture.

Drake the mature scholar could now clearly identify the merits of the Chinese culture of different historical periods. He appreciated the ancient religion of the Shang dynasty as "a personal relationship between men and God." Also, its source seemed "to be an intuitive belief in God and in life after death."[53] He pointed out that "The 'Ti' (*Di* 帝) or 'Shang Ti' (*Shangdi* 上帝)—God—of the Shang period was conceived as an Eternal Being ruling the world in righteousness, and requiring righteousness of men, rather than ritualistic sacrifice. In this respect, early Chinese religion is in keeping with the teaching of the Hebrew prophets."[54]

For the early Chinese classics of the Zhou dynasty, Drake found that they started a movement of naturalistic and materialistic tendency. But he insisted that "in spite

---

47. F. S. Drake, "The Contribution of Chinese Religious Thought," *Chinese Recorder* 72, no. 9 (September 1941): 496–505; Drake, "The Contribution of Chinese Religious Thought (Concluded)," *Chinese Recorder* 72, no. 10 (October 1941): 537–45.
48. Drake, "Contribution of Chinese Religious Thought," 496–97.
49. Drake, "Contribution of Chinese Religious Thought," 497.
50. Drake, "Contribution of Chinese Religious Thought," 497.
51. Drake, "Contribution of Chinese Religious Thought," 497.
52. Drake, "Contribution of Chinese Religious Thought," 497.
53. Drake, "Contribution of Chinese Religious Thought," 498.
54. Drake, "Contribution of Chinese Religious Thought," 499.

of this deterioration of the idea of Heaven, the original spiritual idea of a Conscious, Ethical Will, a Power making for Righteousness, always persisted alongside the more materialistic and mechanical idea, even to the present day."[55] He summarized the main schools of thought in the Pre-Chin period into four: the Confucian, the Taoist, the Mohist, and the Legalist schools.[56] Among them, Confucianism triumphed. He emphasized that the triumph means that the Chinese were concerned with moral character and human relationships,[57] moral government and education,[58] and the equality of life.[59] In each of the above characteristics, Drake found positive aspects. For Confucian moral cultivation, he suggested that,

> From this it is apparent that in Confucian thinking intellectual and moral truth are not distinguished; there is One Truth running through the Universe, expressing itself in physical and moral laws; it is for men by earnest study and constant practice, to bring his individual, social and political life into accord with these.[60]

For the moral government, he said,

> Here is the democratic spirit expressed in clear and definite terms. The final authority is the voice of the people; not however swayed irresponsibly by the word of the demagogue, but as expressing the moral principles of the Universe implanted in the heart of Man.[61]

For the equality of life, he claimed that,

> Hence the Chinese have been called Humanists, and humanists they are in the best sense of the term: the sense in which Christ was a humanist, putting the claims of men before the claims of Church or State or creed. "The Sabbath was made for man, not man for the Sabbath." "Whosoever shall give to drink unto one of these little ones a cup of cold water only, in the name of a disciple . . . he shall in no wise lose his reward." "Inasmuch as ye did it unto one of these my brethren, even these least ye did it unto me." "Where two or three are gathered together in my name, there am I in the midst of them."[62]

This last quotation is the most telling passage. Drake directly linked the Confucian teaching with the teaching of Christ, and he described it as "Humanism."

---

55. Drake, "Contribution of Chinese Religious Thought," 499–500.
56. Drake, "Contribution of Chinese Religious Thought," 500.
57. Drake, "Contribution of Chinese Religious Thought," 503.
58. Drake, "Contribution of Chinese Religious Thought," 504.
59. Drake, "Contribution of Chinese Religious Thought," 505.
60. Drake, "Contribution of Chinese Religious Thought," 504.
61. Drake, "Contribution of Chinese Religious Thought," 505.
62. Drake, "Contribution of Chinese Religious Thought," 505.

Drake cited *The Doctrine of the Mean* (*Zhongyong* 中庸) to further explain that the essence of Confucian Humanism is that "human nature consists of moral principles conferred by Heaven."[63] He then quoted a statement from Zhu Xi and asserted that Confucian Humanism is in accordance with the Christian teaching of the image of God.

> "The source of the Way is in Heaven and cannot be changed; its concrete embodiment is in ourselves and cannot be neglected" (道之本原出於天而不可易。其實體備於己而不可離). This is another way of saying that man is created in the image of God; the image of God referring of course not to his physical form but to the mental and moral elements of his nature.[64]

Confucianism is exalted in its moral teaching, and it has a religious background—the Way of Heaven—to support it.[65] However, he found that the Chinese people's religious needs could not be fully satisfied by Confucianism. Thus, Taoism, and especially Buddhism, filled this gap.

Drake suggested that the mystic approach to the *Dao* in the *Daode jing* 道德經, "if taken to heart in the West would save us from many of our theological and ecclesiastical controversies."[66] For Buddhism, he recognized that Buddhism enriched the religious life and thought of Chinese people. He pointed out that the division of Buddhist schools in China was much better than the division of Christianity in the West.[67]

Finally, Drake turned to introduce the Neo-Confucian thought of the Song dynasty. As in the 1920s, he held high regard for Zhu Xi. He saw parallels between Zhu and Paul the apostle in teaching.

> "Man's nature is entirely good . . . but when I wish to act accordingly, alas! I am carried away by human desire" (人性無不善……但則是我要恁地做，不奈何，便是人欲奪了). The language is surprisingly like that of St. Paul: "I delight in the law of God after the inward man: but I see another law in my members, warring against the law of my mind, and bringing me into captivity to the law of sin which is in my members." But what to St. Paul was a central theme, was to Chu Hsi only a single admission. Chu Hsi had not the deep sense of sin of St. Paul, nor the joy of a Deliverer: "O wretched man that I am! who shall deliver me from the body of this death? I thank God through Jesus Christ our Lord."[68]

---

63. Drake, "Contribution of Chinese Religious Thought (Concluded)," 538.
64. Drake, "Contribution of Chinese Religious Thought (Concluded)," 538.
65. Drake, "Contribution of Chinese Religious Thought (Concluded)," 539–40.
66. Drake, "Contribution of Chinese Religious Thought (Concluded)," 540.
67. Drake, "Contribution of Chinese Religious Thought (Concluded)," 542.
68. Drake, "Contribution of Chinese Religious Thought (Concluded)," 544.

Finally, he repeated his earlier claim made in the 1920s that Zhu Xi had approached God with his greatest capacity without the revelation of God in Jesus Christ, and rightly described the ultimate reality of the universe in personal and conscious terms.[69] In conclusion, Drake emphasized that the ethical mind of Zhu Xi is "very much akin to the Mind of Christ."

> They were laymen, brought up in the traditions of Chinese moral education, and bearing the responsibility of Chinese official life. It is therefore the more remarkable that experience of life, accurate observation, and prolonged reflection, led them to see the Universe as the outcome of Creative Love, as the manifestation of an Ethical Mind. If it is true that "Christianity ... was a religion founded by a layman for laymen," we have something here very much akin to the Mind of Christ.[70]

One must notice that in this comment, Drake did not suggest that the Neo-Confucian teaching has inadequacies and flaws. Rather, he suggested that it is a religion much akin to Christianity. Moreover, as he stated in the beginning of the article, the Western world can be corrected and saved by the Chinese culture. He became a missionary of Chinese culture.

"The Christian Teacher in China"[71]

One may question whether the change indicated that Drake had betrayed his early vision of Christian education in China. I do not think that Drake's change was a betrayal of his education ideal. Rather, I consider it a thoughtful reflection on Chinese culture and its relationship with education after his years of service in China. In 1938, he published an article entitled "Problems Before Christian Education in China," in *Religion in Education*, reviewing the history of Christian education in China.[72] He appreciated that China had had schools since ancient times and that Chinese classics provided a broad humanistic education. However, the method of learning by memorizing content without explanation and understanding, and the formal essays required for imperial examinations, negated the educational value of the system. Therefore, when the Western missionaries arrived in China, they established schools to train leaders for the newly founded Chinese churches. The subjects were based on the need to prepare the students to teach Scripture and religion and included both Chinese classics and Western subjects such as mathematics, natural science, mental

---

69. Drake, "Contribution of Chinese Religious Thought (Concluded)," 544–45.
70. Drake, "Contribution of Chinese Religious Thought (Concluded)," 545.
71. F. S. Drake, "The Christian Teacher in China: I. The Ancient Confucian Background," *Religion in Education* 15, no. 1 (1947): 22–25.
72. F. S. Drake, "Problems before Christian Education in China," *Religion in Education* 5, no. 4 (1938): 200–207.

and moral philosophy, history, and geography. The initial educational attempt slowly became a model of modern education in China.[73] After the abolition of the imperial examinations, the Chinese government introduced a modern school system. Drake noticed that one might have thought that "there would be no further need for the maintenance of the secular part of the Christian school system."[74] However, he pointed out that many Christian schools remained in operation. The first reason for a space for Christian education in China was that Chinese Christians recognized the value of the schools in keeping alive a Christian community by training "a body of enlightened Christian men and women, with ideals of service and with trained minds and practical abilities."[75] The second reason is that the character-building of Christian education was generally recognized and attractive to the general public.[76]

After establishing the basis for Christian education in China, Drake discussed the problems facing the Christian schools. He identified four problems: 1. poverty; 2. illiteracy; 3. Christian education's relation to Chinese culture; 4. the question of religion in the Christian school system.[77] For poverty and illiteracy, he argued that Chinese churches and Christians could manage them quite well. Chinese Christians believed in the value of education. They were willing to bear the financial burden for their children's education in Christian schools with a hope of good character-building and career prospect.[78] Regarding the problem of illiteracy, he confidently claimed, "The Christian Church has been a leader in endeavouring to overcome the joint problems of illiteracy and the difficulty of the written language [in China]."[79]

For Chinese Christian schools and colleges, the government's restriction on religious education was a problem in the Republican period. Drake reported that, from 1927 onward, the Chinese government required all schools to be registered, with the requirement that religious courses were forbidden in primary and secondary schools' curricula and were only allowed in universities as electives. Some Christian schools decided to close down as a result of the restrictions.[80] However, he thought that making religious education courses voluntary could meet the challenge. In a report about boys' schools in Qingzhou of BMS in 1928, he noted that the students "gained more than they lost" by voluntary religious education, because "the spirit became more and more sincere."[81] After the war, he still held the view

---

73. Drake, "Problems before Christian Education," 200.
74. Drake, "Problems before Christian Education," 201.
75. Drake, "Problems before Christian Education," 202.
76. Drake, "Problems before Christian Education," 201.
77. Drake, "Problems before Christian Education," 202–7.
78. Drake, "Problems before Christian Education," 202–3.
79. Drake, "Problems before Christian Education," 204.
80. Drake, "Problems before Christian Education," 206.
81. F. S. Drake, "Report of Boys' Schools in the Eastern Association – 1928," January 1929, 3-4, CH/57, BMSA.

that "[b]efore long, statistics showed that the religious results in Middle Schools and Colleges were better under the voluntary than under the compulsory system."[82]

I argue that for Drake, the most weighty and ongoing problem for Christian education in China was its relation to Chinese culture. At this point, we can link his passion for Chinese religions and culture with Christian education. He argued that Chinese culture can be seen as "a revelation."[83] According to Drake, ideals and resources in Confucianism, Neo-Confucianism, Taoism, and Buddhism "are all assets in the troubled world of to-day on the side of a spiritual interpretation of life, and they cannot be ignored by the Christian educationist."[84] Therefore, a good Christian teacher in China should be a teacher that embraces Chinese culture and advances it with new meaning from the Christian faith:

> It is hardly too much to say that one of the finest sights in China to-day is that of a Christian Chinese teacher who is grounded in this culture of his own land and who sees it illumined by the light of his Christian experience, and selects from it and expounds it with new meaning and force.[85]

Indeed, Drake held to this educational ideal. In 1948, he listed the tasks of Christian education in China in detail. He stated that,

> The special tasks of Christian education in China are: first to train leaders for the Christian Church, preachers (lay and cleric, men and women), teachers, doctors and social workers; second, to educate the Christian laity, sending young Christian men and women into all walks of life, and also by a wide spread system of adult education to raise the general level of the Christian community; third, to give a Christian interpretation of the Chinese classics and Chinese civilisation, which is to bring out the full spiritual and ethical meaning inherent in them, by teaching with true spiritual insight the Chinese humanities—this may well become the supreme task of the Christian teacher in China in the future; and fourth, to interpret Christianity to the educated in China by presenting it in relation to the best Eastern and Western thought.[86]

Drake highlighted that interpreting Chinese culture through Christian faith to bring out its "full spiritual and ethical meaning" would be "the supreme task" of the Christian teacher in China. Also, the Christian teacher in China should teach the Christian faith by articulating it in connection with Eastern and Western cultures.

---

82. F. S. Drake, "The Christian Teacher in China: II. The Modern System and the Place of Christian Education," *Religion in Education* 15, no. 2 (1948): 54.
83. Drake, "Problems before Christian Education in China," 205.
84. Drake, "Problems before Christian Education in China," 205–6.
85. Drake, "Problems before Christian Education in China," 206.
86. Drake, "The Christian Teacher in China: II. The Modern System and the Place of Christian Education," 55.

In another article, he likewise mentioned that "the supreme task of the Christian universities of China is to unite in perfect understanding in Christ the spiritual and ethical consciousness of East and West."[87] In the article, he explained how the task can be done in detail. In addition, one can notice that it is the philosophical or theological logic that he proposed in "The Contribution of Chinese Religious Thought."

> It may fairly be argued that Christianity sets the seal to the spiritual and ethical values of the ancient civilization of China; that God, intimately known and loved in Jesus Christ, is the great Being dimly set forth in the Chinese Classics; that Christ is the Perfect Man of Confucianism—but perfect through the Cross; and that the Kingdom of God is the great world order of peace and harmony to which all things were thought to tend; that the moral sense recognized as deeply rooted in human nature is the voice of God; and that the original uncorrupted nature of man, so often emphasized in the Chinese books, is none other than man's creation in the image of God. In the Christian consciousness the ancient humanistic teaching finds its fulfilment and its root; its meaning and its moral power.[88]

From the above quotations, one can see in Drake's own experience as an educational missionary was an experience of putting the ideal into practice. His turn to Chinese religions and culture was a necessary step for him to be a good Christian teacher in China, who had the task of uniting Christian and Chinese cultures.

In my opinion, Drake's thought on this point was not an idealistic fantasy or the result of religious zeal, but a very concrete and respectful suggestion for missionaries working in Christian education in China in the early twentieth century. Li T'ien-Lu (Li Tianlu 李天祿), the president of Cheeloo University from 1927 to 1929, wrote out his expectation for a good educational missionary from the West in a letter to C. E. Wilson in 1928; when the university was facing political unrest, student protests and the pressure of registration. Li emphasized the importance of love for the Chinese people of the missionary teachers. He believed that it was crucial to keep the original Christian educational purpose of the University.

> I am convinced that in seeking to strengthen the foreign staff in the university with men of the right type you are doing the wisest thing to prevent that falling away from the original Christian purpose which has been feared by some of our supporters in the British churches. By men of the right type I mean missionaries with a sympathetic attitude of mind and broad vision, with a deep love for the people to whom they are sent and with a deep, personal spiritual experience. That type of missionary would help a great deal to maintain the Christian character of the

---

87. F. S. Drake, "East and West in Christian Universities in China," *International Review of Mission* 36, no. 3 (1947): 342.
88. Drake, "East and West," 342.

institution and also render good service to the general Christian movement in this country.[89]

Li did not explain what he meant by "a sympathetic attitude of mind and broad vision," but from the above analysis, we can ascertain that Drake the educational missionary had a sympathetic attitude and a broad vision of Chinese culture and religions. He also exhibited a great love for Chinese people by wholeheartedly embracing their culture and tradition. Li's statement testifies that Drake was a teacher that Chinese educators in the early twentieth century wanted to have for a good Christian education.

Finally, I want to point out that Drake's educational vision, for him, bore both real-life and spiritual significance to the world. He presented his educational ideal as a solution to global conflicts and a realization of the Christian hope of salvation of the universe. He stated that,

> In the stress of conflicting world forces, the Christian universities in China are thus making their contribution towards a new social synthesis in these three ways—in life, thought and religion—as centres of growing understanding between East and West, in the Spirit of Jesus Christ, "where there is neither Greek nor Jew, circumcision nor uncircumcision, barbarian, Scythian, bond nor free, but Christ is all, and in all."[90]

The abiding belief that cultural exchange can solve global conflicts reminds us of Drake's early work in 1923. Therefore, one may suggest that his turn to Chinese religions and culture in his educational ministry was a fulfillment of his conviction. For him, education can effectively integrate Chinese culture and the Christian faith together; and generate new resources for dealing with problems in the world. After working in China for over three decades, Drake could concretely explain his vision of Christian education as a cultural synergy. He penetratingly identified that the international cooperation of material form—financial, economic, industrial, commercial, and mechanical—of his time "is usually given rather patronizingly from a stronger to a weaker power." He argued that Christian universities of China can achieve "deeper, more fundamental, more reciprocal" cooperation in social, intellectual, and religious realms.[91] In the social realm, he pointed out that Christian universities form real communities of different races with a common purpose. The communal life helps the members of the universities to live without racial distinction and grow daily in the understanding of one another's life and ways.[92] In the

---

89. "Li Tien-Lu to C. E. Wilson, October 22, 1928," BMSA, CH/33.
90. Drake, "East and West," 343.
91. Drake, "East and West," 339.
92. Drake, "East and West," 340.

intellectual realm, he emphasized that the significant contribution to natural science made by Christian universities of China was due to the fact that "eastern and western members of staff work side by side."[93] In the field of the humanities in Christian universities, he was aware that "the West has something to teach and something to learn; perhaps it has less to teach and more to learn; some would say it has nothing to teach and everything to learn." Thus, they can "include the wisdom of both East and West."[94] In the area of religion, he pointed out that the religious life of Christian universities in China helped to nurture a new Christian consciousness of tolerance and mutual acceptance. The interdenominational cooperation in Christian universities of China showed that differences in belief can be "an enrichment of religious life and thought; for unity can be achieved not by elimination but comprehension." Different denominations can preserve the value of their particular contribution, "not by withdrawing it from the common stock, but by pouring it in."[95] For everyday religious life, he observed that the "universal element is preserved, and the western trappings fall away or, rather gradually give place to more appropriate Chinese forms of expression."[96] In short, all three areas indicate that meaningful cooperation and reciprocal exchanges were being done within the Christian universities of China.

Drake stated that Christian universities in China that were serving the new social synthesis were the places "in the Spirit of Jesus Christ" that "Christ is all, and in all." He gave a deep religious significance to Christian education institutions performing cultural exchange and integration in China as manifestations of the work of the Spirit. Indeed, in his later life, he explicitly asserted that one understands Eastern cultures and religions through a "religious spirit diffused through all."[97] Therefore, for Drake as an educator, turning to Chinese religions and culture was a journey into the spiritual realm where "Christ is all, and in all." "Going forth to teach, we shall have learnt"[98] is a necessary experience for a Christian teacher in China for an education that can change China and the world in the Spirit of Christ.

Bibliography

"Benxiao yange shulue" 本校沿革述略 [A brief account of the development of the University]. *Qilu Daxue fuyuan jinian tekan* 齊魯大學復員紀念特刊 [Special bulletin for demobilization of Cheeloo University], December 25, 1946: 2.

---

93. Drake, "East and West," 340.
94. Drake, "East and West," 341.
95. Drake, "East and West," 343.
96. Drake, "East and West," 343.
97. F. S. Drake, "The Study of Asia: A Heritage and a Task: Inaugural Address Delivered on April 7, 1960," *Journal of the Hong Kong Branch of the Royal Asiatic Society* 1 (1960–61): 17.
98. Drake, "Some Thoughts on China," 202.

"Lin Yangshan jiaoshou furen tushuguan zhang." 林仰山教授復任圖書館長 [Prof. Drake resumed to be the University librarian]." *Qilu Daxue xiaokan* 齊魯大學校刊 [Cheeloo University Bulletin] 64 (1948): 2.

"Notes on Contributors." *Chinese Recorder* 54 (1923): 185.

"Our Missions in China." *Missionary Herald of the Baptist Missionary Society* 104 (1922): 88.

"Our Work in China." *Missionary Herald of the Baptist Missionary Society* 105 (1923): 107.

"Peitaiho Conferences," *Chinese Recorder* 66, no. 10 (October 1935): 635.

"Qilu shenxue jiaoshou Lin Yangshan mushi ming eryue nei laixiao" 齊魯神學教授林仰山牧師明二月內來校 [Rev. Drake, Professor of Cheeloo School of Theology will come to the University in February], *Qilu Daxue xiaokan* 62 (1947): 3.

Corbett, C. H. *Shantung Christian University (Cheeloo)*. New York: United Board for Christian Education in China, 1955.

Dong, Linfu. *Cross Culture and Faith: The Life and Work of James Mellon Menzies*. Toronto: University of Toronto Press, 2005.

Drake, F. S. "A Shang Dynasty Site at Li-ch'êng (歷城) Wan-Shê-Jên-Chuang (王舍人庄) Shantung," *China Journal* 31, no. 3 (1940): 118–20.

Drake, F. S. "City Work in Tsingchowfu (continued)." *Missionary Herald of the Baptist Missionary Society* 102 (1920): 113–15.

Drake, F. S. "City Work in Tsingchowfu." *Missionary Herald of the Baptist Missionary Society* 102 (1920): 91–92.

Drake, F. S. "East and West in Christian Universities in China." *International Review of Mission* 36, no. 3 (1947): 338–43.

Drake, F. S. "Problems before Christian Education in China." *Religion in Education* 5, no. 4 (1938): 200–207.

Drake, F. S. "Religion in a Manchurian City (continued)." *Chinese Recorder* 66, no. 3 (March 1935): 161–70.

Drake, F. S. "Religion in a Manchurian City." *Chinese Recorder* 66, no. 2 (February 1935): 104–11.

Drake, F. S. "Shang Dynasty Find at Ta-hsin Chuang, Shantung." *China Journal* 31, no. 2 (1939): 77–80.

Drake, F. S. "Some Thoughts on China." *Missionary Herald of the Baptist Missionary Society* 105 (1923): 200.

Drake, F. S. "Ta-hsin Chuang Again." *China Journal* 33, no. 1 (1940): 8–10.

Drake, F. S. "The Christian Teacher in China: II. The Modern System and the Place of Christian Education." *Religion in Education* 15, no. 2 (1948): 50–55.

Drake, F. S. "The Contribution of Chinese Religious Thought." *Chinese Recorder* 72, no. 9 (September 1941): 496–505.

Drake, F. S. "The Contribution of Chinese Religious Thought (Concluded)." *Chinese Recorder* 72, no. 10 (October 1941): 537–45.

Drake, F. S. "The Message of a Chinese Philosopher: Dr. Percy Bruce's New Book." *Missionary Herald of the Baptist Missionary Society* 105 (1923): 135.

Drake, F. S. "The Study of Asia: A Heritage and a Task: Inaugural Address delivered on April 7, 1960." *Journal of the Hong Kong Branch of the Royal Asiatic Society* 1 (1960–61): 11–17.
Drake, F. S. "The Tao Yuan (道院): A New Religious and Spiritualistic Movement." *Chinese Recorder* 54, no. 3 (1923): 133–44.
Drake, F. S. "The Taoists of Lao-Shan (continued)." *Chinese Recorder* 65, no. 5 (May 1934): 308–18.
Drake, F. S. "The Taoists of Lao-Shan." *Chinese Recorder* 65, no. 4 (April 1934): 238–45.
Madeley, F. "New Methods." *Chinese Recorder* 51, no. 9 (September 1920): 660.
Regents Park College, Oxford. *Baptist Missionary Society Archives (BMSA)*.
"School History," School of Chinese, The University of Hong Kong, accessed on May 7, 2020 http://web.chinese.hku.hk/main/school-history/.

Bibliography of F. S. Drake

English works

"A Chat with a Taoist Recluse." *Chinese Recorder* 70 (1939): 433–36.
"A Chat with Buddhists." *Chinese Recorder* 67 (1936): 281–85.
"A Sculptured Panel from T'êng-Hsien." *Monumenta Serica* 13 (1948): 389–94.
"A Shang Dynasty Site at Li-ch'êng (歷城) Wan-Shê-Jên-Chuang (王舍人庄) Shantung," *China Journal* 31, no. 3 (1940): 118–20.
"An Inscribed Pottery Vessel of the Chow Dynasty." *Journal of the North-China Branch of the Royal Asiatic Society* 71 (1940): 46–53.
"Ancient Pottery from Shantung." *Monumenta Serica* 4, no. 2 (1940): 383–405.
"China's North-West Passage: The Struggle for the Tarim Basin in the Later Han Dynasty." *Journal of the North-China Branch of the Royal Asiatic Society* 67 (1936): 147–59.
"City Work in Tsingchowfu (continued)." *Missionary Herald of the Baptist Missionary Society* 102 (1920): 113–15.
"City Work in Tsingchowfu." *Missionary Herald of the Baptist Missionary Society* 102 (1920): 91–92.
"East and West in Christian Universities in China." *International Review of Mission* 36, no. 3 (1947): 338–43.
"Foreign Religions of the Tang Dynasty (continued)." *Chinese Recorder* 71 (1940): 643–49.
"Foreign Religions of the Tang Dynasty (continued)." *Chinese Recorder* 71 (1940): 675–88.
"Foreign Religions of the Tang Dynasty." *Chinese Recorder* 71 (1940): 343–54.
"Mohammedanism in The T'ang Dynasty." *Monumenta Serica* 8 (1943): 1–40.
"Nestorian Crosses and Nestorian Christians in China under the Mongols: A lecture delivered on December 11, 1961." *Journal of the Hong Kong Branch of the Royal Asiatic Society* 2 (1962): 11–25.
"Nestorian Literature of the Tang Dynasty (continued)." *Chinese Recorder* 66 (1935): 738–42.
"Nestorian Literature of the Tang Dynasty (continued)." *Chinese Recorder* 66 (1935): 677–87.
"Nestorian Literature of the Tang Dynasty." *Chinese Recorder* 66 (1935): 608–17.

"Nestorian Monasteries of the T'ang Dynasty: And the Site of the Discovery of the Nestorian Tablet." *Monumenta Serica* 2 no. 2 (1937): 293–340.

Preface to *Yin-tai Cheng-pu Jen-wu T'ung-k'ao* 殷代貞令人物通考 [Oracle Bone Diviners of the Yin Dynasty], by Jao Tsung-yi, v–viii. 2 vols. Hong Kong: University of Hong Kong Press, 1958.

"Problems before Christian Education in China." *Religion in Education* 5, no. 4 (1938): 200–207.

"Religion in a Manchurian City (continued)." *Chinese Recorder* 66, no. 3 (March 1935): 161–70.

"Religion in a Manchurian City." *Chinese Recorder* 66, no. 2 (February 1935): 104–11.

"Sculptured Stones of the Han Dynasty." *Monumenta Serica* 8 (1943): 280–318.

"Shang Dynasty Find at Ta-hsin Chuang, Shantung." *China Journal* 31, no. 2 (1939): 77–80.

"Some Thoughts on China." *Missionary Herald of the Baptist Missionary Society* 105 (1923): 200.

"Ta-hsin Chuang Again." *China Journal* 33, no. 1 (1940): 8–10.

"The Christian Teacher in China: I. The Ancient Confucian Background." *Religion in Education* 15, no. 1 (1947): 22–25.

"The Christian Teacher in China: II. The Modern System and the Place of Christian Education." Religion in Education 15, no. 2 (1948): 50–55.

"The Contribution of Chinese Religious Thought (Concluded)." *Chinese Recorder* 72, no. 10 (October 1941): 537–45.

"The Contribution of Chinese Religious Thought." *Chinese Recorder* 72, no. 9 (September 1941): 496–505.

"The Heritage of the North China Peasant." *International Review of Mission* 27 (1938): 174–82.

"The Message of a Chinese Philosopher: Dr. Percy Bruce's New Book." *Missionary Herald of the Baptist Missionary Society* 105 (1923): 135.

"The Nestorian 'Gloria in Excelsis Deo.'" *Chinese Recorder* 66 (1935): 291–300.

"The Shên-T'ung Monastery and The Beginning of Buddhism in Shantung." *Monumenta Serica* 4, no. 1 (1939): 1–39.

"The Study of Asia: A Heritage and a Task: Inaugural Address delivered on April 7, 1960." *Journal of the Hong Kong Branch of the Royal Asiatic Society* 1 (1960–61): 11–17.

"The Tao Yuan (道院): A New Religious and Spiritualistic Movement." *Chinese Recorder* 54 (1923): 133–44.

"The Taoists of Lao-Shan (continued)." *Chinese Recorder* 65, no. 5 (May 1934): 308–18.

"The Taoists of Lao-Shan." *Chinese Recorder* 65, no. 4 (April 1934): 238–45.

Editor. *Symposium on Historical, Archaeological and Linguistic Studies on Southern China, South-East Asia and the Hong Kong Region: Papers Presented at Meetings Held in September 1961 as Part of the Golden Jubilee Congress of the University of Hong Kong.* Hong Kong: Hong Kong University Press, 1967.

With Chow, E. T. "Kuan-Yao and Min-Yao: A Study on Imperial Porcelain and People's Porcelain from K'ang-Hsi to the End of the Ch'ing Dynasty." *Archives of the Chinese Art Society of America* 13 (1959): 54–74.

Chinese works

〈山東大辛莊商代遺址的發現〉。《學術》第3期（1940）：頁14–22。
〈唐代之景教文獻〉。《魯鐸》第7卷（1935）：頁107–20。
〈歷城縣王舍人莊商代遺址的發現〉。《學術》第4期（1940）：頁21–26。
《大學國文講疏》。台北：世界書局，1961。
《中國文選》。修訂五版。香港：香港大學出版社，1975。
《中國美術》。香港：香港大學出版部，1954。
《林仰山教授中文存》。香港：香港大學中文學會，197?。
《教會史》。再版。上海：廣學會，1947。

4
Christianity and Medical Education in China in the Second World War

Gordon King and His Wartime Adventures and the Interconnectedness between China and Hong Kong

Wong Man Kong[1]

Introduction

Hong Kong is located in one of China's southern peripheries. Nevertheless, it occupies a unique position within the broader historical picture of modern Chinese history in general and the history of Christian missions in particular. In the first place, Hong Kong missionaries considered themselves China missionaries. They looked for and created opportunities to extend their influence in China, and vice versa. The reciprocal effects of the development of missionary medicine between Hong Kong and China were much more cordial than the geographical distance might have implied. This chapter is a case study of Dr. Gordon King (Chinese name: Wang Guodong 王國棟). This Chinese name is a combination of literary and homophonic translations. Wang is a literary translation of King, which happens to be a typical Chinese surname. Guodong is a homophonic translation of Gordon, carrying an implicit literary meaning in Chinese as a pillar of the [Chinese] nation, and also a popular name. His full Chinese name makes perfect sense to the Chinese, conveying a topical meaning in the context of the zenith of Chinese nationalism.[2]

---

1. Acknowledgments: The research for writing this chapter is supported by the General Research Fund of the Research Grants Council of Hong Kong, China (project no. 12602818). I am equally grateful to the Centre for Studies in Religion and Society (CSRS), the University of Victoria, Canada, which hosts me as a visiting research fellow. An earlier version of this chapter was presented at the CSRS Thursday Lecture Series on November 4, 2021. I would like to record my gratitude to the Needham Research Institute for granting the permission to use its photo in this chapter. Last but not least, I am very grateful for the comments and suggestions from the two anonymous reviewers.
2. For his biographical information, see Peter Cunich, "Gordon King," in *Dictionary of Hong Kong Biography*, ed. May Holdsworth May and Christopher Munn (Hong Kong: Hong Kong University

His career in China reveals the multifaceted interconnectedness between China and Hong Kong. Thanks to his prior connections, King made possible the exodus of one generation of young medical students from Hong Kong to ensure the continuation of their training under wartime conditions. They would become pillars in the development of modern medicine in postwar Hong Kong. Despite the physical distance between Hong Kong and the Chinese mainland, the Christian missionaries' activities, the spread of the Christian message, and Western medical ideas and practices helped create an extraordinary and enormously consequential interconnectedness between them.

Christianity and the Development of Medical Education in the First Half of Twentieth-Century China: A Background Note

During the first half of the twentieth century, specifically from 1900 to 1945, the Christian influence in China varied widely in scale and scope, going through changes repeatedly and unexpectedly. The Boxers and the ensuing fiasco marked the zenith of xenophobia for some people and, ironically, the beginning of xenomania for others in China. Subsequently, China underwent two decades of a "golden age" of missionary movement that Daniel Bays rightly defines as a period of rapid growth of the "Sino-Foreign Protestant Establishment." The number of foreign missionaries and Chinese Christians increased significantly. There were also waves of revivals in different locations and forms, resulting from stirring emotionalism inspired by the seeming opposites of the usual powerful pulpit teaching and charismatic practices.[3] On the other hand, the May Fourth Movement in 1919 inspired the gradual strengthening of a nationalistic notion of politics that defined a tighter control over the Christian religion, such as registering schools and replacing missionaries with Chinese in some leading positions within the church circle.[4] In short, there were upside-down and inside-out changes in missionary organizations and church institutions in China's first half of the twentieth century.

Press, 2012), 226–27. See also Malcolm Allbrook, "King, Gordon (1900–1991)," *Australian Dictionary of Biography*, National Centre of Biography, Australian National University. Published 2017, accessed November 1, 2021, https://adb.anu.edu.au/biography/king-gordon-24841/text 33420.

3. Daniel H. Bays, *A New History of Christianity in China* (Chichester, West Sussex; Malden, MA: Wiley-Blackwell, 2012).
4. Yip Ka-che, *Religion, Nationalism, and Chinese Students: The Anti-Christian Movement of 1922–1927* (Bellingham: Center for East Asian Studies, Western Washington University, 1980); Jessie Gregory Lutz, *Chinese Politics and Christian Missions: The Anti-Christian Movements of 1920–1928* (Notre Dame: Cross Road Books, 1988).

Christianity was a relatively stable factor in the development of medicine in China throughout these five decades. As revealed in the award-winning study by Sean Hsiang-lin Lei, the first half of the twentieth century saw the growth of biomedicine as the Chinese quest for modernity—in the wake of such a global health crisis as the Manchurian plague—to reposition and even reinvent traditional Chinese medicine.[5] Against the emerging picture of these new trends in the medical history of modern China, missionary medicine deserves special notice.

Missionary medicine could achieve wonders through surgery, which traditional Chinese medicine practitioners did not usually encourage. The pioneering medical practitioners, such as Dr. Peter Parker during the 1830s and 1840s, and Dr. John Kenneth Mackenzie from the 1870s to the 1880s, won the confidence of the general public in China because of their skills in surgery, most notably in curing eye diseases, which were quite prevalent in China. This was of particular significance for two reasons. First, treating eye diseases was relatively low risk. A patient suffering from eye disease might have already had significant visual impairment. If an eye surgery failed, the worst outcome for the patient was the loss of sight, which the patient had already anticipated. As such, it did not easily provoke strong resistance from patients and their families. Second, it could create a powerful conversion experience for Chinese patients, similar to the biblical account of Saul's conversion to Paul the Apostle. To see is to be enlightened, both visually and spiritually.

Medical education had become a more significant aspect of missionary medicine than simply performing possible surgical treatments since 1900. Like most early forms of education, medical missionaries tried out their apprenticeship programs with a few selected Chinese. However, as missionary medicine proved popular and the Christian hospitals successful, some started their medical schools with the help of missionary funding, local donations, and foreign philanthropy. An outstanding example was Dr. Thomas Cochrane, who was instrumental in knitting together his connections in Chinese politics and Christian missions to make the medical college sustainable.[6] His brainchild was the Peking Union Medical College. Its founding and subsequent developments coincided with the growing acceptance of the germ theory for diseases and the rise of biomedicine among the Chinese. Dr. Wu Lien-teh's (Wu Liande 伍連德) remarkable success in combating the Manchurian plague in 1910 was the most welcome testimony to the necessity of germ theory. A Methodist in terms of the Christian denomination, from Penang in British Malaya, Dr. Wu was a Cambridge-trained physician. He started his medical career first in

---

5. Sean Hsiang-lin Lei, *Neither Donkey nor Horse: Medicine in the Struggle over China's Modernity* (Chicago: University of Chicago Press, 2014).
6. Andrew E. Adam, *Thomas Cochrane and the Dragon Throne: Confronting Disease, Distrust and Murderous Rebellion in Imperial China* (London: SPCK, 2018).

Singapore and Penang, and later in Shanghai and North China. No one could dispute that the Western medical training model was needed in China.[7] The College was an instance of the collaboration of Anglo-American missionary societies, such as the London Missionary Society and the American Board of Commissioners for Foreign Missions. The College received a generous funding provision from the Rockefeller Foundation in 1915. Two years later, the foundation remodelled the College after the John Hopkins University School of Medicine. The College was one of the best examples of the "Sino-Foreign Protestant Establishment."

The Medical Missionary Career of Gordon King: Beijing, Jinan, and Hong Kong

A word about Gordon King's background is helpful. On July 7, 1900, he was born into a pious Christian family in Britain. Frederick H. King, his father, was a Baptist minister in London and, subsequently, Bristol. Gordon King studied at the Bristol Grammar School. As required by the military service act of 1916, he joined the army in July 1918 under conscription and was assigned to the Sixth King's Liverpool Regiment. Fortunately for him, the next month saw the rapid deterioration of the Central Powers. The armistice in World War I was signed in November 1918. He returned home unscathed. Soon afterward, he applied for and was admitted to the London Hospital Medical College. From 1919 to 1924, he was an award-winning student who secured prizes in the following subjects: anatomy, clinical pathology, pathology, clinical medicine, and diseases of children. He was qualified in 1924 with the MRCS (Membership of the Royal College of Surgeons) and the LRCP (Licentiate of the Royal College of Physicians). At London Hospital, he worked as a surgical clinical assistant, medical clinical assistant, assistant chemical pathologist, and also as Alston Research Scholar at Hale Clinical Laboratory. In 1926, he was elected a fellow of the Royal College of Surgeons. During his medical education, he developed the notion of Christian service by applying medical knowledge. He became a medical missionary of the Baptist Missionary Society (BMS), which sent him to China in 1925. He underwent Chinese language training at the Yenching School of Chinese Studies in Beijing for nine months. Between July 1927 and January 1930, the BMS seconded him to the PUMC, where he taught obstetrics

---

7. There were eight more Christian medical colleges in the first half of twentieth century, namely the Hackett Medical College for Women in Canton, the St. John's University in Shanghai, Cheeloo University in Jinan, the Mukden Medical College in Shenyang, the West China Union University in Chengdu, the Hsiang-Ya Medical College in Changsha, the Women's Christian Medical College in Shanghai, and the Lingnan University in Canton.

and gynaecology.[8] By then, the PUMC had become China's most significant medical college, with missionary and philanthropic support.[9] After his term at PUMC, he was entitled to a furlough in Britain. Apart from attending church and missionary meetings and events, he maintained his professional connections. His work in China won his cohorts' recognition, and he was elected a Foundation Fellow of the Royal College of Obstetrics and Gynaecology in 1932. After his furlough, the BMS deployed him to take up a professorship and head the Department of Obstetrics and Gynaecology at Cheeloo University, also known as Shantung Christian University, of which the BMS was one of the founders. He was also the medical director of the University Hospital, one of the critical missionary hospitals in China.[10]

Gordon King's pathway to Hong Kong would not have been anticipated, had it not been for the Japanese invasion of Shandong. In a medical conference in Guangzhou in 1935, Prof. William I. Gerrard, dean of Medicine, had extended a personal and cordial invitation to Gordon King to take up the Chair of Obstetrics and Gynaecology at the University of Hong Kong (HKU). Gordon King rejected the offer. He later wrote, "I did not even consider it then, as I was extremely happy in work in Cheeloo and felt my place was there."[11] The Japanese Kwantung Army occupied Manchuria in 1931. The Chinese government tried to persuade the League of Nations to sanction Japan, but to no avail. Gordon King and other missionaries were aware of the growing Japanese ambition in China. Nevertheless, they decided to stay in China. When he finished his furlough in September 1937, in light of the Marco Polo Bridge incident that had taken place two months earlier, he chose to return to Cheeloo University. His wife and children, however, stayed behind in Britain. The King family was aware of the threats and dangers in China. Upon his arrival, he met with waves of refugees taking the opposite direction of travel, leaving Jinan as rumour had it that the Japanese army would soon occupy the city.

---

8. For his biographical information, see "Gordon King" under Folder Title: Gynaecology – Staff (Hu-Le). China Medical Board, Inc. records, RG 1 (FA065) Box 64, Folder 450, Rockefeller Archive Center.
    Besides, it was reported that King had "done practically no service for his mission." The PUMC thus agreed to refund the BMS Gordon King's passage from Britain to China. See a note dated July 12, 1928, from Dr. J. P. Maxwell of PUMC to the China Medical Board, New York. China Medical Board, Inc. records, RG 1 (FA065) Box 64, Folder 450. Rockefeller Archive Center.
9. For details, see Mary Brown Bullock, *An American Transplant: the Rockefeller Foundation and Peking Union Medical College* (Berkeley: University of California Press, 1980).
10. Upon his arrival in 1932, the medical college had already trained up altogether 238 doctors, nearly half of them working in missionary hospitals in 15 different provinces in China. See *The 140th Annual Report of the Baptist Missionary Society for the year ending 31 March 1932* (London: Carey Mission, 1932), 36.
11. A letter of June 21, 1938, from Gordon King to Dr. Clement Chesterman. A letter kept at the "Gordon King papers" Baptist Missionary Society Archives, The Angus Library and Archive, Regent's Park College, the University of Oxford.

There was some combat between the Japanese and Chinese at that time. He carried on with his trip and reported for duty to the university.[12] In December 1937, the Japanese army occupied Jinan. Most students and faculty members had already left for Chengdu in Sichuan Province, where they relaunched the teaching and learning activities. He kept his pledge to take care of the university property and discharged his medical duties to heal the sick and injured people who sought treatment at the University Hospital. At that time, Britain and Japan were still on good terms; the Anglo-Japanese Alliance was in place, signed in 1902 and renewed in 1922. At first, the Japanese army did not cause much nuisance to the British in China. However, their presence caused "the frustrations, annoyances and everlasting compromises of trying to carry on under the Japanese regime in North China."[13] Gordon King's primary call was to engage in medical education. If that was not possible, there was no point for him to stay at Cheeloo University. He wrote:

> I felt that if our students were able to return to us, and teaching work were to open up again in autumn, I should definitely stay on here [senior students had left for Chengdu].... We are hoping to start a premedical course in the autumn, but that means 4 or 5 years before they will have reached the stage of requiring instructions in my subjects. From the teaching point of view, it looks as though my work in this line will be in abeyance for an indefinite period.... I wonder how far I should be justified in giving up for this work to which I have devoted myself for over ten years now.[14]

Gordon King's interest in going to HKU was taking shape in June 1938, but this was a difficult decision. Religion played a role in this decision-making process. In a letter in June, he declared, "I feel that there would be very real opportunities for Christian services [at HKU]."[15] On the other hand, he was of the view that divine intervention would have a role. Specifically, he articulated it as follows: "If this is not God's will for me, I have a firm belief that God will make His way clear to me through the workings of the appointment committee [at HKU]. So I am still praying and waiting for this final guidance." But in two weeks, he changed his mind as he saw some unforeseen developments. Dr. Philip B. Price and Dr. Laurence M. Ingle soon left their postings at Cheeloo University. Gordon King did not want to leave his colleagues at Cheeloo University helpless and withdrew his case from HKU in a collegial spirit. In his letter to the BMS, he asserted,

---

12. "A 'Warm' Reception: Dr Gordon King Arrives Back in Shantung." *Missionary Herald of the Baptist Missionary Society* 120, (March 1938): 50–52.
13. "Escape from Hong Kong: Lieut-Col Gordon King Tells Exciting Tale of Journey into China," [a talk delivered at the Hong Kong Rotary Club Weekly Luncheon on February 26, 1946, Gloucester Hotel] *South China Morning Post and the Hongkong Telegraph*, February 27, 1946.
14. A letter of June 21, 1938, from Gordon King to Dr. Clement Chesterman, Gordon King papers.
15. A letter of June 21, 1938, from Gordon King to Dr. Clement Chesterman, Gordon King papers.

It would be a very severe blow to the Hospital to lose both [Philip B. Price] and me at one fell swoop. [Laurence M.] Ingle and I are now the only two here prepared to undertake major surgery, and with Ingle going on furlough next year the outlook would be pretty bleak. My very great reluctance to sever the ties which bind me to Cheeloo and the BMS are of course factors which weigh with me increasingly and all the time. So, all in all, I have been driven the conclusion that there is only one course open to me now, and this is to withdraw my application for the Hongkong post.[16]

But in another two weeks' time, especially after the negotiation with the Japanese regime, it became crystal clear that Cheeloo University was not allowed to start any course, premedical courses included. Given this situation, Gordon King did not see his place in the delivery of medical education. His wife and children were not returning to Shandong for obvious safety reasons. His appointment case at HKU was reinstated.[17] In mid-September 1938, he finally decided to move to HKU, where he was to become the chair of Obstetrics and Gynaecology at the University of Hong Kong. He could now clearly present his case to the missionary board as the circumstances became more apparent. He stated three reasons:

(1) The conviction that, next to the spiritual mission in life, my main job is as a teacher in my own subjects. The Fellowship which I hold with the British College of Obstetricians and Gynaecologists pledges me to specialist work only in my own subjects, and whilst, during the recent abnormal times, I have been glad to do any work that was necessary, I do not feel that I can continue indefinitely to devote most of my time to work outside of my field.

(2) The prospect that for several years at least I shall be unable to carry out my real jobs at Cheeloo, and shall have no alternative but to continue in the Hospital Superintendency, an administrative office for which I do not feel suited either by training or inclination—whereas in Hongkong, unsought by me, an opportunity has presented itself of being able to give my whole time to teaching and work amongst students, where a missionary motive is perhaps even more needed than in this place.

(3) The fact that I owe it to my family to bring to an end this period of enforced separation as soon as possible (we have had an aggregate of three years' separation since 1930).[18]

He ends his letter with polite rhetoric: "I shall hate to pull up the roots which have taken such a deep hold in Cheeloo." Furthermore, he remarks, "I feel too that, even if I do go to Hongkong for an agreed initial period of three years, the door would not

---

16. A letter of July 10, 1938, from Gordon King to Dr. Clement Chesterman, Gordon King papers.
17. A letter of July 31, 1938, from Gordon King to Dr. Clement Chesterman, Gordon King papers.
18. A letter of September 12, 1938, from Gordon King to Rev. C. E. Wilson, Gordon King papers.

be closed to my return to Cheeloo at the end of that time if I feel that there is a need here which I could and ought to fill."[19] One might argue that it was the usual writing strategy to save him from any accusation of running away from his responsibilities. Yet, there were two main points here. First, he made a substantial donation to the BMS that conveyed his sincere intention to maintain a friendly connection. Second, his connection with the missionary circle in China turned out to be a great help to future medical students studying at HKU.

To Hong Kong he went with a Christian imperative, which was evident in his formal resignation letters, addressing Dr. Clement Chesterman and Rev. Charles Edward Wilson. The former was the BMS medical secretary and medical officer; the latter the BMS Foreign Secretary. In Chesterman's letter, Gordon King declares, "I feel that the need for Christian men on the staff of a Government University [in Hong Kong] is at least as great as at a University like Cheeloo." He stresses a sense of continuity in upholding missionary zeal. In his letter, he remarks, "The same motives and ideals which have inspired me in years past [1927–1938] will continue to inspire me in this new sphere in what, I trust, will be an ever-growing service for the Kingdom of God in China."[20] In his letter to Rev. Wilson, Gordon King speaks in a more pious tone: "This decision has only been reached after a great deal of earnest thought and prayer." Similarly, he states, "I know you will understand me when I say that my service of the [heavenly] Kingdom will always take first place in my life in whatever sphere I find myself." He kept the same conviction that HKU presented itself full of great potential in Christian ministry—"I believe that the spiritual opportunities of service there are not less great than the professional."[21]

The BMS was receptive to Gordon King's sincere letters. In return, it made a friendly gesture, granting a favor that King had not asked for. The official letter says,

> [Committee members] passed a Minute expressing their desire in favour of granting you three years' leave of absence from the BMS so that you will understand that at the end of this period the way is open for you to approach us again and to resume your missionary service with us.[22]

At HKU, Gordon King was not a missionary but still upheld a solid Christian vision. He made it clear to the BMS that HKU did not allow him to stay as a member of the missionary society in any capacity. Yet, he kept his promises to BMS that he

---

19. A letter of September 12, 1938, from Gordon King to Rev. C. E. Wilson, Gordon King papers.
20. A letter of October 6, 1938, from Gordon King to Dr. Clement Chesterman. Gordon King papers.
21. A letter of October 6, 1938, from Gordon King to Rev. C. E. Wilson, Gordon King papers.
22. A copy of the letter of November 3, 1938, from the BMS to Gordon King. Gordon King papers. This letter was addressed to him at the Cheeloo University address. The letter never reached him at HKU. It took over a year for Rev. Wilson to realize that the letter was lost. He sent another letter to King on January 19, 1940. It took almost two months to reach King at HKU. As a result, King's reply letter was dated March 19, 1940.

would not drop Christian ministry should any such occasion arise. He reported the following:

> There are many opportunities for work amongst the students, and there is a fairly active Christian Association here, of which I have been selected President this Year [1940]. There is a service every Sunday morning in one of the Hostel Chapels, attended by some 30 or 40 students. Next Sunday [March 24, 1940,] I am speaking at the Easter service. Mary and I have been holding a Discussion Group recently on Sunday evenings at our house, and have had about a dozen quite keen students attending. So there are many opportunities for service here, and in many respects the work is no easier and no harder than it used to be in Cheeloo.

In the same letter, he instructed the BMS to use his superannuation allowance to settle an outstanding expense incurred by his family's travel costs and donate the remaining sum to the BMS Medical Auxiliary Fund.[23] This is probably the only record available to show the "missionary" aspect of his life in Hong Kong.

Gordon King's Unusual Christian Contribution to Medicine in Hong Kong

Apart from teaching, what did Gordon King actually do in Hong Kong? Under his supervision of the maternity service of HKU—Tsan Yuk Hospital and Queen Mary Hospital, there were 3,161 babies delivered and 320 gynaecological operations in his first year of service. Subsequently, he was appointed the dean of Medicine, which came with many administrative duties. Outside of HKU, he was the chairman of Hongkong Eugenics (subsequently renamed the Hong Kong Family Planning Association). Throughout his term of chairmanship, he was more concerned with birth control and infant health care—targeting not ideological debates on race but on "the elimination of untold suffering to both mothers and children."[24] He spent most of his energy and time on his academic duties and professional activities. His time and energy for Christian duties were understandably limited. It could not have allowed any Christian contribution of significance to medicine in Hong Kong.

The Japanese army's invasion of Hong Kong in December 1941 was a turning point for Gordon King. By early 1942, he was among the few British who would be spared from being forced into an internment camp. His duty was to care for the University Relief Hospital. Yet, his prior experience with the Japanese at Cheeloo University convinced him that working with them meant he had no future in Hong

---

23. A letter March 19, 1940, from Gordon King to Dr Clement Chesterman, Gordon King papers.
24. Gordon King, letter to the editor, *South China Morning Post*, May 11, 1940. Regarding the ideological debates about eugenics in modern China, see Frank Dikötter, *The Discourse of Race in Modern China*, 2nd ed. (New York: Oxford University Press, 2015).

Kong, and he escaped. By mid-April 1942, he reached Chongqing, and he began assisting his students from HKU.[25] He attached great importance to three matters—relief money, uninterrupted medical education, and recognition from both the British Medical Council and the Hong Kong government.

In terms of relief money, Gordon King convinced Horace Seymour, the British Ambassador to China, to support HKU students with a financial scheme offering relief money and setting up loans. He was instrumental in forming the University Relief Work, a sub-section of the activities of the Hong Kong Refugee Relief Bureau. He sometimes distributed the money to the needy students by himself or by his office.

Gordon King discussed the subject of uninterrupted medical education directly with Chen Lifu 陳立夫, the Chinese Minister for Education. Chen knew that King had a good reputation at Peking Medical Union College and Cheeloo University, serving Chinese in different locations for over a decade. Altogether, 140 HKU medical students continued their medical training in four colleges: the National Shanghai Medical College, the National Hsiang Ya Medical College (or Yale-in-China), and the Medical Colleges of Cheeloo University and Lingnan University. Of these four medical colleges, three were Christian colleges. If one could presume the spirit of Christian brotherhood extending to him with sincere understanding and support because of his prior affiliation with BMS and Cheeloo University, the most challenging one would be the secular institution—National Shanghai Medical College. Interestingly enough, however, the College appointed him a visiting professor, for which Gordon King remained grateful. He acknowledged it in a public lecture in Hong Kong. A newspaper recorded it as follows:

> Perhaps, my own personal indebtedness is greatest to Dr H. B. Chu [Chu Heng-bi (Zhu Hengbi 朱恆璧)], the energetic director of the National Shanghai Medical College . . . where I have received every kindness and courtesy. The temporary premises of the College at Koloshan near Chungking will long be remembered by the large number of our medical students who have passed through it.[26]

---

25. Gerald H. Choa and Peter Cunich had written the contributions of Gordon King in assisting HKU medical students to continue their medical training in China. See, Gerald H. Choa, *"Heal the Sick" Was Their Motto: The Protestant Medical Missionaries in China* (Hong Kong: Chinese University Press, 1990), and Peter Cunich, *A History of the University of Hong Kong*, vol. 1, *1911–1945* (Hong Kong: Hong Kong University Press, 2012).
26. He delivered the public lecture entitled "Picking up Threads of Learning" at the HKU library on October 1, 1945. "Hongkong University Address; Lieut-Col. Gordon King Tells Students of Experiences in China – Picking up Threads of Learning," *South China Morning Post & the Hongkong Telegraph*, October 6, 1945.

While acknowledging that wartime medical education was a problematic issue in China, producing a small number of medical graduates,[27] one might consider Gordon King's contribution to HKU medical students exceptionally significant.

Figure 4.1: Gordon King and his colleagues from the Shanghai Medical College, Koloshan (Geleshan 歌樂山), Sichuan Province: (right to left) Chu Heng-bi (Zhu Hengbi 朱恆壁), Gordon King, Jen Pang-che (Ren Bangzhe 任邦哲), and Wang Yu-chi (Wang Youqi 王有琪). Reproduced courtesy of the Needham Research Institute, Cambridge.

In terms of recognition from both the British Medical Council and the Hong Kong government, he worked hard to establish all the records to pave the way for proper recognition after settling his medical students in different colleges. He explained to the General Medical Council,

> My original records in Hong Kong were all burned by the Japanese, but I have succeeded in making new files containing all the essential particulars of each student who is now in Free China. The colleges which our students are attending all rank as Grade "A" colleges . . . under the existing emergency conditions, may be regarded as equivalent to the training which the student would have received in Hong Kong.

---

27. Yip Ka-che, "Health, National Resistance, and National Reconstructions: The Organization of Health Services in China during the Sino-Japanese War, 1937–1945," in *Resisting Japan: Mobilizing for War in Modern China, 1935–1945*, ed. David Pong (Norwalk, CT: EastBridge, 2008), 118–21.

I should like to urge the Members of the General Medical Council to consider favourably this request for recognition and registration of students who are temporarily forced to continue their medical studies outside of Hong Kong.

Not only did King quickly gather all the necessary information from these colleges and send them to the General Medical Council for accreditation purposes, but he also sought help from ministers in London and the British Ambassador to China. The final step was to create an Emergency Committee for the Conferment of Hong Kong Medical Degrees within HKU. When the Japanese surrendered in August 1945, the process for recognition was needed to be done very quickly.[28]

Students' views about Gordon King reveal his Christian contribution through his actions and deeds. Ong Guan Bee (Wang Yuanmei 王源美), an HKU medical student from 1940 to 1947, witnessed the unfolding of events and gained original insights into the life and times of Gordon King. At the outbreak of the Japanese invasion, Ong observed that Gordon King "was the driving force in the organization of care for the sick and wounded." On their exodus to Free China, Ong and some other HKU students traveling from Kwangtung to Kwangsi met up with Gordon King in Kweilin. King asked them "to stay with the Chinese Red Cross, which was under the directorship of Dr. Robert Lim [Chinese name: Lim Kho-Seng (Lin Kesheng 林可勝)]." Lim was a top medical scientist who had headed the Department of Physiology at Peking Union Medical College before he joined the Red Cross in 1937. King knew that Lim was one of the best possible medical mentors for his students in China at that time.[29] Another significant moment when Ong saw King's contribution was when Hong Kong needed to restore its medical services. Ong remarked, "Although the Medical Faculty was not yet functioning [in 1946], he was able to gather together the medical graduates he had trained and posted them as medical officers." Ong observed in 1948 when China was in the zenith of the civil war, "At one stage all the clinical posts in the Kowloon Hospital were filled by graduates of the University of Hong Kong, many of whom had worked and acquired considerable experience in missionary hospitals throughout China."[30] In 1951, HKU medical alumni donated a large sum of money to create an annual scholarship for obstetrics

---

28. Gordon King, "An Episode in the History of the University," in *Dispersal and Renewal: Hong Kong University During the War Years*, ed. Clifford Matthews and Oswald Cheung (Hong Kong: Hong Kong University Press, 1998), 85–103.
29. Yip, "Health, National Resistance, and National Reconstructions," 120. See also Shi-yung Liu (Liu Shiyong 劉士永) and Shih-ching Kuo (Guo Shiqing 郭世清), "Lin Kesheng (1897–1969): Ansheng huiying de Zhongyanyuan yuanshi yu Guofang Yixueyuan yuanzhang" 林可勝 (1897–1969)：闇聲晦影的中研院院士與國防醫學院院長 [Robert K. S. Lim (1897–1969): Academician of Academia Sinica and Chancellor of National Defense Medical Center in Silent Shadow], *Taiwan Historical Research* 臺灣史研究 19, no. 44 (December 2012): 141–205.
30. Guan Bee Ong, "Dispersal and Renewal: Hong Kong University Medical and Health Services," in Matthews and Cheung, *Dispersal and Renewal*, 389–95.

and gynaecology at HKU in his honour.[31] It was a measurement of his impact. In short, Gordon King embodied the values and meanings of compassion and connections in the development of medicine.

Conclusion

Gordon King's missionary call was to engage in medical education. In the first half of his career in China (1927–1938), the Christian character of his work was more explicit because he was a medical missionary. In the second half of his career in China (1939–1956), the Christian character was more implicit through his work as a professor and as dean of Medicine. Yet, these two stages of his career were interconnected. I would argue that his missionary career and experience negotiating with the Japanese rule in Jinan had prepared him to follow the right path while tackling the challenges caused by the Japanese occupation of Hong Kong.

Of all Gordon King's contributions in China, I would consider his determination to deliver uninterrupted medical education for HKU students most important. He had already experienced the time at Cheeloo University in 1937 when a medical education vacuum would inevitably delay one's future growth. Like Ong, many HKU medical students could have wasted their future medical careers while drifting from one place to the other during wartime. It could have been a significant loss to them personally. Ong wrote to the newspaper's editor to express his gratitude in 1951:

> It was Professor King's unselfish energy and hard work that secured admission for those students into the various universities and colleges of Free China. It was his deep understanding and patience that inspired them to continue their studies in spite of the wartime hardship."[32]

Moreover, suppose Hong Kong had lost several generations of medical students from 1941 to 1945. In that case, it could have created a substantial gap in medical services in the reconstruction years in Hong Kong between 1946 and the early 1950s, when the medical service was under tremendous pressure as the population grew from six hundred thousand to over two million. The wartime degree holders and the ongoing medical training that Gordon King facilitated created a pool of medical practitioners of several hundred in numbers and became one of the fundamental backbones of the social development of Hong Kong. Moreover, his exemplary deeds were a powerful testimony to medical professionalism, Christian faith,

---

31. "Dr Gordon King: to Be Honoured by Graduates; Aid During War," *South China Morning Post*, May 22, 1951.
32. "Dr Gordon King (To the Editor, S.C.M. Post) by G. B. Ong," *South China Morning Post*, June 26, 1951.

and personal virtue that King demonstrated to his students. While the demand for fully trained doctors was equally strong for postwar reconstruction anywhere else, this pool of several hundred Hong Kong doctors was essential for Hong Kong, and they carried forward King's model with them.

Gordon King's notable contributions to medical developments in Hong Kong reveal how a person's personality and integrity, imbued and enhanced by the Christian faith, enabled and strengthened an extraordinary interconnectedness between Hong Kong and China in their relationship. There may indeed be other similar episodes in modern Chinese history that merit closer scrutiny by historians.

Bibliography

Allbrook, Malcolm. "King, Gordon (1900–1991)." *Australian Dictionary of Biography*. National Centre of Biography, Australian National University, published 2017, accessed November 1, 2021, https://adb.anu.edu.au/biography/king-gordon-24841/text33420.

Adam, Andrew E. *Thomas Cochrane and the Dragon Throne: Confronting Disease, Distrust and Murderous Rebellion in Imperial China*. London: SPCK, 2018.

Anonymous. "A 'Warm' Reception: Dr Gordon King Arrives Back in Shantung." *Missionary Herald of the Baptist Missionary Society* 120, (March 1938): 50–52.

Anonymous. "Dr Gordon King: to Be Honoured by Graduates; Aid During War." *South China Morning Post*, May 22, 1951.

Anonymous. *The 140th Annual Report of the Baptist Missionary Society for the year ending 31 March 1932*. London: Carey Mission, 1932.

Bays, Daniel H. *A New History of Christianity in China*. Chichester: Wiley-Blackwell, 2012.

Choa, Gerald H. *"Heal the Sick" Was Their Motto: The Protestant Medical Missionaries in China*. Hong Kong: Chinese University Press, 1990.

Cunich, Peter. "Gordon King." In *Dictionary of Hong Kong Biography*, edited by Holdsworth May and Christopher Munn, 226–27. Hong Kong: Hong Kong University Press, 2012.

Cunich, Peter. *A History of the University of Hong Kong*. Vol. 1, *1911–1945*. Hong Kong: Hong Kong University Press, 2012.

Dikötter, Frank. *The Discourse of Race in Modern China*. 2nd ed. New York: Oxford University Press, 2015.

"Gordon King papers." Baptist Missionary Society Archives, The Angus Library and Archive, Regent's Park College, The University of Oxford.

"Gordon King papers." Gynaecology – Staff (Hu-Le). China Medical Board, Inc. records, RG 1 (FA065) Box 64, Folder 450 Rockefeller Archives.

"Joseph Needham Photographs Wartime China, 1943–1946." East Asian History of Science Library, Needham Research Institute, University of Cambridge.

King, Gordon. "An Episode in the History of the University." In *Dispersal and Renewal: Hong Kong University During the War Years*, edited by Clifford Matthews and Oswald Cheung, 85–103. Hong Kong: Hong Kong University Press, 1998

King, Gordon. "Escape from Hong Kong: Lieut-Col Gordon King Tells Exciting Tale of Journey into China." [A talk delivered at the Hong Kong Rotary Club Weekly Luncheon on February 26, 1946, Gloucester Hotel] *South China Morning Post and the Hongkong Telegraph*, February 27, 1946.

King, Gordon. "Hongkong University Address: Lieut-Col. Gordon King Tells Students of, Experiences in China—Picking up Threads of Learning." *South China Morning Post & the Hongkong Telegraph*, 6 October 1945.

King, Gordon. Letter to the editor. *South China Morning Post*, May 11, 1940.

Lei, Sean Hsiang-lin. *Neither Donkey nor Horse: Medicine in the Struggle over China's Modernity*. Chicago: University of Chicago Press, 2014.

Liu, Shi-yung [Liu Shiyong 劉士永] and Shih-ching Kuo [Guo Shiqing 郭世清]. "Lin Kesheng (1897–1969): Ansheng huiying de Zhongyanyuan yuanshi yu Guofang Yixueyuan yuanzhang" 林可勝（1897–1969）：闇聲晦影的中研院院士與國防醫學院院長 [Robert K. S. Lim (1897–1969): Academician of Academia Sinica and Chancellor of National Defense Medical Center in Silent Shadow]. *Taiwan Historical Research* 臺灣史研究 19, no. 4 (December 2012): 141–205.

Lutz, Jessie Gregory. *Chinese Politics and Christian Missions: The Anti-Christian Movements of 1920–1928*. Notre Dame: Cross Road Books, 1988.

Ong, G. B. "Dr Gordon King (To the Editor, S.C.M. Post)." *South China Morning Post*, June 26, 1951.

Ong, G. B. "Dispersal and Renewal: Hong Kong University Medical and Health Services," In Matthews and Cheung's *Dispersal and Renewal*, 389–95.

Wilson, C. E. *The Baptist Missionary Society: How It Works and Why*. London: The Carey Press, 1931.

Yip Ka-che. "Health, National Resistance, and National Reconstructions: The Organization of Health Services in China during the Sino-Japanese War, 1937–1945." In *Resisting Japan: Mobilizing for War in Modern China, 1935–1945*, edited by David Pong, 118–21. Norwalk: East Bridge, 2008.

Yip Ka-che. *Religion, Nationalism, and Chinese Students: The Anti-Christian Movement of 1922–1927*. Bellingham: Center for East Asian Studies, Western Washington University, 1980.

5
Christian Efforts in Mass Education of Republican China
Zhang Xueyan and Xie Songgao's Christian Literary Work as Examples

Chen Jianming

We define "commoners" (*pingmin* 平民) as ordinary people—as opposed to nobles—while mass education is the opposite, but the basis of, elite education. Mass education is education that helps commoners to meet the needs of their daily lives. According to *Is Public Education Necessary?* by the renowned American educator Samuel Blumenfeld, the root of mass education could be traced back to the Reformation, specifically to John Calvin. The Reformers believed that the only way to consolidate Protestantism was to enable people to read the Bible themselves. Blumenfeld said, "The modern idea of popular education—that is, education for everyone—first arose in Europe during the Protestant Reformation when Papal authority was replaced by the Biblical authority. Since the Protestant rebellion against Rome had arisen in part as a result of Biblical study and interpretation, it became obvious to Protestant leaders that if the Reform movement were to survive and flourish, widespread Biblical literacy, at all levels of society, would be absolutely necessary."[1]

During the 1920s and 1930s, a mass education movement spread across China. The Chinese Protestant church participated in this movement in various ways. Y. C. James Yen (Yan Yangchu 晏陽初) and Tao Xingzhi 陶行知 were famous advocates of mass education in modern China and founders of the Chinese National Association of the Mass Education Movement (Zhonghua pingmin jiaoyu cujinhui 中華平民教育促進會). They were both Christians and had an ambition to love and save

---

1. Samuel L. Blumenfeld, *Is Public Education Necessary?* (Boise, Idaho: The Paradigm Company, 1985), 10.

people as Jesus did.[2] To them, the first step to saving a nation was to improve its peoples' qualities. They felt that commoners should be given priority in education. "Commoners" meant people with low social status or farmers in rural areas who did not have many opportunities to obtain an education, if any. Yen and Tao integrated mass education into social reformation and rural development, which contributed to the modernization of China in that precarious socio-political reality. A lot of research has been conducted on Yen's and Tao's mass education programs. However, research on mass education activities of their contemporary Christian intellectuals is lacking. Thus, this chapter examines mass education activities that were carried out through literary work by Zhang Xueyan 張雪岩 (1901–1950), chief editor of the *Christian Farmer* (*Tianjia banyuebao* 田家半月報), and Xie Songgao 謝頌羔 (1895–1974), editor of the Christian Literature Society for China (CLSC, Guangxue hui 廣學會). It is hoped that this chapter will enrich readers' understanding of Christian mass education in Republican China.

I. Brief Introduction of Xie Songgao and Zhang Xueyan

Xie Songgao was the CLSC's general secretary and a member of its executive and publication committees. He earned achievements in literary translation, literary creation, periodical editing, religious instruction, public education, and youth education. From 1926 to 1950, more than 160 of his works were published by the CLSC (mainly translation and compiled works, along with small amounts of writings), most of which were authored by him independently.

Xie, also known as Z. K. Zia, was born in a Christian family in Hangzhou 杭州, Zhejiang 浙江, on April 15, 1895.[3] His pen name was Jize 濟澤. His father was a pastor of a Presbyterian church in Hangzhou, with his home located right next to the church. In 1905, Xie entered the Hangchow Presbyterian College (Hangzhou Yuying Shuyuan 杭州育英書院) to receive secondary education and began his tertiary education in 1912 in the same institution, which later changed its name to Hangchow Christian College (Zhijiang Daxue 之江大學) in 1914. A year later, Xie left Hangzhou for Ningbo 寧波 due to illness and transferred to another Christian university—Soochow University. He graduated from Soochow University in 1917 and then worked at a community service center sponsored by a Presbyterian church in Shanghai. Meanwhile, he assisted in the evangelistic activities of the Pure Heart Church (Qingxin tang 清心堂). In the autumn of the following year, Frank W. Bible

---

2. In 1912, Arthur J. Bowen held a series of evangelical gatherings at the University of Nanking. Fifty students converted to Christianity after the gatherings. and Tao was one of them. Yen was baptized in a Western school operated by the China Inland Mission when he was young.
3. Z. K. Zia, "Memories of My Life," *Ching Wen English Magazine*, no. 27 (1938): 195.

of the American Presbyterian Mission (North) sponsored Xie to study in the United States. Xie studied at the Auburn Theological Seminary, in Auburn, New York, for three years and obtained a Bachelor of Theology. He pursued his postgraduate studies at Boston University and finished writing his first book, *My Ideal People* (*Lixiang zhong ren* 理想中人), during his time in the United States. After obtaining his master's degree in 1922, with his thesis on Confucian civilization, Xie returned to China.[4] He taught at the Nanking Theological Seminary for a year, followed by a year of teaching at the Law Department of Soochow University.[5]

From 1924 to 1926, Xie worked as the editor of *Young People's Friend* (*Qingnian you* 青年友), a magazine published by the Publication Department of the American Methodist Episcopal Church in Shanghai. Meanwhile, he started translating books, working independently or with others. The religious educational books he translated include *Principles of Modern Preaching* (*Jindai xuandaoxue dagang* 近代宣道學大綱), *Parenthood and Child Nurture* (*Ertong jiaoyuxue* 兒童教育學), *Introduction to Religious Education* (*Zongjiao jiaoyu gailun* 宗教教育概論), *Fifty Famous Stories Retold* (*Taixi mingren xiaoshuoji* 泰西名人小說集), *Mahatma Gandhi* (*Gandi xiaozhuan* 甘地小傳), *Scientific Christian Thinking for Young People* (*Kexue de Jiduhua sixiang* 科學的基督化思想), and *The Family: Its History and Problems* (*Jiating de yanjiu* 家庭的研究). Most of them were published by the Publication Department of the American Methodist Episcopal Church in Shanghai. Xie's literary skills were approved by the Christian community.

In June 1926, recommended by H. K. Wright, a missionary of the American Presbyterian Mission (North), and financed by the Canadian Presbyterian Mission, Xie joined CLSC.[6] From 1929 to 1930, Xie and the American missionary Albert J. Garnier served as the general secretaries of CLSC. Hereafter, Xie was a member of the CLSC's executive committee, publication committee, and economics committee in different periods. In 1928, Xie became the editor of the monthly periodical *Shining Light* (*Mingdeng* 明燈), and then the editor of *The People's Magazine* (*Pingmin yuekan* 平民月刊) in 1933. Both magazines were published by the CLSC.

During the War of Resistance against Japan, Xie left the occupied territory for Chengdu through southeast China in the spring of 1942. On September 18, United

---

4. Z. K. Zia, *Wo ruhe de you jinri* 我如何得有今日 [What I owe to the Christian church] (Shanghai: Christian Literature Society for China, 1938), 12–42.
5. Xie Songgao wrote "Wo de dongjia" 我的東家 [My host], a story about his stay in the United States, for *Young People's Friend*. He signed off with "Law Department, Soochow University, Shanghai, 1 January 1924." See *Young People's Friend* 4, no. 2 (1924): 39.
6. Z. K. Zia, "Memories of My Life," *Ching Wen English Magazine*, no. 32 (1939): 35; Z. K. Zia, *The Glad Tidings of Peace: The Thirty-ninth Annual Report of the Christian Literature Society for China* (Shanghai: Christian Literature Society for China, 1926), 8–9. The Christian Literature Society for China was cofounded by missionary societies in China. Therefore, the living expenses of the editors were almost without exception reimbursed by the missionary society to which the editor belonged.

Christian Publishers was officially established, and Xie took part in its affairs as the representative of the CLSC. A few months later, in January 1943, he was appointed as the interim vice-general secretary of the CLSC; when M. E. Terry, the general secretary, was not in Chengdu, Xie would perform the general secretary's duties. In February 1946, Xie returned to the CLSC in Shanghai and left the organization five years later. On September 13, 1974, Xie died alone in Shanghai, aged eighty.[7]

Zhang Xueyan was an eminent Chinese Christian activist, the chief editor of *Christian Farmer*, and one of the founders of the Jiusan Society (Jiusan xueshe 九三學社). He authored a huge number of writings, translations, and commentaries. By my count, Zhang's works included four hundred ninety-nine papers, six books, one doctoral thesis (English), five translation works, and three edited books. The total word count was approximately 1,690,000 characters.

Zhang was born in Dachangtuan 大常疃 Village, Guti 固堤 Town, Weixian 濰縣 (now Hanting 寒亭 District in Weifang 濰坊) in Shandong. He was born into a peasant family, and his mother died when he was five. Financed by his relatives, Zhang studied in a mission primary school in his village starting at age eight. In 1914, he began his secondary education in Wenhua Shuyuan 文華書院 in Weixian.[8] In his early days there, Zhang was sponsored by Zhang Guandao 張貫道, an elder of a church of the American Presbyterian Mission.[9] He quit half a year later and became a teacher in his hometown in 1915. He worked as a clerk in a pharmacy after that. In 1916, he was recruited by the British recruitment mission to be a Chinese laborer in Europe. He put great effort into studying English after work and served as a translator for a time. After returning to China in late 1919, he was appointed by Wenhua Shuyuan as an English teacher. In 1922, he worked for Zhengji 政記 Shipping Company, first in Yantai 煙台 and then in Tianjin. After resigning from the company in May 1928, he first joined Zhang Zuolin's 張作霖 army and then the local military but left soon after.

During August and September 1928, Zhang worked as assistant editor of the CLSC in Shanghai. In the following year, with the help of Ralph C. Wells of the American Presbyterian Mission (North), Zhang was admitted to the Nanking

---

7. Zhao Xiaohui 趙曉暉, "Jiang tianguo jian zai renjian (xia)" 將天國建在人間 (下) [Building the Kingdom of God in the human world (Part 2)], *Tianfeng* 天風, no. 4 (2017): 39.
8. Wenhua Shuyuan began as a boys' school founded by Robert M. Mateer in 1883 in the Courtyard of the Happy Way (Ledaoyuan 樂道院), a mission compound of the American Presbyterian Mission (North) in Shandong. It was renamed Wenhua Middle School in 1915. In 1931, it was combined with Wenmei 文美 Girls' Middle School to form Guangwen 廣文 Middle School. Its name changed again to Weifang Second Middle School in 1952.
9. Cui Derun 崔德潤, "Huiyi laoyou Zhang Xueyan" 回憶老友張雪岩 [In memory of my old friend Zhang Xueyan], in *Zhang Xueyan shiliao xuanbian* 張雪岩史料選篇 (Weifang: CPPCC Weifang City Hanting District Culture and History Committee, 1991), 24.

Theological Seminary.[10] Independent of his schoolwork, Zhang started to translate or write some poems and prose, which revealed his literary talent. In 1932, his paper "The Life of Jesus" (*Yesu shengping* 耶穌生平) won second place in the Timothy Richard essay contest, which was organized by the National Christian Council of China.[11] After graduating from the seminary in June 1933, Zhang went to Shanghai and worked as religious education secretary of the General Assembly of the Church of Christ in China.

In August 1934, along with Sun Ensan 孫恩三, he founded the *Christian Farmer*, a periodical of the North China Christian Rural Service Union (Huabei Jidujiao nongcun shiye cujinhui 華北基督教農村事業促進會) based in Jinan. Zhang successively served as the periodical's deputy editor-in-chief, editor-in-chief, and publisher. Three years later, in August 1937, Zhang left China to study abroad. He attended the University of Toronto in Canada and Cornell University in the United States. He obtained a doctoral degree in sociology from Cornell University. In September 1940, Zhang returned to China and arrived in Chengdu, leading the office of the *Christian Farmer* (Tianjiashe 田家社). Apart from being a longtime editor of the *Christian Farmer*, Zhang also taught at universities like Cheeloo University and Yenching University.

In 1944, Zhang, Xu Deheng 許德珩, Pan Shu 潘菽, and others organized the Forum on Democracy and Science (renamed as Jiusan 九三 Forum on September 3, 1945) in Chongqing 重慶. On May 4, 1946, the Jiusan Society was officially established in Chongqing, and he was elected as a member of its council. On May 12, he was chosen to be a standing member of the council. In early 1948, he was invited to give lectures abroad. From the winter of 1948 to the spring of 1949, Zhang "accomplished his lecturing tour across North America, spreading the good news of the liberated areas of China, and won international sympathy and friendship."[12]

Invited by the Central Committee of the Communist Party of China (CPC), Zhang visited Beiping 北平 to discuss state affairs in the summer of 1949. On September 21, Zhang attended the First Plenum of the Chinese People's Political Consultative Conference (PCC) as a representative of the religious sector and was elected to be a member of the Drafting Committee of the *Common Program* (*Gongtong gangling* 共同綱領). Unfortunately, a few months later, on January 28,

---

10. Zhang Songwu 張松武, "Zhang Xueyan de qingshaonian shidai" 張雪岩的青少年時代 [Zhang Xueyan's adolescence], in *Zhang Xueyan shiliao xuanbian*, 40.
11. Zhang Xueyan 張雪岩, "Yesu shengping" 耶穌生平 [The life of Jesus], *Zhonghua gui zhu* 中華歸主, no. 136 (May 1933): 3.
12. Dong Mofang 董謨芳, "Zhuhe Tianjia fukan jinian Zhang Xueyan tongzhi" 祝賀田家復刊紀念張雪岩同志 [In celebration of the *Christian Farmer*'s reissue and in memory of Comrade Zhang Xueyan], *The Christian Farmer* 17, nos. 1–2 (November 1951): 5.

1950, Zhang died due to a cerebral hemorrhage. The Chinese government held a public memorial ceremony for him on February 2.

II. Zhang Xueyan's Mass Education Efforts

As rural areas in China were confronting an economic crisis during the 1930s, some intellectuals promoted and joined the rural construction movement, which was aimed to "bring relief to rural communities" (*jiuji xiangcun* 救濟鄉村), "revive rural communities" (*fuxing xiangcun* 復興鄉村), and "build the capacity of rural communities" (*jianshe xiangcun* 建設鄉村). From July 7 to 20, 1933, the National Christian Council of China held a conference on literacy education and rural construction in Ding County (Dingxian 定縣) of Hebei Province, a county known for its mass education. The theme of the conference was "How Should Christianity Contribute to Rural Construction?" The conference discussed farmers' need for literacy and proposed solutions to the problem of illiteracy. After the conference, Hebei, Shanxi, Shandong and other provinces also held similar conferences, and members of the conferences came to the conclusion "to set up a literature department in the North China Christian Rural Service Union to publish Christian reading materials for farmers."[13] Sun Ensan, secretary of the National Christian Council of China, pointed out that

> for five or six years, the need for a distinctly Christian journal for village people has been felt by Christian leaders throughout the country. The urgency of this need has increased considerably in more recent years as a result of the steady growth in literacy, both inside the church and among the country people in general. According to our latest estimate there are at least 100,000 new literates and semi-literates in the church alone who are in great need of some paper that is within their power to read and possess and which brings regularly to them such help as they need in their daily religious and secular life. To this pressing need we are now addressing ourselves.[14]

Zhang was interested in this rural construction movement. One day in January 1934, Zhang met Sun in a Western-style restaurant on Museum Road in Shanghai. During the meeting, Sun mentioned his plan to use literary work to promote rural construction. He insisted on inviting Zhang to join the program, and Zhang agreed. After a few months of preparation, the trial issue of the *Christian Farmer* was published in July, and the first issue of the magazine was published on August 1. In

---

13. D. W. Lyon, "Wenzi shiye" 文字事業 [Literary work], in vol. 12 of *Zhonghua jidujiaohui nianjian* 中華基督教會年鑑 (Shanghai: Christian Literature Society, 1933): 125.
14. T. H. Sun 孫恩三 [Sun Ensan 孫恩三], "'The Christian Farmer,' A Prospectus," *West China Missionary News* 36, nos. 7–8 (1934): 21.

August 1938, Sun applied for a two-year leave to study in the United Sates, and the magazine was put in Zhang's charge.

The *Christian Farmer* was a sextodecimo, semi-monthly periodical. It had twenty-four issues per year and consisted of twenty pages per issue. The magazine was published on the first and fifteenth of every month, and was subject to the influence of such factors as war, inflation, financial crisis, church sponsorship, and location change. As a result, the pages and the publishing time might differ. The magazine was divided into standard columns and supplements. The standard columns included commentaries, news, general knowledge, arts, religion, readers' zone, Q & A, and miscellaneous, while topics of the supplements included hygiene, children, family, and livelihood.

The *Christian Farmer* had two stated purposes: "Firstly, to strive to serve the needs of our fellow countrymen in rural areas, especially farmers, comprehensively. Secondly, to strive to promote the Christian spirit of sacrifice and love, making people in touch with the magazine, no matter in personal or public life, experience an 'abundant life' given by Jesus."[15] Zhang insisted on "speaking the truth and spreading our voice for justice; treating farmers as the basis of the country, [and believing that] knowledge is the power," which were the founding principles of the *Christian Farmer*. Zhang followed the aim to serve the rural population by implementing literacy education and imparting scientific and cultural knowledge through the magazine. Zhang also emphasized that the magazine should move with the times and spread the new culture that would meet the needs of the contemporary era. In his *Tianjia zhanwang* 田家瞻望 written during the War of Resistance against Japan, Zhang said that "the *Christian Farmer* was born of the needs of the times. A beautiful child of the current era, it was born of demand for mass literacy; it is a tool of mass education and a powerful weapon of religious service. It should take up the responsibility as a newspaper or magazine and the mission of being a leader of the mass, and promote the new culture that meets the needs of the contemporary era."[16]

Due to Zhang's careful management, the *Christian Farmer* was well-received among farmers. It was distributed all over China and even to foreign countries including the UK, the United States, Korea, and Thailand. The *Christian Farmer*'s circulation reached 50,000, and it had more than 400,000 readers at its peak.[17] It was estimated that from 1946 to 1947, around 750,000 people in China read the

---

15. "Benbao wuzhounian jinian" 本報五週年紀念 [The fifth anniversary of the *Christian Farmer*], *Christian Farmer* 6, 15–16 (August 1939): 2.
16. Zhang Xueyan, *Tianjia zhanwang* 田家瞻望 [The aspirations of the *Christian Farmer*] (Chengdu: Tianjiashe, 1942), 3.
17. As of September 1, 1937, the number of subscriptions increased to 35,000, with the readership at more than 400,000.

Christian Farmer, 60 percent of those being farmers, and Christian pastors in rural areas could not even work without the magazine.[18]

To accomplish the magazine's mission, Zhang pointed out:

> The magazine is born to fulfill the needs of the rural population in the country. Therefore, the content of the magazine should have much to do with reality and be relevant to their lives. This is a conclusion based on our observation, not imagination. The logic of our conclusion is that the most urgent need of the farmers is a means to learn—literacy. Having literacy as capital, they can acquire various modern products of knowledge, so as to become equipped minds and modern citizens; having literacy as key, they can open the door to the treasure of knowledge, gaining convenient access to knowledge. Although universal education has not yet materialized, thanks to the promotion of mass education in both the public and private sectors in recent years, there are fewer illiterate people than before. Increasingly more people in rural areas can read and write. Since this has laid a foundation [for our work], it is unjustified for us to give up a good cause. We should no doubt speed up our work, introducing through a popular publication to the general rural literate public, who have acquired the essential tool (literacy) for their quest for knowledge and innovation, extensive and interesting material relevant to their life systematically and regularly, so that they will have an opportunity to conveniently undertake self-education and keep improving themselves. This, on the one hand, can complement mass education; on the other hand, this can indirectly arouse illiterates' interest in literacy and passion for learning, as these could emerge after they see their friends and relatives' self-improvement brought by literacy.[19]

The *Christian Farmer* aimed to serve the rural population and rural churches, and its three types of prospective readers were church members who could read the Gospels without great difficulty, graduates of literacy classes and similar schools for adults, and the general rural literate public.[20] When editing the magazine, Zhang, along with his colleagues, strove to use simple words and material that was easily understood, to match its audience's reading level. They made sure that most of the words in the magazine were included in the *Thousand Character Primer for Peasants* (*Nongmin qianzike* 農民千字課). They also provided phonetic notation of important yet difficult words at the page margin and footnotes, explaining uncommon or difficult phrases and sentences.

---

18. He Kaili 何凱立, *Jidujiao zai Hua chubanshiye (1912–1949)* 基督教在華出版事業, 1912–1949 [Original in English: *Protestant Missionary Publications in Modern China 1912–1949: A Study of Their Programs Operations and Trends*], trans. Chen Jianming and Wang Zaixing (Chengdu: Xichuan daxue chubanshe, 2004), 261.
19. Zhang, *Tianjia zhanwang*, 23–24.
20. Sun, "'The Christian Farmer,' A Prospectus," 21.

Zhang also often offered advice on how to acquire literacy to farmers. In "Good Ways to Popularize Literacy" (Shi renren dou shizi de haofazi 使人人都識字的好法子), Zhang pointed out why it was difficult for adults to acquire literacy: for the elderly, it could be due to their poor memories; sometimes, adults were too busy to learn; it was also possible that it was inconvenient for young women to learn from male teachers. To solve these problems, Zhang suggested that literate children be little teachers.[21] In "Good Ways to Teach Mothers to Read" (Jiao muqin shizi de miaofa 教母親識字的妙法), Zhang related the story of Aihua 愛華, a primary school student, teaching his mother to read, thereby introducing a good example of how to promote literacy education among farmers.[22]

The *Christian Farmer* received enthusiastic responses from its readers. Some people wrote to the magazine saying that their knowledge was enhanced through reading it. Realizing that the magazine was planning to set up its publishing fund, many readers made donations to it. A reader from Luoyang 洛陽 in Henan 河南 was satisfied with the *Christian Farmer* when he first read it. He wrote to the magazine commending it, stating:

> It is a perfect reading material for Chinese commoners. The wording is easy to understand, and the content is brilliant and comprehensive. More importantly, thanks to the low price of the magazine, the general public can have an affordable means to learn news about national affairs. The magazine can thus contribute greatly to the dissemination of the message of national salvation. Apart from current news, the magazine includes much essential knowledge for the people. From this thin magazine, we can find, for example, information on treatments for lung diseases, the Q&A section about medicine, knowledge of poultry and livestock farming and sericulture, and so on. It is not hard to tell from the *Christian Farmer* that the magazine contributes to not only our resistance against Japanese aggression but also the happiness and health of people from all over the world![23]

Besides serving as the *Christian Farmer*'s editor, Zhang engaged in other mass education initiatives. In the summer of 1935, Cui Derun 崔德潤, principal of Guangwen 廣文 Middle School in Weixian, discussed with Zhang how to engage students of Cui's school in the rural construction movement. Zhang suggested that Cui's school could host a summer camp organized by the Young Men's Christian Association for students of Christian middle schools. The summer camp would be held in a village

---

21. Zhang Xueyan, "Shi renren dou shizi de haofazi" 使人人都識字的好法子 [Good ways to popularize literacy], *Christian Farmer* 1, no. 6 (October 1934): 9.
22. Zhang Xueyan, "Jiao muqin shizi de miaofa" 教母親識字的妙法 [Good ways to teach the mothers to read], *Christian Farmer* 2, no. 15 (August 1935): 30.
23. Zhang Songyun 張松筠, "Kanjian *Tianjia banyuekan* hou de ganxiang" 看見田家半月報後的感想 [My thoughts after reading the *Christian Farmer*], *Christian Farmer* 7, no. 18 (1940): 5.

and discuss how to solve rural problems. Eventually, the summer camp was held at Yuhetou 虞河頭, a village near Ledaoyuan 樂道院 (the Courtyard of the Happy Way). Zhang left Jinan 濟南 for the summer camp and gave a speech to it. Liang Shuming 梁漱溟 was also a speaker at the summer camp, and he made a speech on the importance of rural construction, the future of Chinese rural areas, and the dos and don'ts in the study of rural problems. Zhang and Liang joined the students' field trip too. The students attended a seminar in the mornings and visited the peasant families in groups in the afternoons. By doing so, the students gained a realistic understanding of the rural areas in China.[24] After the summer camp, Zhang went back to Jinan and reported the event in the *Christian Farmer*. He wrote that the summer camp

> selected a village (Yuhetou) as the base. The village was about five *li* 里 away from the host school, Guangwen Middle School. The tasks of the field trip covered five areas, namely public hygiene, mass education, family reform, cooperative training, and instruction. Because the students were not there to be self-important teachers but to learn from and make friends with the villagers, they were welcomed by the villagers, who were willing to work with them. Whenever the students were there, the villagers prepared food and drinks for them. The villagers also sincerely accepted the students' advice about hygiene and family reform, as well as being attentive students of the students' literacy class.[25]

The office of *Christian Farmer* moved to Chongqing in late August 1944, and after the War of Resistance against Japan, to Beiping in September 1946.

III. Xie Songgao's Mass Education Efforts

Xie Songgao's most notable mass education activity was editing *The People's Magazine*. The first issue of *The People's Magazine* was published in July 1924 by the Publication Department of the Methodist Episcopal Church. Its founding editor remains unknown. *The People's Magazine* was initially a weekly and later a monthly magazine. The magazine's wording was confined to the scope of the *People's 1,000 Character Primer* (*Pingmin qianzike* 平民千字課). Its editor from 1927 to 1928 was Luo Yunyan 羅運炎, followed by Xu Zuotong 許佐同.[26] In 1933, *The People's Magazine* became a publication of CLSC, edited by Xie Songgao.

---

24. Cui, "Huiyi laoyou Zhang Xueyan," 25–26.
25. Zhang Xueyan, "Yige shixing dao minjian qu de xuesheng xialingying" 一個實行到民間去的學生夏令營 [A student summer camp held among the commoners], *Christian Farmer* 2, no. 14 (July 1935): 12.
26. Tang Yin 湯因, "Zhongwen Jidujiao zazhi qikan mulu suoyin (er)" 中文基督教雜誌目錄索引（二）[Index of Chinese Christian magazines and periodicals (2)] 1949, p. 55. Shanghai Municipal Archives U133-0-34; Nie Wenhui 聶文匯, "Zhongguo jiaohui dingqi kanwu diaochabiao"

The People's Magazine identified itself as a "friend of commoners." It aimed to "popularize mass education and expand the commoners' knowledge." Xie claimed that "we [intellectuals] are eager to be friends of commoners since we know they are hardworking, kind and genuine. We also know that if we befriend them, they are very reliable and very willing to endeavour for us."[27] In "The New Year's Mission Statement of The People's Magazine" published in the third issue of 1934, The People's Magazine claimed that "we still need to be friends of commoners; we have to think of means to guide them and help improve their prospects. We would like to be friends of more primary students, winning their sympathy and friendship."[28] In August 1936, The People's Magazine claimed that it could be "1. a supplementary reading for children aged about ten; 2. a textbook for servants; 3. introductory material for evangelists to distribute among strangers; 4. a textbook or reading material for church literacy classes; 5. a gift of Sunday schools [for their students]."[29] Therefore, we can say that the magazine targeted the less educated and their children.

The contents of the magazine were rich, covering current affairs, politics, domestic news, daily life knowledge, moral cultivation, and so on, interspersed with some Christian teachings. The magazine included articles for children and youth in addition to adults. Children and youth were also its targeted readers because its editor hoped that it could reach and influence the commoners' children. For instance, the twelfth issue of its twelfth volume included columns like illustrations, calligraphies, commentaries, dialogues, short essays, people, sanitary knowledge, knowledge of farming practices, folk customs, stories, poems, jokes, and riddles. Many columns of the magazine were relevant to the commoners' daily life. There was a column in this issue, for instance, entitled "Soil is Vital for Raising Chickens and Cows." It can be said that it was tailor-made for farmers. In addition, the columns on folk customs, stories, riddles, and jokes not only entertained adults, but were also welcomed by children of farming families.

Because the readers of the magazine were mostly commoners with a relatively low literacy level, its articles were usually written in simple language and included some colloquial expressions. For instance, the article "Act More, Talk Less" (Duo zuoshi shao shuohua 多做事少説話) went: "When I visited Nanjing with Mr. Mi Xingru 米星如 last time, we came across a friend Mr. Chang. He was very attentive. Although he served in the government, he did not agree with his colleagues, for he

---

中國教會定期刊物調查表 [Survey on the periodicals of Chinese churches], in vol. 10 of Zhonghua jidujiaohui nianjian (Shanghai: Christian Literature Society, 1928), 59.
27. "Pingmin zhi you" 平民之友 [Friend of commoners], The People's Magazine 10, no. 4 (1934): 1.
28. "Benkan de xinnian shiming" 本刊的新年使命 [The New year's mission statement of The People's Magazine], The People's Magazine 10, no. 3 (1934): 3.
29. "Pingmin yuekan de yongchu" 平民月刊的用處 [The use of The People's Magazine], The People's Magazine 12, no. 8 (August 1936): i.

thought they talked too much and did too little. Mr. Chang said, 'We should now act more and talk less.' I could tell he acted more than talked. He rushed about every day, busy working."[30]

In January 1937, considering that *The People's Magazine* and the *Woman's Star* (*Nu xing* 女星) shared similar aims and were published by the same organization, CLSC decided to merge these two magazines.[31] After the merger, "Woman's Star" was printed as the magazine's name on its front cover and as its running title, while "Woman's Star and The People's Family Magazine" (Nu xing yu pinmin jiating yuekan 女星與平民家庭月刊) appeared on the magazine's title page as its name. Xie was no longer a member of the magazine's editorial team after the merger.

Xie was the editor of the influential six-volume *C.L.S Readers for Illiterates* (*Guangxue duben* 廣學讀本), published from 1931 to 1936. CLSC's publications catalog introduced the *readers* as follows: "Each volume of the readers is divided into several lessons which are all easy to read. It aims to teach students to read as well as inculcating important moral ideas and Christian truth. Since the *readers* talk about questions of life, they are welcomed by their readers. Therefore, many children's summer schools and mass education schools have used these *readers* as textbooks."[32] To provide simple reading materials to commoners, Xie compiled *The Story Readers for the Common People* (*Pingmin gushi duben* 平民故事讀本), of which volumes 1–4 were published between February 1938 and July 1940, while the publication dates of volumes 5 and 6 were unknown. Xie also edited *Art Pictures for the Common People* (*Pingmin zihua ji* 平民字畫集), which included works by Feng Zikai 豐子愷 and others, and was published in 1940.

Xie also organized literacy classes and mass education schools. Because of the January 28 incident in 1932, Xie's house in Zhuangjiage 莊家閣 was burnt to ashes. He regretted not using his house to do something useful for the poor. After having rebuilt his house a few months later, he held literacy classes for the poor in the ruins of his house and in Gaoqiao 高橋 of Pudong 浦東. More than seventy people attended his literacy classes at its peak. His classes also became a shelter for homeless people. "Miserable beggars could be made good citizens" there.[33] In 1936, together with his friend Wu Zhixiong 吳志雄, Xie established a mass education school. Xie also worked with his father, who was a Christian pastor, to establish a school in his hometown, donating several thousand copies of *C.L.S Readers for Illiterates* to the

---

30. "Duo zuoshi shao shuohua" 多做事少說話 [Act more, talk less], *The People's Magazine* 10, no. 1 (October 1934): 11.
31. "Nu xing yuekan yu Pingmin yuekan hekan qishi" 女星月刊與平民月刊合刊啟事 [Notice about the merger of the *Woman's Star* and *The People's Magazine*], *Woman's Star* 6, no. 1 (January 1937): 2.
32. *Guangxuehui tushu mulu* 廣學會圖書目錄 [Catalogue of Christian Literature Society for China] (Shanghai: Christian Literature Society for China, 1938): 10.
33. Z. K. Zia, "Huoshui yuan" 活水院 [Huoshui Courtyard], in *Wo ruhe de you jinri*, 92–93.

school as its textbooks.³⁴ After the Battle of Shanghai in 1937, Shanghai, excluding its International Settlement and French Concession, was occupied by the Japanese army. Since Xie's house was in the occupied area, his literacy classes were forced to discontinue. In early 1939, Xie ran two free schools. He expressed his thought on free education by saying that "I am interested in giving free education to poor country children... As I see it, to give is more blessed than to receive so far as education is concerned."³⁵

As noted by Lu Yuanding 陸元鼎, "Dr. Xie is a Christian. He likes to befriend commoners, often visiting slums in person frequently. For the welfare of the poor, he ran a mass education school in his house in west Shanghai. The tuition fee there was one dollar for a semester, including the textbooks and stationery. For those in dire poverty, tuition was free, so that they could have an opportunity to receive education."³⁶ Xie once told his friend, "I have four types of interests: 1. assisting in the work of orphanages, children's welfare associations and disaster relief; 2. helping commoners and going to rural areas to make friends with farmers there; living like a commoner and befriending commoners, I will never forget where I came from; 3. undertaking education as the theme of my career ... My work at CLSC and schools is related to education. 4. participating in church work, for example, assisting in the work of the Fitch Memorial Church (Hongde Tang 鴻德堂). These are the four goals of my life that I will never give up."³⁷ This passage outlines the major areas of Xie's career: serving his community, helping commoners, educating youth, and participating in evangelism.

IV. Features of Zhang Xueyan and Xie Songgao's Mass Education Efforts

Although Zhang and Xie did not work together in the same organization and almost did not cross paths with each other, their mass education efforts shared many similarities.

First of all, they were both born into lower-class families. They understood the sufferings of commoners and sympathized with them. Xie's grandmothers lived in the rural areas of Ningbo. He would sometimes live with them during his childhood.

---

34. Z. K. Zia, "Wo dui pingmin xuexiao de xingqu" 我對平民學校的興趣 [My Interest in mass education schools], *The People's Magazine* 12, no. 5 (May 1936): 8.
35. Z. K. Zia, "Wo de geren xingqu" 我的個人興趣 [My personal interests], *Xuetu zhi you* 學徒之友 1, no. 2 (1939): 32.
36. Lu Yuanding 陸元鼎, "Ji Xie Songgao boshi zhi jiating" 記謝頌羔博士的家庭 [Dr. Xie Songgao's family], *Jiankang jiating* 健康家庭 2, no. 2 (1940): 38.
37. Z. K. Zia, "Wo de sizhong gongzuo" 我的四種工作 [Four types of my work], *The People's Magazine* 12, no. 5 (May 1936): 8.

According to Xie's recollection in his memoirs, "I have a great impression of my childhood in the countryside. The most memorable place for me is Gaoqiao 高橋 Town . . . there I could receive gifts from nature. I liked to make friends with the people there, and I liked to go fishing too," he said. He added, "Farmers there would distribute their freshly made dumplings to their neighbours. They were close to each other, and I would never forget how sincere, honest and hardworking they were."[38] Xie was born into an ordinary pastor's family. When he was a kid, he met many people from the lower class in church. In his memoirs, he mentioned a skillful young carpenter, a plasterer named Baogen 保根, a shoemaker called A'Cai 阿才, and a diligent and sincere farmer known as Brother Shen (Shen Dage 沈大哥). They were all Christians and impressed Xie very much.

Moreover, in his memoirs, Xie explained why he was interested in commoners:

> I was born a commoner. Later, I studied abroad. After returning to China, I taught at a university, considering myself a literatus. I was wrong. Whoever forgets commoners will never have a bright future . . . Commoners are our friends. They are where our food, clothing and houses come from. Isn't it a big mistake to be arrogant because of living on the ninth floor [of the Christian Literature Society Building]? . . . All of the great people were friends of commoners. Jesus, St. Francis and Gandhi did not despise commoners. If they had done so, their greatness would have been diminished. . . . I had the inclination to live like a commoner. Sometimes, I would sit and drink tea with commoners, having a pot of tea costing 80 *wen* 文; sometimes, I would have soya milk with them. I don't take it as a personal degradation . . . I am still happy to be a friend of commoners, and I wish I could always be until the day I am called home.[39]

Xie thought that writers "should not write all day, engaging in idle theorizing and writing empty words. They should do concrete things, suffering with commoners and doing some kinds of lower-class work . . . God does not commend my arrogance. He wants me to be with ordinary people."[40] Hence, although Xie was busy with his literary work, he still spent time on social services and evangelism.

Unlike Xie, who was more concerned with commoners in cities, Zhang paid more attention to farmers. Born in a village, Zhang had a miserable childhood and deeply understood the pain and hardship of farmers. Zhang considered farmers as

> the greatest benefactors of human beings because all basic living necessities are the results of their work. Even the most modern and scientific mechanized industries depend on raw materials produced by farmers. Therefore, it is not overstating that farmers are the foundation of human civilization and the origins of cultural

---

38. Zia, *Wo ruhe de you jinri*, 8–9.
39. Zia, *Wo ruhe de you jinri*, 76–78.
40. Zia, *Wo ruhe de you jinri*, 58.

development... Nowadays, well-equipped people are concentrated in metropolises; cultural, educational, economic and welfare policies and facilities are mostly planned for the equipped people in metropolises. However, people ought not to ignore or even look down upon farmers, who, since ancient times, have made tremendous contributions to producing living necessities and fostering cultural development.[41]

Zhang wrote numerous editorials and essays to call attention to farmers.

Secondly, while establishing mass education schools was not the major work of Zhang and Xie's careers, their thoughts and practices were consistent with the aim of mass education, namely improving the overall qualities of citizens.

Tao Xingzhi emphasized that the importance of mass education rested on "enabling the illiterate and intellectually inadequate people to be people who are literate and intellectually adequate," and "empowering all countrymen with the intellectual capacity to be the master of our country, so that a solid foundation can be laid for the building of an innovative country."[42] Y. C. James Yen pointed out that "the people are the roots of a country; the roots firm, the country is tranquil" (*min wei bang ben* 民為邦本, *ben gu bang ning* 本固邦寧). He thought that mass education aimed to "eliminate illiteracy, educate new citizens," and exploit the people's "intellectual mine," equipping the people with productivity, knowledge, solidarity, and health, and turning them into smart and enterprising Chinese citizens.[43]

Xie linked enlightenment of thoughts to the modernization of China. He expressed the thought that "if we want to build an ideal country, we must popularize education to eliminate illiteracy... so that all the people can understand their duties as citizens and engage in patriotic efforts. When these happen, an ideal country can be built before long."[44] Xie also wrote,

> We should develop the people's intelligence and popularize education. This work should be conducted not only at schools but in any institution that is closely connected to the people. For example, in villages, teahouses are where people would gather at leisure. There villagers listen to living performances of Chinese storytellers (*shuo xiaoshu, chang pinghua de* 說小書, 唱評話的), which is the most popular entertainment for them. By utilizing the storytellers to impart knowledge to the people, we may achieve better outcomes, since school education is boring

---

41. Zhang Xueyan, "Yesu yu nongmin" 耶穌與農民 [Jesus and farmers], *Christian Farmer* 13, no. 8 (1946): 1.
42. Tao Xingzhi 陶行知, *Tao Xingzhi jiaoyu wenji* 陶行知教育文集 [A collection of Tao Xingzhi's essays on education], complied by Hu Xiaofeng 胡曉風 (Chengdu: Sichuan jiaoyu chubanshe, 2017), 96.
43. Zhang Shiwen 張世文. *Dingxuan nongcun gongye diaocha* 定縣農村工業調查 [Investigation on the rural industry in Ding County] (Chengdu: Sichuan renmin chubanshe, 1991).
44. Z. K. Zia, *Lunli de yanjiu* 倫理的研究 [A study on ethics] (Shanghai: Christian Literature Society for China, 1927), 273.

and mechanical, whereas teaching through storytelling is more entertaining and appealing, easily and unwittingly imparting knowledge to villagers. Teahouses are also where views on current affairs and critique of customs are expressed. Youths who have the ambition of developing the people's intelligence should visit this kind of public places during holiday time, joining the local community and their conversations. When the villagers have misconceptions, the youths can attempt to correct them; when they have outworn opinions, the youths can attempt to change them. Educating the illiterates by osmosis is highly effective."[45]

To nurture qualified citizens, Xie edited books including *A Short Introduction to Elementary Civics* (*Gongmin changshi xiaojian* 公民常識小簡) and *Fifteen Lectures in Elementary Civics* (*Gongmin changshi shiwu jiang* 公民常識十五講).

As for Zhang, he hoped to popularize literacy education and promote scientific knowledge of livelihood, farming, and sanitation through the *Christian Farmer*, to enhance the educational and moral development of farmers, improve their living standard and productivity, and reform rural society. To enable farmers to read and write was to popularize education in rural areas nationwide. Zhang was convinced that it could equip farmers with scientific knowledge, enterprising thought, reasonable attitudes, and the capacity to act constructively, so that their overall standards of living could reach a level as high as represented by those enjoyed by citizens of modern, powerful countries.[46] In July 1943, to commemorate the Double-Seventh Incident in 1937, Zhang wrote "Commemoration of the Double-Seventh Incident and the *Christian Farmer*" ("Qiqi" jinian yu benbao "七七" 紀念與本報). In this article, he pointed out that "as [our country] is winning the War of Resistance against Japan, the *Christian Farmer* ought to tread the path to nation-building, being ready to undertake the more important mission of cultural nation-building. It aims to make Chinese farmers' intellectual level improving day by day until they reach the level a great power's citizens should achieve, as well as equipping Chinese citizens with not only viability but also creativity to promote our culture and let it shine in every corner of the earth."[47] To protect the farmers' fundamental rights, Zhang intentionally educated the *Christian Farmer*'s readers about the ideas of democracy and legal awareness. He also reminded readers that they should fully use law to defend their democratic rights.

Furthermore, Zhang and Xie's thoughts on mass education were rooted in their Christian faith. The disciples of Jesus should fulfill his great commission, which is to spread the Gospel and teach all nations to follow the teachings of Jesus Christ

---

45. Z. K. Zia, *Gongmin yu shehui de yanjiu* 公民與社會的研究 [A short study of civics and sociology] (Shanghai: Christian Literature Society for China, 1929), 24–25.
46. "Jinji qishi" 緊急啟事 [Emergency notice], *Christian Farmer* 9, no. 24 (December 1942): 12.
47. Zhang Xueyan, "'Qiqi' jinian yu benbao" "七七" 紀念與本報 [Commemoration of the Double-Seventh Incident and the *Christian Farmer*], *Christian Farmer* 10, no. 13 (July 1943): 1.

until the Parousia. Peter Au (Ou Yingyu 區應毓) wrote in *The Ideas of Education Concept and the View on Christian Education* (*Jiaoyu linian yu Jidujiao jiaoyuguan* 教育理念與基督教教育觀), "Christian education has the Christian faith as its basis and whole person education as its means; it starts with knowledge and ends with morality; its essence is knowledge, which can be applied to daily life. We cannot put the cart before the horse or attend to the trifles but neglect the essentials. We have to be consistent and clearly differentiate between essence and application. By doing so, we can fulfill the great educational commission of Jesus Christ."[48] Likewise, Zhang and Xie equated evangelization with education. They considered the two to be complementary and equally important, believing that the goal of the two was the same, which was to cultivate a noble personality in the Chinese people.

As mentioned above, the aim of the *Christian Farmer* was to strive to promote the Christian spirit of sacrifice and love, making people who were connected with the magazine, in both their personal or public life, experience an "abundant life" given by Jesus. The *Christian Farmer* "aim[ed] to preach through literary work, enabling the Chinese farmers to understand the truth, to obey and follow the loving Christ. When all the Chinese farmers become truth seekers and loving people because of reading the *Christian Farmer*, the society can be developed well, and the country can progress."[49]

In "My Religious Views" (Wo de zongjiaoguan 我的宗教觀), Xie wrote, "I am in my forties, and I know that religion is an indispensable thing. My religious views are centred on Jesus' religious views. Jesus loves commoners, and so do I."[50] Xie attached great importance to religious education. He expressed the thought that, "Religious education is spiritual education. It is the most significant component of moral education and the highest goal of character education."[51] He said, "Religious education is not confined to schools. It can be implemented anytime and anywhere. People receive education throughout their lives. The period from childhood to adulthood is simply the most significant one for education."[52] Xie translated a series of books on religious education after he returned to China, such as *Principles of Modern Preaching* (*Jindai xuandao xue dagang* 近代宣道學大綱), *How to Teach Religion* (*Zongjiao jiaoshou fa* 宗教教授法), *Introduction to Religious Education*

---

48. Ou Yingyu 區應毓, *Jiaoyu linian yu Jidujiao jiaoyuguan* 教育理念與基督教教育觀 [The ideas of education and the view on Christian education] (Sichuan: Sichuan University Press, 2005), 308.
49. Zhang Xueyan, "Huiguo hou de guangan" 回國後的觀感 [My feelings after returning to the country], *Christian Farmer* 7, no. 19 (1940): 2.
50. Z. K. Zia, "Wo de zongjiaoguan" 我的宗教觀 [My Religious Views], in *Chuncaotang zaji* 春草堂雜記 (Shanghai: Christian Literature Society for China, 1937), 6–7.
51. Z. K. Zia, "Zongjiao jiaoyu shi shenme?" 宗教教育是甚麼？ [What is religious education?], *Young People's Friend* 3, no. 4 (1923): 39.
52. Z. K. Zia, *Jiduhua rensheng de yanjiu* 基督化人生的研究 [A study on a Christianized life] (Shanghai: Christian Literature Society for China, 1928), 10.

(*Zongjiao jiaoyu gailun* 宗教教育概論), and *Parenthood and Child Nurture* (*Ertong jiaoyuxue* 兒童教育學). He later included these translations into a book series on religious education. His translation works of short novels had the theme of family education and social education from a religious perspective too.

Last but not least, Zhang and Xie were both patriotic and made a great effort to promote patriotism. Xie once wrote a paper in English, aimed at youth. In the paper, he said, "I love my country, because I do not care to be some other nation's subject. I do not care to be a Westerner, for I know I cannot be one. I do not care to be called a Japanese, for no one in China would consider it an honor to be called such. I must love my country, for that is the only place where I can breathe freely and love peacefully."[53] Xie studied the life of Jesus and inferred that Jesus was patriotic. He grieved over his motherland and was opposed to Roman imperialism. Hence, he came to the conclusion: "Anyone who does not love his or her country cannot be considered as a disciple of Christ. Only the ones who love their country can love the world."[54] In January 1937, Xie published an article entitled "Christians and Patriotism" (Jidutu yu aiguo 基督徒與愛國), in which he appealed to Christians to be patriotic: 1. If a Christian is an official, he definitely will not aim to make a fortune; 2. If he has a fortune, he definitely will not want to keep it, as it will do evil to his offspring. 3. When he is in a position of power, he definitely will think of the sufferings of commoners. 4. If he is a university teacher, he will befriend commoners and keep modest. 5. If he achieves great fame, he will attribute the glory to God. All in all, a Christian will follow Christ from the beginning to the end. Christ never betrayed his country; he only cried for Jerusalem.[55] In his semi-autobiographical fiction, *My Ideal People* (*Lixiang zhong ren* 理想中人), first published by the Mission Book Company in 1925 and republished by CLSC in 1933, he created a character named Wang Liugong 王六功 (later renamed Wang Bade 王八德), who was a persevering orphan. Although Wang lost his parents when he was a child, as a devout Christian, he had faith in God and followed the right path. He studied in America. After returning to his motherland, he contributed to it and served his community.

Facing Japan's invasive military operations in China before the outbreak of the War of Resistance against Japan, Zhang published several statements expressing his patriotism through the *Christian Farmer*. During the war, propagating the idea of "resisting Japan and loving the country" was an important issue for Zhang. He thought that the solidarity of the people had great significance to China's resistance to Japan. He stated: "What the enemy fears most is not our government or army but

---

53. Z. K. Zia, *Why I Love My Country and Other Simple Essays* (Shanghai: Zhonghua Book Company, 1937), 1.
54. Zia, *Wo ruhe de you jinri*, 58–59.
55. Z. K. Zia, "Jidutu yu aiguo" 基督徒與愛國 [Christians and patriotism], *Woman's Star* 6, no. 1 (January 1937): 21.

the solidarity of our people. Wake up, my farmer friends! Our unity is not only a backup to our army but also the only way to turning China from a weak country to a strong one."[56] Guided by this thought, Zhang attempted to arouse the people's zeal for fighting against the enemy through the *Christian Farmer*. He also encouraged people to contribute to China's resistance against Japan by, for example, giving clothes to the soldiers on the front line and donating to them. In a letter to the readers of the *Christian Farmer* dated October 1, 1939, Zhang wrote, "To accomplish the ultimate goal of 'winning the War of Resistance [*kangzhan bisheng* 抗戰必勝], [and] succeeding in building the nation' [*jianguo bicheng* 建國必成], we should make a particular effort to call for love and sacrifice for our country, apart from keeping up our effort to achieve the original goal. It is hoped that every reader of the *Christian Farmer* is a warrior against the enemy and a proficient participant in the building of our nation, regardless of whether he directly or indirectly contributes to the causes."[57]

In addition to the aforementioned similarities, both Zhang and Xie gained an initial understanding of Western culture at church schools, studied theology abroad, and had deep insights into Western culture and education. They both took literary work (translating, writing, and editing) as their means of mass education and yielded fruitful results. When we study mass education in Republican China, we cannot ignore the model of Christian literary work as represented by Zhang and Xie.

Bibliography

"Benbao wuzhounian jinian" 本報五週年紀念 [The fifth anniversary of *Christian Farmer*]. *Christian Farmer* 6, nos. 15–16 (August 1939): 2.

Bi, Yuanqing 畢願清. *Zhang Xueyan shiliao xuanbian* 張雪岩史料選編 [Selected historical materials of Zhang Xueyan]. Weifang: CPPCC Weifang City Hanting District Culture and History Committee, 1991.

Blumenfeld, Samuel L. *Is Public Education Necessary?* Boise: The Paradigm Company, 1985.

Cui Derun 崔德潤. "Huiyi laoyou Zhang Xueyan" 回憶老友張雪岩 [In memory of my old friend Zhang Xueyan]. In *Zhang Xueyan shiliao xuanbian* 張雪岩史料選篇, edited by Bi Yuanqing 畢願清. Weifang: CPPCC Weifang City Hanting District Culture and History Committee, 1991.

Dong Mofang 董謨芳. "Zhuhe Tianjia fukan jinian Zhang Xueyan tongzhi" 祝賀田家復刊紀念張雪岩同志 [In celebration of the *Christian Farmer*'s reissue and in memory of Comrade Zhang Xueyan]. *Christian Farmer* 17, nos. 1–2 (November 1951): 5.

"Benkan de xinnian shiming" 本刊的新年使命 [The new year's mission statement of *The People's Magazine*]. *The People's Magazine* 10, no. 3 (1934): 2–3.

---

56. Zhang Xueyan, "Nongyou men! Women gai zhenme ban ne?" 農友們！我們該怎麼辦呢？ [Farmers! What should we do?], *Christian Farmer* 3, no. 23 (December 1936): 10.

57. Zhang Xueyan, "Yi feng wenhou de xin" 一封問候的信 [A letter of regards], *Christian Farmer* 6, no. 21 (November 1939): 6.

"Duo zuoshi shao shuohua" 多做事少說話 [Act more, talk less]. *The People's Magazine* 10, no. 1 (October 1934): 11.

Guangxuehui tushu mulu 廣學會圖書目錄 [Catalogue of the Christian Literature Society for China]. Shanghai: Christian Literature Society for China, 1938.

He, Kaili 何凱立. *Jidujiao zai Hua chuban shiye (1912–1949)* 基督教在華出版事業, 1912–1949 [Original in English: *Protestant Missionary Publications in Modern China 1912–1949: A Study of Their Programs, Operations, and Trends*]. Translated by Chen Jianming and Wang Zaixing. Chengdu: Xichuan Daxue Chubanshe, 2004.

"Jinji qishi" 緊急啟事 [Emergency notice]. *Christian Farmer* 9, no. 24 (December 1942): 12.

Lu, Yuanding 陸元鼎. "Ji Xie Songgao boshi zhi jiating" 記謝頌羔博士的家庭 [Dr. Xie Songgao's Family]. *Healthy Home* 健康家庭 2, no. 2 (1940): 38.

Lyon, D. W. "Wenzi shiye" 文字事業 [Literary work]. In vol. 12 of *Zhonghua jidujiaohui nianjian* 中華基督教會年鑑. Shanghai: Christian Literature Society for China, 1933.

Nie, Wenhui 聶文匯. "Zhongguo jiaohui dingqi kanwu diaochabiao" 中國教會定期刊物調查表 [Survey on the periodicals of Chinese churches]. In vol. 10 of *Zhonghua jidujiaohui nianjian*, Shanghai: Christian Literature Society for China, 1928.

"Nu xing yuekan yu Pingmin yuekan hekan qishi" 女星月刊與平民月刊合刊啟事 [Notice about the merge of the *Woman's Star* and *The People's Magazine*]. *Woman's Star* 6, no. 1 (January 1937): 2.

Ou, Yingyu 區應毓. *Jiaoyu linian yu Jidujiao jiaoyuguan* 教育理念與基督教教育觀 [The ideas of education and the view on Christian education]. Sichuan: Sichuan University Press, 2005.

"Pingmin yuekan de yongchu" 平民月刊的用處 [The use of *The People's Magazine*]. *The People's Magazine* 12, no. 8 (August 1936): i.

"Pingmin zhi you" 平民之友 [Friend of commoners]. *The People's Magazine* 10, no. 4 (1934): 1–2.

Sun, T. H [Sun Ensan 孫恩三]. "'The Christian Farmer,' A Prospectus." *West China Missionary News* 36, nos. 7–8 (1934): 21–23.

Tang Yin 湯因. "Zhongwen Jidujiao zazhi qikan mulu suoyin (er)" 中文基督教雜誌目錄索引 (二) [Index of Chinese Christian Magazines and Periodicals (2)], 1949, 55. Shanghai Municipal Archives U133-0-34, p. 55.

Tao Xingzhi 陶行知. *Tao Xingzhi jiaoyu wenji* 陶行知教育文集 [A collection of Tao Xingzhi's essays on education], complied by Hu, Xiaofeng 胡曉風. Chengdu: Sichuan jiaoyu chubanshe, 2017.

Zhao, Xiaohui 趙曉暉. "Jiang tianguo jian zai renjian (xia)" 將天國建在人間 (下) [Building the Kingdom of God in the human world (Part 2)]. *Tianfeng* 天風, no. 4 (2017): 37–39.

Zhang, Shiwen 張世文. *Dingxian nongcun gongye diaocha* 定縣農村工業調查 [Investigation on the rural industry in Ding County]. Chengdu: Sichuan renmin chubanshe, 1991.

Zhang Songwu 張松武. "Zhang Xueyan de qingshaonian shidai" 張雪岩的青少年時代 [Zhang Xueyan's adolescence]. In *Zhang Xueyan shiliao xuanbian* 張雪岩史料選篇, edited by Bi Yuanqing 畢願清. Weifang: CPPCC Weifang City Hanting District Culture and History Committee, 1991.

Zhang Songyun 張松筠. "Kanjian *Tianjia banyuekan* hou de ganxiang" 看見田家半月報後的感想 [My thoughts after reading the *Christian Farmer*]. *Christian Farmer* 7, no. 18 (1940): 5–6.

Zhang Xueyan 張雪岩. "Huiguo hou de guangan" 回國後的觀感 [My feelings after returning to the country]. *Christian Farmer* 7, no. 19 (1940): 2.

Zhang Xueyan 張雪岩. "Jiao muqin shizi de miaofa" 教母親識字的妙法 [Good ways to teach the mothers to read]. *Christian Farmer* 2, no. 15 (August 1935): 30.

Zhang Xueyan 張雪岩. "Nongyou men! Women gai zhenme ban ne?" 農友們！我們該怎麼辦呢？ [Farmers! What should we do?]. *Christian Farmer* 3, no. 23 (December 1936): 10.

Zhang Xueyan 張雪岩. "'Qiqi' jinian yu benbao" "七七" 紀念與本報 [Commemoration of the Double-Seventh Incident and the Christian Farmer]. *Christian Farmer* 10, no. 13 (July 1943): 1.

Zhang Xueyan 張雪岩. "Shi renren dou shizi de haofazi" 使人人都識字的好法子 [Good ways to popularize literacy]. *Christian Farmer* 1, no. 6 (October 1934): 9.

Zhang Xueyan 張雪岩. *Tianjia zhanwang* 田家瞻望 [The aspirations of the *Christian Farmer*]. Chengdu: Tianjia Press, 1942.

Zhang Xueyan 張雪岩. "Yesu shengping" 耶穌生平 [The life of Jesus]. *Zhonghua gui zhu* 中華歸主. no. 136 (May 1933): 3–10.

Zhang Xueyan 張雪岩. "Yesu yu nongmin" 耶穌與農民 [Jesus and farmers]. *Christian Farmer* 13, no. 8 (1946): 1.

Zhang Xueyan 張雪岩. "Yi feng wenhou de xin" 一封問候的信 [A letter of regards]. *Christian Farmer* 6, no. 21 (November 1939): 6–7.

Zhang Xueyan 張雪岩. "Yige shixing dao minjian qu de xuesheng xialingying" 一個實行到民間去的學生夏令營 [A student summer camp held among the commoners]. *Christian Farmer* 2, no. 14 (July 1935): 12.

Zia, Z. K. (Xie Songgao 謝頌羔). *Lunli de yanjiu* 倫理的研究 [A study on ethics]. Shanghai: Christian Literature Society for China, 1927.

Zia, Z. K. *Gongmin yu shehui de yanjiu* 公民與社會的研究 [A short study of civics and sociology]. Shanghai: Christian Literature Society for China, 1929.

Zia, Z. K. *Jiduhua rensheng de yanjiu* 基督化人生的研究 [A study on a Christianized life]. Shanghai: Christian Literature Society for China, 1928.

Zia, Z. K. "Jidutu yu aiguo" 基督徒與愛國 [Christians and patriotism]. *Woman's Star* 6, no. 1 (January 1937): 21.

Zia, Z. K. "Memories of My Life." *Ching Wen English Magazine*, no. 27 (1938): 195–96.

Zia, Z. K. "Memories of My Life." *Ching Wen English Magazine*, no. 32 (1939): 35–36.

Zia, Z. K. *The Glad Tidings of Peace: The Thirty-ninth Annual Report of the Christian Literature Society for* China Shanghai: Christian Literature Society for China, 1926.

Zia, Z. K. *Why I Love My Country and Other Simple Essays*. Shanghai: Zhonghua Book Company, 1937.

Zia, Z. K. "Wo de dongjia" 我的東家 [My host]. *Qingnian you* 青年友 4, no. 2 (1924): 37–39.

Zia, Z. K. "Wo de geren xingqu" 我的個人興趣 [My personal interests]. *Xuetu zhi you* 學徒之友 1, no. 2 (1939): 32.

Zia, Z. K. "Wo de sizhong gongzuo" 我的四種工作 [Four types of my work]. *The People's Magazine* 12, no. 5 (May 1936): 8.

Zia, Z. K. "Wo de zongjiaoguan" 我的宗教觀 [My religious views]. In *Chuncaotang zaji* 春草堂雜記. Shanghai: Christian Literature Society for China, 1937.

Zia, Z. K. "Wo dui pingmin xuexiao de xingqu" 我對平民學校的興趣 [My interest in mass education schools] *The People's Magazine* 12, no. 5 (May 1936): 8.

Zia, Z. K. *Wo ruhe de you jinri* 我如何得有今日 [What I owe to the Christian church]. Shanghai: Christian Literature Society for China, 1938.

Zia, Z. K. "Zongjiao jiaoyu shi shenme?" 宗教教育是甚麼？ [What is religious education?]. *Qingnian you* 3, no. 4 (1923): 39.

6
An Unfulfilled Ideal
Zhu Jingnong's Educational Ideas and Practices[1]

Jiafeng Liu

Preface: A Forgotten All-Around Educator

Zhu Jingnong 朱經農 (King Chu, 1887–1951), with ancestry from Baoshan 寶山 (today Shanghai 上海) in Jiangsu 江蘇 Province, was born in Pujiang 浦江 County in Zhejiang 浙江 Province, where his father was the county magistrate. When Zhu was eight years old, his father died. Following his father's death, the family sought refuge with his uncle Zhu Qiyi 朱其懿, an official in Hunan 湖南 Province. In 1904, Zhu traveled to Japan to further his studies. A year later, Zhu was introduced to the Chinese Revolutionary Alliance (Tongmenghui 同盟會) by Huang Xing 黃興. Around the end of the same year, the Japanese government issued an order regulating Chinese students' admission to schools in Japan, which led to many Chinese students in Japan withdrawing collectively from their schools in protest. Zhu then returned to Shanghai and participated in the establishment of the China College (Zhongguo gongxue 中國公學). After the 1911 Revolution, Zhu went to Beijing and worked as an editor of the *Democracy Daily* (*Minzhu bao* 民主報) and the *East Asia News* (*Yadong xinwen* 亞東新聞). In 1916, Zhu was admitted to the University of George Washington while serving as secretary to the Chinese Educational Mission in the United States (Liu Mei xuesheng jianduchu 留美學生監督處). After graduation, he entered Columbia University and while studying there, was deeply influenced by John Dewey's educational philosophy.

---

1. The Chinese original of this chapter was published as Liu Jiafeng 劉家峰, "Zhuangzhi weichou: Zhu Jingnong de jiaoyu linian yu shijian" 壯志未酬：朱經農的教育理念與實踐, *Aomen ligong xuebao: renwen shehui kexue ban* 澳門理工學報（人文社會科學版）79 (2020): 78–89. Reused with permission.

Invited by Cai Yuanpei 蔡元培 in 1921, Zhu became a professor of education at Peking University. In 1922, he joined the Commercial Press in Shanghai as an editor, compiling textbooks and teachers' reference books to support the new curriculum of the Chinese school system. Many primary and secondary schools used these books. In 1924, he became the head of the Chinese department and a professor of education at the Shanghai Baptist College (later known as the University of Shanghai; Hujiang daxue 滬江大學). After the Shanghai massacre of 1925, he was involved in establishing Kwanghua University (Guanghua Daxue 光華大學) and became its dean and later vice-president. He was appointed the commissioner of education of the Special Municipality of Shanghai in 1927. In 1928, he became the director of the office of general education at the Ministry of Education and Research (Daxueyuan 大學院) of the Nationalist government. After the ministry was reorganized as the Ministry of Education (Jiaoyubu 教育部), he became the director-general of its department of general education. In 1930, he was appointed the administrative vice minister of the ministry. In 1931, he served as the acting president of China College for a short period of time before becoming president of Cheeloo University. In the next year, he was appointed the commissioner of education of the Hunan Provincial Government. He held this post for ten and a half years. In 1943, Zhu became the dean of the National Central University and later the political vice minister of the Ministry of Education. After the War of Resistance against Japan, Zhu returned to Shanghai and worked concurrently as the general manager of the Commercial Press and the president of Kwanghua University. In 1946, Zhu attended the National Constituent Assembly as a representative of the educational profession. In November 1948, he was sent as China's chief delegate to the general conference of the UNESCO in Lebanon. Afterward, he resided in the United States and spent time lecturing and writing. In 1950, he joined the faculty of the Hartford Seminary, researching the history of education in China. On March 9, 1951, Zhu died of a heart attack in his apartment in the United States, aged sixty-five.[2]

Since he began his education career at twenty years old, Zhu Jingnong dedicated himself to teaching, editing, and working as an education administrator in schools or government for forty-five years. All his jobs were directly or indirectly related to education. After Zhu's death, Wang Yunwu 王雲五 commended him for his contributions to education in China: "To my best knowledge, very few [educators] in China can be comparable to Zhu in terms of diligence and devotedness,

---

2. Important sources of Zhu's biographical materials include *Aishanlu shichao* 愛山廬詩鈔 [Selected poems from Aishan Mansion] (Taipei: Taiwan Commercial Press, 1965), compiled by his son Zhu Wenchang 朱文長, and Zhang Daren's 張達人 "Zhu jingnong xiansheng nianpu (chugao)" 朱經農先生年譜（初稿）[The chronicle of Zhu Jingnong (first draft)] serialized in volume 11, no. 4 and volume 12, nos. 1/2 of *Hunan wenxian* 湖南文獻.

achievements, and the breadth of areas involved." Wang also praised Zhu as an "all-around educator."[3]

Unfortunately, such a renowned educator, publisher, scholar, and poet is almost forgotten in contemporary China. Compared with Zhu's contemporaries like James Yen (Yan Yangchu 晏陽初) and Tao Xingzhi 陶行知, Zhu has attracted only scant scholarly attention, which is not commensurate with his contributions to education in China. This lack of attention may be due to Zhu's long service in the Nationalist government and his promotion of the aim of education based on the Three Principles of the People (*sanmin zhuyi* 三民主義). In recent years, however, some research on Zhu's life has been conducted and published.[4] Building on previous scholarship on Zhu and focusing on his educational ideas and practices, this chapter aims to offer additional information about Zhu's Christian faith and the formation of his educational ideas, which are lacking in discussions of his life in previous scholarship. In addition, by investigating Zhu's moves from academia to government and vice versa in his education career, this chapter aims to shed light on whether Zhu performed his roles in academia and government with skill and ease, or if indecisiveness led him to make these career changes. Looking into these questions will help us to gain better understanding of Zhu, a man who had a lifelong interest in education and regarded it as his vocation.

---

3. Wang Yunwu 王雲五, "Wo suo renshi de Zhu Jingnong xiansheng" 我所認識的朱經農先生 [The Mr. Zhu Jingnong I know], in *Aishanlu shichao*, 152.
4. Major scholarly articles on Zhu's life include Zhi Xiaomin 智效民, "Shiming yinggong huanming qing: guanyu Zhu Jingnong" 詩名應共宦名清——關於朱經農 [One's reputation as a literatus and an official should be equally untarnished: On Zhu Jingnong], *Zhuanji wenxue* 傳記文學, no. 472 (September 2001), 51–58. This article is also included in his *Hushi he tade pengyou men (zengbu ben)* 胡適和他的朋友們（增補本）[Hu Shih and his friends (updated and expanded edition)] (Beijing: Shijie zhishi chubanshe 世界知識出版社, 2020); Li Mao 李卯, "Zhu Jingnong jichu jiaoyu kecheng sixiang ji shijian yanjiu" 朱經農基礎教育課程思想及實踐研究 [A study of Zhu Jingnong's thoughts and practices about basic education curriculum] (master's thesis, Hunan Normal University, 2011); Li Mao, "Jindai jiaoyujia Zhu Jingnong jiaoyu sixiang de quanmian jiedu" 近代教育家朱經農教育思想的全面解讀 [A comprehensive interpretation of the modern Chinese educator Zhu Jingnong's educational thoughts], *Journal of Jianghan University (Social Science Edition)* 31, no. 1 (2014): 116–20, 129; Xu Baoan 徐保安 and Li Meng 李萌, "Shiming haishi huanming? Cong Zhu Jingnong kan Minguo zhishi fenzi de zhiye xuanze yu rensheng chujing" 詩名還是宦名？——從朱經農看民國知識份子的職業選擇與人生處境 [Reputation of being a good scholar or reputation of being a good official? A study of career choices and life situations of intellectuals in the Republican Era: The case of Zhu Jingnong], *Studies on Republican China* 26, no. 2 (2014): 148–66; and Han Shu 韓戍, "Zhanhou Zhongguo sili daxue de zhili kunjing: Yi Zhu Jingnong zhizhang Guanghua Daxue weili (1946–1949)" 戰後中國私立大學的治理困境——以朱經農執掌光華大學為例（1946–1949）[The governance difficulties of private universities in post-war China: A case study of Kwanghua University under Zhu Jingnong's administration (1946–1949)], *Historical Research in Anhui*, no. 5 (2018): 76–84.

Religious Education in the Eyes of a Christian

Zhu Jingnong was a Protestant Christian. This fact is seldom mentioned in his chronicle or any other biographical materials about him. His eldest son Zhu Wenchang 朱文長 wrote in an obituary of his father, "My father was a devout Christian, especially in his later years."[5] However, we lack reliable information on when Zhu converted to Protestantism, which denomination he belonged to, and how he encountered the Christian faith. The main reason is that Zhu Jingnong seldom talked about his faith. In an article on religious education published in 1926, Zhu mentioned that he "had no chance to hear the Gospel until the age of eighteen or nineteen, and had no experience in compulsory attendance on any sort of religious service."[6] We can therefore infer that his first encounter with Christianity was around 1905.

More information about Zhu's faith is provided in his speech at a banquet hosted by the Changsha Christian Employees' Union (Changsha Jidujiao zhiyuan lianhehui 長沙基督教職員聯合會) in 1932, when he was the commissioner of education of the Hunan Provincial Government in Changsha. In his speech, he says, "Thirty years ago, I studied the Christian faith in a church in Shanghai, and I was baptized. Since then, I have kept a close association with the Church wherever I went."[7] We could also say that he had converted to Protestantism before studying in Japan in 1904 or 1905. As for the church in Shanghai he referred to in his speech, since it was published in a weekly of the American Methodist Episcopal Mission (South) called *China Christian Advocate* (*Xinghua zhoukan* 興華週刊), we can infer that Zhu probably belonged to this denomination. After his return to China in 1921, Zhu served in two different Christian universities, as head of the Chinese department at Shanghai Baptist College and president of Cheeloo University. He also served as a senior education official of the Nationalist government. These experiences earned Zhu a high reputation among Christian educators in China and, particularly, with overseas missionary societies. As a representative of the Chinese educational profession, he deeply engaged in the work of the China Christian Educational Association (Zhongguo Jidujiao jiaoyuhui 中國基督教教育會) and its Council of Higher Education. From the late 1920s—when he became an advisor of the Correlated Program for Christian Higher Education in China—to the postwar period, Zhu played an influential role in the formulation of a program for cooperation and coordination among Christian universities in China.

---

5. Zhu Jingnong, *Aishanlu shichao*, annotated by Zhu Wenchang, 126.
6. King Chu, "Compulsory Religious Instruction," *Chinese Recorder* 57, no. 5 (1926): 342.
7. "Zhu tingzhang Jingnong yanjiang" 朱廳長經農演講 [A speech by Commissioner Zhu Jingnong], *Chinese Christian Advocate* 興華週刊 29, no. 41 (1932): 30.

Soon after Zhu returned to China, the Anti-Christian Movement and the Restore Educational Rights Movement broke out. As an educator and a Christian, Zhu was against irrational opposition to Christianity and Christian education. In 1921, Professor Ernest D. Burton of the Divinity School of the University of Chicago led a commission comprising members from Britain and the United States to China to investigate Christian education. After the visit, Burton expressed his view on the role of Christian schools in the new education system. Zhu immediately translated Burton's words into Chinese and published them in *Xin jiaoyu* 新教育 (*The New Education*). Burton suggested that Christian education should adapt to the needs of the Chinese. Christian schools should be handed over to the Chinese as soon as possible; both public and Christian schools were indispensable to the Chinese education system. As they had their own strength and weaknesses, they should collaborate with each other.[8] Zhu agreed with these ideas, and he maintained this stance throughout his life.

During the Anti-Christian Movement, the Nationalist Group (*guojia zhuyi pai* 國家主義派), which consisted of mainly members of the Chinese Youth Party (Zhongguo qingnian dang 中國青年黨), were the ones who pulled out all the stops to promote the idea of transferring the right to educate students from foreigners to the Chinese government. Represented by Li Huang 李璜, Yu Jiaju 余家菊, and Chen Qitian 陳啟天, the Nationalist Group illustrated their education ideas through books like *Education of Nationalism* (*Guojia zhuyi de jiaoyu* 國家主義的教育), *Education: From the Nationalists' Point of View* (*Guojia zhuyi jiaoyu xue* 國家主義教育學), and the weekly *Awakening Lion* (*Xingshi* 醒獅). They demanded the entire and unconditional prohibition of Christian education and colonial education and the restoration of national sovereignty over education. In February 1925, Zhu Jingnong criticized the Nationalist Group's stance on education in a speech at the National Institute of Self-Government (Guoli zizhi xueyuan 國立自治學院). This provoked the Nationalist Group's interest in debating with Zhu, since there had been no criticism from the educational circles against their idea of nationalist education for two years until Zhu spoke up. Chen published a long article in *Awakening Lion*, asking Zhu whether he really agreed with the policy of nationalist education and why he did not support the restoration of education rights.[9]

---

8. Ernest D. Burton, "Jidujiao xuexiao zai Zhongguo jiaoyu xitong zhong suozhan diwei" 基督教學校在中國教育系統中所占地位 [The position of Christian schools in the education system of China], translated by Zhu Jingnong, *New Education* 4, no. 3 (1922): 355–61. When the Education Rights Restoration Movement was intensifying, this Chinese translation was reprinted by several periodicals like *Henan jiaoyu gongbao* 河南教育公報.
9. Chen Qitian 陳啟天, "Qingwen zancheng guojia zhuyi de Zhu Jingnong jun" 請問贊成國家主義的朱經農君 [A question for Mr. Zhu Jingnong who supports nationalism], *Xingshi* 醒獅, no. 21 (1925): 1–2.

Replying to Chen's questions, Zhu explained that he supported nationalism because "legitimate nationalism does not contradict isonomy." On the restoration of education rights, he argued that it should be understood at different levels. First, schools with political aggression implications should immediately be taken over. Second, church schools should be allowed to continue to exist after registering with the government, since these schools were only a type of private school, of which the existence was generally permitted in most civilized countries. Moreover, education in China had not yet been universalized. The more schools China had, the more educational opportunities children would get. Therefore, primary and secondary schools run by churches should be allowed to exist if they followed the curricula stipulated by the government.[10] Zhu further elaborated on this in another speech. He pointed out that church schools had many problems and defects, and the main problem was that they did not follow the curricula of the new education system. Zhu thought that until the universalization of education in China was realized, churches should temporally be allowed to run primary schools as long as they obey the government's regulations. In addition, churches should be allowed to run some good experimental secondary schools with dedicated efforts, and these schools could serve as examples for other public secondary schools. To Zhu, a university was an inclusive place of learning; it should be open-minded and tolerant, allowing different religious beliefs to exist on campus unless they went against the national interest. Every school must register with the government and operate under the national regulations. Also, compulsory participation in religious rituals should be prohibited, and Chinese culture should be emphasized in schools. Zhu tried to convince the Nationalist Group that there was a practical reason for allowing church schools to exist: the development of education in China was still in its embryonic stage. It required a massive number of teachers and a lot of financial support. "Christian education could supply what we lacked. However, to agree to the society's demand, we could ask Christian educational institutions to improve so as to meet our regulations."[11]

In his debate with non-Christians, Zhu Jingnong developed his view of religious education. He believed that religion had a unique function in education. On the one hand, religious faith was a personal choice; "Forcing others to convert to a religion should always be disapproved of; however, it is also wrong to force others not to believe in any religion." He thought that in any civilized country, freedom of religion is protected by its constitution. Students should have the freedom to choose

---

10. Zhu Jingnong, "Wei guojia zhuyi de jiaoyu dafu Chen Qitian jun" 為國家主義的教育答復陳啟天君 [My answer to Mr. Chen Qitian on nationalist education], *Zhonghua jiaoyujie* 中華教育界 14, no. 11 (1925): 4–7.
11. Zhu Jingnong, "Zhongguo jiaohui xuexiao gailiang tan—zai Nanfang Daxue jiangyan" 中國教會學校改良譚——在南方大學講演 [On reforming church schools in China: A speech at Southern University], *Zhonghua jidujiao jiaoyu jikan* 中華基督教教育季刊 1, no. 2 (1925): 9.

the religion they want to follow; it should not be determined by their parents or teachers. He also suggested that religious faith and national sovereignty are two separate things, and the former was completely different from political invasion. On the other hand, religious education was an experiment of moral education, and the aims of religion were to "exhort people to be virtuous, learn the Way (*dao* 道) and love others. It does not bear meaning in relation to political invasion, and it seems unnecessary to ban religion entirely."[12] In his opinion, religious education should be permitted in church schools, but it should never be compulsory. To Western missionaries, a system of voluntary religious instruction would weaken the outcome of religious education. However, Zhu referred to his personal conversion experience as an example to show that the worry was unnecessary. He once said that he "would have no chance to become a Christian if his parents had had their way in directing his religious belief." To a modern educated person, "religion, just as marriage, is a matter of one's own choice." Parents should not have the right to choose a religion for their child. Therefore, Zhu thought that compulsory religious education did not suit Chinese sentiment; a student's heart would be won only if there was "heart-to-heart contact of personality" between them and their teacher.[13]

Zhu was slightly different from contemporary Christian educators like James Yen and Tao Xingzhi. Religion was an important concern in his life, and he publicly advocated the importance of religion to education. In early 1923, there were debates over science and metaphysics (*xuanxue* 玄學) in the intellectual and cultural circles in China. Zhu actively participated in the debates through writing an article challenging the view of Zhang Junmai 張君勱, one of the representative figures of the Metaphysician School (*xuanxue pai* 玄學派), from eight perspectives, especially Zhang's distinction between matter and spirit.[14] After that, Zhu did not stop. He wrote another article in March 1924 called "Science and Religion" (Kexue yu zongjiao 科學與宗教) and submitted it to *Endeavour Monthly* (*Nuli yuebao* 努力月報), which was about to be issued by Hu Shi 胡適. In his letter to Hu, Zhu described his article as follows: "Eighty percent [of its contents] are to defend science, and the remaining twenty percent are to defend religion. I did so because I am a devout religious believer while with extreme admiration for science. I know that you and

---

12. Zhu, "Wei guojia zhuyi de jiaoyu da Chen Qitian jun," 6.
13. Chu, "Compulsory Religious Instruction," 342–43.
14. Zhu Jingnong, "Du Zhang Junmai lun renshengguan yu kexue de liangpian wenzhang hou suo fasheng de yiwen" 讀張君勱論人生觀與科學的兩篇文章後所發生的疑問 [Questions I have after reading Zhang Junmai's two articles on the philosophy of life and science], *Nuli zhoubao* 努力週報, no. 55 (1923): 2–3. This article was also published in *Chenbao fukan* 晨報副刊 on June 18, 1923, and later in *Kexue yu renshengguan* 科學與人生觀 edited by Wang Mengzou 汪孟鄒.

your fellow colleagues may not accept the content of my defense for religion. Feel free to point out my mistakes, but please do not take it personally."[15]

Zhu first criticized the Metaphysicians for bringing irrelevant charges against science, such as the claim that "science triggered the outbreak of the First World War." He also pointed out the Metaphysicians' misunderstanding of "science" and the "scientific method." At the same time, he noted the limitations of science: "Regarding the mystery of the universe, science only discovered the reason of the 'second step' and the fundamental problem has yet to be solved." Since the mystery of the universe remained unsolved, one appealed to God. From Zhu's perspective, this was the origin of religion:

> Since people in the world cannot rely merely on reason and be entirely unsentimental, they feel uncomfortable if they cannot find the origin of the "void and empty" universe and the creatures that "come for no reason." The hundred years of one's lifetime are a short span of time, like the brief appearance of night-blooming cereus. Where are we from? Do we still exist after death? The future is dim and distant, and we do not have an eternal home. Exploring in such darkness, through which can we express our strong feelings? Therefore, there are assumptions about the unknowable realm. The endpoint of science is the starting point of religion. Religion is a wonderful thing for soothing one's emotion. It is good for people, and it is not incompatible with science.

Then, Zhu concluded, "Religion and science should be complementary to [one another] instead of attacking each other." Scientists should not "break into the unknown realm and repudiate religion" for no reason. On the other hand, religionists (*zongjiao jia* 宗教家) should not deny facts proven scientifically out of thin air, and they should not treat science as their enemy without reason.[16]

Zhu also integrated his thinking on science and religion into his book *Educational Thoughts* (*Jiaoyu sixiang* 教育思想). In the chapter "Science and Religion" (Kexue yu zongjiao 科學與宗教) of this book, which was finished during the War of Resistance against Japan, Zhu's points of view are basically the same as those mentioned previously. But in "Science and Religion," Zhu referred to Wang Yangming 王陽明 and Wen Tianxiang 文天祥 to illustrate his understanding of religious faith. According to Zhu, Wang Yangming's "intuitive knowledge" (*liangzhi* 良知) means the heavenly principle that transcends time and space, and this is the Word (*logos*) in the

---

15. Research Office on the History of the Republic of China at Chinese Academy of Social Sciences, comp., *Hushi laiwang shuxin xuan (shang)* 胡適來往書信選 (上) [Selected correspondence of Hu Shih (volume 1)], compiled by (Beijing: Social Sciences Academic Press, 2013), 175. However, *Endeavour Monthly* eventually failed to be published for several reasons. As a result, "Kexue yu zongjiao" 科學與宗教 [Science and Religion] was published in *Wenshe yuekan* 文社月刊 (volume 1, combined issue of nos. 11 and 12) in October 1926.
16. Zhu, "Kexue yu zongjiao," 19.

Gospel of John ("In the beginning was the Word" [1:1]). Although Wang did not refer to God directly, the "principle" (li 理) he talked about was omnibenevolent, without a beginning and omnipresent, which was very similar to the Holy Spirit of Christianity. The best principle is the Word in Christianity. Referring to Wen Tianxiang, Zhu pointed out that the upright spirit (*zhengqi* 正氣) in heaven and earth described in *The Song of Upright Spirit* (*Zhengqi ge* 正氣歌) "dwells between heaven and earth, and creates mountains, rivers, the sun, the moon and stars. When revealed in humans, it becomes the upright spirit, [the eight virtues of] loyalty, filial piety, benevolence, love, faithfulness, righteousness and love of peace, and the four cardinal principles of a nation (*guo zhi siwei* 國之四維), namely propriety, righteousness, integrity, and sense of shame." Zhu thought that this was a faith, and the founding spirit of the Chinese nation. Although we refer to this with different names such as *shen* 神, *shangdi* 上帝, Allah, or Buddha, "in our faiths there exist an omniscient, omnipotent, benevolent and loving God who created the universe and all creatures."[17] Therefore, Zhu emphasized that we should not deny the role of religion in the process of education, because education is living, and religious elements are essential to our lives. During the War of Resistance against Japan, Zhu proposed that the country should put up not only a "physical national defense" with science but also a "spiritual national defense" that includes not ignoring religion, because "the upright spirit in heaven and earth and wisdom in our mind both originated from religious faith . . . It will be difficult [for our country] to have citizens who 'look upon death as returning home (*shi si ru gui* 視死如歸),' 'sacrifice their lives to achieve benevolence (*shai sheng cheng ren* 殺身成仁)' and 'die for the sake of justice (*cong rong jiu yi* 從容就義)' if religion is not promoted and [people in our country] do not believe in any religion."[18]

More notably, Zhu used prayer-like language in *Educational Thoughts*: "We pray that God will grant us have greater wisdom, love, and comprehension to clarify misunderstandings and know the true way of heaven."[19] When Zhu was the president of Kwanghua University, he actively promoted "education of love": "Teachers and students, and students themselves should cooperate with each other in the spirit of love and sincerity." Zhu objected to "education of hatred": "One should not come here if he or she comes with hatred and an intention to revolt, shed the blood of man, instigate conflicts and liquidate people."[20] Although the idea of "education of

---

17. Zhu Jingnong, *Jiaoyu sixiang* 教育思想 [Educational Thoughts] (Shanghai: Commercial Press, 1948), 78.
18. Zhu, *Jiaoyu sixiang*, 91.
19. Zhu, *Jiaoyu sixiang*, 85.
20. Zhu Jingnong, "Shixing aide jiaoyu de Guanghua Daxue" 施行愛的教育的光華大學 [The Kwanghua University that implements love education], transcript of a speech recorded by Wang Gongxia 汪公暇, *Shanghai jiaoyu* 上海教育 5, no. 11–12 (June 15, 1948): 9.

love" was advocated with the intention of keeping students from political conflicts among parties and cliques, it is obviously inseparable from his Christian faith. His emphasis on religious education is an important feature of Zhu's educational view that sets him apart from other educators of his day.

The Basis of Zhu's Educational Ideas: From Democracy to the Three Principles of the People

Zhu was a productive writer. However, most of his writings and speeches on education were scattered in newspapers and periodicals. He published only two books, namely *Seven Lectures on Modern Educational Thoughts* (*Jindai jiaoyu sichao qijiang* 近代教育思潮七講, 1941) and *Educational Thoughts* (*Jiaoyu sixiang* 教育思想, 1944). Published during the War of Resistance against Japan, they can be taken as the *magnum opuses* of his educational research. Scholars have summarized Zhu's educational thoughts in five areas: thoughts on child-based basic education; thoughts on vocational education that combines pragmatism and personal cultivation; thoughts on art education that unites aesthetic and reality; thoughts on civil education that emphasizes both theories and practice; and thoughts on science education that pays equal attention to knowledge and spirit.[21] This summation is relatively comprehensive and quite accurate. This chapter will not make specific elaborations of Zhu's educational thoughts in any of these five areas. Instead, it investigates Zhu's educational thoughts manifested in his educational philosophy. The term "education ideas" refers to fundamental principles and goals of education: one's educational ideas are closely connected to his faith and values, and the national aim of education will also affect an individual's educational ideas.

In April 1919, the Education Investigation Committee of the Ministry of Education (Jiaoyubu jiaoyu diaochahui 教育部教育調查會) passed Shen Enfu 沈恩孚 and Jiang Menglin's 蔣夢麟 proposal, affirming that the aim of education in the Republic of China was to "cultivate a healthy personality" (*yangcheng jianquan renge* 養成健全人格) and "develop a republican spirit" (*fazhan gonghe jingshen* 發展共和精神). The "healthy personality" mainly includes four areas: 1. Private virtue as the foundation of establishing oneself while public virtue as the foundation of serving the society and the nation, 2. knowledge and skills necessary for one's life, 3. a healthy and lively physique, and 4. graceful and joyful emotions. The "republican spirit" includes advocating democracy so that all people would know that a government by the people is the foundation of their nation, and developing the habit of civic self-governance so that all people can bear responsibilities toward their

---

21. Li, "Jindai jiaoyujia Zhu Jingnong jiaoyu sixiang de quanmian jiedu," 116–20, 129.

society and nation.²² This new educational aim was published in the newly issued *Xin jiaoyu*, a periodical edited by Jiang, manifesting the spirit of the quest for science and democracy since the New Culture Movement, and representing the educational ideas upheld by Dewey's Chinese students. In 1924, three years after returning to China, Zhu further elaborated on this educational aim. Having combed through Western scholars' views on the purpose of education, Zhu expressed the thought that "nurturing healthy individuals and creating a progressive society (*yangcheng jianquan de geren, chuangzao jinhua de shehui* 養成健全的個人，創造進化的社會)," which was stated in the first issue of *New Education*, expressed the aim of education very well. He listed nine criteria for a "healthy individual." In addition to those suggested by Shen and Jiang for a "healthy personality," Zhu suggested that a healthy individual should be able to cooperate with others, have basic civic knowledge and skills, understand world and domestic economies, maintain family harmony, ensure that their children receive education, be able to exercise their mind to create and invent, and have an appropriate belief, etc.. In terms of a "progressive society," Zhu directly borrowed Dewey's idea that in such a society, all members of an organization could cooperate fully with each other, and all organizations could be open and honest to each other, in order to bring forth peaceful social reform.²³ In short, Zhu completely followed the idea of "democracy" in Dewey's educational philosophy. This was also the core of his educational ideas throughout his life.

In response to the problems of Chinese society at the time, Zhu pointed out some educational areas that should be strengthened, namely physical and health education, civic education, personality cultivation, science education, education in rural areas, compulsory education, and mass education.²⁴ These terms can be regarded as the keywords of education in the 1920s, and Zhu was one of their main advocates. He assisted Zhu Qihui 朱其慧 and Xiong Xiling 熊希齡 (Zhu's aunt and uncle) as well as James Yen in establishing the Chinese National Association of the Mass Education Movement (Zhonghua pingmin jiaoyu cujinhui 中華平民教育促進會). Moreover, Zhu and Tao Xingzhi compiled the *Easy Chinese Lesson for the Illiterates* (*Pingmin qianzike* 平民千字課), the first thousand-character primer for the masses. Zhu himself also compiled a series of primary and secondary school textbooks for the new curriculum of the Chinese school system when working at the Commercial Press, introducing ideas of civic education, personality cultivation, and science education into the textbooks, influencing one generation of teenagers after another. Later, as the political situation of China changed rapidly, Zhu kept

---

22. *New Education* 1, no. 3 (April 1919): title page.
23. Zhu Jingnong, "Jiaoyu de mudi" 教育的目的 [The purpose of education], *Shun Pao Educational Supplement* 申報：教育與人生週刊, no. 16 (January 28, 1924): 165.
24. Zhu, "Jiaoyu de mudi," 166.

switching jobs, and his ideas and expressions on education also changed. One of the most notable changes was the integration of the aim of education based on the Three Principles of the People into his educational ideas. This can easily be observed in his works.

The concept of the aim of education based on the Three Principles of the People originated in the First National Education Meeting hosted by the Ministry of Education and Research in May 1928. In the meeting, all attendees agreed to adopt the new concept of the education of the Three Principles of the People in place of the idea of "partified education" (*danghua jiaoyu* 黨化教育). Having recently transferred from Shanghai to head the office of general education at the Ministry, Zhu participated in drafting the new aim of education. According to him, education in China under the leadership of the Nationalist Party should have an aim "that entirely suits the actual situation, serving as a standard for determining how to lead the whole nation to go through the political tutelage stage and adopt constitutionalism."[25] There were four articles in the Ministry's bill of the new education aim. The first three articles stipulate that various forms of educational measures should be adopted to incorporate the principle of nationalism (*minzu zhuyi* 民族主義), the principle of the rights of the people (democracy) (*minquan zhui* 民權主義), and the principle of the people's livelihood (*minsheng zhuyi* 民生主義). The fourth article allowed for promotion of internationalism in the hope of advancing into a stage of total peace (*datong* 大同). In April 1929, the Nationalist government officially promulgated the *Aim of Education in the Republic of China and Directions for Its Enforcement* (*Zhonghua Minguo jiaoyu zongzhi ji qi shishi fangzhen* 中華民國教育宗旨及其實施方針). Its description of the aim of education based on the Three Principles of the People was generally the same as Zhu's. Afterward, Zhu adopted the Three Principles of the People as the guiding thoughts of his educational research. This will be illustrated with the contents of his *Seven Lectures on Modern Educational Thoughts* as examples.

Seven Lectures on Modern Educational Thoughts was a collection of Zhu's lecture notes when he was the president of Cheeloo University. In January 1932, he carried the manuscript to Shanghai and was ready to send it to the Commercial Press for publishing. Unfortunately, the manuscript was destroyed because of the January 28 Incident. After returning to Jinan 濟南, he redrafted the manuscript. The contents of its introductory and other four chapters were successively published in *Cheeloo Monthly* (*Qida yuekan* 齊大月刊). Despite this, Zhu was not able to convert the manuscript into a monograph during his tenure at Cheeloo. It became even harder

---

25. Zhu Jingnong, "Zhonghua Minguo jiaoyu de zongzhi" 中華民國教育的宗旨 [The aim of education in the Republic of China], with notes of Zheng Jingzhong 鄭精忠, *Jiaoyu yuekan* 教育月刊 1, no. 12 (1928): 1.

for him to do so after becoming the commissioner of education of the Hunan Provincial Government. In the summer of 1939, while serving as a lecturer on modern educational thoughts in a training course for executive officers in Hunan, Zhu made "deletions and additions" to his redrafted manuscript to adapt it into a series of lecture notes. These lecture notes were published two years later as *Seven Lectures on Modern Educational Thoughts*.

In the introductory chapters of both the manuscript and the published version, Zhu stated that although educational thoughts in the West were actively publicized and discussed, they represented different stances, and many different schools of thought about education were derived from them. Therefore, for his work, Zhu selected only those educational thoughts that had significant impact on the modern trends in education and were closely related to modern education in China. Other than that, he looked at whether an educational thought suited China's situation. The educational thoughts covered in his work were selected for the sake of education in China, and they aimed to help him achieve his ultimate goal of solving the problems of education in China.[26] This is similar to the concept of "rooting education in the Chinese soil" (*zha gen Zhongguo dadi ban jiaoyu* 紮根中國大地辦教育) promoted by mainland Chinese educators in recent years. It is noteworthy that having undergone the baptism of the Three Principles of the People, all Western educational thoughts selected by Zhu were eventually reformed into a set of education ideas that Zhu believed were most suitable for China. The following are some examples.

Zhu regarded the child-based approach to education as the educational thought that provided the greatest contribution to the development of modern education. Although according to its educational regulations, the Nationalist government "[strove] to develop a child-based education," only a few experimental primary schools had some understanding of choosing teaching materials and improving teaching practices in accordance with child psychology. Most of the educators insisted on thinking from an adult's perspective and imposed several learning materials inappropriate for children's physical and mental development. Some authors of primary school textbooks opposed not only the use of story, but also the use of the vernacular Chinese (*baihua* 白話). The education bureaus of the large cities even required primary schools to carry out more instructions in Chinese classical texts. They attempted to make primary students remember important moral principles in these texts, such as the eight steps of self-cultivation in *The Great Learning* (*Daxue* 大學), through rote learning. Students were required to recite the moral principles in front of people like parrots. To Zhu, all these were faulty educational practices that

---

26. Zhu Jingnong, *Jindai jiaoyu sichao qijiang* 近代教育思潮七講 [Seven lectures on modern educational thoughts] (Changsha: Commercial Press, 1941), 1.

violated the spirit of the child-based approach to education.[27] Hence, child-based education was the topic of the first chapter of his book. Having combed through the thoughts on child education of naturalists like Jean-Jacques Rousseau, Ellen Key, and Leo Tolstoy, Zhu pointed out their compatibility and incompatibility with the situation of China. At the end of the chapter, Zhu referred to the aim of education based on the Three Principles of the People, pointing out some educational principles such as "to allow a child's body and mind to immerse and develop in the education of the Three Principles of the People"; "to allow a child's personality and sociability to develop evenly under the guidance of education of the Three Principles of the People"; "to equip children with the basic knowledge and skills necessary for their life under the education of the Three Principles of the People"; and so on. Here we can see that Zhu shrewdly blended the aim of education based on the Three Principles of the People with Western naturalists' thoughts on child-based education.

Zhu basically followed the same structure to present his ideas in other chapters of his book. For example, in the chapter on science education, Zhu opined that science education was the second-most influential educational thought in the modern era. He began with introducing the thoughts of George Combe, Herbert Spencer, Aldous Huxley, and Francis Bacon. Then, he referred to the ideas of science education proposed by the "advanced people of the party-state" (*dangguo xianjin* 黨國先進) such as Sun Yat-sen and Chiang Kai-shek. Finally, Zhu integrated these ideas into directions for education aiming at success in the War of Resistance against Japan and constructing the Chinese nation-state.

If we compare the structures of the manuscript and the Commercial Press edition of the *Seven Lectures on Modern Educational Thoughts* as shown in the table above, it is not difficult to recognize the similarity between their contents. The "deletions and additions" were simply the elimination of a chapter titled "Pragmatism and Vocational Education" and the addition of a chapter called "Three Principles of the People and Education Policy." The added chapter offers a detailed introduction to the main ideas of the Three Principles of the People, the formulation of the Nationalist Party's education policy and the directions for its implementation, the *Provisional Constitution for the Period of Political Tutelage* (*Xunzheng shiqi yuefa* 訓政時期約法) and national education, the *Program of the War of Resistance and National Construction* (*Kangzhan jianguo gangling* 抗戰建國綱領) and the plan of implementation of the wartime education policy. All of them highlighted the characteristics of wartime education.

Moreover, the chapter titled "Democracy and Universal Education" in the manuscript became the chapter called "Nationalist Thought and Universal Education"

---

27. Zhu, *Jindai jiaoyu sichao qijiang*, 2–3.

Table 6.1: The structures of the manuscript and the Commercial Press edition of *Seven Lectures on Modern Educational Thoughts*

1932 Manuscript[1]		1941 Commercial Press Edition	
Chapter I	Introduction ※	Lecture I	An Overview of Modern Educational Thoughts
Chapter II	Naturalism and Child-Centered Education ※	Lecture II	Naturalism and Child-Centered Education
Chapter III	Realism and Science Education ※	Lecture III	Realism and Science Education
Chapter IV	Democracy and Universal Education ※	Lecture IV	Nationalist Thought and Universal Education
Chapter V	Pragmatism and Vocational Education ※	Lecture V	Historical Materialism and Labor Education
Chapter VI	Humanism and Art Education	Lecture VI	Neo-Idealism and Personality Education
Chapter VII	Historical Materialism and Labor Education	Lecture VII	Three Principles of the People and Education Policy
Chapter VIII	Neo-Idealism and Personality Education	Appendix I	Humanism and Art Education
Chapter IX	Contributions of Psychology to Educational Thoughts	Appendix II	Contributions of Psychology to Education

1. The chapters marked with "※" were published in *Cheeloo Monthly*.

in the Commercial Press edition. The term "democracy" (*minben* 民本) became "nation" (*minzhu* 民族). In an article published in the *Cheeloo Monthly*, Zhu first explained that democracy was the third-most significant educational thought in the modern era. In politics, democracy refers to ideas like "people are the foundation of a country" and "popular sovereignty." In the cultural sphere, it means equal educational opportunities. In the education sphere, it was a guide for young people to cultivate a habit of working with others, staying together through thick and thin, and converting weaknesses into strengths by learning from others.[28] As I mentioned before, this was the idea of democratic education guided by Dewey's education thought that Zhu actively promoted after returning to China from the United States.

---

28. Zhu Jingnong, "Minben zhuyi yu puji jiaoyu" 民本主義與普及教育 [Democracy and universal education], *Cheeloo Monthly* 2, no. 8 (1932): 768.

He emphasized that universal education was the way of social reform and the basis for democracy since the realization of democracy could not be alienated from universal education.[29]

In the fourth lecture of the Commercial Press edition, Zhu claimed that "nationalist thought" was people's motivation to love their nation, also known as patriotism. If there was no national consciousness in a nation, when it was in crisis, its people would not realize the great significance of the ideas of "national supremacy" and the concept that "the nation is the first priority"; they would also not be willing to sacrifice their own interests and overcome their prejudice to save their endangered nation and love their disaster-stricken country. Zhu cited the Franco-Prussian War as an example of wars of education. He pointed out that the rise of Germany was due to Fichte's advocacy of new education and promotion of the idea that education built a nation.[30] Quoting Sun Yat-sen as saying, "China has regressed to its current state because of losing the nationalist spirit," Zhu suggested that as the nation was in crisis, the government should follow the *Program of the War of Resistance and National Construction*, speed up the universalization of education, and develop the people's national consciousness, so as to enhance their sentiment of resisting and reinforce the power of defense against Japan. Eventually, the missions of defeating Japan and constructing the nation could be accomplished.[31] However, the fourth lecture of the Commercial Press edition had a completely different emphasis from its counterpart in the manuscript, which talked about how the thought of democracy brought out the universalization of education, which in turn would strengthen the democratic society. On the other hand, in the fourth lecture of the Commercial Press edition, Zhu focused only on the notion that the purpose of universal education was to cultivate nationalism. The difference between the two editions shows the influence of wartime thinking on Zhu's educational ideas.

Zhu extensively quoted sayings from Sun Yat-sen and Chiang Kai-shek in *Seven Lectures on Modern Educational Thoughts* and *Educational Thoughts*. In chapters three, five, and six of *Seven Lectures*, Zhu devoted individual sections to the views of the "advanced people of the party-state" on science, labor, and personality education, taking them as grounds for his argument. The *Seven Lectures* often reiterated the superiority of the words of the party-state leaders. Zhu pointed out that all education policies of the Nationalist Party and their implementation plans must adopt the Three Principles of the People and the bequeathed teachings of Sun Yat-sen (*Zhongli yijiao* 總理遺教) as the fundamental principles. Zhu was an early revolutionary. Following Sun Yat-sen throughout his life, Zhu had a strong faith in

---

29. Zhu, "Minben zhuyi yu puji jiaoyu," 768.
30. Zhu, *Jindai jiaoyu sichao qijiang*, 5.
31. Zhu, *Jindai jiaoyu sichao qijiang*, 64–65.

the Three Principles of the People and published studies on the principles. He was an important explicator of the principles.[32] Hence, it is reasonable for Zhu, a key member of the education administration system of the Nationalist government, to integrate the aim of education based on the Three Principles of the People into Western educational philosophy and put these ideas into practice.

Nevertheless, we should also note that Zhu persistently objected to the Nationalist Party's attempt to control university education. He advocated for academic independence and freedom of thought. These ideas were clearly expressed in his letter to Hu Shi on February 1, 1931: "Now, politicians in China see potential in education, so they want to manipulate education . . . If the Nationalist Party wants to make public universities partified, there may not be any good results. Universities are not military forces. Freedom of thought and teaching cannot be disallowed."[33] Moreover, during the War of Resistance against Japan, the Nationalist Party implemented a policy of "education control" (*jiaoyu tongzhi* 教育統制), which severely undermined academic independence. After the war, Zhu, who was then vice minister of education, showed great concern for that implementation. He publicly expressed that "political parties should withdraw from schools, and thoughts cannot be controlled. Academic independence and freedom of thought must be upheld in university education."[34] Although Zhu was a loyal supporter of the aim of education based on the Three Principles of the People, he did not blindly follow the Nationalist Party's education policy. We can still see glimpses of the "democracy" he pursued in his early days throughout his life.

Withdrawing from Academia and Becoming an Official: Versatility or Indecisiveness?

During the twenty-seven years from 1921—when Zhu returned from the United States to teach at Peking University—to 1948, when he was sent as China's chief delegate to the general conference of the UNESCO in Lebanon, Zhu spent almost a half of the period on education administration, whereas he worked in universities or for the Commercial Press for the other half. He made several career changes, switching between academia and government. From the memoirs written by Zhu's friends,

---

32. Zhu Jingnong, *Sun Zhongshan xiansheng xueshuo de yanjiu* 孫中山先生學説的研究 [Research on the thoughts of Mr. Sun Yat-sen] (Shanghai: Xin shidai cubanshe, 1928).
33. "Zhu Jingnong zhi Hu Shi (can)" 朱經農致胡適（殘）[A letter to Hu Shih from Zhu Jingnong on February 1, 1932 (fragment)], in *Hu Shi laiwang shuxin xuan (zhong)* 胡適來往書信選（中）(Beijing: Social Sciences Academic Press, 2013), 430.
34. "Jiaoci Zhu Jingnongshi tan sixiang buneng tongzhi" 教次朱經農氏談思想不能統制 [The Vice Minister of Education, Mr. Zhu Jinnong, talks on the impossibility of controlling thoughts], *Dagang bao* 大剛報, February 11, 1946.

we can see that Zhu was highly regarded for his scholarship and administrative competence. Yu Ke 俞可 praised Zhu for "being a scholar and an official with skill and ease."[35] Xu Baoan 徐保安, on the other hand, analyzed Zhu's career choices and inner struggle between choosing an academic and an official career. According to Xu, Zhu did not have consistent career planning throughout his life. He was indecisive about serving in government or academia, and life and family pressure affected his vocational decisions.[36] The views of Yu and Xu are both reasonable yet debatable. It was not uncommon for scholars to work in the government in Zhu's time. Notable examples include Ding Wenjiang 丁文江 and Weng Wenhao 翁文灝. This phenomenon was partly in the scholar-officials' tradition of "excelling in learning and then entering public service" (*xue er you zhe shi* 學而優則仕). However, it was more likely that modern Chinese intellectuals chose to do so to achieve their aspiration toward "national salvation through scholarship" (*xueshu jiuguo* 學術救國). In the following discussion of this issue, I will refer to Zhu's several critical career switches.

When the Special Municipality of Shanghai was established in January 1927, Huang Fu 黃郛 was the mayor. He sought renowned scholars and experts to serve in the government, and Zhu was appointed Shanghai's commissioner of education. In his inaugural speech, Huang talked about his selection criteria for positions in his municipal government: "The only selection criteria are the candidate's professional knowledge and work experience. However, since the situation of Shanghai is unpleasant, I have also to give particular attention to one's virtue." Among the high-ranking officials of the municipal government of Shanghai at that time, there were those whom Huang had already known for a long time. Yet, there were also those who had never met Huang before.[37] Zhu belonged to the latter group. His appointment shows that he was considered a specialist in his field and had a good reputation. However, there is another explanation of why Zhu was appointed: right before the triumph of the Northern Expedition, Zhu had gone to Guangzhou 廣州 to establish contact with the central committee of the Nationalist Party. After returning to Shanghai, he started secretly engaging in party affairs with people such as Wu Zhihui 吳稚暉 and Yang Xingfo 楊杏佛. This made him a trustworthy "comrade" of the senior members of the Nationalist Party.[38] Zhu was also the vice-president

---

35. Yu Ke 俞可, "Zhu Jingnong: weixue weizheng youren youyu de quan mianjiao yujia" 朱經農：為學為政遊刃有餘的全面教育家 [Zhu Jingnong: A comprehensive educator who performed his roles in academia and government with skill and ease] *Shanghai Education*, no. 12 (2015), 68–69.
36. Xu and Li, "Shiming haishi huanming?"
37. Shen Yi 沈怡, "Shanghai shi gongwuju shinian" 上海市工務局十年 [Ten years in the Shanghai Bureau of Public Works], *Zhuanji wenxue* 傳記文學, no. 99 (1970): 11–12.
38. Han Shu 韓戍, "Beifa qianhou de xiaoyuan zhengzhi yu xuesheng yundong—yi Shanghai Guanghua Daxue wei zhongxin." 北伐前後的校園政治與學生運動——以上海光華大學為中心 [Campus politics and student movements before and after the Northern Expedition: Centered on Kwanghua University in Shanghai], *Historical Review*, no. 1 (2018): 153–64.

of Kwanghua University and the head of the philosophy and education section of the Editorial Department of the Commercial Press. According to Wang Yunwu, the director of the Editorial Department, the Shanghai municipal government "considered Jingnong the only suitable person to oversee education in the largest metropolitan city of China. It invited Zhu several times, and he felt that it was his duty not to decline the invitation."[39] It was the first time Zhu entered the realm of education administration. With only sixteen subordinates and a very stringent budget, he managed to get proper resources for the educational framework of Greater Shanghai. During his tenure as Shanghai's commissioner of education, Zhu lectured concurrently at several private universities. This caused Wang Yunwu to not only admire Zhu's scholarship, but also admit that he also had "outstanding administrative ability." A colleague of Zhu at that time, Pan Gongzhan 潘公展, commented on Zhu in his memoir, saying, "He was self-confident and did not go in quest for quick success; he kept his feet on the ground and finished his tasks step by step, laying a good foundation for the future."[40] However, soon after breaking new ground, Huang Fu resigned, and Zhu also stepped down.

Indeed, it can be said that Zhu stepped down reluctantly. According to Han Shu 韓戍, when Zhu worked at Kwanghua University, he suppressed students belonging to the Nationalist Party, who, through the Shanghai Students' Union (Shanghai xuesheng lianhehui 上海學生聯合會), accused him of organizing the University Association (Daxue tongzhi hui 大學同志會) to participate in "anti-revolutionary" activities. The students also charged Zhu with being a "hardcore anti-revolutionist" and "running dog of warlords." The Shanghai Party Purification Committee (Shanghai shi qingdang weiyuanhui 上海市清黨委員會) summoned Zhu, and Zhu denied all the accusations. He claimed that he joined the University Association as a representative of Kwanghua University. He also denied the charge of suppressing the students from the Nationalist Party. However, the students did not accept Zhu's defense and published a series of proclamations requesting the government remove Zhu from the position of commissioner of education. Zhu was then forced to resign.[41]

In 1928, the Nationalist government set up the Ministry of Education and Research, and Cai Yuanpei invited Zhu to serve as the director of its office of general education. Later, the ministry was reorganized, and the Ministry of Education was formed. Zhu became the director-general of its department of general education. Soon, he was promoted to the position of administrative vice minister. Zhu's

---

39. Wang, "Wo suo renshi de Zhu Jingnong xiansheng," 157.
40. Pan Gongzhan 潘公展, "Jinian yiwei Zhongguo jiaoyujia" 紀念一位中國教育家 [In memory of a Chinese educator] in *Aishanlu shichao*, 150.
41. For more, see Han Shu, "Beifa qianhou de xiaoyuan zhengzhi yu xuesheng yundong—yi Shanghai Guanghua Daxue wei zhongxin," *Historical Review*, no. 1 (2018): 153–64.

official career had gone smoothly to that point. However, because of the factional strife in the National Central University, Jiang Menglin, the minister of education, had a conflict with senior members of the Nationalist Party, like Wu Zhihui. On December 4, 1930, Jiang was removed from his position. Zhu resigned subsequently and became a commissioner of the Examination Yuan (Kaoshiyuan 考試院). At the same time, student protests took place repeatedly in China College. Because of this and also owing to the lack of funding, the college almost stopped functioning. Zhu was invited to find out the solutions. However, the problems facing the college were very complicated, and the students were in constant conflict with the Party. Zhu was stuck in the middle. He once complained to Hu Shi in a letter that "it is an unenviable work that pleases no one and exhausts me." He was looking for an opportunity to leave the college.[42]

The opportunity came soon after that. In 1929, Cheeloo University's failure to register with the Ministry of Education triggered a student movement and later a strike, stopping the university from functioning. To assist the university, Luella Miner, the university's dean of women, sought help from H. H. Kung (Kong Xiangxi 孔祥熙), then minister of industry. During the Boxer Rebellion, Miner praised Kung as a "guardian of faith" (*hujiao yingxiong* 護教英雄) for his protection of missionaries. She sponsored Kung to study in the United States afterward.[43] Kung was thankful for Miner's help in the past. Therefore, Kung became the chairman of the university's board of governors to help it register with the government as soon as possible, and as of March 1931, he also served as the university's president. However, because Kung was unable to be on campus frequently, he recommended that Zhu become president. The university's board of governors and its related mission societies in Britain and the United States approved Zhu's appointment shortly afterward. Zhu was welcomed not only because he used to be a vice minister of education and thus was closely connected to the central government, but also because he was a famous educator and was praised as a "Christian gentleman." Therefore, Zhu was widely accepted by both Chinese and foreign members of Cheeloo University.[44] Zhu took up his position in July 1931, and the university's registration with the government was completed in December. After one and a half years of vacancy, the post of president was filled by an ideal candidate.

During his time at Cheeloo University, everything went well for Zhu, and he enjoyed a peaceful life there. According to Zhu, the administrative work was carried out by the deans of colleges. There was not much work for the president. It was a

---

42. "Zhu Jingnong zhi Hu Shi (can)," 445.
43. Luella Miner, *Two Heroes of Cathay, an Autobiography and a Sketch* (New York: Fleming H. Revell Company, 1903).
44. "Mr. King Chu's Resignation," *Cheeloo Monthly*, no. 1 (September 1933), Archives of United Board of Christian Higher Education in Asia, Yale Divinity School Library, RG11-265-4263.

good opportunity for him to teach and write. He originally "wanted to take this opportunity to read books he had yet to read and to conduct systematic research on the culture of Chinese education."[45] However, the good days did not last long. In 1932, the provincial government of Hunan and the central government asked him to serve as the commissioner of education in Hunan to reform education in the region. At first, Zhu firmly turned down the request; he had no intention of taking up any official position again. Despite this, the Executive Yuan (Xingzhengyuan 行政院) ignored Zhu's wishes and publicly announced Zhu's appointment on August 15, 1932. Considering his ancestors' involvement in the education enterprise in Hunan, Zhu agreed to hold this office for an initial six months—one year at most. He also promised that once he established a new education system in Hunan, he would return to Cheeloo University. The university's board of governors permitted Zhu's leave to assist the national development of education in China but required Zhu to sign a written promise to resume his presidentship at the university as planned.

In June 1933, two months before the promised deadline for Zhu to return to Cheeloo University, the university and the Hunan provincial government started a heated exchange through telegraph.[46] On June 6, He Jian 何健, provincial governor of Hunan, wrote to Kung asking for allowing Zhu to continue serving as the commissioner of education in the province. However, Cheeloo University firmly rejected He's request. Given his multiple identities in Cheeloo and Government, Kung became the target of lobbyists from both sides. He was initially on the university's side. However, after receiving Chiang Kai-shek's telegram requiring Zhu to remain in Hunan, Kung changed his mind and suggested that the university grant Zhu another year of leave. Stuck between the university and the Hunan provincial government, Zhu was unsure about what he should do. Back-and-forth negotiations between the two parties through telegraph took place. While this process was rather exciting, this chapter will not go into detail.[47] In short, weighing the pros and cons of his different options again and again, Zhu had to make up his mind. He left Hunan for Cheeloo University on August 2 without prior notice. However, important figures of the party-state, including Chiang Kai-shek and Wang Jingwei 汪精衞, kept pressuring him. Eventually, Zhu had to resign from the university and return to Hunan. This career shift from academia to government was the most difficult and painful decision Zhu made in his life.

---

45. Zhu Jingnong, "Shinian huiyi" 十年回憶 [Reminiscence of ten years]. *Hunan jiaoyu yuekan* 湖南教育月刊, no. 33/34 (October 13, 1942): 1.
46. For the contents of the telegrams, see the aforementioned "President Chu's Resignation," RG11-267-4273. A twenty-page booklet compiled by Cheeloo University after the "Zhu Jingnong Incident," it included telegrams issued by the parties involved in the incident. The booklet has never been published.
47. Xu and Li, "Shiming haishi huanming?"

Cheeloo University was established with the support of more than ten British, American, and Canadian missionary societies. The relationships among the missionary societies as well as between the university's Chinese and foreign members were complicated. These parties were also in constant conflict. It was fortunate for the university to have a president like Zhu, who was deemed very satisfactory by all stakeholders of the university. Zhu's resignation was a heavy blow to the university, which just began to proceed on the right track. Considering the price that the university paid for its search for Zhu's successor—someone deemed to be satisfactory by all its stakeholders, which included more than three years of searching, and the subsequent internal schism, it is not difficult to understand why the university felt it was unfair to them that Zhu resigned owing to pressure from important figures of the party-state.[48]

Of course, Hunan needed Zhu too. The population of the province was much bigger than that of a university. The provincial government used the province's population as the main argument to persuade Zhu to stay in Hunan. As an intellectual aspiring to contribute to his country through his scholarship, Zhu had no excuse for declining the request, as staying in Hunan could help address the needs of educational development of China.

The loss of Cheeloo University was the gain of Hunan. Unexpectedly, Zhu served as the commissioner of education of the Hunan provincial government for ten and a half years, working under three different provincial governors. Zhu might be the longest-serving official administering educational affairs at provincial level during the Republican era. After taking up the post, Zhu overhauled the education system in Hunan and promptly won the trust of He Jian and the people in the province. To address the problem of insufficient funds, Zhu proposed a creative solution known as "raising funds from fields and hills" (*mutian mushan* 募田募山): "To fix the problem permanently, we should first raise funds from fields and hills. We can collect rice from fields and fields grow crops. We can grow coarse grains and fruits in hills, which also helps solve financial difficulties."[49] Instead of listing Zhu's achievements in Hunan in numerical terms, I would like to refer to a passage written by Zhu's colleague Yu Xianli 余先礪:

> In those ten years, the reform of the education system, the establishment of new schools and the improvement of teaching methods all made us feel like seeing the light at the end of the tunnel after passing through bramble thickets, peaches and

---

48. Liu Jiafeng 劉家峰, "Xiaoyuan zhengzhi yu Zhongxi boyi: Qilu daxue lian qianhou de yichang fengbo" 校園政治與中西博弈：齊魯大學立案前後的易長風波 [Campus politics and Sino-Western power game: The saga of Cheeloo University's replacement of president before and after its registration with the Chinese government], *Journal of Sun Yat-sen University (Social Science Edition)* 58, no. 2 (2018): 76–84.
49. Zhu, "Shinian huiyi," 2.

plums flourishing in gardens and the sounds of strumming and singing continuing unabated. Despite the unsettling socio-political realities and the instability of governmental funding at that time, with the spirit of a wise man free from perplexities, a virtuous man free from anxiety and a courageous man free from fear, Zhu strove for peace in upheavals and progress in difficulties. He was a sincere and simple man who created miracles.[50]

During Zhu's tenure, he completed the project of popularizing the national compulsory education in Hunan ahead of schedule, establishing "a central school in every town and a primary school for every hundred households." Considering the less developed economic conditions of Hunan and the wartime situation, it was a true "miracle" to have achieved this.

However, Zhu's educational work in Hunan saw some hindrances too. Apart from the lack of funding and talent, Zhu faced the problem of factional strife within the Nationalist Party in the province, which extended to the field of education. He did his best to prevent schools from being affected by it, greatly contributing to the province's political stability and the implementation of the central government's policies in Hunan.[51]

In February 1943, Chiang Kai-shek, then president of the Executive Yuan, was also serving as the president of the National Central University at the time. He appointed Zhu to be the vice-chancellor (*jiaoyu zhang* 教育長), overseeing the operations of the university. This move demonstrates that Zhu was trusted by Chiang and Chen Lifu 陳立夫, then minister of education. Some people labeled Zhu as a member of the Central Club Clique of the Nationalist Party because of this.[52] In March 1944, Chiang resigned from the presidency, and Zhu became the political vice minister of the Ministry of Education under Chen's arrangement. After the War of Resistance against Japan, Zhu resigned from the post. According to his eldest son's recollection, Zhu had been working in the government for so long and was tired of the vicissitudes of official life. At that time, as Wang Yunwu entered officialdom, he invited Zhu to head the Commercial Press. Despite his lack of experience and confidence in managing workers, Zhu was persuaded by Wang to join the

---

50. Yu Xianli 余先礪, "Xiangsheng jiaoyu de huihuang shiye: jinian Zhu Jingnong shishi shizhounian." 湘省教育的輝煌史頁——紀念朱經農逝世十周年 [A glorious page in the history of education in Hunan: in commemoration of the tenth anniversary of the death of Zhu Jingnong], in *Aishanlu shichao*, 148.
51. Lai Jinghu 賴景瑚, "Yidai hongru" 一代鴻儒 [A great scholar], *Hunan wenxian* 湖南文獻 11, no. 2 (April 1983). Lai was a special commissioner of the Nationalist Party in Hunan around the War of Resistance against Japan. He worked closely with Zhu.
52. Liu Shouqi 劉壽祺, "Zhu Jingnong yu Hunan jiaoyu." [Zhu Jingnong and education in Hunan], *Hunan wenshi* 湖南文史 34, no. 2 (1982): 159.

Commercial Press again. He also concurrently served as the president of Kwanghua University, returning to the frontline of education.

In November 1948, as a delegate of the Chinese government, Zhu attended the general conference of UNESCO in Lebanon. It was the last time he would engage in public service. He did not return to China after the conference as he foresaw the defeat of the Nationalist Party. Instead, he decided to reside in the United States and spend time lecturing and writing. In August 1950, Zhu became a professor at the Hartford Seminary. *Aishanlu shichao* 愛山廬詩鈔 included a photo of him with E. H. Cressy, a longstanding leading figure of the China Christian Educational Association and its Council of Higher Education, who knew Zhu well. From this, we could infer that it should be at Cressy's invitation that Zhu joined the faculty of the Hartford Seminary.

Zhu's frequent career switches indicate that his official positions changed at the will of the government. While Zhu accepted some of the appointments in accordance with his will, such as those at the Shanghai municipal government and the Ministry of Education, at other times, he accepted appointments after repeated contemplation, such as his transfer from Cheeloo University to the Hunan provincial government. Sometimes, he took up an appointment at the invitation of someone in power or his old friend. Most of his career decisions were made under external influence, and some of them were against his will. In the workplace, Zhu came across many difficulties and obstacles from different parties. Therefore, the view that Zhu performed his roles in academia and government with skill and ease as well as having everything under control is not consistent with history, even though when Zhu's contemporaries said so, they meant it as a compliment to him.

On the other hand, it is true that Zhu's career switches were frequent, Zhu appeared to be indecisive as a result. His longest-serving position was the commissioner of education of the Hunan provincial government, a position he held for ten and a half years, whereas in some other institutions, his periods of service were shorter, averaging one year or six months. The great frequency of Zhu's career switches also represents the unsettled socio-political reality of Republican China. However, I wish to clarify that I do not mean that Zhu simply followed the herd and did not have any career aspirations. In his later days, Zhu recounted his professional learning experience in a speech. He stated that while studying abroad, he was first interested in topics in politics such as comparative constitution, government, and international law. However, he soon realized that "there must be a political ideal behind every political transformation." Thus, his interest shifted from politics to intellectual history. As he subsequently realized that "ideas cannot be disseminated without education," he changed his mind and concentrated his studies on education and the history of the evolution of human thoughts. He said, "Until now, these have still interested me."⁵³ Education was Zhu's interest and vocation for life. He always worked in the field of education, irrespective it being in academia or government. Zhu was not a theoretical educator. He had an aspiration for national salvation and put it into practice. Taking this into consideration, we may understand why Wang Yunwu praised Zhu as an "all-around educator."

Conclusion: Sounds of Strumming and Singing, or a Dream in Vain?

In September 1942, the education bureau of Hunan convened a meeting in Leiyang 耒陽 to celebrate the tenth anniversary of Zhu as the commissioner of education. A couplet, hung on a theater stage, was cowritten by Yu Xianli and a colleague of his in recognition of Zhu's achievements in those ten years. The couplet goes:

> Planting trees is easy, but nurturing people is difficult.
> After his ten years of effort, we dare to say students are now everywhere in Hunan.
> The breeze of autumn is gentle, and the moon of autumn is clear.
> Thanks to an education reform, the sounds of strumming and singing are widespread in thousands of families.⁵⁴

In response to praises from different quarters, Zhu evaluated himself differently: "Figures on education have added up year by year, and everyone's perception of education has changed. However, facing this opportunity of times, I am repeatedly bothered that my ability is poor, but my responsibilities are heavy. I hate myself for not achieving our ideal yet."⁵⁵

On February 27, 1951, ten days before his death, Zhu commented on his own life in his diary as follows:

> I was a member of the Chinese Revolutionary Alliance and then transferred to the Nationalist Party in 1912. Since then, I have consistently been loyal to the Party. When the Party was ruling, I faithfully complied with the Party's regulations and did not attempt to contend for power. When the Party failed, I drifted from place to place and did not betray the Party. The Nationalist Chinese government was established in 1927 after the initial success of the national revolution. Because of my affiliation with the Party, I left academia and became an official, experiencing ups and downs for over twenty years. Looking back, I feel that I made a huge

---

53. Zhu Jingnong, "Wo zenyang qiuxue" 我怎樣求學 [How I pursued studies], *Dushu tongxun* 讀書通訊, no. 155 (May 1948): 15.
54. The Chinese original reads: "樹木易，樹人難，十載辛勤，敢云七澤三湘，遍栽桃李；秋風清，秋月朗，一場粉墨，藉使千門萬戶，廣被弦歌。" Yu, "Xiangsheng jiaoyu de huihuang shiye: jinian Zhu Jingnong shishi shizhounian," 148.
55. Zhu, "Shinian huiyi," 8.

sacrifice. If I had spent those years concentrating on academic work and writing, my achievements would have gone beyond what I achieved. My accomplishments as an official in those twenty some years were all destroyed by wars. As I am now recalling my memory, it seems that everything I have done is just a dream. I am now old and weak. Although I want to write, I no longer have the stamina to do so. Sigh.[56]

This diary entry can be taken as Zhu's self-confession. He regretted having given up his academic career to become an official, which led to his limited achievements in scholarship. In fact, he had revealed this view before: "After returning to China, I spent most of my time on education administration—either on local education affairs or university administrative affairs. I did not have a chance to read as many books worth reading as possible. I also did not have time to organize my thoughts that are worth publishing into systematic works. I hope that soon I can get rid of all administrative work, focus on reading in a secluded place and write a few basic books. As the old saying goes, 'if you want to be good, learn till [you are] old.' I am ashamed that I have not conducted thorough studies on any topics."[57]

In his final years, Zhu was stranded in the United States, moving from the East Coast to the West Coast. He suffered from poverty and sickness. However, whenever his health got slightly better, he immediately "worked hard reading and continued to write." It seemed that he finally got a chance to focus on studying. Unfortunately, he passed away before finishing his planned work, "A Brief History of Chinese Educational Thoughts" (Zhongguo jiaoyu sixiang jianshi 中國教育思想簡史) and left several manuscripts. Given his thirty-some years' experience in education in China and profound knowledge of ancient and modern educational thoughts in China and the West, if he had enough time, he might have finished his planned work, which would have been a contribution to education in China.

However, Zhu's regret could not be fully ascribed to his personal choices. It was the inevitable outcome of "national salvation through education" and "national salvation through scholarship," practiced by Chinese intellectuals at that time. Wang Yunwu, an old friend of Zhu, said, "Zhu devoted himself to education while not forgetting his country and the people." Zhu's colleague Pan Gongzhan 潘公展 said Zhu was "an educator who taught people not only by words but also by deeds."[58] How could an educator with aspirations like Zhu be satisfied with simply writing in a study? Regardless of being a teacher or an education administrator, all Zhu did was to realize his dream of "national salvation through education." It was only his

---

56. Zhu Wenchang and Zhu Wenhua 朱文華, "Xianjun Jingnong gong shishi qianhou" 先君經農公逝世前後 [Before and after the death of our father Zhu Jingnong], in *Aishanlu shichao*, 126.
57. Zhu, "Wo zenyang qiuxue," 15.
58. Pan, "Jinian yiwei Zhongguo jiaoyujia," 150.

personal encounters and social reality that prevented him from realizing his dream and made him sigh, "it was just a dream."

Zhu lamented, "as I am now recalling my memory, it seems that everything I have done is just a dream." This does not entirely reflect reality. At the very least, he left legacies in Hunan, the Commercial Press, Cheeloo University, and many other places. In addition, the numerous well-received textbooks he edited, as well as his commentaries and writings on education, have become a treasure trove of educational thoughts for today's Chinese educators. They are waiting for the educators' exploration.

Liu Shouqi 劉壽祺 (1901–1990), a famous educator in Hunan and Zhu's contemporary, worked under Zhu for a long time. In 1935, he served as the director of the experiment district of compulsory education (Yiwu jiaoyu shiyan qu 義務教育實驗區) and a secretary of the mass training guidance office (Minzhong xunlian zhidao chu 民眾訓練指導處) in Hunan. When Zhu was transferred to the National Central University and the Ministry of Education, Liu followed him and served as his secretary and an education inspector. He was Zhu's helpful and trusted assistant. Liu joined the Communist Party of China in 1938 in secret and made use of his public identity as a Nationalist party-state official to protect some progressive youths and underground communist organizations. The following is his comment on Zhu:

> He was a knowledgeable scholar, well-versed in both Chinese and Western studies. Despite floating in the sea of officialdom for a while, he was not a politician who excelled at maneuvering among various political groupings. He was not only an upright, selfless, loyal and courageous patriot. He was also a sincere and diligent educator who established himself and others. No matter in Leiyang or Chongqing, thanks to him, some of our Party's underground agents were sheltered and some progressive youths protected. Although he did not do so consciously or take the initiative to do so, his deeds benefited the Party and the people.[59]

While the comment does not represent the Communist Party's definitive and official evaluation of Zhu's place in history, it is a comment of a senior member of the Communist Party on a more senior member of the Nationalist Party, which goes beyond ideological differences and political partisanship, and can be said to be objective and accurate.

---

59. Liu, "Zhu Jingnong yu Hunan jiaoyu," 173.

Bibliography

Burton, Ernest D. "Jidujiao xuexiao zai zhongguo jiaoyu xitong zhong suozhan diwei" 基督教學校在中國教育系統中所占地位 [The position of Christian schools in the education system of China], translated by Zhu Jingnong. *New Education* 新教育 4, no. 3 (1922): 355–61.

Chen, Qitian 陳啟天. "Qingwen zancheng guojia zhuyi de Zhu Jingnong jun" 請問贊成國家主義的朱經農君 [A question for Mr. Zhu Jingnong who supports nationalism]. *Xingshi* 醒獅, no. 21 (1925): 1–2.

Chu, King [Zhu Jingnong 朱經農]. "Compulsory Religious Instruction." *Chinese Recorder* 57, no. 5 (1926): 341–44.

Han, Shu 韓戌. "Beifa qianhou de xiaoyuan zhengzhi yu xuesheng yundong—yi Shanghai Guanghua Daxue wei zhongxin." 北伐前後的校園政治與學生運動——以上海光華大學為中心 [Campus politics and student movements before and after the Northern Expedition: Centered on Kwanghua University in Shanghai]. *Historical Review* 史林, no. 1 (2018): 153–64.

Han, Shu. Zhanhou Zhongguo sili daxue de zhili kunjing—yi Zhu Jingnong zhizhang Guanghua Daxue weili (1946–1949) 戰後中國私立大學的治理困境——以朱經農執掌光華大學為例（1946–1949）[The governance difficulties of private universities in post-war China: A case study of Kwanghua University under Zhu Jingnong's administration (1946–1949)]. *Historical Research in Anhui* 安徽史學, no. 5 (2018): 76–84.

Lai, Jinghu 賴景瑚. "Yidai hongru" 一代鴻儒 [A great Confucianist]. *Hunan wenxian* 湖南文獻 11, no. 2 (April 1983).

Li, Mao 李卯. Zhu Jingnong jichu jiaoyu kecheng sixiang ji shijian yanjiu 朱經農基礎教育課程思想及實踐研究 [A study of Zhu Jingnong's thoughts and practices about basic education curriculum]. Master's thesis, Hunan Normal University, 2011.

Li, Mao. "Jindai jiaoyujia Zhu Jingnong jiaoyu sixiang de quanmian jiedu" 近代教育家朱經農教育思想的全面解讀 [A comprehensive interpretation of the modern Chinese educator Zhu Jingnong's educational thoughts]. *Journal of Jianghan University (Social Science Edition)* 31, no. 1 (2014): 116–20.

Liu, Jiafeng 劉家峰. "Xiaoyuan zhengzhi yu zhongxi boyi: qilu daxue lian qianhou de yichang fengbo" 校園政治與中西博弈：齊魯大學立案前後的易長風波 [Campus politics and Sino-Western power game: The saga of Cheeloo University's replacement of president before and after its registration with the Chinese government]. *Journal of Sun Yat-sen University (Social Science Edition)* 中山大學學報 58, no. 2 (2018): 76–84.

Liu, Shouqi 劉壽祺. "Zhu Jingnong yu Hunan jiaoyu" 朱經農與湖南教育 [Zhu Jingnong and education in Hunan]. *Hunan wenshi* 湖南文史 34, no. 2 (1982).

Miner, Luella. *Two Heroes of Cathay, an Autobiography and a Sketch*. New York: Fleming H. Revell Company, 1903.

"Mr. King Chu's Resignation." *Cheeloo Monthly Bulletin*, no. 1 (September 30, 1933). Archives of United Board of Christian Higher Education in Asia, Yale Divinity School Library, RG11-265-4263.

"President Chu's Resignation." Archives of United Board of Christian Higher Education in Asia, RG11-267-4273.

Research Office on the History of the Republic of China at Chinese Academy of Social Sciences, comp. *Hu Shi laiwang shuxin xuan (shang)* 胡適來往書信選（上）[Selected correspondence of Hu Shih (volume 1)]. Beijing: Social Sciences Academic Press, 2013.

Shen, Yi 沈怡. "Shanghai shi gongwuju shinian" 上海市工務局十年 [Ten years in the Shanghai Bureau of Public Works]. *Zhuanji wenxue* 傳記文學, no. 99 (1970): 11–18.

Xu, Baoan 徐保安 and Li Meng 李萌. "Shiming haishi huanming? Cong zhu jingnong kan minguo zhishi fenzi de zhiye xuanze yu rensheng chujing" 詩名還是宦名？——從朱經農看民國知識份子的職業選擇與人生處境 [Reputation of being a good scholar or reputation of being a good official? A study of career choices and life situations of intellectuals in the Republican Era: The case of Zhu Jingnong]. *Studies on Republican China* 民國研究 26, no. 2 (2014): 148–66.

Yu, Ke 俞可. "Zhu Jingnong: weixue weizheng youren youyu de quan mianjiao yujia," 朱經農：為學為政遊刃有餘的全面教育家 [Zhu Jingnong: A comprehensive educator who did research and administrative works with ease]. *Shanghai Education* 上海教育 12 (2015): 68–69.

Zhang, Daren 張達人. "Zhu jingnong xiansheng nianpu(chugao)" 朱經農先生年譜（初稿）[The chronicles of Zhu Jingnong (first draft)]. *Hunan wenxian* vol. 11, no. 4 (1983) and vol. 12, nos. 1–2 (1984).

Zhi, Xiaomin 智效民. *Hushi he tade pengyou men (zengbu ben)* 胡適和他的朋友們（增補本）[Hu Shih and his friends]. Beijing: Shijie zhishi chubanshe 世界知識出版社, 2020.

Zhi, Xiaomin 智效民. "Shiming yinggong huanming qing—guanyu zhu jingnong" 詩名應共宦名清──關於朱經農 [One's reputation as a literatus and an official should be equally untarnished: On Zhu Jingnong]. *Zhuanji wenxue* 傳記文學, no. 472 (September 2001): 51–58.

Zhu, Jingnong 朱經農. *Aishanlu shichao* 愛山廬詩鈔 [Selected poems from Aishan Mansion], compiled and annotated by Zhu Wenchang 朱文長. Taipei: Taiwan Commercial Press, 1965.

Zhu, Jingnong 朱經農. "Du Zhang Junmai lun renshengguan yu kexue de liangpian wenzhang hou suo fasheng de yiwen" 讀張君勱論人生觀與科學的兩篇文章後所發生的疑問 [Questions I have after reading Zhang Junmai's two articles on the philosophy of life and science]. *Nuli zhoubao* 努力週報, no. 55 (1923): 2–3.

Zhu, Jingnong 朱經農. "Jiaoci Zhu Jingnong shi tan sixiang buneng tongzhi" 教次朱經農氏談思想不能統制 [The Vice Minister of Education, Mr. Zhu Jinnong, talks on the impossibility of controlling thoughts]. *Dagang bao* 大剛報, February 11, 1946.

Zhu, Jingnong 朱經農. "Jiaoyu de mudi" 教育的目的 [The purpose of education]. *Shun Pao Educational Supplement* 申報：教育與人生週刊, no. 16 (January 28, 1924): 165–66.

Zhu, Jingnong 朱經農. "Jiaoyu sixiang" 教育思想 [Educational Thoughts]. Shanghai: Commercial Press, 1948.

Zhu, Jingnong 朱經農. *Jindai jiaoyu sichao qijiang* 近代教育思潮七講 [Seven lectures on modern educational thoughts]. Changsha: Commercial Press, 1941.

Zhu, Jingnong 朱經農. "Kexue yu zongjiao" 科學與宗教 [Science and Religion]. *Wenshe yuekan* 文社月刊 1, no. 11/12 (October 1926): 5–20.

Zhu, Jingnong 朱經農. "Minben zhuyi yu puji jiaoyu" 民本主義與普及教育 [Democracy and universal education]. *Cheeloo Monthly* 2, no. 8 (1932).

Zhu, Jingnong 朱經農. "Shinian huiyi" 十年回憶 [Reminiscence of ten years]. *Hunan jiaoyu yuekan* 湖南教育月刊, no. 33/34 (October 13, 1942).

Zhu, Jingnong 朱經農. "Shixing aide jiaoyu de Guanghua Daxue" 施行愛的教育的光華大學 [The Kuanghua University that implements love education], transcript of a speech recorded by Wang Gongxia 汪公暇. *Shanghai jiaoyu* 上海教育 5, no. 11/12 (June 15, 1948): 8–9.

Zhu, Jingnong 朱經農. "Sun Zhongshan xiansheng xueshuo de yanjiu" 孫中山先生學說的研究 [The research on the thoughts of Mr. Sun Yat-sen]. Shanghai: Xin shidai cubanshe, 1928.

Zhu, Jingnong 朱經農. "Wei guojia zhuyi de jiaoyu dafu Chen Qitian jun" 為國家主義的教育答復陳啟天君 [My answer to Mr. Chen Qitian on nationalist education]. *Zhonghua jiaoyujie* 中華教育界 14, no. 11 (1925): 4–7.

Zhu, Jingnong 朱經農. "Wo zenyang qiuxue" 我怎樣求學 [How I pursued studies]. *Dushu tongxun* 讀書通訊, no. 155 (May 1948): 15.

Zhu, Jingnong 朱經農. "Zhongguo jiaohui xuexiao gailiang tan—zai Nanfang Daxue jiangyan" 中國教會學校改良譚——在南方大學講演 [On reforming church schools in China: a speech at Southern University]. *Zhonghua jidujiao jiaoyu jikan* 中華基督教教育季刊 1, no. 2 (1925): 5–9.

Zhu, Jingnong 朱經農. "Zhonghua Minguo jiaoyu de zongzhi" 中華民國教育的宗旨 [The aim of education in the Republic of China], with notes of Zheng Jingzhong 鄭精忠. *Jiaoyu yuekan* 教育月刊 1, no. 12 (1928): 1–6.

Zhu, Jingnong 朱經農. "Zhu Jingnong zhi Hu Shi (can)" 朱經農致胡適（殘）[A letter to Hu Shih from Zhu Jingnong on February 1, 1932 (fragment)]. In *Hu Shi laiwang shuxin xuan (zhong)* 胡適來往書信集（中）, compiled by Research Office on the History of the Republic of China, Institute of Modern History, Chinese Academy of Social Sciences. Beijing: Social Sciences Academic Press, 2013.

Zhu, Jingnong 朱經農. "Zhu tingzhang Jingnong yanjiang" 朱廳長經農演講 [A speech by Commissioner Zhu Jingnong]. *Chinese Christian Advocate* 興華週刊 29, no. 41 (1932): 30–31.

Part Three: New Initiatives

7
A Project of National Transformation in China
Yu Rizhang's Promotion of Social Education

Peter Chen-main Wang

Chinese intellectuals who lived at the turn of the century were vexed by alarming phenomena—ongoing foreign encroachment and unceasing internal corruption and malfunction. Repeated reforms in the late Qing dynasty and even the Revolution of 1911 failed to turn the tide. China seemed to be in a deep whirlpool that no one knew how to escape. Against this background, Yu Rizhang 余日章 (David Z. T. Yui, 1882–1936), a prominent leader of the YMCA in China, distinguished himself by presenting a set of social education ideals and projects to address the evils and to restore the prosperity and power of China.

In China, social education (*shehui jiaoyu* 社會教育) usually denotes all educational activities of cultural and social institutions outside of family and schools.[1] This definition, though different from that used by modern scholars in America and Europe, was appropriate for an underdeveloped country with few schools available and low literacy in the nineteenth and early twentieth centuries.[2] The launch of

---

1. Even up to today, the Department of She-hui jiao-yu (社會教育學系) of National Taiwan Normal University, the first and probably the only department in this field in Taiwan, still holds this definition of social education. Interestingly, the department does not use the literal translation of its English name but adopts the name "The Department of Adult & Continuing Education," which is close to the definition of the social education in China. See the website of the department, "Department of Adult & Continuing Education (社會教育學系)," National Taiwan Normal University," accessed June 20, 2020, http://www.ace.ntnu.edu.tw/en/mem-bers/teacher.php?class=130,100,110,120.
2. Social education, in modern times, usually suggests "a socially centered school curriculum" and is often used as a synonym for "social studies." For example, see Christine Woyshner, Joseph Watras, and Margaret Smith Crocco, eds., introduction to *Social Education in the Twentieth Century: Curriculum and Context for Citizenship* (New York: Peter Lang, 2004), ix–xii; Jacob W. Neumann, "Social Education—Sacrality in Education," in *Journeys in Social Education: A Primer*, ed. Cameron White (Rotterdam: Sense Publishers, 2011), 49–66; David L. Grossman and Looe Tin-Yau Lo, eds., introduction to *Social Education in Asia: Critical Issues and Multiple Perspectives* (Charlotte, NC: Information Age Pub, 2008), 1–4.

social education in China at the beginning of the twentieth century was extraordinarily significant because the illiteracy rate in China at that time was roughly 85–90 percent. Social education was seen to be the only way for the masses to become literate; to understand their society, their country, and the outside world; and to grasp civil liberty and modern citizenship. Yet even now, few people in education are aware that the inception of social education in China came from a Christian leader—Yu Rizhang.[3]

An examination of Yu Rizhang's efforts in social education will not only reveal the origin of general education in modern China, but also serve to illustrate a Christian intellectual's response to his changing context. This chapter explores the subject in three parts. The first part introduces Yu Rizhang's school life at Boone School in Wuhan, St. John's University in Shanghai, and Harvard University in Boston, with an emphasis on his nationalist and Christian identity. The second part addresses Yu Rizhang's early career at the YMCA, which ignited his vision for saving China through social education. The third part discusses the mass education movement and the citizenship movement of the Chinese YMCA that culminated from Yu's efforts.

A Nationalistic Youth

Nationalism and Christianity were two major threads throughout Yu Rizhang's youth. He was born in 1882 into a pastor's family. His father, Yu Wenqing 余文卿, was a pastor of the Episcopal Church in Hubei. Because of Pastor Yu's assignments in various cities in Hubei, the family moved often and did not have a settled life. Yu Rizhang was educated either at home or at church-affiliated schools. Fortunately, Pastor Yu was serious about Rizhang's study and character, and Rizhang was a diligent student from his early years onward. The Yu family finally settled down at Wuchang in 1885, and Rizhang was admitted to Bishop Boone Memorial School (hereafter Boone School), an Episcopal boarding school.[4] For the next five years, Rizhang enjoyed his school life and performed with distinction in his studies.

---

3. Many scholars, when they discuss the history of social education in China, fail to recognize that the origin of social education in modern China had close relations with Christian activities. For example, see, Li Jianxing 李建興, *Zhongguo shehui jiaoyu fazhan shi* 中國社會教育發展史 (Taipei: Sanmin shuju, 1986); and Guoli Taiwan shifan taxue shehui jiaoyu xuexi 國立臺灣師範大學社會教育學系, ed., *Bainian lai shehui jiaoyu de huigu yu zhanwang: Li Jianxing jiaoshou qizhi huadan zhuanji* 百年來社會教育的回顧與展望：李建興教授七秩華誕專輯 (Taipei: Shida shuyuan, 2011).

4. This boarding school, founded at Wuchang in 1871, was named after Bishop William Jones Boone (1811–1864), the first Episcopal Bishop of China. It began to offer college education in 1905, while still a high school. "Boone College, Wuchang, China," *An Episcopal Dictionary of the Church*, accessed June 21, 2020, https://episcopalchurch.org/library/glossary/boone-college-wuchang-china.

The outbreak of the Boxer Rebellion at the end of the nineteenth century can be regarded as a disguised blessing in Yu Rizhang's life. This uprising, with the slogan of "supporting the Qing government and exterminating the foreigners," launched its attacks on foreigners and Christians in 1899 and caused heavy casualties: more than 32,000 Chinese Christians and 200 Western missionaries were killed.[5] While the violence was centered in North China, Christians and Christian institutions in other parts of China also felt the threat and made plans to protect themselves. Boone School moved its faculty and students to St. John's College in Shanghai—another Episcopal educational institution.[6]

Shanghai and St. John's College captivated Yu Rizhang both intellectually and emotionally and later played an important role in his life. When the Boxer Rebellion came to an end, Yu Rizhang and his fellow classmates at Boone School petitioned and were permitted by the church to continue their studies at St. John's. Yu was admitted to the college from the preparation school (high school) in early 1902 and graduated from St. John's in early 1905.

Yu, like many Chinese youth in early twentieth-century China, was very concerned with state affairs. These youth were distressed by the Qing government's inability to defend national sovereignty against foreign encroachment and contemplated how to build up a China of wealth and power. A series of articles that Yu Rizhang wrote for the campus journal, *St. John's Echo*, vividly demonstrated his nationalistic thinking.

He first highlighted the desperate and deteriorating situation in China, attributing the blame to the Qing government. China was weak and helpless, he wrote, because the Qing government failed to respond to the crisis and made mistakes again and again in its dealing with domestic and foreign affairs. Yu did not hide his disdain for the weak and disgraceful performance of the Qing government which, in his eyes, was "quasi-moribund."[7] The Qing government was blamed for its surrender of national interest and for bringing humiliation to the country. For example, in the

---

5. There are numerous studies on the Boxer Rebellion. Here are some classics on this topic: Paul A. Cohen, *History in Three Keys: The Boxers as Event, Experience, and Myth* (NY: Columbia University Press, 1997); Joseph W. Esherick, *The Origins of the Boxer Uprising* (Berkeley: University of California Press, 1987); Victor Purcell, *The Boxer Uprising: A Background Study* (London: Cambridge University Press, 1963).
6. According to the website of the Episcopal Church, "The Episcopal Church began an institution for boys in Shanghai around 1851. It was the foundation for St. John's. The school was founded by the Rt. Rev. Samuel Isaac Joseph Schereschewsky, Bishop of Shanghai, 1877–1883. . . . St. John's College opened on Sept. 1, 1879." For more information, see "St John's University, Shanghai," An Episcopal Dictionary of the Church, accessed June 21, 2020, https://episcopalchurch.org/library/glossary/st-johns-university-shanghai.
7. Yui Z. T. [Yu Rizhang], "The Benefits of the Russo-Japanese War to China," *St. John's Echo*, April 1905, 8.

case of the Russo-Japanese War in 1904–1905, many Chinese intellectuals felt deeply humiliated because China became a prize and even a battlefield for foreign powers. Yu mentioned that China's sovereignty was "infringed by allowing the fighting to take place on our territory."[8] Regarding Great Britain's expansion in Tibet in 1904, Yu wrote, "the Chinese suzerainty was actually defied," and Chinese sovereignty was slighted. He commented that "the Yellow Dragon pays no attention to whether any foreign power is exerting any influence in her dependencies or not—nay, not even in China Proper.... China does not know yet how to protect herself, to say nothing of protecting her colonies."[9] Yu found similar cases in Qing's dealing with railroad contracts and concluded, "The fact is our sovereignty has been repeatedly violated by foreign countries, and will continue to be so until the paralysis of our government has been cured."[10]

Even as a college student, Yu recognized that China's problem was not only foreign invasion, but also the inability of the masses to unite for any efforts for China. He pointed out that "there is little or none of that cohesion which is essential to national strength."[11] The secret to wealth and power for China, according to Yu, lay in the awakening of the Chinese mind. The victory of Japan in the Russo-Japanese War demonstrated the importance of vigorous spirit and active will among the people for building a great power. Therefore the Chinese mind should be awakened "in noticing and recognizing the importance of a well-disciplined and intelligent army and navy, in seeing the good fruits of a constitutional form of government, in desiring the unification of the Yellow Race, in disseminating a general and wide education, in developing a strong love of country, and in making us pledge ourselves for self-defence and independence."[12] Although Yu did not state how to awaken the Chinese mind, his writings from his college time always held great expectation for the rise of a modern China with power and dignity.

Yu's writings also occasionally revealed some Christian ideas. For example, regarding British expansion into Tibet, he noted one benefit would be to "open another field for the spread of Christianity which was formerly strictly forbidden," so that many would "receive the light of the Gospel."[13] Yu hoped that Great Britain would accept China's suzerainty over Tibet and revise the treaty between her and Tibet. Yu concluded, "To this prayer to the Almighty who presides over the destinies

---

8. Yui, "Benefits of the Russo-Japanese War," 8.
9. Yui Z. T. [Yu Rizhang], "Great Britain and Tibet," *St. John's Echo*, November 1904, 24, 26.
10. Yui, "Benefits of the Russo-Japanese War," 9.
11. Yui Z. T. [Yu Rizhang], "The Railways in China," *St. John's Echo*, August 20, 1904, 14.
12. Yui, "Benefits of the Russo-Japanese War," 10. As for Japanese influence on China, see also Yui Z. T. [Yu Rizhang], "Japanese Influence," *St. John's Echo*, June 20, 1904, 15–19.
13. Yui, "Great Britain and Tibet," 26–27.

of nationals, doubtless every patriotic Chinese will fervently say, 'Amen' and every well-wisher of the Celestial Empire will rejoin, 'So be it.'"[14]

Yu accepted the offer of Boone College to teach after his graduation in 1905. In the next three and a half years, he married Liu Qiongyin 劉瓊瑛, a graduate of St. Hilda's School for Girls in Wuhan, and two children were born. In addition to his teaching, Yu was busy organizing extracurricular activities, including organizing a marching band, a campus newspaper, an English-speaking club, and an outpost of the Salvation Army. The band would perform every Sunday afternoon to attract people to evangelistic events.

Yu's efforts to bring new ideas to his hometown unexpectedly aroused the suspicion of the local authorities about his connection with the anti-Qing organization. Yu was an active member of the Daily Progress Society, which was organized by leading members of local churches to promote modern thought among young intellectuals. Because a local revolutionary leader, Liu Jing'an 劉靜庵 (1875–1911), a teacher of the Boone Divinity School, also joined the society, the Qing government arrested Liu and aimed to put down the society by putting Yu on a second warrant.[15]

The American Episcopal Church intervened at this juncture. Bishop Logan H. Roots (1870–1945), Episcopal Bishop of Hankow, contacted the American Minister in Beijing to express concern about this case.[16] Once the American Minister took up the matter vigorously, regional Viceroy Zhang Zhidong 張之洞 (1837–1909) postponed Liu's death sentence and revoked the second warrant. Probably to avoid Yu's involvement in any further trouble, Bishop Roots arranged, through church connections, for Yu to study in the United States.[17] Yu was admitted to Harvard and made his trip to Cambridge in the fall of 1908. Yu earned his master's degree in education, with honors, in two years and won a Bowdoin prize for his essay "The Schools of Old China."

Quite a few Chinese Christian students in the United States had a burning interest in promoting Christianity in China and formed the Chinese Students' Christian Association in North America in 1909. The purpose of this Association was to provide fellowship and encouragement through campus groups, yearly conferences,

---

14. Yui, "Great Britain and Tibet," 27.
15. Yuan Fanlai 袁訪賚, *Yu Rizhang zhuan* 余日章傳 (Hong Kong: Jidujiao wenyi chubanshe, 1970), 20.
16. "Logan Roots to John Wood, February 11, 1907," 3, RG64-75, American Episcopal Church Archives.
17. Under the request of Bishop Roots, the secretary of the Board of the Missions of the Episcopal Church, John W. Wood, wrote letters to Ann Arbor and Cambridge regarding Yu Rizhang's graduate study in the United States. "Logan Roots to John Wood, July 18, 1907," 1–2, RG64-75, American Episcopal Church Archives.

and a monthly journal.[18] Yu co-founded the Association and was appointed as associate general secretary in the autumn of 1910.[19] When Yu received his degree, he got an offer to become a traveling secretary to establish branches on various campuses. However, word of his younger brother's sickness led him to rush back to China in December 1910. Upon his return, he became headmaster of Boone School.

China's situation at that time gave Yu a good opportunity to involve himself in "saving the nation." When Yu returned to China in December 1910, China's politics were so fluid that Yu switched roles several times to meet the challenges of the time. When the Republican revolution broke out first in Wuhan, Yu organized a Red Cross effort to take care of wounded soldiers, bury the dead, and transport food to the city. At that time, President Li Yuanhong's 黎元洪 (1864–1928) revolutionary government was short of specialists. Through the recommendation of Yu's friends, he briefly assisted Li Yuanhong in dealing with foreign affairs.[20] He was invited by the Minister of Education to attend an education conference in Peking in July 1912, and later worked briefly for the *Peking Gazette* as an associate editor. In January 1913, Yu Rizhang received a career-changing invitation from his old friend, Wang Zhengting 王正廷 (C. T. Wang, 1882–1961), who had assumed the post of associate general secretary of the YMCA in China.

First Step in Social Education: The Lecture Department

The changing context of China in the second half of the nineteenth century paved the way for studying Western science and technology, and later Western learning in general. Christianity, long considered a part of the West, became more acceptable to many Chinese at the turn of the century. Furthermore, the abolition of the civil service examination by the Qing government in 1905 was a determined step in giving up Confucianism—the bedrock of Chinese traditional culture. From this time on, without much resistance from political and cultural circles, Christianity moved into a golden period of its history in China.[21] This change will be vividly demonstrated

---

18. For more information about the Chinese Students' Christian Association, see Stacey Bieler, *"Patriots" or "Traitors"?—A History of American-Educated Chinese Students* (Armonk, NY: M. E. Sharpe, 2004), 222–23.
19. See "Yu Jih-chang" [Yu Rizhang], in vol. 4. of *Biographical Dictionary of Republican China*, ed. Howard Lyon Boorman and Richard C. Howard (New York: Columbia University Press, 1970), 65.
20. The official title of Yu's post is Commissioner for Foreign Affairs in Hubei. "Yu Jih-chang," 65.
21. For the warm and friendly response to Christianity in China, see Peter Chen-main Wang, "Missionary Attitudes toward the Abolition of the Imperial Civil Service Examination in Late Qing: A Study of the Discourse on Educational Reform in Chinese Recorder," in *Western Tides Coming Ashore in a Changing World—Christianity and China's Passage into Modernity* [Chinese], ed. Huang Wenjiang 黃文江 [Wong Man Kong], Zhang Yunkai 張雲開, and Chen Zhiheng 陳智衡 [Chan Chi-hang] (Hong Kong: Alliance Bible Seminary), 103–20.

by the case of the Young Men's Christian Association (hereafter YMCA) in China. Twenty-five years after its establishment, YMCA became one of the most successful Christian societies in China. In 1920, the Chinese YMCA had 174 student associations and 31 city associations with a total membership of 60,500.[22]

The YMCA was founded by George Williams (1821–1905) in London in 1844. The early purpose of this group was to develop a healthy "body, mind, and spirit" to help contemporary youth avoid indulging in modern urban life. This society immediately won the attention of Christian people and spread widely in Europe and North America. The International Committee of YMCAs of North America was formed in the United States.[23]

Because of the widespread reputation and meaningful programs of the YMCA in Europe and America, foreign missionaries in China began to establish some experimental associations in their schools as early as 1885.[24] They then decided to invite the International Committee to send representatives to China to develop activities similar to those that had proved so successful in America.[25] The International Committee answered the call, and the Rev. D. W. Lyon (1870–1949) was sent to China in 1895 to spread the ideas and program of the YMCA.[26] A year later, Mr. John R. Mott (1865–1955), General Secretary of the International Committee, went to China and helped found a base for a national YMCA in China.

The early activities of the YMCA in China could be divided into two main areas. The first consisted of evangelism, which included Bible study classes and evangelical conventions. The second area of YMCA activities was educational, including further education, sport, student summer camps, and public lectures. A particularly popular and successful YMCA program at the time was the science lectures program, which represented the Chinese YMCA's ideal of social education. When Mott visited China in 1896, he felt the need to introduce science and technology into China to educate the Chinese. Mott successfully persuaded Clarence H. Robertson (1871–1960), a

---

22. Kenneth S. Latourette, *A History of Christian Missions in China* (New York: Macmillan, 1929), 584–90; Milton T. Stauffer, ed., *The Christian Occupation of China* (Shanghai: China Continuation Committee, 1922), 371–75; Jessie G. Lutz, "The YWCA-YMCA and China's Search for a Civil Society," in *Proceedings of International Symposium on Christianity and Modernization of China*, ed. Lin Chih-ping [Lin Zhiping 林治平] (Taipei: Cosmic Light, 1995), 628. See also F. Rawlinson, "The Young Men's Christian Association in China," *Chinese Recorder* 51, no. 5 (May 1920): 342–48.
23. Kenneth S. Latourette, *World Service: A History of the Foreign Work and World Service of the Young Men's Christian Association of the United States and Canada* (New York: Association Press, 1957), 26.
24. Shirley S. Garrett, *Social Reformers in Urban China: The Chinese YMCA 1895–1926* (Cambridge, MA: Harvard University Press, 1970), 25–27.
25. David Z. T. Yui [Yu Rizhang], *The Indigenization of the YMCA in China* (Shanghai: YMCA, 1926), 1.
26. D. W. Lyon, *An Outline History of the Chinese YMCA in the Past 25 Years* (Shanghai: YMCA, 1920), 3.

professor of mechanical engineering at Purdue University, to take on this mission in 1902.[27]

Although the educated Chinese had a great interest in modern science, how to attract them to the YMCA and the Christian message remained a problem. The Qing government had already been conducting modernization programs for several decades. What could Clarence Robertson add? It took him quite a while to work out a large-scale lecture program. He experimented with the first science lecture in 1904 and added a lecture about health in 1908. In 1910, Robertson left for America and Europe to seek out scientific subjects that would be most interesting and helpful at the present time in China. He also invested heavily in purchasing apparatus to illustrate the lectures.[28] His preparations proved worthwhile. The first grand lecture tour conducted in 1911 was well received in a number of major cities, first in South China and then in Central China. The second grand lecture tour started in March 1912 and received "the highest welcome" everywhere, even reaching North China and Manchuria.[29]

The subjects of the science lectures in 1911 included the gyroscope, aviation, and the modern development of electricity.[30] Robertson's lectures were famous for scholarly thoroughness and popularity, as demonstrated by real apparatus. They immediately attracted great enthusiasm from the educated Chinese. Invitations came to the YMCA from government schools, chambers of commerce, boards of education, gatherings of officials, and special meetings of the literati. It is worthwhile to note that Robertson's science lectures were associated with evangelistic campaigns. Over three years, from 1911 on, nearly half of his lectures were followed by evangelistic campaigns.[31]

---

27. According to the library website of Purdue University, Clarence H. Robertson obtained a degree in mechanical engineering in 1895 and his master's degree in 1897 from Purdue University. Upon graduating from Purdue, Robertson was an assistant in the Department of Experimental Engineering. From 1895 to 1902, he was a teacher in the Mechanical Engineering Department at Purdue. Robertson resigned from this position to go to China as a missionary. He returned to Purdue University in 1943 as a physics professor. "Clarence H. Robertson papers," Purdue University Archives and Special Collections, accessed June 20, 2020, https://archives.lib.purdue.edu/repositories/2/resources/1010.
28. Yu Rizhang 余日章, "Zhonghua Jidujiao Qingnianhui jiangyanbu shilue" 中華基督教青年會講演部事略, in vol. 1 of Zhonghua Jidu jiaohui nianjian 中華基督教會年鑑 (Shanghai: China Continuation Committee, 1914), 99a–b.
29. Yu, "Zhonghua Jidujiao Qingnianhui jiangyanbu shilue," 100a–b.
30. In the 1911 YMCA report, they were preparing other subjects for future lectures, such as the marvels of astronomy, high-pressure electrical phenomena, experimental psychology, the wonders of sound, and the telautograph, air as a lubricant, the wireless telephone and other wireless phenomena. *1911 Among Young Men in the Middle Kingdom: A Report of the Work of the Young Men's Christian Associations of China and Korea* (Shanghai: General Committee of the Young Men's Christian Associations of China and Korea, 1912), 19.
31. Latourette, *History of Christian Missions*, 588.

Several cases will demonstrate the value and respect accorded to the science lectures in China in the 1910s. In May 1911, while Foochow (Fuzhou 福州) was experiencing political unrest and the threat of foreign invasion, the local YMCA badly needed to secure $45,000 (Mexican dollars) for two association building sites. The YMCA president, members of the Board of Directors, many missionaries, and the manager of the largest foreign bank saw no hope at all for raising these funds. Yet the funds were raised after a successful presentation of the YMCA lecture, "Wireless and High-Pressure Electrical Phenomena," which was attended by a number of important local officials, members of several guilds such as timber, Cantonese, bankers, tea, and so on, and many wealthy men of the city. The lecture helped to generate appreciation and friendship that were important for future connections in Chinese society, and the YMCA received $48,000 by the end of the month.[32]

Some places that had been famous for anti-Christian sentiment now also opened their doors for science lectures. For example, in Taiyuan 太原, fifty missionaries were executed in 1900. Yet Robertson was deeply impressed that science lectures and the follow-up evangelistic meetings there in June 1911 were well-received by the governor of Shanxi 山西, local officials, and many government school students. Among them, 159 signed cards as truth-inquirers at the end of the evangelistic meeting.[33]

The Revolution of 1911, which broke out in October 1911 and aroused a series of uprisings in China, did not affect the unique role of the science lectures. Even as the revolutionary government was being set up in Nanjing in early 1912, a science lecture there could attract a large number of senators, the military governor of Nanking, the acting head of the board of the Interior, and the president of the Senate. Furthermore, the representatives of the new coalition cabinet also came to the lecture, including Premier Tang Shao Yi (Tang Shaoyi 唐紹儀, 1862–1938), Minister of Justice Dr. Wang Chung Hui (Wang Chonghui 王寵惠, 1881–1958), Minister of Education Tsai Yuen Pei (Cai Yuanpei 蔡元培 1868–1940), and even Dr. Sun Yat-sen (Sun Yixian 孫逸仙, 1866–1925), the founder of the Republic.[34] All of them pledged their support and future promotion of the science lectures.[35]

Given such an honorable and influential role in China, the science lectures were naturally elevated to a strategic position in the organization of the YMCA. Robertson was very excited to report to the readers of *The Chinese Recorder* that the Lecture Department was added to the General Committee in March 1912, placed on the equal level as six other major departments—Business, Field Supervision,

---

32. C. H. Robertson, "The Lecture Department of the Young Men's Christian Associations," *Chinese Recorder* 43, no. 7 (July 1912): 412–13.
33. Robertson, "Lecture Department," 413–14.
34. Robertson, "Lecture Department," 414.
35. Yu, "Zhonghua Jidujiao Qingnianhui jiangyanbu shilue," 100b.

Physical Education, Student Work, Publications, and Religious Work.[36] A massive, impressive plan was laid out in Robertson's report. In addition to training lecturers, Robertson contemplated expanding lecture subjects to areas such as personal and national health, physical education, principles of education, fundamentals of a government, conservation, and special illustrated lectures. Moreover, the center of the work would be developed from the great city associations of the YMCA to future great city associations, colleges and universities, other mission centers, and special locations such as conferences and resorts.[37]

Yu Rizhang took charge of the lecture program at this juncture and grew his career in the Chinese YMCA over the next two decades. He accepted an invitation from Wang Zhengting, the associate general secretary of the Chinese YMCA, to become the director of the newly founded Lecture Department on January 1, 1913. Yu held this position for three years before he was promoted to acting general secretary of the YMCA in 1916. Yu's leadership at the Lecture Department not only elevated it to its full potential, but also made it more suitable for a nationalistic context.

According to Yu Rizhang's reports on the activities of the Lecture Department, this new office experienced its busiest time from 1913 to 1916. The first step was to organize a more structured office with a clear division of labor. At the top of the department, there was a board that comprised five distinguished Christians in China.[38] When Yu Rizhang took over the department, there were only two divisions (Physics and Education) for him and Robertson. He added three more divisions, with a team of five lecturers, each responsible for a subject (education, physics, illustrations, health, and agriculture and forestry).[39] When we examine it's formation, the new department was significant for contemporary China. It turned a one-man show of science lectures into a team that paid attention to more aspects of Chinese society. While maintaining Robertson's specialty in physics, the Department recognized that education, health and hygiene, and agriculture and forestry were also subjects in which China badly needed to acquire modern knowledge and technology

---

36. Robertson, "Lecture Department," 410–11. However, D. W. Lyon mistook the founding date as December 1912 in his history of the first twenty-five years of the Chinese YMCA. Lyon, *An Outline History*, 11.
37. Robertson, "Lecture Department," 415–20.
38. These five distinguished Christians were Zhuo Kangcheng 卓康成 (Engineer of Chuan-Han Railway), Francis Lister Hawks Pott (President of St. John's College), Zhang Boling 張伯苓 (Principal of Nankai High School), Zhou Yichun 周詒春 (Y. T. Tsur) (Principal of Tsinghua College), and F. D. Gamewell (General Secretary of China Christian Educational Association).
39. Yu, "Zhonghua Jidujiao Qingnianhui jiangyanbu shilue," 104a–b. Actually, Ling Daoyang 凌道揚 (1888–1993) who obtained his MS degree from Yale and returned to China in 1914. In other words, the division of "agriculture and forestry" was not established until 1914. Wikipedia, s.v. "Ling Daoyang" 凌道揚, accessed June 20, 2020, https://zh.wikipedia.org/wiki/%E5%87%8C%E9%81%93%E6%8F%9A.

from the West. China was still an agricultural country with traditional agricultural knowledge. Ling Daoyang, with a degree in forestry from Yale, was invited to take charge of the agriculture division. Yu Rizhang himself, a Harvard-trained education specialist, took care of the division of education. W. W. Peter, a medical missionary in Wuchang who was interested in public health education, joined the YMCA to be the head of the health division.[40] An illustrations division, headed by G. H. Cole, was created to provide illustrations and films so that the audience might have visual images for the content of each lecture.

Some statistics will help us better understand the popularity of the YMCA Lecture Department in China. In the year 1913, Robertson spent five months giving 123 lectures with a total audience of 86,717 in 11 cities.[41] His load of lectures did not become lighter when other divisions were created. For example, in the year from October 1915 to September 1916, five lecturers gave 514 lectures in total. A chart of their lectures is as follows:

Table 7.1: Programs of the Chinese YMCA Lecture Department, October 1915–September 1916[1]

Division	Lecturer	Places	Times	Audience
Education	Yu Rizhang	14 cities	137 lectures	39,696
Physics	C. H. Robertson	29 cities	125 lectures	38,989
Health	W. W. Peter	10 cities	129 lectures	50,872
Agriculture and Forestry	Ling Daoyang	20 cities	53 lectures	18,924
Illustrations	G. H. Cole	11 cities	70 lectures	16,710

1. "Jiangyan wei shehui jiaoyu zhi liqi" 講演為社會教育之利器, in vol. 3 of *Zhonghua Jidu jiaohui nianjian* (Shanghai: China Continuation Committee, 1916), 41.

In addition to their own lectures, the Lecture Department used indirect means to enlarge the spread of modern knowledge in China. They not only began to train their people to give lectures, but also assisted the Jiangsu Provincial Education Association training lecturers in May 1916. The twenty-two lecturers from this training in turn attracted 166,519 people to 305 lectures. The Lecture Department, through direct and indirect means, reached an audience of 331,710 in 819 lectures in

---

40. For the work of W. W. Peter, please see Bu Liping 卜麗萍, "Cultural Communication in Picturing Health W. W. Peter and Public Health Campaigns in China, 1912–1926," in *Imagining Illness: Public Health and Visual Culture*, ed. David Serlin (Minneapolis: University of Minnesota Press), 24–39.
41. Yu, "Zhonghua Jidujiao Qingnianhui jiangyanbu shilue," 103a.

one year from October 1915 to September 1916, according to Yu's report.[42] Yu never wanted to miss any opportunity to get advanced information for China's betterment or improvement. That might be the reason that, in addition to the five divisions, he made another effort to establish a distinguished lecturer program to get lectures from distinguished foreign people who visited China.

As a patriotic Chinese, Yu Rizhang would not be satisfied with simply disseminating new knowledge while China was in serious trouble. The overthrow of the Qing dynasty and the establishment of the Republic did not bring democracy or improved conditions for the Chinese people. Although Yuan Shikai 袁世凱 (1859–1916) compromised with the revolutionaries and became President, his travesty of the Republic and attempt to become an emperor caused his downfall and left the nation in chaos. As early as 1914, Yu responded by adding politics and administration, physical education, and society to the subjects of the public lectures.[43] This indicates his idea that educating modern citizens and providing them with basic knowledge would help to save China.

Yu formally presented his idea of social education to the public in 1916. He published an article, "Lecture is a Useful and Effective Instrument of Social Education," in the third issue of the *China Church Year Book* (1916). He first pointed out the poverty and weakness of the country, which, he considered, was the result of no improvement in people's welfare and also of no change in social custom. It was a consensus among insightful people that this problem could be dealt with by the expansion of education. Yet, there were neither enough facilities nor enough time to educate millions of illiterate Chinese through school education. Therefore, in Yu's eyes, social education was the best method to enlighten the people of contemporary China.[44] Among the popular methods of social education, the lecture was the best instrument to enlighten the people without the restriction of time and place. The Lecture Department of the YMCA was outstanding in making contributions in this matter because of its ideal program with specialists as lecturers, eloquent delivery, demonstrations by apparatus and illustration, and well-orchestrated arrangements.[45] One more reason for the success of the YMCA lectures, added Yu, was that the lecturers are sincere Christians without any bias or private purposes in their presentations.

Yu Rizhang not only considered that the Lecture Department played a role in social education; he turned the YMCA into an organization of social education. In September 1916, Yu Rizhang, on behalf of the National Committee of the YMCA, paid a visit to President Li Yuanhong, who had acceded to the presidency

---

42. Yu, "Jiangyan wei shehui jiaoyu zhi liqi" 講演為社會教育之利器, in vol. 3 of *Zhonghua Jidu jiaohui nianjian*, (Shanghai: China Continuation Committee, 1916), section *wei*, 40.
43. Yu, "Zhonghua Jidujiao Qingnianhui jiangyanbu shilue," 101b.
44. Yu, "Jiangyan wei shehui jiaoyu zhi liqi," 40.
45. Yu, "Jiangyan wei shehui jiaoyu zhi liqi," 40–42.

when Yuan Shikai died three months previously.[46] Yu presented President Li with a volume entitled *Jiahui qingnian* 嘉惠青年 (*Benefits to the Youth*), which listed all the YMCA's achievements in 1915. The preface of that volume clearly states that the YMCA entrusted itself with the duty of social education, with the wish to cultivate the youth through programs for the body, mind, and spirit. In the twenty-one-year history of the YMCA in China, it founded over one hundred thirty YMCAs in schools and about thirty city associations. If they continued with these efforts, Chinese nationals could reach the level of Americans and Europeans so that China would be built on a solid foundation of wealth and power.[47] At this time, the YMCA had a new direction in China: it was no longer limited as a Christian organization to save souls and to save Christians, but also looked to save the nation and its people.

Next Step in Social Education: From Character Building to Citizenship Education

Yu Rizhang made great efforts to establish the goal of social education for the Chinese YMCA. Yet he still needed a concrete and much larger plan to realize this goal. Yu's strategy of transforming the people did not mature until the 1920s. Yu's method of helping China had a strong connection with the rising tide of nationalistic spirit in China in the 1920s. The YMCA, under Yu's leadership, launched three related programs—the character-building movement, mass education movement, and citizenship education movement—to reach the goal of transforming the people. Apparently, to Yu, these programs were consistent with his thinking of a "revolution of the heart" that would produce a new generation of Chinese citizens to build up a China with power and wealth.

For Yu, the first step was to connect the YMCA programs with China's nationalistic context. When the YMCA was introduced in China, it followed its Western tradition of not becoming involved in politics.[48] However, this tradition could not be maintained when the entire nation was caught up in the nationalistic waves of the May Fourth Movement. While students and intellectuals were aggravated by the post–World War I Paris conference that turned over former German interests in

---

46. After two years as the director of the Lecture Department, Yu first became the associate general secretary of the national committee when Wang Zhengting took over the post of general secretary from Fletcher S. Brockman (1867–1944) in 1915. Then, the next year, Yu became the acting general secretary when Wang assumed his position of vice speaker of the Senate. Yu was formally elected as the general secretary of the national committee in 1917.
47. Fan Yi 范禕 [Fan Zimei 范子美], "Qing Nianhui" 青年會, in vol. 3 of *Zhonghua Jidu jiaohui nianjian* (Shanghai: China Continuation Committee), section *wei*, 127–32.
48. Xie Fuya 謝扶雅, *Jidujiao Qingnianhui yuanli* 基督教青年會原理 (Shanghai: Association Press, 1923), 1–8.

Shandong to Japan, some YMCA secretaries were criticized for their indifference to nationalism and lack of participation in patriotic activities. To solve the differences among the YMCA secretaries, the national committee of the YMCA issued a statement declaring that the YMCA would not interfere with individuals' civic rights.[49]

Yu, who was the general secretary of the YMCA national committee, was not satisfied with this statement, which did not express concern for the critical situation of the nation. Nor did it touch on the relationship between the YMCA and national affairs. He expressed his opinion at the Eighth Convention of the Chinese YMCA in April 1920. He said,

> We all hope that China will become a nation of wealth and power in the future. However, it is a nice thing to have wealth and power, but difficult to maintain them. We can understand this by observing the situation in Europe after the European War [WWI]. Therefore, a strong nation can only be achieved by building its people with a heart of justice, kindness, peace, service, sacrifice and resolution. The purpose of the YMCA is to cultivate the above virtues. If we want to find a way of saving our nation, we must urgently promote the ideas and programs for the YMCA. We should strive together and make China become a nation of justice, of devotion, of Jesus Christ. That is China of Heaven.[50]

Yu definitely considered that saving China should start with building up an ideal character for modern Chinese. A week later, Yu wrote "Renge jiuguo" 人格救國 (Character saves the nation) in the memorial pamphlet at the opening of the new building of the national committee of the YMCA.[51] This term, originally authored by Yu, later became the most important slogan of the YMCA in China in the 1920s. From then on, *Qingnian jinbu* 青年進步 (Association Progress), the official publication of the Chinese YMCA, published several articles on this topic.[52]

Because of Yu's continuous promotion of the idea, the Ninth Convention of the Chinese YMCA in 1923 decided to use "character building" as its motto. Although Yu was not able to attend the meeting because of health problems, he wrote a long letter to all the participants. In this letter, he sincerely appealed to them that the "character building movement" was the only way to save the country and that this idea should be used to awaken the four hundred million countrymen.[53] Because the YMCA's fourfold program (body, mind, spirit, and social relations) was identical to

---

49. Xie, *Jidujiao Qingnianhui yuanli*, 33–34.
50. *Zhonghua Jidujiao Qingnianhui ershiwu zhounian diba ci quanguo daibiao dahui jiyao* 中華基督教青年會二十五週年第八次全國代表大會紀要 (Tientsin: Qingnianhui, 1920), 25–26.
51. Yu Rizhang 余日章, "Zhi Zhonghua Jidujiao Qingnianhui dijiu ci quanguo dahui zhu tongzhi shu" 致中華基督教青年會第九次全國大會諸同志書, in *Zhonghua Jidujiao Qingnianhui quanguo dahui—dahui guicheng* 中華基督教青年會全國大會—大會規程 (Canton: Qingnianhui, 1923), 1.
52. See *Qingnian jinbu* 青年進步, nos. 49, 59, 66, 90.
53. Yu, "Zhi Zhonghua Jidujiao Qingnianhui dijiu ci quanguo dahui zhu tongzhi shu," 1.

the character-building program, Yu believed that this mission should be shouldered by the YMCA and by all YMCA members of the time.⁵⁴ The convention adopted Yu's advice and resolved that the YMCA should contribute to what the nation needed most. The participants decided that the YMCA should not evade its important duty of devoting itself to the national cause.⁵⁵ This was the first time that the YMCA combined the national duty and the mission of the YMCA together.

Yu's vision was that "Saving China" should not stop with the program of character. An ideal modern Chinese citizen should also be equipped with an adequate education. To address the serious illiteracy problem in China, another major effort that Yu promoted was the "mass education movement." The origin of this movement came from the YMCA's assistance to the Chinese labor corps in Europe during World War I. There were about 140,000 Chinese laborers who were hired to work in Europe, and most laborers had problems acclimatizing to the foreign environment.⁵⁶ The YMCA of North America appealed to the Chinese YMCA and Chinese students in the United States to assist these Chinese laborers. There were about eighty Chinese and sixty foreign people who organized the YMCA of the Chinese labor corps and served them in accordance with the YMCA's fourfold program.⁵⁷ The service soon became famous for its incredible achievements, when the YMCA secretaries taught the illiterate Chinese laborers 1,000 "foundation characters," which basically enabled them to read, write, and communicate with others.⁵⁸

When Yu learned that the YMCA in France was very successful in teaching Chinese characters to Chinese laborers, he wanted to apply the same method in China. Yu always believed that the greatest handicap to the progress of the Chinese nation was the illiteracy of the vast majority of China's people. The nation would be

---

54. Yu, "Zhi Zhonghua Jidujiao Qingnianhui dijiu ci quanguo dahui zhu tongzhi shu," 2–4.
55. *Zhonghua Jidujiao Qingnianhui quanguo xiehui dijiu ci quanguo dahui baogao shu*, 5–9.
56. As for the Chinese labor corps in Europe, see Chen Sanjing 陳三井, *Huagong yu Ouzhan* 華工與歐戰 (Taipei: Academia Sinica, 1986); Xu Guoqi 徐國琦, *Strangers on the Western Front: Chinese Workers in the Great War* (Cambridge, MA: Harvard University Press, 2011); Peter Chen-main Wang, "Caring Beyond National Borders: The YMCA and Chinese Laborers in World War I Europe," *Church History: Studies in Christianity and Culture* 78, no. 2 (June 2009): 1–23.
57. Chen, chapter 5 in *Huagong yu Ouzhan*. See also Fu Ruoyu 傅若愚, "Qingnianhui duiyu Ouzhan huagong di gongxian 青年會對於歐戰華工的貢獻," in *Zhonghua Jidujiao Qingnianhui wushi zhounian jinianji* 中華基督教青年會五十週年紀念集 (Shanghai: National Committee of the Chinese YMCA, 1935), 78; Chen Weixin 陳維新, "Zhu Fa huagong Qingnianhui jiyao" 駐法華工青年會紀要, in vol. 9 of *Zhonghua Jidu jiaohui nianjian*, (Shanghai: National Christian Council of China, 1927), 207–8; Charles W. Hayford, *To the People: James Yen and Village China*. (New York: Columbia University Press, 1990), 22–27. According to a YMCA report, there were 109 YMCA secretaries working for the Chinese laborers in Europe. R. M. Hersey, "General Statement Regarding the Y.M.C.A. Work for the Chinese laborers in France," March 1919, 7, YMCA Archives of the USA.
58. It is said that the literacy level of the laborers increased to 38 percent. Garrett, *Social Reformers*, 154–56.

unable to develop, Yu wrote, if "the overwhelming majority of the people cannot read or write, do not possess the fundamental knowledge of modern life in all its aspects, are not aware of their privileges and responsibilities as citizens, and even refuse to take an active interest in the welfare of the country."[59] Yu, therefore, decided to "put the Association's energy and resources behind a mass education experiment."[60] He recruited teachers who had worked in Europe, such as Yan Yangchu 晏陽初 (James Yen, 1893-1990) and Fu Ruoyu 傅若愚 (Daniel Fu, 1892-?), and established the section of mass education under the Education Department of the Chinese YMCA. The experimental campaigns were so successful that they attracted nationwide attention. Distinguished scholars such as Hu Shi 胡適 (1891-1962), Tao Xingzhi 陶行知 (1891-1946), and Zhu Jingnong 朱經農 (1887-1951) organized the Chinese National Association of the Mass Education Movement in 1923 and invited Yan Yangchu as the general secretary to promote the mass education program in China.

Although a national organization was promoting mass education, Yu and the YMCA proceeded with their plan. There were at least two reasons for the Chinese YMCA to continue their program. First, what the YMCA offered was more than a literacy program. Their work did not stop when students from their popular education schools graduated. Supplemental courses were prepared for the graduates of the one-thousand-character courses to enable them to return for education in such elementary subjects as geography, history, arithmetic, letter-writing, hygiene, and science. In this way, the graduates of the YMCA schools would become fairly well-educated in the course of two or three years by gradually enlarging their vocabulary and thus accumulating knowledge.[61] The second reason was that the final goal of the YMCA was to propagate Christianity. The YMCA claimed that that was the major difference between the YMCA's movement and that of the National Mass Education Association.[62] Thousands of Chinese people benefited from this movement. Up to 1926, the Chinese YMCA sold approximately 1.5 million copies of books on mass education.[63] Fu Ruoyu, who took over Yan's position at the YMCA, claimed in 1935 that a quarter-million people had attended the YMCA's mass education programs.[64]

---

59. Yui, *Present Tendencies in the Chinese Y.M.C.A.* (New York: Foreign Division, YMCA of the US and Canada, 1924), 3.
60. Garrett, *Social Reformers*, 157-58.
61. *Constructive Activities of the Young Men's Associations of China* (Shanghai: The National Committee of the YMCA, 1925), 5.
62. Yui, *Indigenization of the YMCA*, 8-9; see also *Jidujiao yu pingmin jiaoyu yundong* (Shanghai: National Christian Council of China, 1930), 9-10.
63. Herman C. Liu and Daniel C. Fu, "The Association and Citizenship Training," in *The Young Men's Christian Association and the Future of China*, ed. Publications Department, National Committee YMCAs of China (Shanghai: Association Press of China, 1926), 36.
64. Fu, "Qingnianhui duiyu Ouzhan huagong di gongxian," 48.

When Yu raised the idea of the character-building movement and the mass education movement, he soon felt the necessity of promoting citizenship education. In 1921, Yu was asked by different groups in China to oversee the negotiation by government representatives at the Washington Conference (November 12, 1921–February 6, 1922). Later, when he reviewed the results of the Washington Conference, he felt that China failed to attain its aspiration, in part because the people's power did not have full play in China.[65] The awakening of Chinese citizens was necessary to correct this unsatisfactory situation.[66] Therefore, he began to promote citizenship training in the Chinese YMCA. His idea was approved by the national convention of general secretaries of the YMCA in 1922 and passed as a resolution in the Ninth National Convention of the YMCA in 1923.[67]

In 1922, the Association made "citizenship education" one of its central programs. The objectives were to promote the civil spirit and participation in civil affairs; to enlighten the people as to social, economic, and political theories, principles, and practices; and to teach people to study home, community, national, and international problems. The key goal of this effort, as Liu Zhanen 劉湛恩 (Herman C. E. Liu, 1896–1938) put it, was "turning of national shame into civic spirit and getting things done within the nation that are crying for the solution rather than stirring up hatred against others."[68]

The YMCA citizenship education movement formally started in 1924, declaring that because of the problem of internal rebellion, corruption, and inefficiency, as well as foreign invasion, China could meet its demise at any time. The movement adopted an old dictum, "Every man is responsible for his country" (*tianxia xingwang, pifu youze* 天下興亡，匹夫有責) to appeal to every citizen to fulfill their citizenship.[69] What China needed most was certainly good citizens—citizens who possessed fundamental knowledge about their country and who were aware of their responsibilities and privileges.

---

65. Yu's open letter to the Chinese about this conference, see, Yuan, *Yu Rizhang zhuan*, 100–106.
66. Yu Rizhang 余日章, "Zhongguo zai guoji jian di diwei" 中國在國際間的地位, *Qingnian jinbu*, no. 73 (May 1924): 3.
67. Yu Rizhang 余日章, "Qingnianhui chuangban gongmin jiaoyu yundong zhi yuanqi ji jinxing" 青年會創辦公民教育運動之源起及進行, in vol. 9 of *Zhonghua Jidu jiaohui nianjian*, 136; Liu Zhanen 劉湛恩, "Wunian lai zhi gongmin jiaoyu yundong" 五年來之公民教育運動, *Qingnian jinbu*, no. 99 (February 1927): 246. A recent article has approached the Citizenship Education Movement from the angle of "citizen" in modern China, yet the whole picture of YMCA's efforts of transforming the Chinese people will not be clear if we do not study this three-fold educational program, from character building to mass education and then to citizenship education. For this recent article, see Bai Yucheng, "God's Model Citizen: The Citizenship Education Movement of the YMCA and Its Political Legacy," *Studies in World Christianity* 26, no. 1 (2020): 42–62.
68. *Constructive Activities of the Young Men's Associations of China*, 6.
69. Quanguo xiehui zhiyu bu 全國協會智育部, "Gongmin jiaoyu yundong di xuanyan ji jihua" 公民教育運動的宣言及計畫, *Qingnian jinbu*, no. 71 (March 1924): 97.

The citizenship education movement soon attracted nationwide attention. Christians, non-Christians, and even anti-Christian leaders approved it heartily. The YMCA received encouragement and support from people like Hu Shi, Feng Yuxiang 馮玉祥 (1882–1948), Gu Weijun 顧維鈞 (Wellington Koo, 1888–1985), and Wang Zhengting. Shortly after, when the May Thirtieth Incident took place, and the Anti-Christian Movement reemerged, the citizenship program "saved the day" for the Associations in many cities.[70] There was a consensus among the YMCA leaders to speed up and strengthen this movement. The Emergency General Secretaries' National Conference held in Shanghai in August 1925 passed the following resolution:

> It is the conviction of this group that the main emphasis in our program in this emergency should be placed on citizenship training aimed to develop a consciousness of moral need, the ability for corporate action and clear thinking. Such a program of citizenship training ought to be planned progressively for a period of years within a sustained emphasis on the elements of good citizenship and a varying emphasis expressed through study of China's current national and international problems.[71]

Subsequently, practically every city and student association carried out some phase of the citizenship training program. The citizenship education movement was a major project of the Chinese YMCA in the 1920s and the early 1930s. However, this movement had an abrupt ending when Japan launched another wave of invasion in China in the 1930s. The national disaster and continuous fights against Japan attracted the attention of everyone, including the YMCA and Yu Rizhang. While the Chinese YMCA moved toward relief programs for war-zone residents and wounded soldiers, Yu Rizhang devoted all his spirit and strength to dealing with the crisis through domestic and international efforts. He suffered a cerebral hemorrhage during a meeting with US Secretary of State Henry Stimson (1867–1950) on January 4, 1933. He never completely recovered his health and passed away on January 22, 1936.

Conclusion

Scholars tend to relegate all social activities of church leaders and church institutions to the category of charitable service and thus ignore their impact and significance for society and scholarship. The ideas and practices of social education of Yu Rizhang and the YMCA under his leadership are a case in point. Their contributions

---

70. Liu and Fu, "The Association and Citizenship Training," 69.
71. Liu and Fu, "The Association and Citizenship Training," 69.

to contemporary society cannot be found in standard histories of social education in China. The above discussion gives us a solid foundation to evaluate their achievements, which were extraordinarily important and meaningful to social education as well as church history.

Firstly, the YMCA's program marked the first time that Chinese Christians tried to influence and transform Chinese people through social education on a large scale. While the Chinese government was too poor and powerless to take care of millions of illiterate people in the early twentieth century, the YMCA found a role in meeting the needs of the people. John R. Mott had the credit for initiating the YMCA's science lecture program. Then Yu Rizhang creatively enriched the lecture program in accordance with the Chinese context. It gradually developed into a full-fledged educational program, from character building to mass education and then to citizenship education. The program was not empty talk or theological theory but actually put its teachings into practice and benefited hundreds of thousands of Chinese people.

Secondly, in the context of church history, Yu Rizhang and the YMCA made a bold move in pushing their programs of social education. At the beginning of the twentieth century, Christianity was still the "foreign religion" in the eyes of most Chinese. The Boxer uprising in 1900 had just taken the lives of hundreds of missionaries and thousands of Chinese Christians. Yet the Chinese YMCA secretaries dared to devote themselves as Christians to bring about a program of transformation for the Chinese people. They did not give up their religion but believed that the Christian spirit would be reflected through their service. They could not know the results when they launched these programs and may not have had full support from their Christian fellows. However, what they achieved was fruitful and extremely impressive from today's perspective.

Thirdly, although the YMCA was an organization that placed a strong emphasis on non-involvement in politics, that did not mean that Christians, both missionaries and Chinese believers, could ignore the suffering of the people and leave the people and society in backward conditions. Yu and the YMCA addressed China's troubles at their roots in poverty, weakness, and disorder. By cultivating good character, literacy, and citizenship, the YMCA's educational programs made real contributions to society and also to the nation. Yu and his followers recognized a problem and devoted their energy and efforts to a meaningful mission that deserves the attention of modern people, both regarding secular and church history.

Bibliography

1911 Among Young Men in the Middle Kingdom: A Report of the Work of the Young Men's Christian Associations of China and Korea. Shanghai: General Committee of the Young Men's Christian Associations of China and Korea, 1912.

Bai, Yucheng. "God's Model Citizen: The Citizenship Education Movement of the YMCA and Its Political Legacy," *Studies in World Christianity* 26, no. 1 (2020): 42–62.

Bieler, Stacey. *"Patriots" or "Traitors"?—A History of American-Educated Chinese Students.* Armonk: M. E. Sharpe, 2004.

"Boone College, Wuchang, China." An Episcopal Dictionary of the Church." Accessed June 21, 2020. https://episcopalchurch.org/library/glossary/boone-college-wuchang-china.

Bu, Liping 卜麗萍. "Cultural Communication in Picturing Health W. W. Peter and Public Health Campaigns in China, 1912–1926." In *Imagining Illness: Public Health and Visual Culture,* edited by David Serlin, 24–39. Minneapolis: University of Minnesota Press, 2010.

Chen, Sanjing 陳三井. *Huagong yu Ouzhan* 華工與歐戰. Taipei: Academia Sinica, 1986.

Chen, Weixin 陳維新. "Zhu Fa huagong Qingnianhui jiyao" 駐法華工青年會紀要. In vol. 9 of *Zhonghua Jidu jiaohui nianjian* 中華基督教會年鑑. Shanghai: National Christian Council of China, 1927.

"Clarence H. Robertson papers." Purdue University Archives and Special Collections. Accessed June 20, 2020. https://archives.lib.purdue.edu/repositories/2/resources/1010.

Cohen, Paul A. *History in Three Keys: The Boxers as Event, Experience, and Myth.* New York: Columbia University Press, 1997.

Constructive Activities of the Young Men's Associations of China. Shanghai: The national committee of the YMCA, 1925.

"Department of Adult & Continuing Education (社會教育學系)." National Taiwan Normal University." Accessed June 2020, http://www.ace.ntnu.edu.tw/en/members/teacher.php?class=130,100,110,120.

Esherick, Joseph W. *The Origins of the Boxer Uprising.* Berkeley: University of California Press, 1987.

Fan, Yi 范禕 [Fan Zimei 范子美]. "Qing Nianhui" 青年會. In vol. 3 of *Zhonghua Jidu jiaohui nianjian* 中華基督教會年鑑, section *wei*, 127–32, Shanghai: China Continuation Committee, 1916.

Fu, Ruoyu 傅若愚. "Qingnianhui duiyu Ouzhan huagong di gongxian" 青年會對於歐戰華工的貢獻. In *Zhonghua Jidujiao qingnianhui wushi zhounian jinianji* 中華基督教青年會五十週年紀念集. Shanghai: National Committee of the Chinese YMCA, 1935.

Garrett, Shirley S. *Social Reformers in Urban China: The Chinese YMCA 1895–1926.* Cambridge, MA: Harvard University Press, 1970.

Grossman, David L. and Looe Tin-Yau Lo, eds. 2008. *Social Education in Asia: Critical Issues and Multiple Perspectives.* Charlotte, NC: Information Age Pub.

Guoli Taiwan shifan taxue shehui jiaoyu xuexi 國立臺灣師範大學社會教育學系, ed. *Bainian lai shehui jiaoyu de huigu yu zhanwang: Li Jianxing jiaoshou qizhi huadan zhuanji* 百年來社會教育的回顧與展望：李建興教授七秩華誕專輯. Taipei: Shida shuyuan, 2011.

Hayford, Charles W. *To the People: James Yen and Village China*. New York: Columbia University Press, 1990.

Hersey, R. M. "General Statement Regarding the Y.M.C.A. Work for the Chinese laborers in France," March 1919. YMCA Archives of the USA

Jidujiao yu pingmin jiaoyu yundong 基督教與平民教育運動. Shanghai: National Christian Council of China, 1930.

Latourette, Kenneth S. *A History of Christian Missions in China*. New York: Macmillan, 1929.

Latourette, Kenneth S. *World Service: A History of the Foreign Work and World Service of the Young Men's Christian Association of the United States and Canada*. New York: Association Press, 1957.

Li, Jianxing 李建興. *Zhongguo shehui jiaoyu fazhan shi* 中國社會教育發展史. Taipei: Sanmin shuju, 1986.

Liu, Herman C. and Daniel C. Fu. "The Association and Citizenship Training," in *The Young Men's Christian Association and the Future of China*, edited by Publications Department, National Committee YMCAs of China. Shanghai: Association Press of China, 1926.

Liu, Zhanen 劉湛恩. "Wunian lai zhi gongmin jiaoyu yundong" 五年來之公民教育運動. *Qingnian jinbu* 青年進步, no. 100 (February 1927): 244–49.

Wikipedia, s.v. "Ling Daoyang" 凌道揚. Accessed June 20, 2020. https://zh.wikipedia.org/wiki/%E5%87%8C%E9%81%93%E6%8F%9A.

"Logan Roots to John Wood, February 11, 1907." RG64-75, American Episcopal Church Archives.

"Logan Roots to John Wood, July 18, 1907." RG64-75, American Episcopal Church Archives.

Lutz, Jessie G. "The YWCA-YMCA and China's Search for a Civil Society." In *Proceedings of International Symposium on Christianity and Modernization of China*, edited by Lin Chih-ping [Lin Zhiping 林治平]. Taipei: Cosmic Light, 1995.

Lyon, D. W. *An Outline History of the Chinese YMCA in the Past 25 Years*. Shanghai: YMCA, 1920.

Neumann, Jacob W. "Social Education – Sacrality in Education." In *Journeys in Social Education: A Primer*, edited by Cameron White. Rotterdam: Sense Publishers, 2011.

Purcell, Victor. *The Boxer Uprising: A Background Study*. London: Cambridge University Press, 1963.

Quanguo xiehui zhiyu bu 全國協會智育部. "Gongmin jiaoyu yundong di xuanyan ji jihua" 公民教育運動的宣言及計畫. *Qingnian jinbu*, no. 71 (March 1924).

Rawlinson, F. "The Young Men's Christian Association in China." *Chinese Recorder* 51, no. 5 (May 1920): 342–48.

Robertson, C. H. "The Lecture Department of the Young Men's Christian Associations." *Chinese Recorder* 43, no. 7 (July 1912): 412–20.

Stauffer, Milton T., ed. *The Christian Occupation of China*. Shanghai: China Continuation Committee, 1922.

"St John's University, Shanghai." An Episcopal Dictionary of the Church. Accessed June 21, 2020. https://episcopalchurch.org/library/glossary/st-johns-university-shanghai.

"The Department of Adult & Continuing Education." National Taiwan Normal University. Accessed June 21, 2020. http://www.ace.ntnu.edu.tw/en/members/teacher.php?class=130,100,110,120.

Wang, Chen-main. "Caring Beyond National Borders: The YMCA and Chinese Laborers in World War I Europe." *Church History: Studies in Christianity and Culture* 78, no. 2 (June 2009): 1–23.

Wang, Chen-main. "Missionary Attitudes toward the Abolition of the Imperial Civil Service Examination in Late Qing: A Study of the Discourse on Educational Reform in Chinese Recorder." In *Western Tides Coming Ashore in a Changing World—Christianity and China's Passage into Modernity* [Chinese], edited by Huang Wenjiang 黃文江 [Wong Man Kong], Zhang Yunkai 張雲開 [Paul W. Cheung], and Chen Zhiheng 陳智衡 [Chan Chi-hang], 103–20. Hong Kong: Alliance Bible Seminary, 2015.

Woyshner, Christine, Joseph Watras, and Margaret Smith Crocco, eds. *Social Education in the Twentieth Century: Curriculum and Context for Citizenship*. New York: Peter Lang, 2004.

Xie, Fuya 謝扶雅. *Jidujiao Qingnianhui yuanli* 基督教青年會原理. Shanghai: Association Press, 1923.

Xu, Guoqi. *Strangers on the Western Front: Chinese Workers in the Great War*. Cambridge, MA: Harvard University Press, 2011.

"Yu Jih-chang" [Yu Rizhang]. In vol. 4. of *Biographical Dictionary of Republican China*, edited by Howard Lyon Boorman and Richard C. Howard. New York: Columbia University Press, 1970.

Yu, Rizhang 余日章 [Yui, Z. T.]. "Jiangyan wei shehui jiaoyu zhi liqi" 講演為社會教育之利器. In vol. 3 of *Zhonghua Jidu jiaohui nianjian* 中華基督教會年鑑, section *wei*. Shanghai: China Continuation Committee, 1916.

Yu, Rizhang 余日章 [Yui, Z. T.]. "Qingnianhui chuangban gongmin jiaoyu yundong zhi yuanqi ji jinxing" 青年會創辦公民教育運動之源起及進行. In vol. 9 of *Zhonghua Jidu jiaohui nianjian* 中華基督教會年鑑. Shanghai: National Christian Council of China, 1927.

Yu, Rizhang 余日章 [Yui, Z. T.]. "Zhi Zhonghua Jidujiao Qingnianhui dijiu ci quanguo dahui zhu tongzhi shu" 致中華基督教青年會第九次全國大會諸同志書. In *Zhonghua Jidujiao Qingnianhui quanguo dahui – dahui guicheng* 中華基督教青年會全國大會——大會規程. Canton: Qingnianhui: 1923.

Yu, Rizhang 余日章 [Yui, Z. T.]. "Zhongguo zai guoji jian di diwei" 中國在國際間的地位. *Qingnian jinbu*, no. 73 (May 1924): 1–4.

Yu, Rizhang 余日章 [Yui, Z. T.]. "Zhonghua Jidujiao Qingnianhui jiangyanbu shilue" 中華基督教青年會講演部事略. In vol. 1 of *Zhonghua Jidu jiaohui nianjian* 中華基督教會年鑑. Shanghai: China Continuation Committee, 1914.

Yuan, Fanlai 袁訪賚. *Yu Rizhang zhuan* 余日章傳. Hong Kong: Jidujiao wenyi chubanshe, reprinted, 1970.

Yui, Z. T [Yu Rizhang]. "Great Britain and Tibet." *St. John's Echo*, November 1904.

Yui, Z. T [Yu Rizhang]. "Japanese Influence." *St. John's Echo*, June 20, 1904.

Yui, Z. T [Yu Rizhang]. *Present Tendencies in the Chinese Y.M.C.A.* New York: Foreign Division, YMCA of the US and Canada, 1924.

Yui, Z. T [Yu Rizhang]. "The Benefits of the Russo-Japanese War to China." *St. John's Echo*, April 1905.

Yui, Z. T [Yu Rizhang]. *The Indigenization of the YMCA in China.* Shanghai: YMCA, 1926.

Yui, Z. T [Yu Rizhang]. "The Railways in China." *St. John's Echo*, August 20, 1904.

Zhonghua Jidujiao Qingnianhui ershiwu zhounian diba ci quanguo daibiao dahui jiyao 中華基督教青年會二十五週年第八次全國代表大會紀要. Tientsin: Qingnianhui, 1920.

8
A Protestant Response to the Drive for Mass Literacy in Early Republican China
The Phonetic Promotion Committee and Its Work, 1918–1922

George Kam Wah Mak

In 1918, the China Continuation Committee (CCC) (Zhonghua xuxing weibanhui 中華續行委辦會),[1] a Protestant Christian organization in Republican China which aimed at fostering greater cooperation among mission groups, appointed a special committee to promote the widespread use of *zhuyin zimu* 注音字母 (National Phonetic Alphabet, or, as shown in Christian publications, National Phonetic Script), a set of phonetic symbols officially promulgated by the Ministry of Education of the Republic of China in the same year to standardize Mandarin pronunciation; it was hoped that the special committee's work would improve biblical and general literacy in China.[2] Throughout its years of existence, the special committee, known as the Phonetic Promotion Committee (PPC) (Zhonghua xuxing weibanhui zhuyin zimu teweihui 中華續行委辦會注音字母特委會 or Jidujiao tichang zhuyin zimu weiyuanhui 基督教提倡注音字母委員會), undertook a range of projects to achieve its

---

1. Established in 1913, the CCC was a national branch of the Continuation Committee of the World Missionary Conference held in Edinburgh in 1910. It eventually led to the formation of the National Christian Council of China in 1922. Brian Stanley, *The World Missionary Conference, Edinburgh 1910* (Grand Rapids; Cambridge: Eerdmans, 2009), 110, 311, 323; F. Rawlinson, Helen Thoburn, and D. MacGillivray, eds., *The Chinese Church as Revealed in the National Christian Conference held in Shanghai, Tuesday, May 2, to Thursday, May 11, 1922* (Shanghai: Oriental Press, 1922).
2. "Conference on Simplified Chinese Writing," *Chinese Recorder* 49, no. 10 (October 1918): 685. *Proceedings of the Seventh Annual Meeting of the China Continuation Committee, Shanghai, April 25–30, 1919,* 58–59, MRL 6: China Continuation Committee Records, 1912–1922 (hereafter abbreviated as CCCR), Box 1, Folder 3, The Burke Library at Union Theological Seminary, Columbia University in the City of New York. For the background of the promulgation of *zhuyin zimu*, see Ping Chen, *Modern Chinese: History and Sociolinguistics* (Cambridge: Cambridge University Press, 1999), 16–19.

aim, such as developing materials and methods for teaching *zhuyin zimu*, preparing promotional materials to publicize the phonetic script, and, in collaboration with Bible societies, preparing biblical texts in the phonetic script.³ After the CCC was dissolved in 1922, the PPC eventually functioned as an independent organization, even though it received support for its work in 1923 from the National Christian Council of China (Zhonghua quanguo Jidujiao xiejinhui 中華全國基督教協進會), the successor to the CCC.⁴ While it is uncertain when the PPC came to an end owing to the lack of primary sources on its work after its independence, existing sources indicate that the PPC remained in operation in the 1930s.⁵ For example, the PPC was "working on a phonetic edition of the Old Testament" in the mid-1930s to make the Old Testament "available to thousands who cannot read the [Chinese] characters."⁶

The PPC was one of the few non-governmental organizations specializing in promoting the use of *zhuyin zimu* in Republican China. However, its work has not yet received sufficient attention from researchers on the phonetic script. In his *Minguo zhuyin zimu zhengce shilun* 民國注音字母政策史論, the first monograph-length study of the history of the implementation of *zhuyin zimu* in Republican China, Yu Jinen 于錦恩, for instance, basically ignored Christian contributions in this regard, not to mention the PPC, despite briefly examining the activities of James Yen's (Yan Yangchu 晏陽初) mass education movement as a means of experimenting with *zhuyin zimu* in literacy education.⁷ Uluğ Kuzuoğlu's doctoral dissertation

---

3. *The Chinese National Phonetic Script: Origin and Progress* (1923), 9, MRL 6: Phonetic Promotion Committee Records, 1919–1930 (hereafter abbreviated as PPCR), Series 1, Box 1, Folder 14, The Burke Library at Union Theological Seminary, Columbia University in the City of New York.
4. The National Christian Council of China did not include the PPC among its standing committees because it intended to have a small number of committees and leave "education, training of missionaries, medical work, etc." to experts. "Changing China Christian Movement as Seen in the National Christian Council Meeting," *Chinese Recorder* 54, no. 6 (June 1923): 316; "The National Christian Council, A Five Years' Review, 1922–1927," 13, MRL 6: National Christian Council of China Records, Series 4, Box 1, Folder 2, The Burke Library at Union Theological Seminary, Columbia University in the City of New York; Minutes of the Meeting of the Phonetic Promotion Committee, 26 May 1922, CCCR, Box 1, Folder 9.
5. This is attested by the advertisement the PPC placed in *Quanguo guoyu yundong dahui huikan di yi qi* 全國國語運動大會會刊第一期 (Shanghai: Quanguo guoyu yundong dahui zong choubeichu 全國國語運動大會總籌備處, 1925), between pp. 28–29 and the publication of *Memoranda Regarding the Progress of the National Phonetic Movement* (July 1930), PPCR, Series 1, Box 2, Folder 1. See also Charles Luther Boynton and Charles Dozier Boynton, eds., *1936 Handbook of the Christian Movement in China Under Protestant Auspices* (Shanghai: Kwang Hsueh Publishing House, 1936), 207.
6. Frank Rawlinson, ed., *The China Christian Year Book 1934–1935* (Shanghai: Christian Literature Society, 1935), 390.
7. Yu Jinen, *Minguo zhuyin zimu zhengce shilun* (Beijing: Chung Hwa Book Company, 2007), 218–23. For details about James Yen and his mass education movement, see Charles W. Hayford, *To the People: James Yen and Village China* (New York: Columbia University Press, 1990).

on the global history of Chinese script reforms is worth mentioning, as its section on missionaries and *zhuyin zimu* includes a discussion of the PPC's work drawing on archival sources from the CCC's and PPC's records held in the Burke Library at Union Theological Seminary in New York. Nevertheless, Kuzuoğlu did not fully capitalize on these materials in his discussion of the PPC's work and devoted only a few pages to it.[8] The same goes for Janet Y. Chen, as she mentioned the PPC's work briefly in the first chapter of her *The Sounds of Mandarin*, and, despite using the PPC's records, she only referred to the PPC's bulletins, as well as a pamphlet and a pronunciation primer published by the PPC.[9]

This chapter aims to address this lacuna of previous research on *zhuyin zimu* and to explore the formation of the PPC and its work from its inception to 1922, when it ceased to be the CCC's special committee.[10] Relying on archival materials about the PPC held in the Burke Library and relevant published sources, this chapter illustrates that the PPC emerged and operated as an organization of what Daniel H. Bays referred to as the Sino-Foreign Protestant Establishment (SFPE) in early Republican China (1912–1927).[11] It argues that the PPC's work, which represents an organized effort of mission-related Protestant groups in China to tackle mass illiteracy, shows that the PPC participated in the nation-building of modern China through facilitating the nurturing of modern Chinese citizens by means of promoting their communicative competence in Mandarin, the national language of modern China.

Illiteracy as a Nationwide Problem in Late Qing and Early Republican China

Although the literacy rate of mid and late nineteenth century China could be, according to Evelyn Rawski, as high as 30 to 45 percent of the male population and 2 to 10 percent of the female population,[12] it is generally held that in late Qing China, most of the Chinese population were illiterate, which means that they did not have a full literacy in literary Chinese, the standard at the time for written Chinese, in

---

8. Uluğ Kuzuoğlu, "Codes of Modernity: Infrastructures of Language and Chinese Scripts in an Age of Global Information Revolution" (PhD diss., Columbia University, 2018), 133–41.
9. Janet Y. Chen, *The Sounds of Mandarin: Learning to Speak a National Language in China and Taiwan, 1913–1960* (New York: Columbia University Press, 2023), 30, 56–57, 301, 303–4, 362.
10. The last meeting minutes of the PPC kept in the Burke Library were dated on May 26, 1922. See Minutes of the Meeting of the Committee for the Promotion of Phonetic Writing, 1919–1922, CCCR, Box 1, Folder 9.
11. Daniel H. Bays, *A New History of Christianity in China* (Chichester: Wiley-Blackwell, 2012), 99–104.
12. Evelyn Rawski, *Education and Popular Literacy in Ch'ing China* (Ann Arbor: University of Michigan Press, 1979), 23, 140.

which proficiency served as a benchmark for literacy.[13] Illiteracy was increasingly recognized as a social problem after the first Sino-Japanese War (1894–1895), as it was seen as a root cause of China's weakness. This led to advocacy for simplifying the writing of the Chinese language to promote mass literacy. Chinese Protestants and Western missionaries were among the advocates. A notable example is Wang Yuchu 王煜初 (Wang Bingyao 王炳耀) of To Tsai Church (Daoji huitang 道濟會堂) in Hong Kong,[14] who devised a phonetic script based on stenography called *pinyin zipu* 拼音字譜 in the late nineteenth century.[15] This kind of activism in promoting mass literacy surely could be due to individual Protestants' commitment to social betterment. Nevertheless, it could also be understood in religious terms: Protestants believe in the Bible's supreme authority as the standard of faith and practice, as well as an individual's right to read and interpret the Bible. Sufficient literacy to read the Bible and other Christian books is seen as practically a necessity for converts.[16]

In early Republican China, most of the national population remained illiterate, no matter whether proficiency in literary Chinese or Mandarin, the new national standard, was considered as the benchmark of literacy. It was estimated that in 1918, China's national literacy rate was about 10 percent of her total population. Chinese Protestants had a higher literacy rate; about 25 percent of adult Protestants were literate, even though literacy here referred to one's ability to read the New Testament with ease.[17] This could be attributed to the continuing efforts of Protestant churches to offer literacy education to their members. A noteworthy example is the work of Ernest J. Peill and Sidney G. Peill, medical missionaries of the London Missionary Society (LMS) in North China, who entered the field in 1901 and 1905 or 1906,

---

13. Elisabeth Kaske, *The Politics of Language in Chinese Education, 1895–1919* (Leiden; Boston: Brill, 2007), 34–35.
14. Carl T. Smith, *Chinese Christians: Elites, Middlemen, and the Church in Hong Kong* (Hong Kong: Hong Kong University Press, 2005), 4.
15. Wang Bingyao, *Pinyin zipu* (Beijing: Wenzi gaige chubanshe 文字改革出版社, 1954). Wang's book was originally completed in 1896 and published in 1897.
16. George Kam Wah Mak, *Protestant Bible Translation and Mandarin as the National Language of China* (Leiden; Boston: Brill, 2017), 163–64.
17. "Geguo shizizhe baifen bili tu" 各國識字者百分比例圖, *Zhonghua Jidujiaohui nianjian* 中華基督教會年鑑 [*China Church Year Book*] 5 (1918): 276; Sidney G. Peill and F. G. Onley, "Illiteracy in the Christian Church in China and the Use of Phonetic Script," in *The China Mission Year Book 1918*, ed. E. C. Lobenstine and A. L. Warnshuis (Shanghai: Kwang Hsüeh Publishing House, 1918), 170; D. Willard Lyon, "Christian Literature Conditions in China To-day," in Lobenstine and Warnshuis, *The China Mission Year Book 1918*, 219; "Editorial: Illiteracy and Church Life," *Chinese Recorder* 49, no. 8 (August 1918): 493. See also Kaske, *The Politics of Language in Chinese Education*. Meimei Wang, Bas van Leeuwen and Jieli Li reminded us that "quantifying education in the nineteenth and early twentieth century is difficult due to the lack of systematic education statistics." Meimei Wang, Bas van Leeuwen, and Jieli Li, *Education in China, ca. 1840–Present* (Leiden; Boston: Brill, 2020), 15.

respectively.[18] In 1913, the Peill brothers began using a modified form of Wang Zhao's 王照 Mandarin Syllabary (Guanhua hesheng zimu 官話合聲字母) in the hospitals in their mission fields in Cangzhou 滄州 and Xiaozhang 蕭張.[19] It was suggested that in the 1910s, using Mandarin Bibles printed in the modified version of Wang Zhao's Mandarin Syllabary prepared by the Peill brothers, the churches of the LMS in North China enabled 90 percent of their members to read the Bible.[20]

While the Chinese government at the time, also known as the Beiyang 北洋 government, was not able to sufficiently provide for national compulsory education for school-age children and adult education, which would promote literacy nationwide, an effort in standardizing the Mandarin-based national language was made in its early years. Developed in 1913 by the Commission on the Unification of Pronunciation (Duyin tongyihui 讀音統一會) of the Ministry of Education, *zhuyin zimu* was the official phonetic script derived from Chinese characters for standardization of Mandarin pronunciation and sound annotation. Partly owing to the political turmoil of the period, it was not officially promulgated until 1918.[21] Nonetheless, between 1915 and 1918, two non-official organizations, namely the Society for the Promotion of Zhuyin Zimu (Duyin tongyi qicheng hui 讀音統一期成會, established in 1915) and the Association for the Study of the National Language (Guoyu yanjiuhui 國語研究會, established in 1916), paved the way for the official adoption of *zhuyin zimu* by offering training courses, publishing monthly journals, and organizing petitions for its official promulgation. Eventually, in June 1918, the Ministry of Education ordered the national higher teachers' colleges to offer *zhuyin zimu* training to their students, so as to nurture teachers of the national

---

18. Norman Goodall, *A History of the London Missionary Society, 1895–1945* (London; New York: Oxford University Press, 1954), 194. The Peill brothers were known as "Pan daifu xiongdi" 潘大夫兄弟 in Chinese, since both were medical doctors. According to some sources, Sidney G. Peill's year of first arrival in China was 1905 instead of 1906. See, for example, *The Hundred and Twentieth Report of the London Missionary Society* (London: London Missionary Society, 1915), 378–79; Lobenstine and Warnshuis, *The China Mission Year Book 1918*, xi.
19. Sidney G. Peill, "'Open Vision' in China: Scriptures in Phonetic for Illiterate Chinese People," in *The Beloved Physician—and Others*, ed. J. Peill (Westminster: London Missionary Society, 1922), 159; Goodall, *A History of the London Missionary Society*, 195.
20. Mak, *Protestant Bible Translation and Mandarin*, 195. See also E. J. Peill and Sidney G. Peill, "The Scriptures in Phonetic for North China," *Chinese Recorder* 47, no. 5 (May 1916): 329–38. The use and effectiveness of the Wang Zhao—Peill script in the LMS churches in North China were discussed in Melissa Wei-Tsing Inouye, "Cultural Technologies: The Long and Unexpected Life of the Christian Mission Encounter, North China, 1900–30," *Modern Asian Studies* 53, no. 6 (2019): 2031–33.
21. Chen, *Modern Chinese*, 17, 180.

language. This was followed by the Ministry of Education's official promulgation of *zhuyin zimu* in November.[22]

The aim of the Beiyang government's promulgation of *zhuyin zimu* was not "to teach illiterates to read, but to unify the pronunciation of the Chinese language and make provincial schools conform to a standard system of enunciation."[23] It was stated explicitly in the Ministry of Education's order of the promulgation of *zhuyin zimu* that the phonetic script was only to serve an auxiliary role in relation to Chinese characters, or in other words, to annotate the pronunciation of characters.[24] Nevertheless, Chinese Protestants participating in the development of phonetic scripts for the Chinese language saw the value of *zhuyin zimu* as a type of simplified writing that would enable illiterates "to read and write intelligently simple Mandarin" without first mastering Chinese characters.[25] A notable example is Wang Pu 王璞. Affiliated with the American Methodist Episcopal Mission (AMEM) (North), he was a disciple of Wang Zhao, the inventor of the Mandarin Syllabary. Like his teacher, Wang Pu was a Zhili 直隸 representative at the Commission on the Unification of Pronunciation. He was also a co-founder of the Society for the Promotion of Zhuyin Zimu.[26] In an article on *zhuyin zimu* published in the 1918 issue of *Zhonghua Jidujiaohui nianjian* 中華基督教會年鑑 (*China Church Year Book*), Wang Pu and his co-author Chen Enrong 陳恩榮 (Chen Zhefu 陳哲甫), another Protestant serving at the Commission, argued that *zhuyin zimu*, a set of phonetic symbols consisting of twenty-four initials, twelve finals and three medials that represents all the sounds of Mandarin, is much easier to learn than Chinese characters. It would empower the lower classes and women to write and read, thus elevating the national literacy level. Moreover, the nationwide use of *zhuyin zimu* would promote economic development and facilitate dissemination of governmental orders and policies, because the phonetic script would be used and understood across social classes, and thus would be an effective medium of communication. The authors did not support the idea that *zhuyin zimu* would supersede Chinese characters; rather, they believed that its widespread use would facilitate the learning of Chinese characters. This view was probably due to their understanding that it would co-exist with Chinese characters,

---

22. Li Jinxi 黎錦熙, *Guoyu yundong shigang* 國語運動史綱 (Shanghai: Commercial Press, 1934), 50–77; *Zhengfu gongbao* 政府公報 865 (21 June 1918) (Beijing: Yinzhuju 印鑄局, 1918), 11–14, 21–22.
23. John Darroch, "Phonetic Systems," in *The China Christian Year Book 1926*, ed. Frank Rawlinson (Shanghai: Christian Literature Society, 1926), 376.
24. Chen, *Modern Chinese*, 181. The wording in the Ministry of Education's order is *"yi dai fanqie zhi yong"* 以代反切之用. Li, *Guoyu yundong shigang*, 77.
25. "Conference on Simplified Chinese Writing," 685.
26. Kaske, *The Politics of Language in Chinese Education*, 136, 417.

as indicated by their hope that in ten years' time, there would be a newspaper in which both *zhuyin zimu* and Chinese characters were used in a mixed manner.[27]

The Formation of the PPC

Against such a background and as part of its work of nurturing a literate church membership, the CCC established the PPC.[28] The roots of the PPC go back to the CCC's annual meeting in April 1918, at which upon the recommendations of the special committees on Christian Literature and on Religious Education, the CCC appointed a special committee to make recommendations with regard to the problem of a simplified system of writing Chinese, which was related to the subject of teaching church members to read the Bible and other literature.[29] Through extensive correspondence and personal consultation with those well-versed in the subject, the special committee collected a large amount of information that was discussed at a conference called by the CCC and held on September 24 and 25.[30] Four types of simplified writing systems were considered by the conference: the Romanization, an adaptation of the Braille system proposed by S. J. Garland of the China Inland Mission (CIM), Wang Zhao's Mandarin Syllabary, and *zhuyin zimu*.[31] Eventually, the conference unanimously decided to recommend *zhuyin zimu* for general use in teaching illiterates.[32] In October 1918, the executive committee of the CCC, upon the special committee's recommendation, established the PPC to "promote the use of this system of phonetic writing and to supervise the necessary editorial work."[33]

It is not surprising that *zhuyin zimu* was recommended by the September conference and eventually adopted as *the* phonetic script promoted by the PPC. Although *zhuyin zimu* had not yet been officially promulgated when the September conference was convened and the PPC was established, Protestant missionaries affiliated with the CCC at that time were not ignorant of the possibilities offered by *zhuyin zimu* as a phonetic writing system endorsed by the Beiyang government, as

---

27. Wang Pu and Chen Enrong, "Shuo zhuyin zimu" 説注音字母, *Zhonghua Jidujiaohui nianjian* 5 (1918): 166–67.
28. E. C. Lobenstine, "The Work of the China Continuation Committee," in Lobenstine and Warnshuis, *The China Mission Year Book 1918*, 274–75.
29. *Proceedings of the Sixth Annual Meeting of the China Continuation Committee, Shanghai, April 19–24, 1918*, 11–12, CCCR, Box 1, Folder 3.
30. *Proceedings of the Seventh Annual Meeting of the China Continuation Committee*, 58.
31. T. F. Carter, "Phonetic Writing of Chinese," *Chinese Recorder* 50, no. 1 (January 1919): 39–40. Garland's Braille system was one for Mandarin. It was known as the "Tsinchow code," as Tsinchow (Qinzhou 秦州) in Gansu 甘肅 was her mission station. Marshall Broomhall, *The Jubilee Story of the China Inland Mission* (London: Morgan & Scott, 1915), 294.
32. "Conference on Simplified Chinese Writing," 685–86.
33. *Proceedings of the Seventh Annual Meeting of the China Continuation Committee*, 59.

they were in touch with Chinese language reformers advocating the use of *zhuyin zimu* who, according to Kuzuoğlu, supported missionary efforts in this regard and even in part relied on them because of the CCC's organizational power, the experience of mission presses in printing phonetic texts, and the government's lack of funds to promote the phonetic script.[34] Yet, we should not overlook one thing: the connection between these Chinese language reformers and the missionaries could be also due to their religious faith, as Wang Pu and Chen Enrong were Protestants. Indeed, they were appointed advisory members of the PPC in 1919.[35]

Whereas the September conference voted unanimously to recommend the use of *zhuyin zimu* "to all missions and churches, Bible and literature societies and other Christian agencies,"[36] by no means was it undisputed within the Protestant circles in China. As mentioned previously, Sidney G. Peill, the PPC's first chairman (1918–1919), was famous for using Wang Zhao's Mandarin Syllabary to teach illiterate Protestants in North China to read the Bible by themselves. Peill did not entirely oppose the conference's choice, as he was determined to give *zhuyin zimu* a thorough trial. However he was not prepared to abandon Wang Zhao's system till *zhuyin zimu* proved to be better.[37] Contrary to what Kuzuoğlu suggested in his doctoral dissertation, Peill was never a "dedicated supporter" of *zhuyin zimu* but opposed to its adoption as *the* phonetic script used in Chinese Protestant churches.[38] In a letter to Garland, the PPC's secretary, dated April 8, 1920, Peill, based on his successful experience in North China, argued that Wang Zhao's system should not be suppressed, owing to its better legibility and practical results. He stated that by using

---

34. Kuzuoğlu, "Codes of Modernity," 135.
35. *Proceedings of the Seventh Annual Meeting of the China Continuation Committee*, 97.
36. Carter, "Phonetic Writing of Chinese," 40. Kuzuoğlu wrongly regarded the decision as one made at the CCC's "sixth annual meeting on September 24–25, 1918." Obviously, he mixed up the September conference and the CCC's sixth annual meeting, because the annual meeting was held from April 19 to 24, 1918. Kuzuoğlu, "Codes of Modernity," 133, note 235.
37. Minutes of Editorial Sub-Committee, December 4, 1918, Archives of the British and Foreign Bible Society, Bible Society's Library, Cambridge University Library, BSA/C17/1/41–46. The minutes are used with the permission of the Bible Society's Library, Cambridge University Library.
38. Kuzuoğlu, "Codes of Modernity," 136. In a letter to S. J. Garland dated July 6, 1919, which is also cited in Kuzuoğlu's doctoral dissertation, Peill expressed that he was "still quite convinced that quicker and more widespread results can be attained by the use of Kuan Hua Tzu Mu if only as a stepping stone to Chu Yin later, on," even though according to Kuzuoğlu, Peill praised the wonders of *zhuyin zimu*. Letter from Sidney G. Peill to S. J. Garland, July 6, 1919, CCCR, Box 1, Folder 8. Moreover, in a letter to Peill dated April 19, 1920, Elwood G. Tewksbury wrote, "I know very clearly that you do not regard Chuyin as the best system for illiterates." Letter from E. G. Tewksbury to Sydney G. Peill, April 19, 1920, CCCR, Box 1, Folder 8. Peill highlighted the advantages of using Wang Zhao's Mandarin Syllabary "amongst illiterates, under the pressure of ordinary working conditions" in the chapter "'Open Vision' in China" of *The Beloved Physician—and Others*, 155–58. See also S. G. Peill, "No Competition with the Government," *Chinese Recorder* 49, no. 3 (March 1918): 206–7.

it, the illiterate could learn to read easily and fluently, which would ensure "their continuing to read when left to themselves." Peill also revealed that his resignation of the PPC's chairmanship in 1919 was due to his fear that "exclusive attention to this one unproved system [i.e., *zhuyin zimu*] ... might result in harm" to the widespread use of "whatever form of phonetic [that] can be most successfully employed for teaching illiterate people in large numbers to read the Scriptures."[39]

Peill's discontent at *zhuyin zimu* very likely led to the following expression of the PPC's position on the relationship between *zhuyin zimu* and other writing systems, as stated in the proceedings of the CCC's annual meeting in 1920: The PPC acknowledged the effectiveness of the Romanization and other writing systems in promoting literacy among church members in some areas, recognizing these systems as "valuable allies." However, considering that "a more adequate supply of helpful literature is certain to be produced" in *zhuyin zimu* than in any other systems, "where other systems are used," books should be prepared in parallel columns, "so as to enable readers of these systems to pass over to the study of the National literature."[40] In other words, the PPC maintained its stance on *zhuyin zimu* as *the* phonetic script to be promoted among Protestant churches in China, although it "had no intention of attempting to interfere with any work being done by others in using Romanized or any other form of Phonetic writing."[41] On the other hand, probably owing to Peill's influence, the illiteracy committee of the LMS recommended in the same year that all those using Wang Zhao's Mandarin Syllabary "continue to do so." It also recommended that learners using this system should be given the key to *zhuyin zimu* to allow them access to its literature.[42] According to Peill, this arrangement was made because it was obvious that the ability to write and decipher *zhuyin zimu* was "of value to everyone," given its status as a government-backed phonetic script.[43]

The PPC as a SFPE Organization

Like its parent organization, the PPC was a SFPE organization. According to Bays, who coined this term, the SFPE was a group of influential Chinese Protestant leaders and Western missionaries who worked as partners to promote "self-management, self-support and self-propagation" in Protestant churches in China during the first half of the twentieth century. Well-educated, well-connected, and articulate, this

---

39. Letter from Sidney G. Peill to S. J. Garland, April 8, 1920, CCCR, Box 1, Folder 8.
40. *Proceedings of the Eighth Annual Meeting of the China Continuation Committee, Shanghai, May 3–7, 1920*, 60, CCCR, Box 1, Folder 3.
41. Minutes of the Meeting of the Committee for the Promotion of Phonetic Writing, April 23, 1920, CCCR, Box 1, Folder 9.
42. "Gleanings from Correspondence and Exchanges," *Chinese Recorder* 51, no. 5 (May 1920): 365.
43. Letter from Sidney G. Peill to S. J. Garland, April 8, 1920.

group of Western and Chinese Protestants constituted an elite policy-setting and decision-making "establishment" in the mission-related Protestant churches. An individual became part of the SFPE mainly because of factors such as status, tradition, force of personality, eloquence and persuasiveness, and control of or access to resources.[44]

As a special committee of the CCC, the PPC drew its membership from the SFPE (see Table 8.1 for its membership from 1918 to 1922), as indicated by the inclusion of famous names in the Protestant circles in China at the time like Edwin C. Lobenstine, the CCC's foreign secretary, and Cheng Jingyi 誠靜怡, Chinese secretary of the same committee, who gained international fame at the World Missionary Conference in Edinburgh in 1910. The PPC's SFPE background gave it an interdenominational and interorganizational character, which facilitated its functioning as a network hub connecting Protestant groups to promote the use of *zhuyin zimu*. The affiliations of the PPC's members included mission-related Christian literature agencies like the British and Foreign Bible Society (BFBS) and the Religious Tract Society (RTS), the China Sunday School Union (CSSU), the Young Men's Christian Association (YMCA), and major Protestant missionary societies in China like the American Presbyterian Mission (North) and the CIM. Despite being a missionary of the AMEM (North), J. H. Blackstone served on the PPC mainly because of his role as trustee of the Milton Stewart Evangelistic Fund, which was the PPC's major benefactor, as illustrated later in this chapter.

Whereas Bays argued that the SFPE was not "a matter of foreign and Chinese Christian leaders sitting down as equals to plan and set priorities,"[45] the PPC's leadership was not entirely foreign. After Peill's resignation, John Darroch served as the PPC's chairman for a short spell. He was succeeded by Fong Foo Sec (Kuang Fuzhuo 鄺富灼) in 1920. Fong was the longest-serving chairman of the PPC when it was the CCC's special committee. He resigned in April 1922, shortly before the National Christian Conference held in the same year that marked the end of the CCC.[46] Fong's chairmanship was unusual, considering that the CCC's special committees

---

44. Bays, *A New History of Christianity in China*, 99–104; Daniel H. Bays, "The Growth of Independent Christianity in China, 1900–1937," in *Christianity in China: From the Eighteenth Century to the Present*, ed. Daniel H. Bays (Stanford, CA: Stanford University Press, 1996), 308, 311. Short bibliographies of some Chinese members of the SFPE are included in Daniel H. Bays, "Leading Protestant Individuals," in *Handbook of Christianity in China, Volume Two: 1800–Present*, ed. R. G. Tiedemann (Leiden: Brill, 2009), 613–20.
45. Bays, *A New History of Christianity in China*, 100.
46. Minutes of the Meeting of the Phonetic Promotion Committee, April 21, 1922, CCCR, Box 1, Folder 9. For details about Fong's career, see Michael Gibbs Hill, "Fong Foo Sec 鄺富灼 and the Business of Teaching English," *China Heritage Quarterly* 30/31 (2012), http://www.chinaheritage-quarterly.org/features.php?searchterm=030_hill.inc&issue=030.

Table 8.1: Members of the Phonetic Promotion Committee (PPC) as the China Continuation Committee's (CCC) Special Committee (1918–1922)[1]

A. Chinese Members

Chinese Name	English Name	Position and Year of Service	Affiliation
誠靜怡	C. Y. Cheng	Ex-officio Member, 1919–1922[2]	China Continuation Committee (CCC)
陳哲甫/陳恩榮	Chen Che-fu	Advisory Member, 1919–1921	Union Church, Beijing
陳頌平/陳懋治	S. P. Chen	Advisory Member, 1921–1922	Ministry of Education, Beijing
全紹武	S. Peter Chuan	Member, 1920–1922[3]	CCC
范玉榮	F. Fan[4]	Member, 1919–1921	Young Women's Christian Association (YWCA)
鄺富灼	Fong Foo Sec	Member, 1919–1920; Chairman, 1920–1922	CCC; Commercial Press; Young Men's Christian Association (YMCA)
郭	S. Y. Kwo	Member, 1920–1921	YMCA
劉宣三	Liu Hsuan San	Advisory Member, 1921–1922	Canadian Methodist Mission
潘子放	T. F. Pan	Member, 1919–1922	China Sunday School Union (CSSU)
沈彬	Marcus W. Sund	Member, 1921–1922	Chung Hwa Book Company
N/A	S. M. Tong	Member, 1921–1922	YMCA

(continued on p. 179)

1. Sources: The PPC's meeting minutes from 1919 to 1922, CCCR, Box 1, Folders 8 and 9, and the proceedings of the CCC's annual meetings from 1918 to 1921. This list of membership is by no means exhaustive, as it is prepared from incomplete available sources. Also, the PPC's membership after the National Christian Conference 1922 is not included.
2. Cheng was the CCC's Chinese secretary.
3. Quan became the PPC's chairman after the National Christian Conference 1922. However, it is uncertain when his chairmanship ended.
4. Fan was commonly known as "Fan Yu-jung" in English. See, for example, Rawlinson, Thoburn, and MacGillivray, *The Chinese Church as Revealed in the National Christian Conference*, 526.

Table 8.1 (continued)

Chinese Name	English Name	Position and Year of Service	Affiliation
王璞	Wang Pu	Advisory Member, 1919–1922	American Methodist Episcopal Mission (AMEM) (North); Ministry of Education, Beijing
楊錫珍/楊芳	Grace Yang	Member, 1921–1922	YWCA
嚴家麟	B. C. Yen	Member, 1918–1919	American Protestant Episcopal Mission (APEM)
余牧師	E. S. Yui	Member, 1919–1922	AMEM (North)

B. Foreign Members

English Name	Chinese Name	Position and Year of Service	Affiliation
T. D. Begg	柯向榮	Member and Treasurer, 1921–1922	British and Foreign Bible Society (BFBS)
J. H. Blackstone	宋合理	Advisory Member, 1918–1919; Member, 1919–1922	AMEM (North); Milton Stewart Evangelistic Fund
G. H. Bondfield	文顯理	Advisory Member, 1918–1921	BFBS; CCC
A. Mildred Cable	蓋女士/蓋群英	Advisory Member, 1921–1922	China Inland Mission (CIM)
T. F. Carter	賈德/賈牧師	Member, 1918–1919; Advisory Member, 1919–1922	American Presbyterian Mission (APM) (North)
G. A. Clayton	雷振華	Advisory Member, 1918–1922	Wesleyan Methodist Missionary Society (WMMS)
John Darroch	竇樂安	Advisory Member, 1918–1919; Chairman, 1919–1920; Member, 1920–1922	CIM; CSSU; Religious Tract Society
O. Espegren	鄭明道	Advisory Member, 1919–1922	Norwegian Lutheran Mission
S. J. Garland	賈素珍/賈素參	Secretary, 1918–1922	CIM

(continued on p. 180)

Table 8.1 (continued)

English Name	Chinese Name	Position and Year of Service	Affiliation
J. Sidney Helps	赫永襄	Advisory Member, 1919–1922	WMMS
Mrs. F. S. Joyce	趙夫人/趙理明夫人	Advisory Member, 1919–1922	CIM
C. S. Keen	欽嘉樂	Advisory Member, 1919–1921	American Baptist Foreign Mission Society
George Carleton Lacy	力宣德	Member, 1921–1922	American Bible Society
Mary Leaman	李大/李美琳	Advisory Member, 1919–1922	APM (North)
Mrs. Spencer Lewis	盧夫人/鹿依士夫人	Advisory Member, 1919–1922	AMEM (North)
Edwin C. Lobenstine	羅炳生	Ex-officio member,[5] 1919–1922	APM (North); CCC
A. Lutley	陸義全	Advisory Member, 1918–1921	CIM
D. W. Lyon	來會理	Advisory Member, 1918–1919	YMCA
A. R. MacKenzie	金扶濟	Advisory Member, 1919–1922	United Free Church of Scotland
F. G. Onley	文勵益	Advisory Member, 1918–1919	London Missionary Society (LMS)
E. J. Peill	潘爾靚	Member, 1920–1921	LMS
Sidney G. Peill	潘爾濟	Chairman, 1918–1919; Member, 1919–1921	LMS
W. B. Pettus	裴德士	Advisory Member, 1919–1921	YMCA
Harry Price	貝牧師	Advisory Member, 1921–1922	Christian Missions in Many Lands (Plymouth Brethren)
L. H. Roots	吳德施	Ex-officio Member, 1919–1922[6]	APEM; CCC

(continued on p. 181)

5. Lobenstine was the CCC's foreign secretary.
6. Roots was the CCC's chairman.

Table 8.1 (continued)

English Name	Chinese Name	Position and Year of Service	Affiliation
Elwood G. Tewksbury	都春圃	Member, 1918–1922	American Board of Commissioners for Foreign Missions; CSSU
Joshua Vale	斐有文	Member, 1919–1922	CIM; CSSU
P. de Vargas	王克私	Member, 1919–1921; Corresponding Member, 1921–1922	YMCA
A. L. Warnshuis	宛禮文/苑禮文	Vice-chairman and Treasurer, 1918–1919; Ex-officio Member, 1919–1921[7]	CCC; Reformed Church in America

7. Warnshuis was the CCC's national evangelistic secretary.

were predominantly chaired by Western missionaries.[47] We may argue that Fong's appointment was mainly due to the PPC's nature as a specialized committee, which means that relevant expertise and connections that could benefit literacy education with the use of phonetic script were instrumental factors in determining one's authority in the committee. Although Fong was not a key figure of the Protestant activism in the simplification of the Chinese language, his reputation as an educator and the chairman of the national committee of the YMCA in China as well as his connection with the Commercial Press were more than enough to compensate for his "weakness." The latter was particularly important to the PPC's work, as evidenced by the fact that some of the PPC's publications were printed by the Commercial Press, such as Bible posters, or produced in "the combination Character—Phonetic [i.e., *zhuyin zimu*] type prepared by the Commercial Press."[48]

---

47. For example, only three of the CCC's special committees were chaired by Chinese Protestants for the years 1920–1921 and 1921–1922. "Officers of Special Committees," *Proceedings of the Eighth Annual Meeting of the China Continuation Committee*; *Proceedings of the Ninth Annual Meeting of the China Continuation Committee, Shanghai, May 5–10, 1921* (Shanghai: China Continuation Committee, 1921), 107–11. I would like to thank Professor Fuk-tsang Ying for allowing me to consult his copy of the 1921 proceedings.
48. Boynton and Boynton, *1936 Handbook of the Christian Movement in China*, 207. The appointment of Marcus W. Sund (Shen Bin 沈彬) as a member of the PPC in 1921 was very likely due to his affiliation with the Chung Hwa Book Company, another major publisher of *zhuyin zimu* teaching materials.

It is also noteworthy that the independent sector of Chinese Protestant Christianity, which included the True Jesus Church (Zhen Yesu jiaohui 真耶穌教會) and the China Christian Independent Church Federation (Zhongguo Yesujiao zilihui 中國耶穌教自立會),[49] was not represented in the PPC, as none of these churches' leaders were members. True to its nature as a SFPE organization, when conducting its work, the PPC relied heavily on the network of Protestant churches and organizations related to foreign missions.

The PPC's Work

The PPC served both Chinese Protestants and non-Protestants, as indicated in its reports for the years 1919–1920 and 1920–1921, which stated that the objectives before it were that "every church member a reader of the Bible" and "every church member a teacher of illiterates."[50] Teaching illiterates *zhuyin zimu* was considered as a means for Protestants as Christian citizens to carry out "patriotic work," since it would not only help the Church to equip its members with sufficient literacy to read the Bible, but would also help the Chinese nation to nurture literate citizens.[51] However, by no means did the PPC conceal promoting evangelism as an objective of its work. As stated in Garland's article introducing the PPC's work that was published in *The China Mission Year Book 1919*, *zhuyin zimu* was a means to "spread amongst the illiterate masses, with a fullness and clearness never before possible, the knowledge of the Truth which alone can make men or nations really free."[52]

Given this, it is unsurprising that the PPC received financial support from the Milton Stewart Evangelistic Fund, which was established by its namesake in Los Angeles to support direct evangelistic campaigns in the mission fields of the East, with China as the fund's main serving mission field.[53] The fund was the PPC's major

---

49. For an introduction to the independent sector, see Bays, "The Growth of Independent Christianity in China, 1900–1937."
50. *Proceedings of the Eighth Annual Meeting of the China Continuation Committee*, 31; *Proceedings of the Ninth Annual Meeting of the China Continuation Committee*, 92.
51. Mak, *Protestant Bible Translation and Mandarin*, 173–182; S. J. Garland, "Promotion of Phonetic Writing in China," in *The China Mission Year Book 1919*, ed. E. C. Lobenstine and A. L. Warnshuis (Shanghai: Kwang Hsüeh Publishing House, 1920), 182–83.
52. Garland, "Promotion of Phonetic Writing in China," 182.
53. J. H. Blackstone, "The Milton Stewart Evangelistic Funds," in *The China Mission Year Book 1917*, ed. E. C. Lobenstine (Shanghai: Christian Literature Society for China, 1917), 366–71; J. H. Blackstone, "The Milton Stewart Evangelistic Fund," in Lobenstine and Warnshuis, *The China Mission Year Book 1918*, 359–66; See also B. M. Pietsch, "Lyman Stewart and Early Fundamentalism," *Church History* 82, no. 3 (2013): 628, 633.

benefactor, as it "provided for almost the entire work" of the PPC.[54] In addition to providing annual grants to the PPC, the fund considered requests for financial help in connection with phonetic teaching that were received and referred by the PPC, such as grants for salaries of itinerant teachers and holding *zhuyin zimu* classes.[55] The fund's literary department headquartered in Shanghai helped handle the PPC's publications and stock, and received orders of PPC-produced materials.[56] According to the CCC's official statistics, it disbursed 3,934.62 silver dollars for the PPC's activities from its inception to the end of May 1922. The amount covered only a part of the PPC's work; Garland's salary as its secretary was covered by the CIM, while the fund paid a substantial part of the PPC's budget.[57] For example, the fund's financial support for the PPC's work in 1921 amounted to 10,000 silver dollars, while the PPC's total expenditure of the year was 11,110.56 silver dollars.[58]

The PPC also received financial support from the Federation of Woman's Boards of Foreign Missions of North America, which was acknowledged for its "donation of gold, one thousand dollars" in the PPC's report submitted to the CCC's annual meeting in 1920.[59] The donation was to be used for the preparation of *zhuyin zimu* literature for women and girls, including books on subjects such as "Better Homes," and "Health Education," and short biographies.[60]

The PPC was defined as one of the CCC's special committees appointed to do definite "promotional" work.[61] To promote and facilitate the use of *zhuyin zimu* in literacy work, the PPC undertook a variety of activities that included the following areas of work:

---

54. Milton T. Stauffer, Tsinforn C. Wong, and M. Gardner Tewksbury, *The Christian Occupation of China: A General Survey of the Numerical Strength and Geographical Distributon [sic] of the Christian Forces in China Made by the Special Committee on Survey and Occupation, China Continuation Committee, 1918–1921* (Shanghai: China Continuation Committee, 1922), 378.
55. Minutes of the Meeting of the Phonetic Promotion Committee, February 11 and April 21, 1922.
56. Minutes of the Meeting of the Committee on the Promotion of Phonetic Writing, January 13, 1920, CCCR, Box 1, Folder 9; *Bulletin No. 6, Phonetic Promotion Committee*, April 1921, PPCR, Series 1, Box 1, Folder 1.
57. Rawlinson, Thoburn, and MacGillivray, *The Chinese Church as Revealed in the National Christian Conference*, 71, 74.
58. Minutes of the Meeting of the Phonetic Promotion Committee, December 29, 1921, CCCR, Box 1, Folder 9.
59. *Proceedings of the Eighth Annual Meeting of the China Continuation Committee*, 60.
60. Minutes of Meeting of Phonetic Promotion Committee, March 4, 1921, CCCR, Box 1, Folder 8; *Proceedings of the Ninth Annual Meeting of the China Continuation Committee*, 91.
61. Rawlinson, Thoburn, and MacGillivray, *The Chinese Church as Revealed in the National Christian Conference*, 56.

1. Preparation of teaching materials

Throughout its years as the CCC's special committee, the PPC published more than ten types of *zhuyin zimu* teaching materials for use in literacy classes. These include primers, syllabary charts, wall charts for teaching Mandarin, a scripture reader, a teachers' manual, a pupil's lesson book, and anagrams.[62] Because the PPC did not have a permanent editorial team, it relied on the volunteer service from missionaries experienced in literacy education to produce these materials. Women missionaries of the CIM were particularly active in this cause. For example, published in 1919, *Daozi zhuyin keben* 道字注音課本 (*Workbook of Pronouncing Phonetic Symbols*) was written by E. O. Trench.[63] Similarly, *Zimu pinyin keben* 字母拼音課本 (*Phonetic Spelling Book, with Easy Sentences*) was written by Evangeline French or Francesca French and first published in 1920.[64] These two primers also served the purpose of evangelism, as biblical excerpts were used as lesson texts.[65] Another example is the *First Steps in Teaching National Phonetic Script* produced by Mrs. F. S. Joyce of the CIM and Mrs. J. C. Griffith of the Presbyterian Church in Canada. Written in English, it served as a guide for Western missionaries who "desire to begin the work of teaching illiterate women."[66]

2. Pedagogy and teacher training

The PPC engaged in the study of the teaching and learning of *zhuyin zimu*. It arranged test classes in teaching *zhuyin zimu* which aimed to "glean more specific information as to the length of time required to master the system in different districts and under varying conditions," as well as determining "the relative merits of the different teaching methods" followed in the primers published by the PPC.[67] The PPC's

---

62. *The Secret of a Strong Church* (Phonetic Promotion Committee, Report 1918–1922), Bulletin No. 8, Phonetic Promotion Committee, 22, PPCR, Series 1, Box 1, Folder 2.
63. "Foreword," *Daozi zhuyin keben* (Shanghai: Phonetic Promotion Committee, 1919), PPCR, Series 1, Box 1, Folder 3.
64. "Foreword," *Zimu pinyin keben* (Shanghai: Phonetic Promotion Committee, 1920), PPCR, Series 1, Box 1, Folder 6. Evangeline (Eva) and Francesca French worked in Huozhou 霍州 in Shanxi 山西 and founded a Bible school for women there in 1904. Irene Chang et al., eds., *Christ Alone: A Pictorial Presentation of Hudson Taylor's Life and Legacy* (Hong Kong: OMF Hong Kong, 2005), 142–43. Having checked the section "Our Book Table" in *Chinese Recorder* 51 (1920) and 52 (1921), I cannot be certain which of the French sisters was the author of this primer. Another edition of *Zimu pinyin keben* was published in 1921. It consists of thirty-seven chapters whereas the 1920 edition consists of thirty-six chapters. Mak, *Protestant Bible Translation and Mandarin*, 191.
65. Examples of biblical excerpts in *Zimu pinyin keben* are discussed in Mak, *Protestant Bible Translation and Mandarin*, 191–192.
66. "Foreword," *First Steps in Teaching National Phonetic Script*, PPCR, Series 1, Box 2, Folder 5.
67. Bulletin No. 5, *Phonetic Promotion Committee*, January 1921, PPCR, Series 1, Box 1, Folder 1.

efforts to develop pedagogy of *zhuyin zimu* resulted in five primers introducing four different teaching methods, namely the analytic word method, the teaching without spelling method, the syllabary method, and the picture method.[68] Moreover, to help the English-speaking missionaries "gain just conception of the merits" of *zhuyin zimu*, the PPC commissioned an English translation of the first part of *Guoyuxue jiangyi* 國語學講義 (*Chinese Phonetic System and Language*, 1919) written by Li Jinxi 黎錦熙, a famous language reformer of the day and a member of the Preparatory Commission on the Unification of the National Language (Guoyu tongyi choubei hui 國語統一籌備會) of the Ministry of Education. The English translation was, at the PPC's request, translated by A. R. MacKenzie, a missionary of the United Free Church of Scotland and advisory member of the PPC. It was published in 1921 by the Commercial Press.[69]

The PPC also invited missionaries experienced in literacy education to hold normal classes for the training of *zhuyin zimu* teachers, considering the lack of properly qualified teachers. It was not easy to secure their service in this regard, as these missionaries were often heavily occupied with the work at their mission stations. Yet, some of them offered alternative solutions. For example, Evangeline French of the CIM and her colleague A. Mildred Cable were willing to receive students for training at their Bible Training Institute in Huozhou 霍州 in Shanxi 山西.[70]

It is noteworthy that the PPC contributed to establishing a literacy standard by introducing *zhuyin zimu* standard tests for illiterates. One could gain a diploma issued by the PPC if he or she, using *zhuyin zimu*, could write a letter of two hundred words spelled correctly and "adequately phrased, punctuated and hyphenated" or reading "intelligently at sight a passage of not less than 200 words of simple narrative not seen before."[71]

3. *Liaison with the Chinese government*

According to F. Rawlinson, a member of the CCC, in the PPC's work the CCC was carrying out "its principle of co-operation by co-operating with the Chinese

---

68. *The Chinese National Phonetic Script* (1923), 9; Quan Shaowu 全紹武, ed., *Jidujiao quanguo dahui baogaoshu* 基督教全國大會報告書, reprinted in *Dongchuan fuyin* 東傳福音, ed. Zhongguo zongjiao lishi wenxian jicheng bianzuan weiyuanhui 中國宗教歷史文獻集成編纂委員會 (Hefei: Huangshan shushe, 2005), 19: 759. For example, *Zimu pinyin keben* is the primer representing the syllabary method.
69. Li Chin-shi, *Chinese Phonetic System and Language*, trans. Alex. R. MacKenzie (Shanghai: Commercial Press, 1921), i; Foreword to ibid.
70. Minutes of Meeting of the Phonetic Promotion Committee, May 10 and October 3, 1921; *Bulletin No. 7, Phonetic Promotion Committee*, July 1921, PPCR, Series 1, Box 1, Folder 1.
71. *Bulletin No. 4, Phonetic Promotion Committee*, June 1920, PPCR, Series 1, Box 1, Folder 2.

Government."[72] Thanks to the close connection of Elwood G. Tewksbury, one of the longest-serving members of the PPC, with the government, the PPC was able to keep abreast of the work on *zhuyin zimu* that was being conducted by the Ministry of Education.[73] At the same time, the PPC solicited opinions and suggestions on the standard of spelling and tone-marking, phrasing, and hyphenating from Protestant workers of literacy education who used *zhuyin zimu* through questionnaires, in aspects of the usage of *zhuyin zimu* in which no official rules were promulgated, such as distinctive marks for the names of deity, or in which new measures were introduced by the Ministry of Education, such as the use of the final letter 'ㄛ'.[74] These opinions and suggestions were discussed at the PPC and conveyed to the Ministry of Education, in the hope that they would be considered by the government for adoption, so as to help improve the legibility of the phonetic script and thus promote its nationwide use.[75] For example, during a meeting with Li Jinxi in November 1920, a sub-committee of the PPC submitted to him "revised lists of all characters which in [the PPC's] Phonetic literature vary either in spelling or tone from the national Phonetic dictionary." Li agreed to forward these to his colleagues who were revising the dictionary for consideration of incorporation in the revised dictionary as alternative readings.[76] In addition, the PPC decided in the same year to publish a *zhuyin zimu* edition of the Gospel of Mark, "asking the members of the Government Phonetic Committee to help . . . by marking the book according to the rules which they propose for adoption for Phonetic literature." By widely circulating this edition of the Gospel of Mark, the new method of linking words together promulgated by the Ministry of Education "may be put to practical test."[77]

Given the good working relationship between the PPC and the authorities, it was not surprising that also in the same year, the PPC wrote to the governor of

---

72. F. Rawlinson, "Christian Co-operation for a Nation-wide Task: Eighth Annual Meeting of the China Continuation Committee," *Chinese Recorder* 51, no. 6 (June 1920): 423.
73. Minutes of the Meeting of the Phonetic Promotion Committee, November 19, 1920. Tewksbury was also commended for his time and labour given to the work of preparing the type of *zhuyin zimu* and of adapting the symbols of *zhuyin zimu* to typewriters, such as the Hammond and Underwood typewriters. Indeed, many of the first styles of the type of *zhuyin zimu* for printing were designed by him and used both for the publications of the PPC and the China Sunday School Union. *The Chinese National Phonetic Script: Origin and Progress, Hints on Teaching*, 9, PPCR, Series 1, Box 1, Folder 7; *The Chinese National Phonetic Script* (1923), 10; Garland, "Promotion of Phonetic Writing in China," 177.
74. Minutes of a Special Meeting of the Committee on the Promotion of Phonetic Writing, November 13, 1919; Minutes of a Meeting of the Committee on the Promotion of Phonetic Writing, January 13, 1920; Minutes of Sub-Committee of Phonetic Promotion Committee, January 27, 1920.
75. Minutes of the Phonetic Promotion Committee, September 23, 1920.
76. Minutes of the Meeting of the Phonetic Promotion Committee, November 19, 1920; *The Chinese National Phonetic Script: Origin and Progress, Hints on Teaching*, 7, PPCR, Series 1, Box 1, Folder 7.
77. Minutes of the Meeting of the Phonetic Promotion Committee, November 19, 1920.

Zhejiang 浙江 to ask him to allow the circulation of a newspaper published in *zhuyin zimu* throughout schools and educational institutions in the province. According to Fong Foo Sec, the governor instructed the China Christian Educational Association to "take the matter in hand and urge the educationalists to see that this is done."[78] The rapport between the PPC and the authorities is also attested to by the fact that Li Jinxi assisted in the preparation of the partial English translation of his *Guoyuxue jianyi*. Li examined the translated text before its publication in 1921 and endorsed it as "an accurate translation" in his preface to the translation.[79]

4. Preparation of the Zhuyin Zimu editions of the Chinese Bible

In addition to publishing 65,000 copies of *Shengjing xuandu* 聖經選讀 (*Scripture Reader*), a thirty-two-page booklet including the Beatitudes and parables, as a *zhuyin zimu* teaching material from 1919 to 1922, the PPC worked with Bible societies to prepare the *zhuyin zimu* editions of the Chinese Bible.[80] Among the Bible societies working in China, the BFBS was the most active in supporting the PPC's work in this regard. Scriptural portions in *zhuyin zimu* were published by the BFBS in most of the years of the PPC as the CCC's special committee. As early as in 1919, the BFBS published the Gospels of Mark and John as well as the Epistle of James and the First Epistle of John in *zhuyin zimu*. The *zhuyin zimu* editions of the other two Gospels and the Acts of the Apostles came out in 1920.[81] In 1921, the BFBS and the American Bible Society published their first editions of the New Testament of the Mandarin *Union Version* in *zhuyin zimu*.[82] In preparing the *zhuyin zimu* edition of the Chinese New Testament, the PPC obtained help from Harry Price of the Christian Missions in Many Lands, who, assisted by his wife, proofread the whole New Testament text in the phonetic script.[83] Indeed, Price was also responsible for

---

78. Fong F. Sec, "Government Education," *Educational Review* 12, no. 2 (1920): 186.
79. Li, "Author's Preface to the English Translation," in *Chinese Phonetic System and Language*, i.
80. "Report of the Special Committee on the Promotion of Phonetic Writing," CCCR, Box 1, Folder 9; Quan, *Jidujiao quanguo dahui baogaoshu*, 19: 759–760.
81. Mak, *Protestant Bible Translation and Mandarin*, 195; Garland, "Promotion of Phonetic Writing in China," 181.
82. Hubert W. Spillett, *A Catalogue of Scriptures in the Languages of China and the Republic of China* (London: British and Foreign Bible Society, 1975), 98; Stauffer, Wong, and Tewksbury, *The Christian Occupation of China*, 453; Mak, *Protestant Bible Translation and Mandarin*, 195. In 1921, George Carleton Lacy, who became the secretary of the China agency of the American Bible Society in the same year, was appointed to the PPC. Minutes of the Meeting of the Phonetic Promotion Committee, October 3, 1921.
83. Minutes of a Special Meeting of the Committee on the Promotion of Phonetic Writing, October 25 and November 13, 1919, CCCR, Box 1, Folder 9; Minutes of Meeting of the Phonetic Promotion Committee, April 5, 1921, CCCR, Box 1, Folder 9.

the final revision of the manuscripts of the *zhuyin zimu* scriptural portions such as the Gospel of Matthew.[84]

5. Publicity

To promote the use of *zhuyin zimu* and appeal to Protestant churches in China for their support, the PPC issued a range of publicity materials. Among them included pamphlets such as *China's Modern Goliath and Her David*, published in 1919. Comparing illiteracy and Protestants to Goliath and David respectively, it aimed to encourage Protestants to beat illiteracy and save their illiterate countrymen from "darkness."[85] Other publicity materials prepared by the PPC include bulletins, phonetic news sheets, bookmarks, pictorial central scrolls (*zhongtang* 中堂), and Bible posters.[86] These materials were not only available for orders from the Protestant circles but also sent to non-Christian schools.[87]

6. Grants-in-aid

The PPC occasionally received proposals from Protestant missionaries to publish books or pamphlets in *zhuyin zimu*, which indicated its reputation as a Protestant organization specializing in producing *zhuyin zimu* publications. However, positioning itself as an organization promoting the use of *zhuyin zimu* to help illiterates to write and read, the PPC rejected these proposals when the subjects of the proposed publications were not related to literacy education with *zhuyin zimu*, even though the PPC gave help "in not a few cases in the preparation of manuscripts and proof reading" of "more general Christian literature."[88] Nonetheless, the PPC offered grants-in-aid for distributing *zhuyin zimu* hymnals, probably owing to the common use of hymnals in literacy classes. For example, Harriet M. Turner of the English Baptist Mission received a subsidy from the PPC to "forward the wider circulation"

---

84. Minutes of a Meeting of the Phonetic Promotion Committee, May 10, 1920; *The Chinese National Phonetic Script* (1923), 11.
85. *China's Modern Goliath and Her David*, PPCR, Series 1, Box 1, Folder 8. The pamphlet does not indicate its publication year, which was, however, mentioned in *The Chinese National Phonetic Script* (1923), 11.
86. *The Secret of a Strong Church*, 22.
87. Minutes of the Meeting of the Phonetic Promotion Committee, October 3 and December 29, 1921. The PPCR include several Bible posters. Some other posters, such as the one entitled "Lihao de genji jiushi Yesu Jidu" 立好的根基就是耶穌基督 (Jesus Christ is the Firm Foundation), are available to view online on the website "Chinese Christian Posters": https://ccposters.com/pg/home/.
88. Minutes of a Meeting of the Committee on the Promotion of Phonetic Writing, January 13, 1920, CCCR, Box 1, Folder 9; *The Chinese National Phonetic Script* (1923), 12.

of the mission's *zhuyin zimu* hymnal, the first of its kind, in 1922.[89] Other *zhuyin zimu* hymnals that received the PPC's grants-in-aid for their circulation included those of the CIM and the RTS, as well as the *zhuyin zimu* edition of the Chinese hymnal edited by Henry Blodget and Chauncey Goodrich of the American Board of Commissioners for Foreign Missions.[90]

The Results of the PPC's Work as the CCC's Special Committee

Although it is difficult to give a fair assessment of the PPC's achievements as the CCC's special committee owing to lack of relevant primary sources, statistics from its own reports and those of other Christian organizations in the early 1920s offer us some idea of the results of its work. According to its report submitted to the 1922 National Christian Conference, the PPC published 804,000 copies of teaching and publicity materials from 1919 to 1922.[91] This figure omits some other types of publications, as according to T. F. Pan (Pan Zifang 潘子放), the PPC distributed about four million copies of leaflets between 1919 and 1920.[92] The BFBS, which collaborated with the PPC in preparing the *zhuyin zimu* editions of the Chinese Bible, circulated more than 150,000 copies of scriptural portions in *zhuyin zimu* from 1919 to 1921.[93] The literacy rate of Chinese Protestants in 1922 was 60 percent of the men and 40 percent of the women,[94] compared with not more than 25 percent of adult Protestants in 1918. It was possible that the PPC's work contributed to such an increase, although this needs to be substantiated by further studies.

Nevertheless, in his contribution to *The China Mission Year Book 1924*, Elijah S. Nieh (Nie Shaojing 聶紹經) of the Christian Literature Society wrote that "the [national] phonetic [script] helps to solve, to some extent, the problem of illiteracy,

---

89. *The Secret of a Strong Church*, 21.
90. Minutes of the Meeting of the Phonetic Promotion Committee, April 21, 1922. It is uncertain which *zhuyin zimu* edition of Blodget and Goodrich's Chinese hymnal received the PPC's subsidy, as it was simply referred to as "Blodget and Goodrich Hymn Book" in the meeting minutes. The *zhuyin zimu* hymnal concerned could be the selection of hymns from Blodget and Goodrich's hymnal prepared by Robert E. Brown of the American Methodist Episcopal Mission (North), which was printed with Chinese character and *zhuyin zimu* on opposite pages. "Gleanings from Correspondence and Exchanges," 367.
91. Quan, *Jidujiao quanguo dahui baogaoshu*, 19: 759–760. According to the PPC's English report on its work between 1918 and 1922, the figure was indeed an approximate dating from September 1919 to April 1922. *The Secret of a Strong Church*, 22.
92. Pan Zifang, "Jiaohui tichang zhuyin zimu de liyou ji jinbu" 教會提倡注音字母的理由及進步, *Zhonghua Jidujiaohui nianjian* 6 (1921): 104.
93. *Proceedings of the Ninth Annual Meeting of the China Continuation Committee*, 90.
94. Rawlinson, Thoburn, and MacGillivray, *The Chinese Church as Revealed in the National Christian Conference*, 291.

but it does not help to increase the percentage of readers in the whole nation."[95] This suggests that as regards improving the national literacy rate, the PPC as the CCC's special committee might not have achieved great results. A number of reasons, such as the PPC's inadequate manpower, could be suggested to account for this, but it appears that the main obstacle was that there was a limited amount of printed matters and literature in *zhuyin zimu* in the late 1910s and early 1920s. Books and newspapers were mostly printed in Chinese character, not coupled with the phonetic script. This problem, which remained in the 1920s, as suggested by Herman Liu (Liu Zhanen 劉湛恩), the president of University of Shanghai, resulted in another problem: "There was no occasion to use it when one had learned the phonetic. It was easily forgotten since there was not much printed matter and very few people knew it."[96]

Conclusion

Chinese Protestants and Western missionaries were among the advocates for simplifying the writing of the Chinese language to promote mass literacy in late nineteenth and early twentieth centuries. Developed in 1913 by the Commission on the Unification of Pronunciation of the Ministry of Education in Republican China and eventually officially promulgated in 1918, *zhuyin zimu* was a phonetic script designed for standardization of Mandarin pronunciation and sound annotation. However, it was considered by Chinese Protestants and Western missionaries who promoted the use of phonetic scripts in literacy education as not only "a good means leading people to church to learn the sacred teachings" but also a tool for "enhancing one's general knowledge as a citizen" since after learning it, one could use it "to read newspapers, study, take notes, and write letters and accounting ledgers."[97] The PPC's establishment can be regarded as part of their continuing efforts for the cause and a response of mission-related Protestant groups to the drive for mass literacy in early Republican China. As indicated by its membership including influential Western missionaries and prominent Chinese Protestant leaders with relevant expertise and connections, the PPC had a background from the SFPE, which gave it an interdenominational and interorganizational character that facilitated its functioning as a network hub connecting different Protestant groups for promoting the use of *zhuyin zimu* in literacy work through various means, including, but not limited to preparing teaching and publicity materials, developing the pedagogy, teacher training, acting

---

95. Elijah S. Nieh, "The Present Situation with regards to Christian Literature," in *The China Mission Year Book 1924*, ed. Frank Rawlinson (Shanghai: Christian Literature Society, 1924), 442.
96. Herman C. E. Liu, "Mass Education and Phonetic Character," in *The China Christian Year Book 1931* (Shanghai: Christian Literature Society, 1931), 215.
97. Quan, *Jidujiao quanguo dahui baogaoshu*, 19: 759.

as a liaison between the government and Protestant workers of literacy education, and providing grants-in-aid. While the results of the PPC's work as the CCC's special committee might not be exceptionally outstanding, the PPC still can be seen as a case of how Chinese Protestants and Western missionaries of the SFPE collaborated to serve the needs of the nascent Chinese republic with enthusiasm, expertise, and experience, contributing to the promotion of mass literacy and the spread of Mandarin as the Chinese national language, and thus the nation-building of modern China.

Bibliography

Bays, Daniel H. "The Growth of Independent Christianity in China, 1900–1937." In *Christianity in China: From the Eighteenth Century to the Present*, edited by Daniel H. Bays. Stanford, CA: Stanford University Press, 1996.

Bays, Daniel H. "Leading Protestant Individuals." In *Handbook of Christianity in China, Volume Two: 1800–Present*, edited by R. G. Tiedemann. Leiden: Brill, 2009.

Bays, Daniel H. *A New History of Christianity in China*. Chichester: Wiley-Blackwell, 2012.

Blackstone, J. H. "The Milton Stewart Evangelistic Funds." In *The China Mission Year Book 1917*, edited by E. C. Lobenstine. Shanghai: Christian Literature Society for China, 1917.

Blackstone, J. H. "The Milton Stewart Evangelistic Fund." In Lobenstine and Warnshuis, *The China Mission Year Book 1918*.

Boynton, Charles Luther, and Charles Dozier Boynton, eds. *1936 Handbook of the Christian Movement in China Under Protestant Auspices*. Shanghai: Kwang Hsueh Publishing House, 1936.

Broomhall, Marshall. *The Jubilee Story of the China Inland Mission*. London: Morgan & Scott, 1915.

Carter, T. F. "Phonetic Writing of Chinese." *Chinese Recorder* 50, no. 1 (January 1919): 39–44.

Chang, Irene, et al., eds. *Christ Alone: A Pictorial Presentation of Hudson Taylor's Life and Legacy*. Hong Kong: OMF Hong Kong, 2005.

"Changing China Christian Movement as Seen in the National Christian Council Meeting." *Chinese Recorder* 54, no. 6 (June 1923): 311–18.

Chen, Janet Y. *The Sounds of Mandarin: Learning to Speak a National Language in China and Taiwan, 1913–1960*. New York: Columbia University Press, 2023.

Chen, Ping. *Modern Chinese: History and Sociolinguistics*. Cambridge: Cambridge University Press, 1999.

China Continuation Committee Records, 1912–1922, The Burke Library at Union Theological Seminary, Columbia University in the City of New York. [Abbreviated as CCCR].

The Chinese Recorder 51–52 (1920–1921).

"Conference on Simplified Chinese Writing." *Chinese Recorder* 49, no. 10 (October 1918): 685–86.

Darroch, John. "Phonetic Systems." In *The China Christian Year Book 1926*, edited by Frank Rawlinson. Shanghai: Christian Literature Society, 1926.

"Editorial: Illiteracy and Church Life." *Chinese Recorder* 49, no. 8 (August 1918): 493–97.

Fong, F. Sec. "Government Education." *Educational Review* 12, no. 2 (1920): 182–90.

Garland, S. J. "Promotion of Phonetic Writing in China." In *The China Mission Year Book 1919*, edited by E. C. Lobenstine and A. L. Warnshuis. Shanghai: Kwang Hsüeh Publishing House, 1920.

"Geguo shizizhe baifen bili tu" 各國識字者百分比例圖. *Zhonghua Jidujiaohui nianjian* 中華基督教會年鑑 [*China Church Year Book*] 5 (1918): 276.

"Gleanings from Correspondence and Exchanges." *Chinese Recorder* 51, no. 5 (May 1920): 364–67.

Goodall, Norman. *A History of the London Missionary Society, 1895–1945*. London; New York: Oxford University Press, 1954.

Hayford, Charles W. *To the People: James Yen and Village China*. New York: Columbia University Press, 1990.

Hill, Michael Gibbs. "Fong Foo Sec 鄺富灼 and the Business of Teaching English." *China Heritage Quarterly* 30/31 (2012). http://www.chinaheritagequarterly.org/features.php?searchterm=030_hill.inc&issue=030.

Inouye, Melissa Wei-Tsing. "Cultural Technologies: The Long and Unexpected Life of the Christian Mission Encounter, North China, 1900–30." *Modern Asian Studies* 53, no. 6 (2019): 2007–40.

Kaske, Elisabeth. *The Politics of Language in Chinese Education, 1895–1919*. Leiden; Boston: Brill, 2007.

Kuzuoğlu, Uluğ. "Codes of Modernity: Infrastructures of Language and Chinese Scripts in an Age of Global Information Revolution." PhD diss., Columbia University, 2018.

Li, Chin-shi [Li, Jinxi 黎錦熙]. *Chinese Phonetic System and Language*, translated by Alex R. MacKenzie. Shanghai: Commercial Press, 1921.

Li, Jinxi 黎錦熙. *Guoyu yundong shigang* 國語運動史綱. Shanghai: Commercial Press, 1934.

Liu, Herman C. E. "Mass Education and Phonetic Character." In *The China Christian Year Book 1931*. Shanghai: Christian Literature Society, 1931.

Lobenstine, E. C. "Work of the China Continuation Committee." In Lobenstine and Warnshuis, *The China Mission Year Book 1918*.

Lobenstine, E. C., and A. L. Warnshuis, eds. *The China Mission Year Book 1918*. Shanghai: Kwang Hsüeh Publishing House, 1918.

Lyon, D. Willard. "Christian Literature Conditions in China To-day." In Lobenstine and Warnshuis, *The China Mission Year Book 1918*.

Mak, George Kam Wah. *Protestant Bible Translation and Mandarin as the National Language of China*. Leiden; Boston: Brill, 2017.

Minutes of Editorial Sub-Committee, December 4, 1918. Archives of the British and Foreign Bible Society, Bible Society's Library, Cambridge University Library. BSA/C17/1/41–46.

Nieh, Elijah S. "The Present Situation with regards to Christian Literature." In *The China Mission Year Book 1924*, edited by Frank Rawlinson. Shanghai: Christian Literature Society, 1924.

Pan, Zifang 潘子放. "Jiaohui tichang zhuyin zimu de liyou ji jinbu" 教會提倡注音字母的理由及進步. *Zhonghua Jidujiaohui nianjian* 中華基督教會年鑑 [*China Church Year Book*] 6 (1921): 101-6.

Peill, E. J., and S[idney] G. Peill. "The Scriptures in Phonetic for North China." *Chinese Recorder* 47, no. 5 (May 1916): 329–38.

Peill, S[idney] G. "No Competition with the Government." *Chinese Recorder* 49, no. 3 (March 1918): 206–7.

Peill, Sidney G. "'Open Vision' in China: Scriptures in Phonetic for Illiterate Chinese People." In *The Beloved Physician—and Others*, edited by J. Peill. Westminster: London Missionary Society, 1922.

Peill, Sidney G., and F. G. Onley. "Illiteracy in the Christian Church in China and the Use of Phonetic Script." In Lobenstine and Warnshuis, *The China Mission Year Book 1918*.

Phonetic Promotion Committee Records, 1919–1930, The Burke Library at Union Theological Seminary, Columbia University in the City of New York. [Abbreviated as PPCR].

Pietsch, B. M. "Lyman Stewart and Early Fundamentalism." *Church History* 82, no. 3 (2013): 617–46.

Proceedings of the Ninth Annual Meeting of the China Continuation Committee, Shanghai, May 5–10, 1921. Shanghai: China Continuation Committee, 1921.

Quan Shaowu 全紹武, ed. *Jidujiao quanguo dahui baogaoshu* 基督教全國大會報告書. Reprinted in vol. 19 of *Dongchuan fuyin* 東傳福音, edited by Zhongguo zongjiao lishi wenxian jicheng bianzuan weiyuanhui 中國宗教歷史文獻集成編纂委員會. Hefei: Huangshan shushe, 2005.

Quanguo guoyu yundong dahui huikan di yi qi 全國國語運動大會會刊第一期. Shanghai: Quanguo guoyu yundong dahui zong choubeichu 全國國語運動大會總籌備處, 1925.

Rawlinson, F[rank]. "Christian Co-operation for a Nation-wide Task: Eighth Annual Meeting of the China Continuation Committee." *Chinese Recorder* 51, no. 6 (June 1920): 423.

Rawlinson, F[rank], Helen Thoburn, and D. MacGillivray, eds. *The Chinese Church as Revealed in the National Christian Conference held in Shanghai, Tuesday, May 2, to Thursday, May 11, 1922*. Shanghai: Oriental Press, 1922.

Rawlinson, Frank, ed. *The China Christian Year Book 1934–1935*. Shanghai: Christian Literature Society, 1935.

Rawski, Evelyn. *Education and Popular Literacy in Ch'ing China*. Ann Arbor: University of Michigan Press, 1979.

Smith, Carl T. *Chinese Christians: Elites, Middlemen, and the Church in Hong Kong*. Hong Kong: Hong Kong University Press, 2005.

Spillett, Hubert W. *A Catalogue of Scriptures in the Languages of China and the Republic of China*. London: British and Foreign Bible Society, 1975.

Stanley, Brian. *The World Missionary Conference, Edinburgh 1910*. Grand Rapids; Cambridge: Eerdmans, 2009.

Stauffer, Milton T., Tsinforn C. Wong, and M. Gardner Tewksbury. *The Christian Occupation of China: A General Survey of the Numerical Strength and Geographical Distributon [sic] of the Christian Forces in China Made by the Special Committee on Survey and Occupation, China Continuation Committee, 1918–1921*. Shanghai: China Continuation Committee, 1922.

The Hundred and Twentieth Report of the London Missionary Society. London: London Missionary Society, 1915.

"The National Christian Council, A Five Years' Review, 1922–1927." MRL 6: National Christian Council of China Records, Series 4, Box 1, Folder 2, The Burke Library at Union Theological Seminary, Columbia University in the City of New York.

Wang, Bingyao 王炳耀. *Pinyin zipu* 拼音字譜. Beijing: Wenzi gaige chubanshe 文字改革出版社, 1954.

Wang, Meimei, Bas van Leeuwen, and Jieli Li. *Education in China, ca. 1840–Present*. Leiden; Boston: Brill, 2020.

Wang, Pu, 王璞 and Chen Enrong 陳恩榮. "Shuo zhuyin zimu" 說注音字母. *Zhonghua Jidujiaohui nianjian* 中華基督教會年鑑 [*China Church Year Book*] 5 (1918): 166–67.

Yu, Jinen 于錦恩.. *Minguo zhuyin zimu zhengce shilun* 民國注音字母政策史論. Beijing: Chung Hwa Book Company, 2007.

Zhengfu gongbao 政府公報 865 (21 June 1918). Beijing: Yinzhuju 印鑄局, 1918.

9
A College Student's Rural Journey
Early Sociology and Anthropology in China Seen through Fieldwork on Sichuan's Secret Society[1]

Di Wang

In 1939, residents of Hope Township (Wangzhen 望鎮), a rural village close to Chengdu, watched Lei Mingyuan, a leader of the local chapter of the Paoge 袍哥 (Gowned Brothers) secret society, execute his own teenage daughter because of a rumor that she and a young tailor who worked for his family were having an illicit affair. Despite the brutal and brazen nature of his crime, Lei did not face any charges. Six years later, in the summer of 1945, Shen Baoyuan 沈寶媛, a female college student from the Department of Sociology at Yenching University, arrived in Hope Township to conduct fieldwork and research on the social organization of rural secret societies; she did this as part of a larger set of educational experiments and summertime activism programs that her professors had established, as discussed later in this chapter.

Shen spent more than a month getting to know Lei and his family and recorded previously unknown facts about the murder, the Lei family, and the secret society to which he belonged. In April of the following year, she completed her report, "A Family of the Rural Organization," as her bachelor's degree thesis.[2] From the title

---

1. This chapter was first published as Di Wang, "A College Student's Rural Journey: Early Sociology and Anthropology in China Seen through Fieldwork on Sichuan's Secret Society," *Frontiers of History in China* 12, no. 1 (2017): 1–31. Reprinted by permission.
2. Shen Baoyuan 沈寶媛, "Yige nongcun shetuan jiating" 一個農村社團家庭 (BA thesis, Department of Sociology, Yenching University, 1946), forty-six pages, plus a two-page abstract. The thesis is written on the special stationery printed for Yenching University with 576 Chinese characters on each page. Each page is folded on the center line where it reads "Yanjing Daxue biye lunwen" 燕京大學畢業論文 [Graduation thesis of Yenching University], something like A and B pages of traditional woodblock printed books. The thesis has 43 pages with a total of 24,000 Chinese characters. The last three pages are an appendix, approximately 1,000 characters, including six items: (1) origins of the Paoge and Haidi 海底; (2) definition of Paoge and other names; (3) examples of Paoge secret codes; (4) Paoge internal regulations; (5) examples of Paoge argot; (6) examples of

page of the thesis, we know that her thesis adviser was Xu Yongshun 徐雍舜, and the two reviewers were Lin Yaohua 林耀華, chair of the Department of Sociology, and Zheng Linzhuang 鄭林莊, the dean of the School of Law.[3] In addition, in the preface, Shen offered a special appreciation to Liao Taichu (Liao T'ai-ch'u 廖泰初) for providing her with his English-language paper on secret societies in Sichuan.[4] The professors who supervised Shen's thesis were clearly well-known and respected pioneers in the fields of sociology and anthropology.[5]

Using the lens of Shen's fieldwork and her written report, this chapter focuses on the means, methods, and persons involved with academic investigations of rural society in the Republican period. The aim is not so much to summarize her work and writing, as it is to talk about Shen's intellectual upbringing among the pioneers of Chinese sociology and anthropology. These pioneers called themselves "rural activists" (*nongcun gongzuo zhe* 農村工作者). They tried to understand rural China's reactions to the wave of Westernization and modernization, and they hoped to change Chinese society as guided by their own notions of modernity. Developments in Chinese sociology and anthropology from the 1920s to the 1940s have made it possible for us to have a picture of rural problems in those years. The investigations by academics, and their attention to the indicators of China's modernization, fed into the Rural Reconstruction and Rural Education Movement. It was these academics who entered the countryside and the lives of peasants. The rich accounts and data they left, in turn, became sources for today's research and actual memories of rural China's past. Their accounts displayed how the development of the two disciplines in China also reflected the way that modern intellectual values entered into academic research, and how Western sociology and anthropology became localized to answer the "China questions" and to solve a "Chinese problem."

Paoge canons. Haidi was the canon of Paoge. See Di Wang, *The Teahouse: Small Business, Everyday Culture, and Public Politics in Chengdu, 1900–1950* (Stanford: Stanford University Press, 2008).

3. The Department of Sociology was under the School of Law of Yenching University.
4. It is Liao T'ai-ch'u [Liao Taichu], "The Ko Lao Hui in Szechuan," *Pacific Affairs* 20, no. 2 (June 1947): 161–73. Although Shen Baoyuan did not mention the title, Liao published only one article on the Paoge. Shen completed her thesis in 1946, but Liao's article was published in 1947. Apparently, what Shen read was the draft manuscript of the article before its publication.
5. It should be noted that at that time, there was not a clear distinction between sociology and anthropology. Today, when we review the works done by the Department of Sociology at Yenching University, we will find that, in fact, their methodologies and research objects can hardly be distinguished from those of anthropology. This tradition has even carried on until today. Currently, anthropology in many Chinese universities is part of the Department of Sociology (including Peking University). Therefore, the professors of sociology at Yenching University mentioned in this book were in fact also anthropologists.

The Paoge and the Lei Family

"Paoge" was another name for the "Sworn Brotherhood Society" (Gelaohui 哥老會) in Sichuan, the most influential secret organization in that province, and one that had arisen as early as the Qing dynasty and continued to the Republic.[6] Although early on there were different opinions on the percentage of its members in the male population, almost all believed it was very high. An article in 1946 said, "The power of the Paoge in Sichuan is really huge. It is said that in Chongqing alone, at least more than half of the people had joined the organization, including people in various trades, especially among business and the military."[7] An article in 1947 claimed that in

---

6. Important works of Chinese secret societies include Cai Shaoqing 蔡少卿, *Zhongguo jindai huidang shi yanjiu* 中國近代黨史研究 (Beijing: Zhonghua Book Company, 1987); Cai Shaoqing, *Zhongguo mimi shehui* 中國秘密社會 (Hangzhou: Zhejiang renmin chubanshe, 1990); Dai Xuanzhi 戴玄之, *Zhongguo mimi zongjiao yu mimi huishe* 中國秘密宗教與秘密會社 (Taipei: Commercial Press, 1990); Zhou Yumin 周育民 and Shao Yong 邵雍, *Zhongguo banghui shi* 中國幫會史 (Shanghai: Shanghai renmin chubanshe, 1993); Yu Songqing 喻松青, *Minjian mimi zongjiao jingjuan yanjiu* 民間秘密宗教經卷研究 (Taipei: Linking Publishing, 1994); Li Fuhua 李富華 and Feng Zuozhe 馮佐哲, *Zhongguo minjian zongjiao shi* 中國民間宗教史 (Taipei: Wenchin Publishing, 1994); Zhuang Jifa 莊吉發, *Qingdai mimi huitang shi yanjiu* 清代秘密黨史研究 (Taipei: Liberal Arts Press, 1994); Wang Jianchuan 王見川 and Jiang Zhushan 蔣竹山, eds., *Ming Qing yilai minjian zongjiao de tansuo: Jinian Dai Xuanzhi jiaoshou lunwenji* 明清以來民間宗教的探索——紀念戴玄之教授論文集 (Taipei: Shinning Culture Publishing, 1996); Jean Chesneaux, *Secret Societies in the Nineteenth and Twentieth Centuries* (Ann Arbor: University of Michigan Press, 1971); Jean Chesneaux, ed, *Popular Movements and Secret Societies in China 1840–1950* (Stanford: Stanford University Press, 1972); Fei-Ling Davis, *Primitive Revolutionaries of China: A Study of Secret Societies in the Late Nineteenth Century* (Honolulu: University of Hawai'i Press, 1977); David Ownby and Mary Somers Heidhues, eds., *"Secret Societies" Reconsidered: Perspectives on the Social History of Early Modern South China and Southeast Asia* (Armonk: M. E. Sharpe, 1993); David Ownby, *Brotherhoods and Secret Societies in Early and Mid-Qing China: The Formation of a Tradition* (Stanford: Stanford University Press, 1996); Barend J. Ter Haar, *Ritual and Mythology of the Chinese Triads: Creating an Identity* (Leiden: Brill, 1998); Martin Booth, *The Dragon Syndicates: The Global Phenomenon of the Triads* (New York: Carroll & Graf, 1999). Studies of Paoge in China mainly present general history and information, although there have been a few articles published in English. However, there is no thorough monograph. Regarding studies of the Paoge, see Hu Hansheng 胡漢生, *Sichuan jindai shishi sankao* 四川近代史事三考 (Chongqing: Chongqing chubanshe, 1988); Wang Chunwu 王純五, *Paoge tanmi* 袍哥探秘 (Chengdu: Bashu shushe, 1993); Qin Heping 秦和平, "Ersanshi niandai yapian yu Sichuan chengzhen shuijuan guanxi zhi renshi" 二三十年代鴉片與四川城鎮稅捐關係之認識, in vol. 19/20 of *Chengshi yu yanjiu* (Tianjin: Tianjin shehui kexueyuan chubanshe, 2000), 76–96; Kristin Stapleton "Urban Politics in an Age of 'Secret Societies': The Cases of Shanghai and Chengdu," *Republican China* 22, no. 1 (1996): 23–64; Lee McIsaac, "'Righteous Fraternities' and Honorable Men: Sworn Brotherhoods in Wartime Chongqing," *American Historical Review* 105, no. 5 (2000): 1641–55; Wang Di 王笛, "Chi jiangcha: Chengdu chaguan, paoge yu difang zhengzhi kongjian" 吃講茶：成都茶館、袍哥與地方政治空間, *Journal of Historical Science*, no. 2 (2010): 105–14.

7. Shi De 拾得, "Paoge zai Chongqing" 袍哥在重慶, *Jipu* 吉普, no. 13 (1946): 10–11.

Sichuan, nearly two-thirds of the population were members.[8] An observation made in 1948 said, "Almost all people who participate in social activities are members of the Paoge, no exceptions."[9] Fan Shaozeng 范紹增, a former master (or leader, strongman) of the Paoge in Chongqing, estimated that the members accounted for about 90 percent of male adults in Sichuan.[10] The previously mentioned sources generally relied on reporters' estimates, but the sociologist Liao Taichu—Shen Baoyuan's teacher—estimated in his 1947 research article that more than 70 percent of male adults in Sichuan were Paoge members.[11] It is easy to understand how someone could point out that the Paoge during that time "were the most powerful people in the local society. As long as [the secret society is put to] a good use, it would not be like other gangs, but might become a favorable mass organization."[12]

Shen Baoyuan noticed the Paoge's ability to exert control over local communities and was surprised to see "how powerful and strong its social control was." She found that "in Hope Township, the association is the center of the community," and it "takes responsibility for social sanctions, even the legal, political, religious, and ethical aspects of social sanctions."[13] Shen's statement gives us important hints. In her report, when it came to the Paoge, she always used the term "association," even for the title of her thesis. This term probably reflects serious consideration on her part. The name "Paoge" itself was a sort of Sichuan-area nickname for Gelaohui, which the members of the secret society and local people most frequently used. In fact, in official documents, they were more often called "Gelaohui" or "Rebel Bandit Clique" (*huidang* 會黨). After all, these organizations were social associations, so when Shen Baoyuan attempted to study Paoge from an academic point of view, without prejudice, she used "association" (or social organization) as something she thought to be a neutral descriptor.[14]

Lei Mingyuan was a local Paoge head in Hope Township. In 1937, the year when the War of Resistance against Japan broke out, middle-aged Lei was energetic. In his mind, he always wanted to be "heroic"; he was surrounded by a group of loyal, powerful sworn brothers. His economic situation was good, so a batch of young

---

8. Li Mufeng 李沐風, "Luetan Sichuan de 'Paoge'" 略談四川的袍哥, *Chahua* 茶話, no. 12 (1947): 81–84.
9. Li, "Luetan Sichuan de Paoge," 81–84.
10. Fan Shaozeng 范紹增, "Huiyi wozai Sichuan paoge zhong de zuzhi shenghuo" 回憶我在四川袍哥中的組織生活, in vol. 84 of *Wenshi ziliao xuanji* 文史資料選輯, ed. Wenshi ziliao bianzuan weiyuanhui 文史資料編纂委員會 (Beijing: Wenshi chubanshe, 1982), 148–60.
11. Liao, "The Ko Lao Hui in Szechuan," 162.
12. Zhang San 張三, "Chongqing de canyiyuan" 重慶的參議員, *Xinguang* 星光, no. 3 (1946).
13. Shen, "Yige nongcun shetuan jiating," 7.
14. In this chapter, I use "Paoge" often as a plural term because they had many branches but not under a unified headquarters. Paoge could mean both the organizations and their members. For the latter, sometimes I use the term "Paoge members" or "Paoge brothers."

brothers lived in his house and enjoyed his benefits. One day, when he was alone in a teahouse, nearly twenty armed rival gangsters approached and shot at him. His Paoge brothers rushed to the site, and a bloody battle took place, during which Lei and his followers killed several opponents. That battle strengthened his position in the Paoge.[15]

Shen Baoyuan's thesis lodged criticisms against the Paoge in Hope Township and found that its members often associated with secret agents (implying links with the Guomindang's police forces); furthermore, they "violated the people's interests and opposed democracy" by using bureaucratic structures, meaning that Paoge masters controlled almost all administrative office positions in the township. As such, they implemented high-pressure policies and imposed unreasonable taxes, trafficking in opium, and prohibiting people's thought, speech, association, and even freedom to read newspapers. Such control benefited from the Paoge's dual identities—local administrators and leaders of a secret organization.[16] Moreover, Shen's leftist ideology must be taken into account to understand her criticisms of the Paoge. This sort of connection will be explained as we move forward.

Some other accounts have pointed out that Paoge members acted in favor of the poor. An investigation into the factors of the Paoge's radical growth found that "Paoge possess a strong solidarity that has held for hundreds of years without a break, especially in terms of their righteousness." The most important credo for them was the prohibition against rape and adultery. Any such accused "would be executed." In addition, the Paoge could help members to lead a better life by "sharing happiness and overcoming troubles together." However, one writer pointed out that the above points were not the fundamental reason for growth. "The basic reason for the Paoge's expansion was due to years of civil war in Sichuan, and because the powerful men there were suppressing the lowly and poor, whose livelihoods were seriously affected. Such victims could hardly survive if they did not have a strong organization to protect them." If a person who was bullied wanted to go to court, he knew nothing about the law and also could not afford the time and money for a lawsuit. Therefore, they often invited a Paoge "big brother" as mediator to settle the case. "The 'big brother' had authority, and people always obeyed his judgment."[17] Therefore, we can see a certain complexity of the Paoge: they could be a local protector or a local bully, depending on circumstances.

---

15. Shen, "Yige nongcun shetuan jiating," 17.
16. Shen, "Yige nongcun shetuan jiating," 7.
17. Li, "Luetan Sichuan de Paoge," 81–84.

"Rural Activists"

As a student in the Department of Sociology of Yenching University, Shen Baoyuan's choice to investigate the Paoge was not accidental but rather a part of the Rural Education Movement and a result of the recent emphasis on fieldwork among early Chinese sociologists and anthropologists. In 1926, the Chinese National Association of the Mass Education Movement (Zhonghua pingmin jiaoyu cujinhui 中華平民教育促進會), led by Y. C. James Yen (Yan Yangchu 晏陽初), conducted experiments in rural education in Ding County 定縣, Hebei Province. In the early 1930s, by using funds raised in the United States, Yen moved the headquarters from Beijing to the city of Dingzhou 定州城 and recruited college students to participate in the experiment.[18]

In 1929, Liang Shuming 梁漱溟 founded the Institution for Village Governance (Cunzhi yanjiuyuan 村治研究院) in Hui County 輝縣, north Henan Province, for the purpose of "rural reconstruction." In 1931, he established the Rural Research Reconstruction Institution in Zouping 鄒平 County, Shandong Province, and published the journal *Village Governance* (*Cunzhi* 村治) in Beijing. He wrote several books to express his ideas of rural reconstruction.[19] Entrepreneurs also took part in this movement, including people like Lu Zuofu 盧作孚, who launched an

---

18. Regarding the Movement of Rural Reconstruction, see Zheng Dahua 鄭大華, *Minguo xiangcun jianshe yundong* 民國鄉村建設運動 (Beijing: Shehuikeshe wenxian chubanshe, 2000); Li Weizhong 李偉中, "Zhishi fenzi 'xiaxiang' yu jindai Zhongguo xiangcun biange de kunjing: Dui 1930 niandai xianzheng jianshe shiyan de jiexi" 知識分子"下鄉"與近代中國鄉村變革的困境: 對20世紀30年代縣政建設實驗的解析, *Nankai Journal*, no. 1 (2009): 115–25; Liu Chonglai 劉重來, "Minguo shiqi xiangcun jianshe yundong shulue" 民國時期鄉村建設運動述略, *Chongqing Social Sciences*, no. 5 (2006): 74–85; Lu Zhenxiang 魯振祥, "Sanshi niandai xiangcun jianshe yundong de chubu kaocha" 三十年代鄉村建設運動的初步考察, *CASS Journal of Political Science*, no. 4 (1987): 37–44; Zhao Xudong 趙旭東, "Xiangcun chengwei wenti yu chengwei wenti de Zhongguo xiangcun yanjiu: Weirao' Yan Yangchu mos hi' de zhishi shehui xue fansi" 鄉村成為問題與成為問題的中國鄉村研究: 圍繞"晏陽初"模式的知識社會學反思, *Social Science in China*, no. 3 (2008): 110–17; He Jianhua 何建華, "Yan Yangchu de pingjiao yundong jiqi xianzheng gaige shiyan" 晏陽初的平教運動及縣政改革實驗, *Southeast Academic Research*, no. 1 (2008): 61–68; Charles Wishart Hayford, *To the People: James Yen and Village China* (New York: Columbia University Press, 1990); Martha McKee Keehn, ed., *Y. C. James Yen's Thought on Mass Education and Rural Reconstruction: China and Beyond: Selected Papers from an International Conference Held in Shijiazhuang, China, May 27–June 1, 1990* (New York: International Institute of Rural Reconstruction, 1993).
19. Liang Shuming (1893–1988) taught in Peking University during 1917 and 1924. Regarding studies of Liang and rural construction, see Lu Xinyu 呂新雨, "Rural Reconstruction, the Nation-state and China's Modernity Problem: Reflections on Liang Shuming's Rural Reconstruction Theory and Its Practice," trans. Zhu Ping and Adrian Thieret, in *Culture and Social Transformations in Reform Era China*, ed. Cao Tianyu, Zhong Xueping and Liao Kebin (Leiden: Brill, 2010), 235–56; Stig Thøgersen, "Revisiting a Dramatic Triangle: The State, Villagers, and Social Activists in Chinese Rural Reconstruction Projects," *Journal of Current Chinese Affairs* 38, no.4 (2009): 9–33; Shugang Wu and Binchang Tong, "Liang Shuming's Rural Reconstruction Experiment and Its Relevance for Building the New Socialist Countryside," *Contemporary Chinese Thought* 40, no. 3 (2009): 39–51.

experiment in Beipei 北碚, part of today's Chongqing, and emphasized that education was the highest priority for rural areas. In 1934, he laid out the blueprint for rural reconstruction in his article "The Rural Reconstruction Movement in Jialing and the Three Gorges Areas" (Sichuan Jialingjiang Sanxia de xiangcun jianshe yundong 四川嘉陵江三峽的鄉村建設運動).[20]

After the start of the War of Resistance against Japan (1937–1945), the Great Rear Area (*Dahoufang* 大後方, i.e., southwest and northwest China under the Nationalist government during the war) became an important basis of the Rural Reconstruction Movement. James Yen's Chinese National Association of the Mass Education Movement, for example, shifted its focus to rural education in Sichuan. In the spring of 1936, the Association worked with the Sichuan provincial government to establish a committee devoted to this goal. In April of 1937, the provincial government set up Xindu 新都 as an experimental county that it governed directly. In September 1939, the Nationalist government announced the "Outline of County Organization at All Levels" (Xian geji zuzhi gangyao 縣各級組織綱要), which adopted the experiences of Yen's work in Ding County and Xindu. Given the special circumstances and the important position of Sichuan in the war, the Nationalist government decided, on March 1, 1940, that with the assistance of the Association, Sichuan would be the first province to implement the new outline.[21]

During the 1920s and 1930s, there were over six hundred organizations and institutions nationwide that engaged in activities associated with the Rural Reconstruction Movement. Overall, over a thousand locations and a variety of experiments were undertaken, such as Ding County (Hebei) by James Yen, Zouping County (Shandong) by Liang Shuming, and Qinghe 清河 (Beijing) by Yenching University, mostly dealing with education.[22] In addition to rural education, the experiments involved rural self-government, agricultural reforms, seed-stock improvement, pest control, and other activities. Furthermore, they tried to solve the problem of farmers' loans by establishing cooperatives and credit unions, rural hospitals, and rural public health care systems. They also educated rural people to reform "evil" social customs, such as foot-binding, drug abuse, gambling, child marriage, mercenary marriage, infanticide, and other "bad habits." In this sense, it was important for Shen Baoyuan that when she was in Hope Township during the

---

20. Lu Zuofu (1893–1952) is an entrepreneur, educator, and social activist and founder of the Minsheng Shipping Company. Regarding studies of Lu's ideas of rural construction, see Liu, "Minguo shiqi xiangcun jianshe yundong shulue."
21. Li Zaiquan 李在全, "Guonan zhong de xiangcun shiye: Kangzhan shiqi Sichuan de xiangcun jianshe yundong—yi Pingjiao hui wei zhongxin de kaocha" 國難中的鄉村事業：抗戰時期四川的鄉村建設運動——以平教會為中心的考察, *New Horizons from Tianfu*, no. 2 (2006): 132–36.
22. Liu, "Minguo shiqi xiangcun jianshe yundong shulue"; Cheng Bicheng 成必成, "Minguo xiangcun jiaoyu yundong jiqi dui nongcun jiaoyu gaige de qishi" 民國鄉村教育及其對農村教育改革的啟示, *Teaching and Administration*, no. 2 (2014): 25–27.

summer of 1945, Yenching University had opened a summer school there. Through her work at the latter, Shen sought every opportunity to connect with and to understand Lei Mingyuan and his family.

In addition, to a large extent, Shen Baoyuan's investigation was inseparable from the effects of the national military crisis. After war broke out, many colleges and universities closed down, and the Nationalist government began to relocate them to the interior. In these early years of the war, almost all universities along the southeast coast, except certain missionary institutions such as Yenching and Fu Jen Catholic, moved to southwest and northwest China. According to the statistics of the Ministry of Education of the Nationalist government, seventy-seven colleges and universities moved to these areas and resumed classes, but seventeen were closed. After the World War broke out across the Pacific in December 1941, Yenching University moved from Beijing to Chengdu and resumed classes there in 1942 under the English name "Yen Ching University in Chen[g] Tu."[23]

Li Anzhai 李安宅 and Lin Yaohua served as chairs of the Department of Sociology successively, and they both emphasized social service.[24] Based on the

---

23. Zhou Yong 周勇, ed., *Xinan kangzhan shi* 西南抗戰史 (Chongqing: Chongqing chubanshe, 2006); Yanjing Daxue Chengdu xiaoyou hui 燕京大學成都校友會, "Kangzhan shiqi qian Rong de Yanjing Daxue" 抗戰時期遷蓉的燕京大學, in *Chengdu wenshi ziliao xuanbian: kang Ri zhanzheng juan* 成都文史資料選編・抗日戰爭卷, ed. Chengdu shi zhengxie wenshi xuexi weiyuanhui 成都市政協文史學習委員會 (Chengdu: Sichuan renmin chubanshe, 2007), 339–56; Zhang Huiying 張瑋瑛, Wang Baiqiang 王百強, et al ed., *Yanjing Daxue shigao* 燕京大學史稿 (Beijing: China Renmin University Press, 1999).

24. Li Anzhai 李安宅 (1900–1985) is a scholar of ethnology and sociology. During 1934 and 1936, he studied anthropology at the University of California at Berkeley and Yale University. Later, he returned to China in 1936 and taught at Yenching University. His major works include Li Anzhai, *Meixue* 美學 (Shanghai: Shijie shuju, 1934); Li Anzhai, *Yili yu liji zhi shehuixue de yanjiu* 儀禮與禮記之社會學的研究 (Shanghai: Commercial Press, 1931); Li Anzhai, *Yiyixue* 意義學 (Shanghai; Chongqing: Commercial Press, 1945). Lin Yaohua (1910–2000), one of pioneers of Chinese anthropology, whose major works were on clans and families including: Lin Yaohua, "Zongfa yu jiazu" 宗法與家族, *Beiping chenbao: Shehui yanjiu* 北平晨報・社會研究, no. 79 (1935): 237–44; Lin Yaohua, "Meiyue hunyin zaji"; Lin Yaohua, *Yixu zongzu de yanjiu* 義序宗族的研究 (master's thesis, Department of Sociology, Yenching University, 1935). In 2000, this thesis was published by Sanlian shudian 三聯書店. Lin Yao-hua, *The Golden Wing: A Sociological Study of Chinese Familism* (London: K. Paul, Trench, Trubner & Co., 1947). There are two Chinese translations, one by Song He 宋和 (Taipei: Laureate Book, 1977) and one by Zhuang Kongzhao 莊孔韶 and Lin Zongcheng 林宗成 (Beijing: Sanlian shudian, 1989); Lin Yaohua, *Minzuxue yanjiu* 民族學研究 (Beijing: Zhongguo shehuikexue chubanshe, 1985); Lin Yaohua, *Minzuxue tonglun* 民族學通論 (Beijing: China Minzhu University Press, 1997); Lin Yaohua, "Baizu" 拜祖, in *Yixu zongzu de yanjiu* 義序宗族的研究 (Beijing: Sanlian shudian, 2000), 302–24; Lin Yaohua, *Shehui renleixue jiangyi* 社會人類學講義 (Xiamen: Lujiang chubanshe, 2003); Lin, Yaohua, "New China's Ethnology: Research and Prospects," in *Anthropology in China: Defining the Discipline*, ed. Gregory Eliyu Guldin (Armonk: M. E. Sharpe, 1990), 141–61; Lin Yaohua, "A Tentative Discussion of the Survival of the Concept of Rank in Contemporary Liangshan Yi Areas," *Chinese Sociology and Anthropology* 36, no. 1 (Fall 2003): 46–62. For studies of Lin Yaohua, see Zhang Haiyang 張海洋, "Lin Yaohua

wartime situation, the department encouraged and organized students to participate in social surveys and services. It can hardly be a surprise that Shen Baoyuan chose the topic that she did, namely that of a family of Paoge. Students at Yenching University during that time were deeply influenced by the Chinese Communist Party (CCP), which was expanding among their ranks. On October 15, 1944, "the progressive students" [*jinbu xuesheng* 進步學生 (i.e., leftists)] from various universities, including Yenching students, established the "Association for Democratic Youth in Chengdu" (Chengdu minzhu qingnian xiehui 成都民主青年協會). As we know, the Chinese Communist revolution was based in the countryside, and the CCP encouraged young people to go to rural areas to understand the peasants. Therefore, the Yenching students who went out were not only influenced by their professors, but also were responding to the CCP's call. In the spring of 1945, the Association organized this shift during the summer break, and thus members of "rural work teams" (*nongcun gongzuo dui* 農村工作隊), for example, provided medical service and medicines, organized evening classes, gathered people to support the war, and looked into landlord-tenant relations.[25] Although I did not find direct information to determine whether Shen Baoyuan's investigation was organized by the CCP, a connection is not implausible; in particular, her leftist ideology would have made common ground with that of the Party.

In her investigative report, Shen enthusiastically welcomed the notion that students needed to link their learning to practice in the field, and to mingle with ordinary people. She said that since her childhood, she had yearned for the rural life and liked the environment there; she had little interest in the hustle of urban life. She felt that rural people were honest, and she did not trust "crafty city residents." In fact, she admitted that her participation in the investigation was "for a selfish reason": she could derive no peace in the city, and she longed for "the quietude of the village life." She sympathized with lower-class people and felt guilty for her privileged life when she saw their hardship. She had "compassion and love" for peasants and a desire to "live, play, and work with them."

---

jiaoshou yu Zhongguo de shaoshu minzu he minzu yanjiu," 林耀華教授與中國的少數民族和民族研究, *Journal of Southwest Minzu University (Humanities and Social Sciences Edition)*, no. 1 (2001): 28–31.

25. Wang Xiaoting 王效挺 and Huang Wenyi 黃一文, eds., *Zhandou de licheng, 1925–1949.2, Yanjing Daxue dixiadang gaikuang* 戰鬥的歷程，1925–1949.2 燕京大學地下黨概況 (Beijing: Peking University Press, 1993), 100–101. Regarding Yenching University, see Stuart, J. Leighton, *Fifty Years in China* (New York: Random House, 1946); Dwight W, Edwards, *Yenching University* (New York: United Board for Christian Higher Education in China, 1959); Philip West, *Yenching University and Sino-Western Relations, 1916–1952* (Cambridge, MA: Harvard University Press, 1976). Regarding its student movement, see Elizabeth J. Perry, "Managing Student Protest in Republican China: Yenching and St. John's Compared," *Frontiers of History in China* 8, no. 1 (2013): 3–31.

Obviously, Shen was an idealist and felt uncomfortable with her own background. Shen herself wrote that fieldwork was a response to the slogan that touted "intellectuals going to the countryside" and she tried to "take advantage of this relaxing summer break to sow seeds of rural work, to express my respect to farmers, and to learn from them beyond knowledge from books."[26] Actually, her professors at Yenching had become the direct examples. Professor Liao Taichu in the Department of Education established a rural service station in Hope Township. During four years at the Chengdu campus, Lin Yaohua, chair of the Department of Sociology, spent his three summer breaks in the minority areas of Liangshan 涼山 and Xikang 西康.[27] Therefore, Shen's investigation followed the typical practices undertaken by her teachers and shared class-oriented values that were regularly preached in Communist ideology.

Shen Baoyuan and Leftists

Shen Baoyuan attended Yenching University probably based on family connections. Her father, Shen Zurong 沈祖榮 (Samuel T.Y. Seng, 1883–1977), was the founder of library science in China.[28] Shen's family provided her with the best education and

---

26. Shen, "Yige nongcun shetuan jiating," 1.
27. Zhang and Wang, *Yanjing Daxue shigao*, 1320; Lin, *A Tentative Discussion of the Survival of the Concept of Rank in Contemporary Liangshan Yi Areas*, 457–60.
28. Born poor, Shen Zurong's grandfather was a tracker on the Yangtze River; his father opened a small restaurant on the waterfront, where he worked for many years. At fifteen years old, Shen Zurong worked for the Protestant Episcopal Church in Yichang and then studied at Boone University, a missionary school. After his graduation, he was employed by the Boone Library (*Wenhua gongshulin* 文華公書林) founded by Mary Elizabeth Wood, an American library expert. In 1914, he went to the United States to study library science funded by Wood and earned his bachelor's degree from Columbia University in 1916, who became the first person from China awarded a degree in library science from there. After returning to China, he continued to work for the Boone Library. In 1920, Wood collaborated with Boone University to build a library major, where both Shen and Wood taught courses. In the 1920s, Shen initiated the Chinese Library Association and as the sole representative of China, he participated in the first general assembly of the International Federation of Library Associations. Later he served as president of the Boone Library School. During the 1930s and 1940s, he trained many library professionals. In 1952, his position was incorporated into Wuhan University with the Boone Library School. He died in 1977. In 2005, Shen Baoyuan and her relatives set up the "Shen Zurong and Shen Baohuan Memorial Scholarship" at Sun Yat-sen University. Shen Baohuan was Shen Zurong's eldest son, who went to the US in 1946 and because of the Communist revolution was thereafter separated from his father. Without further news about his son, Shen Zurong did not know that he moved from the United States to Taiwan and continued his father's mission of library development. Shen Baohuan died in 2004 in the United States. See Cheng Huanwen 程煥文, "Shen Zurong guju xunli," 沈祖榮故居巡禮, *Documentation, Information & Knowledge*, no. 6 (2007): 104–7; Chen Weizun 陳維尊, "Wujinde aisi shenshende huainian: Huiyi waizufu Shen Zurong xiansheng" 無盡的哀思深深的懷念：回憶外祖父沈祖榮先生, *Sohu*, updated September 12, 2010, accessed July 2, 2014, http://zwf251.blog.sohu.com/.

gave her a foundation to become an open-minded and new-style young woman. Yet, in contrast to her famous father, she is basically unknown. I discovered that she is still alive and managed to reach her by phone. She has lost most of her memory because of Alzheimer's disease. However, I was able to learn from her daughter that she was born in 1924. When Shen went to Hope Township for her sociological investigation in the summer of 1945, she was twenty-one years old and a junior in the Department of Sociology, Yenching University.

Shen Baoyuan's academic work was not completely separated from politics and ideologies. At the time, Yenching students were greatly influenced not only by the professors of sociology and anthropology (who will be discussed next) but also by the CCP. As just mentioned, late in 1944, left-wing student activists set up the Association for Democratic Youth in Chengdu, and it included Yenching University communists. In the spring of 1945, when the Association was organizing college students in the countryside in order to further their understanding of peasants and rural issues, a participant claimed, "The rural experience for a month decided my life for the future. The rural reality made me join the revolution."[29]

Although we lack direct evidence of Shen's connection with the CCP, one can see clearly that at Yenching she was a left-wing student, specifically an active member of the Petrel Troupe (Haiyan jutuan 海燕劇團) of the university, founded in the fall of 1942 and named after the famous poem "The Song of the Stormy Petrel" by Maxim Gorky—the Russian writer who was famously devoted to the communist revolution. In the Chinese New Year period of 1943, the troupe performed its first drama, *Wind and Clouds beyond the Great Wall* (*Saishang fengyun* 塞上風雲) by Yang Hansheng 陽翰笙, a story about the Han people and Mongols uniting to fight the Japanese. Later, the troupe performed *Fragrant Grass at the Edges of the Sky* (*Fangcao tianya* 芳草天涯) by Xia Yan 夏衍, a drama of modern intellectuals' lives and loves.[30] Furthermore, Shen's name appeared on a statement titled "An Appeal from Chengdu's Cultural Circle about the Current Political Situation" signed by 248 people on September 29, 1945, including many celebrities in Chinese literature and the arts. They demanded the Guomindang government "immediately end the one-party dictatorship," "unconditionally protect basic human rights, including freedom of speech, press, assembly, association, and religions."[31] When the appeal was made, Mao Zedong had arrived in Chongqing for negotiations with Chiang Kai-shek concerning the ongoing civil war. The "Appeal" presumably was aimed to work with the propaganda of the CCP on the Chongqing Negotiation (August 29–October 10, 1945). Later, Shen went to Hong Kong and became a secretary in the Office of

---

29. Wang and Huang, *Zhandou de licheng, 1925–1949, Yanjing Daxue dixiatang gaikuang*, 100–101.
30. Zhang and Wang, *Yanjing daxue shigao*, 558.
31. *Xinhua ribao* 新華日報, September 29, 1945.

Women Workers of the YWCA. In early 1950, five evening schools for women were closed down, affecting more than one thousand women workers; Shen and thirty-three teachers and staff issued "A Letter of Public Appeal," calling for "Christians, co-workers, and all people who enthusiastically support the YMCA" to work together "to save the schools."[32] Shen's name disappeared from the media. Apparently, she did not continue in academia. My chief point here is that despite her seemingly modest career (but excellent family and university influences), the investigation she conducted seventy years ago is valuable to our current understanding of secret societies. Without her report, we would not be able to examine a family associated with the Paoge in such depth.

The Academic Background of Shen's Investigation

An understanding of Shen Baoyuan's academic environment may help us understand her rural sojourn of fieldwork and activism. Her subsequent written investigation can be regarded as a product of early Chinese sociology and anthropology and a result of pioneering efforts since the 1920s and 1930s. China's social research work started in the early twentieth century and was conducted by several foreign professors, especially at missionary universities. In 1917, C. G. Dittmer, an American professor at Tsing-hua College, guided student research into the cost of living of 195 households in the western suburbs of Beijing. During 1918 and 1919, missionary Sidney D. Gamble and Professor John Stewart Burgess of Yenching University launched a survey of the social conditions of Beijing and published *Peking, a Social Survey* in 1921. In the same year, Professor Daniel H. Kulp of the University of Shanghai took students in the Department of Sociology to Phoenix Village, in Chaozhou 潮州, Guangdong Province, where they investigated 650 households and published their report *Country Life in South China* in 1925.[33] In 1922, the Federation of International Famine Relief Commission invited C. B. Malone and J. B. Tagler to lead 61 students from 9 universities in an investigation of 240 villages in Hebei, Shandong, Jiangsu, Zhejiang, and other provinces and published *The Study of Chinese Rural Economy* in 1924.[34] During 1921 and 1925, Professor John Lossing Buck at the University of Nanking organized students to survey 2,866 farms in 17 counties of 7 provinces

---

32. *Xingdao ribao* 星島日報, January 30, 1950.
33. C. G. Dittmer, "An Estimate of the Standard of Living in China," *Quarterly Journal of Economics* 33, (November 1918): 107–28; Sidney D. Gamble and John Stewart Burgess, *Peking, a Social Survey* (New York: George H. Doran, 1921; repr. Leiden: Global Oriental, 2011); Han Mingmo 韓明謨, "Zhongguo shehuixue diaocha fangfa he fangfalun fazhan de sange lichengbei" 中國社會學調查研究方法和方法論發展的三個里程碑, *Journal of Peking University (Philosophy and Social Sciences)*, no. 4 (1997): 5–15.
34. C. B. Malone and J. B. Tagler, *The Study of Chinese Rural Economy* (Peking: China International Famine Relief Commission, 1924).

and published *Chinese Farm Economy* in 1930. Later, Buck organized an even larger investigation of 16,700 farms in 22 provinces and published *Land Utilization in China* in 1937.[35]

During the same period, Chinese sociologists conducted other social surveys. In the 1920s, the board of the Chinese Educational and Cultural Foundation (Zhonghua jiaoyu wenhua jijin dongshihui 中華教育文化基金董事會) established the Office of Social Surveys, which was renamed Institute of Social Surveys in Peiping (Beiping shehui diaochasuo 北平社會調查所) in 1929. Since 1926, with funding from the United States, it conducted many social studies led by Tao Menghe 陶孟和 and Li Jinghan 李景漢, and published over two dozen books. During 1929 and 1930, the Institute of Social Sciences (Shehui kexue yanjiusuo 社會科學研究所) of Academia Sinica, headed by Chen Hansheng 陳翰笙, investigated the rural areas of Wuxi 無錫, Jiangsu province, and Baoding 保定, Hebei Province.[36] Meanwhile, James Yen set up an experimental area in Ding County, Hebei; Li Jinghan took it over in 1928 and later edited *Investigation of the Social Conditions in Ding County* (*Dingxian shehui gaikuang diaocha* 定縣社會概況調查), which became one of the earliest large-scale county-level surveys.[37]

Developments in the fields of sociology and anthropology in China were inseparable from studies being conducted directly in the countryside. The Yenching sociology pioneers, such academics as Yang Kaidao 楊開道, Li Jinghan, Wu Wenzao 吳文藻, and Fei Xiaotong 費孝通 (Wu's student), emphasized rural fieldwork.[38] They

---

35. John Lossing Buck, *Chinese Farm Economy: A Study of 2866 Farms in 17 Localities and 7 Provinces in China* (Chicago: Chicago University Press, 1930). This book was also translated into Chinese by Zhang Lüluan 張履鸞, see *Zhongguo nongjia jingji* 中國農家經濟 (Shanghai: Commercial Press, 1936); John Lossing Buck, *Land Utilization in China* (Shanghai: University of Nanking, 1937).
36. Chen Hancheng (1897–2004), also known as Chen Han-seng and Geoffrey Chen, who was educated in the US and Europe and is considered a pioneer of modern Chinese social science.
37. *Dingxian shehui gaikuang diaocha* 定縣社會概況調查 [An investigation of social general situation of Dingxian], ed. Li Jinghan (Beiping: Chinese National Association of the Mass Education Movement [Zhonghua pingmin jiaoyu cujinhui 中華平民教育促進會], 1933), has seventeen chapters, including geography, history, county government and other local organizations, population, education, health, hygiene, living expenses, rural entertainment, customs and habits, beliefs, finance and taxation, county finance, agriculture, industry and commerce, rural loans, natural disasters and famine, and disasters of war, and so forth. See also, Han, "Zhongguo shehuixue diaocha fangfa he fangfalun fazhan de sange lichengbei."
38. Yang Kaidao (1899–1981) studied at the University of Iowa and the University of Michigan and earned a doctoral degree in sociology. After his return to China, he taught rural sociology in Shanghai and Fudan Universities. In 1928, he began a teaching career in the Department of Sociology of Yenching University and was in charge of the experiment district in Qinghe township in the suburb of Beijing to investigate history, environment, economy, population, families, hygiene, education, customs, folk rituals, village organizations, and so on. The investigation resulted in *Ching Ho: A Sociological Analysis: The Report of a Preliminary Survey of the Town of Ching Ho, Hopei, North China 1930* (Beijing: Department of Sociology & Social Work, Yenching University, 1930). Li Jinghan (1895–1986) studied in the United States in his early years and then taught at the Department

also published several textbooks on rural sociology, such as Yang Kaidao's *Rural Sociology* (*Nongcun shehuixue* 農村社會學).³⁹ These works studied the realities of rural China's society, population, land, economy, finance, education, organizations, self-government, and other issues.

The Department of Sociology at Yenching University was founded in 1922 by John Stewart Burgess and D. W. Edwards, whose purpose was to train experts to engage in social welfare and social services.⁴⁰ After earning his doctoral degree from Columbia University, Wu Wenzao took a position at Yenching in early 1929 and began to devise a methodology for training students working in China. In 1933, Professor Robert Ezra Park from the University of Chicago was invited by Yenching to teach methodologies of community surveys. Aiming to bring together the best practitioners to form the department, Park suggested that Wu Wenzao invite Alfred Reginald Radcliffe-Brown—the founder of the theory of structural functionalism—to give talks at Yenching for three months.⁴¹ Subsequently, Wu arranged for

---

of Sociology of Yenching University. In the mid-1920s, he guided students conducting surveys of population, families, family income, and family lives in four villages in the Beijing suburbs. He later published *Beiping jiaowai zhi xiangcun jiating diaocha* 北平郊外之鄉村家庭調查 [A Survey of Rural Families in the Suburb of Beiping] (Shanghai: Commercial Press, 1929). During 1924 and 1931, he was in charge of the famous survey of Ding County, Hebei and wrote *Dingxian shehui gaikuang diaocha*. Wu Wenzao (1901–1985) earned his doctoral degree from Columbia University in 1929, and then he returned to China and became a professor at Yenching University. By applying methodologies of community studies and field investigation that were employed in British functionalism of cultural anthropology, he promoted studies of rural community. See Wu Wenzao, "Xiandai shequ shidi yanjiu de yiyi he gongyong" 現代地區實地研究的意義和功用, *Beiping chenbao: Shehui yanjiu*, no. 66 (1934); Wu Wenzao, "Zhongguo shequ yanjiu de xiyang yingxiang yu guonei jinkuang" 中國社區研究的西洋影響與國內近況 *Beiping chenbao: Shehui yanjiu*, nos. 101–102 (1935); Wu Wenzao, "Gongneng pai shehui renleixue de youlai yu xianzhuang" 功能派社會人類學的由來與現狀, *Minzhuxue yanjiu jikan* 民族學研究集刊, no. 1 (1936).

39. Similar works include Gu Fu 顧復, *Nongcun shehuixue* 農村社會學 (Shanghai: Commercial Press, 1924); Yang Kaidao, *Nongcun shehuixue* 農村社會學 (Shanghai: Shijie shuju, 1934); Feng Hefa 馮和法, *Nongcun shehuixue dagang* 農村社會學大綱 (Shanghai: Liming shuju, 1932); Yan Xinzhe 言心哲, *Nongcun shehuixue gailun* 農村社會學概論 (Shanghai: Chung Hwa Books, 1934).

40. Lei Jieqiong 雷潔瓊 and Shui Shizheng 水世琤, "Yanjing daxue shehui fuwu gongzuo sanshi nian" 燕京大學社會服務工作三十年, in vol. 4 of *Yanda wenshi ziliao* 燕大文史資料, ed. Yanda wenshi ziliao bianweihui 燕大文史資料編委會 (Beijing: Peking University Press), 49–58.

41. Robert Ezra Park (1864–1944) was an American urban sociologist considered one of the most influential figures in early US sociology. He taught at the University of Chicago from 1914 to 1933, where he played a leading role in the development of the Chicago School of sociology. His works include Robert Ezra Park and Ernest Burgess, *Introduction to the Science of Sociology* (Chicago: University of Chicago Press, 1921); Robert Ezra Park, R. D. McKenzie, & Ernest Burgess, *The City: Suggestions for the Study of Human Nature in the Urban Environment* (Chicago: University of Chicago Press, 1925). Alfred Reginald Radcliffe-Brown (1881–1955), English social anthropologist, one of founders of structural functionalism. His works include *The Andaman Islanders: A Study in Social Anthropology* (Cambridge: Cambridge University Press, 1922) and *Social Organization of Australian Tribes* (Melbourne: Macmillan & Co.).

Li Anzhai to study anthropology at the University of California at Berkeley, and then Li transferred to Yale. Wu also sent Lin Yaohua to Harvard for doctoral studies in anthropology and Fei Xiaotong to the London School of Economics to study under Bronisław Malinowski. After they completed their degrees and came back to Yenching, all became influential.[42]

Under Wu Wenzao's leadership, Yenching's faculty members and students in sociology, who had been guided by the theories and methodologies of community studies and social anthropology, traveled to a wide range of rural areas for their surveys. In 1936, Fei Xiaotong studied Kaixuangong 開弦弓 Village and completed *Peasant Life in China*.[43] Shen Baoyuan's adviser Xu Yongshun published an article titled "Migrants and Crime in Northeast China" (Dongsansheng zhi yimin yu fanzui 東三省之移民與犯罪).[44] In addition, the research of department chair, Lin Yaohua, the dean of the Law College, Zheng Linzhuang, and professor of education Liao Taichu focused on the countryside. It is safe to surmise that their work influenced Shen's investigative methods and techniques. Thus prepared, Shen Baoyuan came to Hope Township. Her Yenching training and the political and ideological trends there had had some sort of real impact on her work.

---

42. Fei Xiaotong (1910–2005) earned his doctoral degree from the University of London in 1938. His works include *Hualanyao shehui zuzhi* 花藍瑤社會組織 (Nanjing: Jiangsu renmin chubanshe, 1988); *Yunnan sancun* 雲南三村 (Tianjin: Tianjin renmin chubanshe, 1990); "Fifty Years Investigation in the Yao Mountains," 17–36 in *The Yao of South China: Recent International Studies*; *From the Soil: The Foundations of Chinese Society*, ed. Jacques Lemoine and Chien Chiao (Paris: Pangu, Editions de l'A.F.E.Y, 1991).There are many studies of Fei Xiaotong's scholarship, such as Zhao, "Xiangcun chengwei wenti yu chengwei wenti de Zhongguo xiangcun yanjiu: Weirao 'Yan Yangchu moshi' de zhishi shehui xue fansi," 110–17; Wang Jianmin 王建民, "Tianye minzuzhi yu Zhongguo renleixue de fazhan: Jinian Fei Xiaotong, Lin Yaohua xiansheng 100 zhounian danchen" 田野民族志與中國人類學的發展——紀念費孝通、林耀華先生100周年誕辰, *Journal of South-Central Minzu University (Humanities and Social Sciences)*, no. 6 (2010): 6–11; R. David Arkush, *Fei Xiaotong and Sociology in Revolutionary China* (Cambridge, MA: Harvard University Asia Center, 1981); Fong Shiaw-Chian [Fang Xiaoqian 方孝謙], "Fei Xiaotong's Theory of Rural Development and Its Application: A Critical Appraisal," *Issues and Studies* 33, no. 10 (October 1997): 20–43; Naigu Pan, "Vitality of Community Study in China: Professor Fei Xiaotong and Community Study," in *Home Bound: Studies in East Asian Society: Papers Presented at the Symposium in Honor of the Eightieth Birthday of Professor Fei Xiaotong*, ed. Chie Nakane and Chien Chiao (Tokyo: Centre for East Asian Cultural Studies, 1993), 33–43.
43. It was written in English. See Fei Hsiao-tung [Fei Xiaotung], *Peasant Life in China: A Field Study of Country Life in the Yangzi Valley* (New York: Oxford University Press, 1939). See also, Han Mingmo, "Zhongguo shehuixue diaocha fangfa he fangfalun fazhan de sange lichengbei."
44. Xu Yongshun, "Dongsansheng zhi yimin yu fanzui" 東三省之移民與犯罪, *Shehuixue jie* 社會學界, no. 5 (1931): 147–65.

Methodologies of Shen's Investigation

As soon as Shen Baoyuan and her classmates arrived in Hope Township, they sought to establish a good foundation based on "friendly exchanges" with villagers. Shen tried to understand "the conditions of rural life, the situation of farm families, and structure of local forces." She knew that to really understand "local forces" in the area, she would have to start from the top and, from there, open channels of access to "local relationships." As suggested by villagers, she first visited the head of the township (*xiangzhang* 鄉長), the security chief (*baoan duizhang* 保安隊長), and heads of the *baojia* 保甲 (a traditional system of local order), who "mostly were members of the society."[45] Here, "the society" means the secret society—Paoge. Her thesis, including the title, often used the two terms "social organization" (*shetuan* 社團) and "society" (*shehui* 社會). The latter has two meanings in Shen's report. One is the most common, with a meaning close to "community"; the other has the same meaning as the "Paoge" or its members.

Shen Baoyuan subsequently discovered that collecting information about Paoge was difficult because their members were "very cautious about leaking secrets of the organization." Therefore, after she became familiar with Lei Mingyuan and his wife, Woman Lei, she "was still afraid to tell them what she was doing, to avoid their suspicion." As their relationship grew closer, she started to ask more questions, but she was dissatisfied with the progress because she "often could not get the needed answers." Sometimes, she had to "circle around" but "failed to gain the slightest material"; or "tried very hard just to get a little sporadic information."[46] Undoubtedly, it was difficult to enter the world of this kind of family.

Shen got to know Lei Mingyuan mostly through his wife. Lei's youngest daughter and son enrolled in summer school, and through this teacher-student relationship, she had more opportunities to become close to the family. She began to treat them "as the beginning of a study of Paoge society." At that time, although peasants' children had opportunities to go to a rural school, they also carried a heavy work burden. They usually needed to work in the fields after school; they did not have tutoring after school, and many had difficulties in learning. When the Yenching college students held summer school there, it was a boon for peasant families. Lei and his wife enthusiastically supported the school and helped set up equipment. They also became "voluntary propagandists for the school." Also, the Lei couple helped keep disciplining students when the school needed it. Shen felt that their methods were "not very appropriate" but that they certainly provided much-needed

---

45. Shen, "Yige nongcun shetuan jiating," 2.
46. Shen, "Yige nongcun shetuan jiating," 6.

support.⁴⁷ As an illiterate man, Lei Mingyuan "respected" educated people and showed "extreme friendliness" to Shen and her classmates. He liked to talk to these young people about guns and military knowledge. He often carried and displayed a Browning pistol, carefully wiping it daily with a piece of cloth. He possessed excellent marksmanship skills and taught shooting to whichever students wanted to learn. He owned this pistol for nearly twenty years and claimed that he had used it to "kill countless lives."⁴⁸

The Lei couple played a "decisive role" in Shen's investigation. Every afternoon, she would investigate and visit all kinds of people, and in the evening, she wrote in her working diary. She gradually discovered that the scope of the investigation should be limited to the Lei family, which would help her understand the Paoge. Therefore, she began to collect and sort her materials in this manner.⁴⁹

In the beginning, Shen experienced difficulties because of the secret nature of the Paoge. Her inquiries faced "either support or obstruction by local forces." Thus, she made an effort to gather all kinds of information through daily chats, "intentionally or unintentionally asking questions" and to try to gain "totally honest answers" in a spontaneous way.⁵⁰ For example, while in the kitchen, she sometimes deliberately asked Woman Lei about traditional medicines or recipes; these were opportunities to learn about the family's life and "the inside stories of Paoge society."⁵¹ She did not explain that she was collecting information for her thesis, only that she acted from "curiosity."⁵² Shen often visited their house. She stated, "In many a long evening, when the sunshine made the rice fields a golden color, I sat in their living room as a guest." When the Lei daughter Shuying asked Shen to be her English tutor, Shen deepened the relationship and "established a friendship."⁵³

Shen stayed in Hope Township for only a month and five days, unlike anthropologists who often lived in a village for a long period. However, it was not a long distance between Hope Township and Chengdu, and she kept in close touch after the end of her fieldwork; some of the stories in her report actually happened after she had left Hope Township. Shen went back several times in August and September 1945, and January 1946. In the fall and winter, Woman Lei and Shuying visited the Chengdu campus of Yenching several times, and Shuying even once watched the student performance of *Fragrant Grass in Skyline* and stayed overnight at the school,

---

47. Shen, "Yige nongcun shetuan jiating," 2.
48. Shen, "Yige nongcun shetuan jiating," 17.
49. Shen, "Yige nongcun shetuan jiating," 2.
50. Shen, "Yige nongcun shetuan jiating," 3.
51. Shen, "Yige nongcun shetuan jiating," 3–4.
52. Shen, "Yige nongcun shetuan jiating," 5.
53. Shen, "Yige nongcun shetuan jiating," 4.

returning home the next day.[54] After Shuying started her middle school, located on the same street as Yenching, the two young women would meet each other almost every day.[55] This ongoing friendship helped Shen complete her materials.

Although Shen did not disclose the name of Shuying's middle school, it would have been Huamei Girls' Middle School, a missionary school on Shaanxi Street. In 1939, because of air raids, the school and a primary school next door were closed and evacuated to the countryside. The Chengdu campus of Yenching University subsequently took over the space of these two sites.[56] Although there is no record of the place Huamei evacuated to, based on other accounts, it probably was Hope Township. Thus, Shuying's having attended Huamei seems quite logical.[57] After the war, the middle school moved back to Chengdu, so Shen and Shuying lived almost in the same place.

I have discussed how Shen did her fieldwork and collected materials, but what methodology did she use in writing? In her thesis, Shen briefly mentioned that Lin Yaohua taught her the "viewpoint of structural functionalism," which regarded society as a complex structure in which all parts work together to function integrally and stably. One may surmise that, to a certain extent, Lin's study of families influenced Shen's choice of topic. The theory of structural functionalism had become popular in the 1930s–1940s in China and gradually dominated Western academic sociology, as seen in the work by Harvard University's Talcott Parsons of the 1930s–1960s and beyond (through his students). When the University of Chicago's Robert Ezra Park visited Yenching, he taught field investigation and community studies, inspiring Wu Wenzao, Lin Yaohua, and Fei Xiaotong to combine the methodologies of sociology and anthropology. During his visit to China, Radcliffe-Brown was the adviser for Lin Yaohua's master's thesis, and under Radcliffe-Brown's influence, Lin advocated the new sociological and anthropological methods of structural functionalist research

---

54. Shen, "Yige nongcun shetuan jiating," 4. The modern drama *Fragrant Grass in the End of the World* (*Fangcao tianya* 芳草天涯) was written by Xia Yan 夏衍. The story is about a group of intellectuals' experiences during the war, their love life, their struggle for survival, and their participation in the War of Resistance. See Xia Yan. *Fangcao Tianya* (Shanghai: Kai Ming Book, 1949).
55. Shen, "Yige nongcun shetuan jiating," 5.
56. On August 15, 1945, the Japanese surrendered and the war in China ended. The Chengdu campus of Yenching University returned to Beiping in the summer of 1946. See Yanjing Daxue Chengdu xiaoyou hui, "Kangzhan shiqi qian Rong de Yanjing daxue," 339–56.
57. According to an entry in his diary on November 18, 1940, Ye Shengtao 葉聖陶 traveled with Gu Jiegang 顧頡剛 (1893–1980) to Chongyiqiao 崇義橋, i.e. Hope Township, to visit Huamei Middle School and was treated to a meal by its president. See Ye Shengtao, vol. 19 of *Ye Shengtao ji* (Nanjing: Jiangsu jiaoyu chubanshe, 2004), 311. Ye Shengtao (1894–1988) was a famous educator; Gu was a very famous historian. Under the jurisdiction of Hope Township, there were thirteen villages, one of which was called "Huamei" 華美, likely getting the name from the time when Huamei Girls' Middle School relocated there. See Chengdu shi difangzhi bianzuan weiyuanhui 成都市地方志編纂委員會, ed, *Chengdu shizhi: Zongzhi* 成都市志・總志 (Chengdu: Shidai chubanshe, 2009), 425.

for the study of families. This advocacy turned immediately to village families in the west, mostly because the war had pushed everything away from the northern and eastern cities.[58]

The training Shen Baoyuan received determined the purpose and techniques of her investigation. In the preface of her thesis, she thanked her adviser Lin Yaohua for teaching her the "Operational Method (*jisuan fangfa* 計算方法) and Functionalism" (this refers to early sociology's structural functionalism). She said that she used the Operational Method to "measure interactions among people." She also explained that the Operational Method was a new approach, coming from critical theory and functionalism in American social anthropology; it resulted from synthesizing both approaches. The new method could be applied using mathematical methods, such as statistics, for studying human phenomena and could "predict the occurrence of future events." She tried to use her thesis to make an "experiment" in this new research method. She believed that the "narrative of relations" (*guanxi xushu* 關係敘述) was important, being "an essential element in the Operational Method."[59] In her view, the two approaches were mutually complementary, because people's relations involved requests, rituals, actions, and contexts, all of which could become data.

However, in reading her thesis, I did not find any actual application of the new methods. The Operational Method generally uses a macro perspective, using statistical theories and mathematical methods to calculate formulas related to changing quantifiable conditions; thus, it determines the increase and decrease in the conditions, which give shape to, or even eliminate, the situation.[60] Shen might have planned to use this approach for the next step, but once she completed her thesis, she did not have a chance to go back to the project. For us, today, I believe that it is not

---

58. During the Chengdu period (1942–1945) of Yenching University, he visited the Yi people's area in Liangshan for three times. See Lin, *Shehui renleixue jiangyi*, 456–60.
59. In his later years, Lin Yaohua wrote *Shehui renleixue jiangyi* [Teaching notes on Social anthropology] in which he reviewed both schools of Critical Theory and Functionalism (*Shehui renleixue jiangyi*, 22–24). Regarding studies of these two schools of anthropology in China, see Qiao Jian 喬健, "Meiguo lishi xuepai" 美國歷史學派 in vol. 1 of *Shehui wenhua renleixue jiangyangji* 社會文化人類學講演集, ed. Zhou Xing 周星 and Wang Mingming 王銘銘 (Tianjin: Tianjin renmin chubanshe, 1996), 137–56. Regarding Franz Boas' specific school, see Franz Boas and George W. Stocking Jr., *A Franz Boas Reader: The Shaping of American Anthropology, 1883–1911* (Chicago: University of Chicago Press, 1974); Franz Boas, *Anthropology and Modern Life* (London: George Allen & Unwin, 1929). Regarding major works of Functionalism, see Radcliffe-Brown, *The Andaman Islanders*; Adam Kuper, ed., *The Social Anthropology of Radcliffe-Brown* (London: Routledge, 2004); Bronislaw Malinowski, *Crime and Custom in Savage Society* (New York: Harcourt, Brace & Company, 1926); Raymond Firth, ed., *Man and Culture: An Evaluation of the Work of Bronislaw Malinowski* (London: Routledge & Kegan Paul, 1957).
60. Cai Jiaqi 蔡家麒, "Shilun minzuxue tianye diaocha de lilun yu fangfa" 試論民族學田野調查的理論與方法, in *Minzu yanjiu wenji: Yunnan sheng minzu yanjiusuo jiansuo sanshi zhounian jinian* 民族研究文集——雲南民族研究所建所三十周年紀念, ed. Yunnansheng minzu yanjiusuo 雲南省民族研究所 (Kunming: Yunnan minzu chubanshe, 1987), 25–52.

important to pursue Shen's methods and theories; thus, I pay more attention to the stories of Lei and his family that Shen recorded. Although she often made comments that reflected her Westernized, educated elite's point of view, she was still trying to understand the Leis' lives and inner world, and make objective observations. In my opinion, she combined microscopic methods, individual visits, and observations, all of which were then being used in field investigations generally.

As stated, Shen Baoyuan said in her thesis that Professor Lin Yaohua taught her mathematical methods, but Lin himself did not say much about this in his book *Teaching Notes on Social Anthropology* (*Shehui renleixue jiangyi* 社會人類學講義), a comprehensive summary of his own lifetime's teaching and research. When he commented on the critical theory adherents (*piping pai* 批評派) in anthropology, he said, "As for methodologies of studies, applying statistics to analyze culture is not beneficial; using it to recover ethnic cultural history is too mechanical."[61] It seems Lin did not give much credit to this methodology. However, the theses written by Lin Yaohua's students repeatedly referred to the use of the theory under Professor Lin's supervision. For instance, in his thesis "A Rural Handicraft Family: A Report on the Du Family in Shiyangchang" (Yige nongcun shougongye de jiating: Shiyangchang Dujia shidi yanjiu baogao 一個農村手工業的家庭：石羊場杜家實地研究報告), Yang Shuyin 楊樹因 said that in the class on social systems during 1942 and 1943, Lin Yaohua "introduced this perspective to students," stressing the use of the comparative mathematical method to "examine the interaction between people using standardized units and predicting the future."[62] Although it requires more study to understand how much Lin Yaohua influenced his students in research methodology, it is clear that Lin set up student sojourns in rural areas so that they would better understand peasant lives. Shen was one of them, and she left valuable records from her field investigation.

Conclusion

This chapter uses Shen Baoyuan's rural investigations of 1945 as a starting point to examine how the academic and ideological trends at Yenching University influenced

---

61. Lin, *A Tentative Discussion of the Survival of the Concept of Rank in Contemporary Liangshan Yi Areas*, 25.
62. Yang Shuyin 楊樹因, "Yige nongcun shougongye de jiating: Shiyangchang Dujia shidi yanjiu baogao" 一個農村手工業的家庭：石羊場杜家實地研究報告 (thesis, Department of Sociology, Yenching University, 1944). Other theses written by Lin Yaohua's students who used this method include "A Study of Factory Workers: A Printing Factory in Chengdu," "The Lama Temple in Zagunao," and so on. See Zhao Li 趙麗 and Zhu Hu 朱滸, "Yanda shehui diaocha yu Zhongguo zaoqi shehuixue bentuhua shijian" 燕大社會調查與中國早期社會學本土化實踐, in *Jindai Zhongguo shehui yu minjian wenhua* 近代中國社會與民間文化, ed. Li Changli 張長莉 and Zuo Yuhe 左玉河 (Beijing: Shehuikexue wenxian chubanshe, 2007), 88–106.

her work. It also provides a window into early Chinese sociologists and anthropologists in their approach to rural communities, how intellectuals in the Republican era tried to solve rural problems, and how the introduction of Western sociology and anthropology influenced them as well. We are given access to an individual (Lei) and his family in a rural community that had little impact on the nation's struggles, but it connects them with prominent scholars who did have an intellectual impact on China. A place as small as Hope Township was linked to the larger Chinese society and to intellectual trends that also had links internationally.

The development of Chinese sociology and anthropology in the 1920s and 1930s made a workable picture of the world of Paoge possible. The rural investigations of the time became an important part of the Rural Reconstruction and Rural Education Movements. Shen Baoyuan, part of this larger academic work, made it clear that her motive was "to study a secret society and the family profile of one of its leaders" and that she wished it to be a "purely academic exploration of personal interest."[63] From the subjects of sociological and anthropological investigations during the time, this topic seems to be relatively quite difficult. Most fieldwork like this at the time concerned aspects such as industry, economy, life, and customs, in which the subjects were not sensitive to a certain social group or organization and much less concerned about any secret to be revealed. But, as she saw the role of the Paoge more clearly, things fundamentally changed in her project. Although the secret society was semi-public, it was still explicitly banned. Furthermore, they maintained stringent rules to protect secrets and to punish violators. Her study involved problems and dangers.

Of course, Shen doing this survey had an advantage: the site was close to Chengdu—unlike her adviser Lin Yaohua, who took three trips to Xiaoliangshan 小涼山 and Xikang 西康 during 1943 and 1945, experiencing long journeys, hardships, and even threats to his life.[64] It is a well-known tragic story that when Fei Xiaotong and his newly married bride Wang Tonghui 王同惠 went together to Yao Mountain (Dayaoshan 大瑤山), Guangxi Province, for their fieldwork in 1935, Wang disappeared forever.[65] Because of the short distance to the big city, Shen could keep frequent contact with the Lei family even after the summer fieldwork. Without such continuing exchanges with Shen, her investigation would have lacked breadth, especially since the events in the Lei family after the summer of 1945 would have been missing.

---

63. Shen, "Yige nongcun shetuan jiating," 6.
64. Lin, *A Tentative Discussion of the Survival of the Concept of Rank in Contemporary Liangshan Yi Areas*, 457–60.
65. Fei got caught in a tiger trap and Wang presumably died while traveling to get help for him. See Fei Xiaotong, *Liushang Yaoshan* 六上瑤山 (Beijing: Minzu University of China Press, 2006), 268–71; Arkush, *Fei Xiaotong and Sociology in Revolutionary China*, 66–67.

Shen acknowledged that she did not have a clear idea of what she would study before she arrived in Hope Township. Subsequently, however, she recognized the Paoge everywhere and found that they occupied the central place of local power This phenomenon caused her to gain an "interest in the study of such an organization and inspired her to take this opportunity to gather information about them," which would only eventually become the "real motivation for this thesis."[66] Apparently, to understand the rural society of the western Sichuan Plain in the 1940s, one simply had to examine the Paoge. Lei Mingyuan and Shen Baoyuan lived in two different worlds, but they did interact in the summer of 1945. The former was investigated and described, and the latter was the investigator and narrator of the former's story. Shen recorded the Lei family's stories as well. Ultimately, we view the Paoge and one of their families through the eyes of a Western-trained student in sociology who exhibited youthful thinking, youthful influences, and a bit of naivete.

Indeed, Shen's thesis is superficial and lacks in-depth analysis and extensive discussion. After all, it was done by an undergraduate student whose theories and methods were still relatively immature. However, its merits are in the data. To some extent, my aim is to continue her task. Although it has been many years since her work, I am surprised to find that today, our understanding of the Paoge is still lacking. Although historical accounts provide a great deal of cases of Paoge activity and presence, no other source brings us so close to them and their organization.[67] Her thesis perhaps was not solid, like what mature academic research would be, but this was due to her lack of ability to process the information more slowly and with deliberation about her methods. Larger events unfolded around Shen, making all that impossible. In the end, she seems more trustworthy because of this: we are not reading dressed-up or doubtful data.

Bibliography

Arkush, R. David. *Fei Xiaotong and Sociology in Revolutionary China*. Cambridge, MA: Council on East Asian Studies, 1981.
Boas, Franz, and George W. Stocking Jr. *A Franz Boas Reader: The Shaping of American Anthropology, 1883–1911*. Chicago: University of Chicago Press, 1974.
Boas, Franz. *Anthropology and Modern Life*. London: George Allen & Unwin, 1929.
Booth, Martin. *The Dragon Syndicates: The Global Phenomenon of the Triads*. New York: Carroll & Graf Publishers, 1999.
Bronislaw Malinowski. *Crime and Custom in Savage Society*. New York: Harcourt, Brace & Company, 1926.

---

66. Shen, "Yige nongcun shetuan jiating," 2.
67. Shen, "Yige nongcun shetuan jiating," 10.

Buck, John Lossing. *Chinese Farm Economy*. Chicago: University of Chicago Press, 1930. [The Chinese translation by Zhang Lüluan 張履鸞. *Zhongguo nongjia jingji* 中國農家經濟. Shanghai: Commercial Press, 1936.]

Buck, John Lossing. *Land Utilization in China*. Shanghai: University of Nanking, 1937.

Cai, Jiaqi 蔡家麒. 1987. "Shilun minzuxue tianye diaocha de lilun yu fangfa" 試論民族學田野調查的理論與方法 [Theories and methodologies of fieldwork in ethnology]. In *Minzu yanjiu wenji: Yunnansheng minzu yanjiusuo jiansuo sanshi zhounian jinian* 民族研究文集——雲南省民族研究所建所三十周年紀念 [An essay collection: The thirtieth anniversary of the establishment of the Institute of Minority Studies in Yunnan], edited by Yunnansheng minzu yanjiusuo 雲南省民族研究所, 22–52. Kunming: Yunnan minzu chubanshe, 1987.

Cai, Shaoqing 蔡少卿. *Zhongguo jindai huidang shi yanjiu* 中國近代黨史研究 [A study of Chinese secret societies]. Beijing: Zhonghua Book Company, 1987.

Cai, Shaoqing 蔡少卿. *Zhongguo mimi shehui* 中國秘密社會 [Chinese secret societies]. Hangzhou: Zhejiang renmin chubanshe, 1990.

Chen, Weizun 陳維尊. "Wujinde aisi shenshende huainian: Huiyi waizufu Shen Zurong xiansheng" 無盡的哀思深深的懷念：回憶外祖父沈祖榮先生 [Endless sadness and deep memory]. Sohu. Updated September 12, 2010, accessed July 2, 2014. http://zwf251.blog.sohu.com/.

Cheng, Bicheng 成必成. "Minguo xiangcun jiaoyu yundong jiqi dui nongcun jiaoyu gaige de qishi" 民國鄉村教育及其對農村教育改革的啟示 [The Rural Education Movement in Republican China and the inspirations of today's rural educational reforms]. *Teaching and administration* [*Jiaoxue yu guanli* 教學與管理], no. 2 (2014): 25–27.

Cheng, Huanwen 程煥文. "Shen Zurong guju xunli" 沈祖榮故居巡禮 [A note of visiting Shen Zurong's former residence]. *Documentation, Information & Knowledge* [*Tushu qingbao zhishi* 圖書情報知識], no. 6 (2007): 104–7.

Chengdu shi difangzhi bianzuan weiyuanhui 成都市地方志編纂委員會, ed. *Chengdu shizhi: Zongzhi* 成都市志・總志 [Gazetteer of Chengdu: General annual]. Chengdu: Chengdu shidai chubanshe, 2009.

Chesneaux, Jean, ed. *Popular Movements and Secret Societies in China 1840–1950*. Stanford: Stanford University Press, 1972.

Chesneaux, Jean. *Secret Societies in the Nineteenth and Twentieth Centuries*. Ann Arbor: University of Michigan Press, 1971.

Dai, Xuanzhi 戴玄之. *Zhongguo mimi zongjiao yu mimi huishe* 中國秘密宗教與秘密會社 [Chinese secret religions and secret societies]. Taipei: Commercial Press, 1990.

Davis, Fei-Ling. *Primitive Revolutionaries of China: A Study of Secret Societies in the Late Nineteenth Century*. Honolulu: University of Hawai'i Press, 1977.

Dittmer, C. G. "An Estimate of the Standard of Living in China." *Quarterly Journal of Economic* 33, (November 1918): 107–28.

Edwards, Dwight W. *Yenching University*. New York: United Board for Christian Higher Education in Asia, 1959.

Fan, Shaozeng 范紹增. "Huiyi wozai Sichuan paoge zhong de zuzhi shenghuo" 回憶我在四川袍哥中的組織生活 [A recall of my organizational life in Sichuan paoge]. In vol. 84 of

Wenshi ziliao xuanji 文史資料選輯 [Selections of historical sources], edited by Wenshi ziliao bianzuan weiyuanhui 文史資料編纂委員會, 148–60. Beijing: Wenshi chubanshe, 1982.

Fei, Hsiao-tung [Fei Xiaotung 費孝通]. *Peasant Life in China: A Field Study of Country Life in the Yangzi Valley*. New York: Oxford University Press, 1939.

Fei, Hsiao-tung. *From the Soil: The Foundations of Chinese Society*. Berkeley: University of California Press, 1992.

Fei, Hsiao-tung. "Fifty Years Investigation in the Yao Mountains." In *The Yao of South China: Recent International Studies*, edited by Jacques Lemoine and Chien Chiao, 17–36. Paris: Pangu, Éditions de l'A.F.E.Y., 1991.

Fei, Xiaotong [Fei, Hsiao-tung]. *Yunnan sancun* 雲南三村 [Three villages in Yunnan]. Tianjin: Tianjin renmin chubanshe, 1990.

Fei, Xiaotong [Fei, Hsiao-tung]. *Liushang Yaoshan* 六上瑤山 [Six trips to the Yao mountain]. Beijing: Minzu University of China Press, 2006.

Feng, Hefa 馮和法. *Nongcun shehuixue dagang* 農村社會學大綱 [Outlines of rural sociology]. Shanghai: Liming shuju, 1932.

Firth, Raymond, ed. *Man and Culture: An Evaluation of the Work of Bronislaw Malinowski*. London: Routledge & Kegan Paul, 1957.

Fong, Shiaw-Chian [Fang Xiaoqian 方孝謙]. "Fei Xiaotong's Theory of Rural Development and Its Application: A Critical Appraisal." *Issues and Studies* 33, no. 10 (October 1997): 20–43.

Gamble, Sidney D., and John Stewart Burgess. *Peking, a Social Survey*. New York: George H. Doran, 1921; reprinted by Leiden: Global Oriental, 2011.

Gu, Fu 顧復. *Nongcun shehuixue* 農村社會學 [Rural sociology]. Shanghai: Commercial Press, 1924.

Guan, Qun 冠群. "Chengdu de 'paoge'" 成都的袍哥 [Gowned Brothers in Chengdu]. *Zhoumo guancha* 周末觀察 3, no. 7 (1948): 14.

Han, Mingmo 韓明謨. "Zhongguo shehuixue diaocha fangfa he fangfalun fazhan de sange lichengbei" 中國社會學調查研究方法和方法論發展的三個里程碑 [Methodologies of Chinese sociology and three milestones in the development of methodologies]. *Journal of Peking University (Philosophy and Social Sciences)* [*Beijing daxue xuebao (shehui kexue ban)* 北京大學學報（社會科學版）], no. 4 (1997): 5–15.

Hayford, Charles Wishart. *To the People: James Yen and Village China*. New York: Columbia University Press, 1990.

He, Jianhua 何建華. "Yan Yangchu de pingjiao yundong jiqi xianzheng gaige shiyan" 晏陽初的平教運動及縣政改革實驗 [James Yen's common education movement and the experience of reforming county administration]. *Southeast Academic Research* [*Dongnan xueshu* 東南學術] no. 1 (2008): 61–68.

Hu, Hansheng 胡漢生. *Sichuan jindai shishi sankao* 四川近代史事三考 [Three chapters on modern Sichuan]. Chongqing: Chongqing chubanshe, 1988.

Keehn, Martha McKee, ed. *Y. C. James Yen's Thought on Mass Education and Rural Reconstruction: China and beyond: Selected Papers from an International Conference Held in Shijiazhuang, China, May 27–June 1, 1990.* New York: International Institute of Rural Reconstruction, 1993.

Kuper, Adam, ed. *The Social Anthropology of Radcliffe-Brown.* New York: Routledge, 2004.

Lei, Jieqiong 雷潔瓊 and Shui Shizheng 水世淨. "Yanjing daxue shehui fuwu gongzuo sanshi nian" 燕京大學社會服務工作三十年 [Thirty years of social service work at Yanching University]. In vol. 4 of *Yanda wenshi ziliao* 燕大文史資料 [Historical materials of Yenching University], ed. Yanda wenshi ziliao bianweihui 燕大文史資料編委會, 49–58. Beijing: Peking University Press, 1989.

Li, Anzhai 李安宅. *Meixue* 美學 [Aesthetics]. Shanghai: Shijie shuju, 1934.

Li, Anzhai 李安宅. *Yili yu liji zhi shehuixue de yanjiu* 儀禮與禮記之社會學的研究 [A sociological study of rituals and rites]. Shanghai: Commercial Press, 1935.

Li, Anzhai 李安宅. *Yiyixue* 意義學 [Significs]. Shanghai: Chongqing: Commercial Press, 1945.

Li, Fuhua 李富華, and Feng Zuozhe 馮佐哲. *Zhongguo minjian zongjiao shi* 中國民間宗教史 [History of popular religions]. Taipei: Wenchin Publishing, 1994.

Li, Jinghan 李景漢. *Beiping jiaowai zhi xiangcun jiating diaocha* 北平郊外之鄉村家庭調查 [A survey of rural families past Beiping's suburbs]. Shanghai: Commercial Press, 1929.

Li, Jinghan 李景漢, ed. *Dingxian shehui gaikuang diaocha* 定縣社會概況調查 [Investigation of the general situation of the society of Dingxian]. Beiping: Association to Promote Chinese Common Education [Zhonghua pingmin jiao cujin hui 中華平民教育促進會], 1933; reprint, 1986.

Li, Mufeng 李沐風. 1947. "Luetan Sichuan de 'paoge'" 略談四川的袍哥 [A brief chat on the Gowned Brothers in Sichuan]. *Chahua* 茶話, no. 12 (1947): 81–84.

Li, Weizhong 李偉中. "Zhishi fenzi 'xiaxiang' yu jindai Zhongguo xiangcun biange de kunjing: Dui 1930 niandai xianzheng jianshe shiyan de jiexi" 知識分子"下鄉"與近代中國鄉村變革的困境：對20世紀30年代縣政建設實驗的解析 [Intellectuals going to the countryside and the difficult situation of rural reform in modern China]. *Nankai Journal* [*Nankai xuebao* 南開學報], no. 1 (2009): 115–25.

Li, Zaiquan 李在全. "Guonan zhong de xiangcun shiye: Kangzhan shiqi Sichuan de xiangcun jianshe yundong-yi Pingjiao hui wei zhongxin de kaocha" 國難中的鄉村事業：抗戰時期四川的鄉村建設運動——以平教會為中心的考察 [Rural programs in the national crisis: the Rural Construction Movement during the War of Resistance against Japanese Seen from the Association for Populace Education]. *New Horizons from Tianfu* [*Tianfu xinlun* 天府新論], no. 2 (2006): 132–36.

Liao T'ai-ch'u [Liao Taichu 廖泰初]. "The Ko Lao Hui in Szechuan." *Pacific Affairs* 20, no. 2 (June 1947): 161–73.

Lin, Yaohua 林耀華. "Zongfa yu jiazu" 宗法與家族 [Laws of clans and families]. *Beiping chenbao: Shehui yanjiu* 北平晨報·社會研究, no. 79 (1935): 237–44.

Lin, Yaohua 林耀華. *Yixu zongzu de yanjiu* 義序宗族的研究 [A study of clans in Yixu]. Master's thesis, Department of Sociology, Yenching University, 1935; published by Sanlian shudian, 2000.

Lin, Yaohua 林耀華. *Jinchi* 金翅 [The golden wing], Translated by Song He 宋和. Taipei: Laureate Book, 1977.

Lin, Yaohua 林耀華. *Minzuxue yanjiu* 民族學研究 [Ethnology]. Beijing: Zhongguo shehuikexue chubanshe, 1985.
Lin, Yaohua 林耀華. *Jinyi: Zhongguo jiazu zhidu de shehuixue yanjiu* 金翼：中國家族制度的社會學研究 [The golden wing: A Sociological study of Chinese familism], translated by Zhuang Kongzhao 莊孔韶 and Lin Zongcheng 林宗成. Beijing: Sanlian shudian, 1989.
Lin, Yaohua 林耀華. *Minzuxue tonglun* 民族學通論 [Introduction to ethnology]. Beijing: China Minzhu University Press, 1997
Lin, Yaohua 林耀華. "Baizu" 拜祖 [Worshipping ancestors]. *Shehui wenti* 社會問題 [Social problems] no. 20 (1929/30): 302–24.
Lin, Yaohua 林耀華. *Shehui renleixue jiangyi* 社會人類學講義 [Teaching notes on social anthropology]. Xiamen: Lujiang chubanshe, 2003.
Lin, Yaohua 林耀華. "New China's Ethnology: Research and Prospects." In *Anthropology in China: Defining the Discipline*, edited by Gregory Eliyu Guldin, 141–61. Armonk: M. E. Sharpe, 1990.
Lin, Yaohua 林耀華. *The Golden Wing: A Sociological Study of Chinese Familism*. London: K. Paul, Trench, Trubner & Co., 1947.
Lin, Yaohua 林耀華. "A Tentative Discussion of the Survival of the Concept of Rank in Contemporary Liangshan Yi Areas." *Chinese Sociology and Anthropology* 36, no. 1 (Fall 2003): 46–62.
Liu, Chonglai 劉重來. "Minguo shiqi xiangcun jianshe yundong shulue" 民國時期鄉村建設運動述略 [A review of the Rural Construction Movement in Republican China]. *Chongqing Social Sciences* [*Chongqing shehui kexue* 重慶社會科學], no. 5 (2006): 74–85.
Liu, Chonglai 劉重來. *Zhongguo xibu xiangcun jianshe de xianqu zhe: Lu Zuofu yu minguo xiangcun jianshe yanjiu* 中國西部鄉村建設的先驅者：盧作孚與民國鄉村建設研究 [The pioneer of rural construction in West China: Lu Zuofu and rural reconstruction in Republican China]. Beijing: Remin chubanshe, 2007.
Lu, Xinyu 呂新雨. "Rural reconstruction, the nation-state and China's modernity problem: reflections on Liang Shuming's rural reconstruction theory and its practice," translated by Zhu Ping and Adrian Thieret. In *Culture and Social Transformations in Reform Era China*, edited by Tianyu Cao, Xueping Zhong, and Kebin Liao, 235–56. Leiden: Brill, 2010.
Lu, Zhenxiang 魯振祥. "Sanshi niandai xiangcun jianshe yundong de chubu kaocha" 三十年代鄉村建設運動的初步考察 [A study of the Rural Construction Movement]. *CASS Journal of Political Science* [*Zhengzhi xue yanjiu* 政治學研究] no. 4 (1987): 37–44.
Malone, C. B., and J. B. Tagler. *The Study of Chinese Rural Economy*. Peking: China International Famine Relief Commission, 1924.
McIsaac, Lee. "'Righteous Fraternities' and Honorable Men: Sworn Brotherhoods in Wartime Chongqing." *American Historical Review* 105, no. 5 (2000): 1641–55.
Ownby, David. *Brotherhoods and Secret Societies in Early and Mid-Qing China: The Formation of a Tradition*. Stanford: Stanford University Press, 1996.
Ownby, David, and Mary Somers Heidhues, eds. *"Secret Societies" Reconsidered: Perspectives on the Social History of Early Modern South China and Southeast Asia*. Armonk: M. E. Sharpe, 1993.

Pan, Naigu. "Vitality of Community Study in China: Professor Fei Xiaotong and Community Study." In *Home Bound: Studies in East Asian Society: Papers Presented at the Symposium in Honor of the Eightieth Birthday of Professor Fei Xiaotong*, edited Chie Nakane and Chien Chiao 33–43. Tokyo: Centre for East Asian Cultural Studies, 1992.

Park, Robert Ezra, and Ernest Burgess. *Introduction to the Science of Sociology*. Chicago: University of Chicago Press, 1921.

Park, Robert Ezra, R. D. McKenzie, and Ernest Burgess. *The City: Suggestions for the Study of Human Nature in the Urban Environment*. Chicago: University of Chicago Press, 1925.

Perry, Elizabeth J. "Managing Student Protest in Republican China: Yenching and St. John's Compared." *Frontiers of History in China* 8, no. 1 (March 2013): 3–31.

Qiao, Jian 喬健. "Meiguo lishi xuepai" 美國歷史學派 [School of American historical anthropology]. In vol. 1 of *Shehui wenhua renleixue jiangyangji* 社會文化人類學講演集 [A collection of lectures of social anthropology], edited by Zhou Xing 周星 and Wang Mingming 王銘銘, 137–56. Tianjin: Tianjin renmin chubanshe, 1996.

Qin, Heping 秦和平. "Ersanshi niandai yapian yu Sichuan chengzhen shuijuan guanxi zhi renshi" 二三十年代鴉片與四川城鎮稅捐關係之認識 [Opium and urban taxes in 1920s and 1930s Sichuan]. In vol. 19/20 of *Chengshi shi yanjiu* 城市與研究 [Series on urban history], 76–79. Tianjin: Tianjin shehui kexueyuan chubanshe, 2000.

Radcliffe-Brown, A. R. *The Andaman Islanders: A Study in Social Anthropology*. Cambridge: Cambridge University Press, 1922.

Radcliffe-Brown, A. R. *Social Organization of Australian Tribes*. Melbourne: Macmillan & Co., 1931.

Radcliffe-Brown, A. R. *The Andaman Islanders*. Cambridge: Cambridge University Press, 1933.

Shen, Baoyuan 沈寶媛. "Yige nongcun shetuan jiating" 一個農村社團家庭 [A family of rural secret society]. BA thesis, Department of Sociology, Yenching University, 1946.

Shi De 拾得. "Paoge zai Chongqing" 袍哥在重慶 [Gowned brothers in Chongqing]. *Jipu* 吉普, no. 13 (1946): 10–11.

Stapleton, Kristin. "Urban Politics in an Age of 'Secret Societies': The Cases of Shanghai and Chengdu." *Republican China* 22, no. 1 (November 1996): 23–64.

Stuart, J. Leighton. *Fifty Years in China*. New York: Random House, 1946.

Ter Haar, Barend J. *Ritual and Mythology of the Chinese Triads: Creating an Identity*. Leiden: E. J. Brill, 1998.

Thøgersen, Stig. "Revisiting a Dramatic Triangle: The State, Villagers, and Social Activists in Chinese Rural Reconstruction Projects." *Journal of Current Chinese Affairs* 38, no. 4 (2009): 9–33.

Wang, Chunwu 王純五. *Paoge tanmi* 袍哥探秘 [Exploring the secrets of Paoge]. Chengdu: Bashu shushe, 1993.

Wang, Jianchuan 王見川, and Jiang Zhushan 蔣竹山, eds. *Ming Qing yilai minjian zongjiao de tansuo: Jinian Dai Xuanzhi jiaoshou lunwenji* 明清以來民間宗教的探索——紀念戴玄之教授論文集 [Studies of popular religions since the Ming and Qing: An essay collection for commemoration of Dai Xuanzhi]. Taipei: Shinning Culture Publishing, 1996.

Wang, Jianmin 王建民. "Tianye minzuzhi yu Zhongguo renleixue de fazhan: Jinian Fei Xiaotong, Lin Yaohua xiansheng 100 zhounian danchen" 田野民族志與中國人類學的發展——紀念費孝通、林耀華先生100周年誕辰 [Field ethnography and development of Chinese anthropology]. *Journal of South-Central Minzu University (Humanities and Social Sciences)* [*Zhongyang minzu daxue xuebao (renwen shehuikexue ban)* 中央民族大學學報（人文科學版）], no. 6 (2010): 6–11.

Wang, Mingming 王銘銘. "Gongneng zhuyi yu Yingguo xiandai renleixue" 功能主義與英國現代人類學 [Functionalism and modern British anthropology]. In vol. 1 of *Shehui wenhua renleixue jiangyangji*, edited by Zhou Xing and Wang Mingming 108–36. Tianjin: Tianjin renmin chubanshe, 1996.

Wang, Xiaoting 王效挺, and Huang Wenyi 黃一文, eds. *Zhandou de licheng, 1925–1949.2, Yanjing Daxue dixiadang gaikuang* 戰鬥的歷程，1925–1949.2 燕京大學地下黨概況 [History of struggling, 1925–1949, underground activities of the CCP of the Yenching University]. Beijing: Peking University Press, 1993.

Wang, Di 王笛. *The Teahouse: Small Business, Everyday Culture, and Public Politics in Chengdu, 1900–1950*. Stanford: Stanford University Press, 2008.

Wang, Di 王笛. "Chi jiangcha: Chengdu chaguan, paoge yu difang zhengzhi kongjian" 吃講茶：成都茶館、袍哥與地方政治空間 [Drinking settlement tea: Teahouses, Gowned Brotherhood, and local political space in Chengdu]. *Journal of Historical Science* [*Shixue yuekan* 史學論刊], no. 2 (2010): 105–14.

West, Philip. *Yenching University and Sino-Western Relations, 1916–1952*. Cambridge, MA: Harvard University Press: 1976.

Wu, Wenzao 吳文藻. "Xiandai shequ shidi yanjiu de yiyi he gongyong" 現代地區實地研究的意義和功用 [Significances and functions of field work in modern community]. *Beiping chenbao: Shehui yanjiu*, no. 66 (December 26, 1934).

Wu, Wenzao 吳文藻. "Zhongguo shequ yanjiu de xiyang yingxiang yu guonei jinkuang 中國社區研究的西洋影響與國內近況 [Western influence of community studies in China]. *Beiping Chenbao: Shehui yanjiu zhoukan*, nos. 101–102 (January 9, 1935).

Wu, Wenzao 吳文藻. "Gongneng pai shehui renleixue de youlai yu xianzhuang" 功能派社會人類學的由來與現狀 [The Origin and current state of the social anthropology of Functionalist school]. *Minzuxue yanjiu jikan* 民族學研究集刊, no. 1 (1936).

Wu, Shugang, and Tong Binchang. "Liang Shuming's Rural Reconstruction Experiment and Its Relevance for Building the New Socialist Countryside." *Contemporary Chinese Thought* 40, no. 3 (Spring 2009): 39–51.

Xia, Yan 夏衍. *Fangcao tianya* 芳草天涯 [Fragrant grass at the edges of the sky]. Shanghai: Kai Ming Book, 1949.

Xingdao ribao 星島日報, January 30, 1950.

Xinhua ribao 新華日報, September 29, 1945.

Xu, Yongshun 徐雍舜. "Dongsansheng zhi yimin yu fanzui" 東三省之移民與犯罪 [Migrants and crimes in Northeastern China]. *Shehuixue jie* 社會學界, no. 5 (1931): 147–65.

Yan, Xinzhe 言心哲. *Nongcun shehuixue gailun* 農村社會學概論 [Introduction to rural sociology]. Shanghai: Chung Hwa Books, 1934.

Yang, Kaidao 楊開道. *Nongcun shehuixue* 農村社會學 [Rural sociology]. Shanghai: Shijie shuju, 1934.

Yang, Shuyin 楊樹因. "Yige nongcun shougongye de jiating: Shiyangchang Dujia shidi yanjiu baogao" 一個農村手工業的家庭：石羊場杜家實地研究報告 [A rural handcraft family: A research report on Tu family in Shiyangchang]. Thesis, Department of Sociology, Yenching University, 1944. Stored at the Library of Peking University.

Yanjing daxue Chengdu xiaoyou hui 燕京大學成都校友會. 2007. "Kangzhan shiqi qian Rong de Yanjing daxue" 抗戰時期遷蓉的燕京大學 [Chengdu campus of Yenching University during the War of Resistance against Japanese]. In *Chengdu wenshi ziliao xuanbian: kang Ri zhanzheng juan* 成都文史資料選編・抗日戰爭卷 [Selections of literature and historical material of Chengtu: The Volume of the Resistance War against Japan], edited by Chengdu shi zhengxie wenshi ziliao xuexi weiyuanhui 成都市政協文史學習股長會, 339–56. Chengdu: Sichuan renmin chubanshe, 2007.

Ye, Shengtao 葉聖陶. Volume 19 of *Ye Shengtao ji* 葉聖陶集 [A collection of Ye Shengtao's works]. Nanjing: Jiangsu jiaoyu chubanshe, 2004.

Yen-ching ta hsüeh, Shê hui hsüeh hsi [Department of Sociology, Yenching University]. *Ching Ho: A Sociological Analysis: The Report of a Preliminary Survey of the Town of Ching Ho, Hopei, North China 1930*. Beijing: Department of Sociology & Social Work, Yenching University, 1930.

Yu, Songqing 喻松青. *Minjian mimi zongjiao jingjuan yanjiu* 民間秘密宗教經卷研究 [Scriptures of folk secret religions]. Taipei: Linking Publishing, 1994.

Zhang, Haiyang 張海洋. "Lin Yaohua jiaoshou yu Zhongguo de shaoshu minzu he minzu yanjiu" 林耀華教授與中國的少數民族和民族研究 [Lin Yaohua and studies of Chinese minorities and ethnicities]. *Journal of Southwest Minzu University* [*Xinan minzu xueyuan xuebao* 西南民族學院學報] no. 1 (2001): 28–31.

Zhang, Huiying 張瑋瑛, Wang Baiqiang 王百強 et al., ed. *Yanjing daxue shigao* 燕京大學史稿 [History of Yenching University]. Beijing: China Renmin University Press, 1999.

Zhang, San 張三. "Chongqing de canyiyuan" 重慶的參議員 [Counselors of Chongqing]. *Xinguang* 星光, no. 3 (1946).

Zhao, Li 趙麗, and Zhu Hu 朱浒. "Yanda shehui diaocha yu Zhongguo zaoqi shehuixue bentuhua shijian" 燕大社會調查與中國早期社會學本土化實踐 [Social surveys of Yenchjing University and localization of early sociology in China]. in *Jindai Zhongguo shehui yu minjian wenhua* 近代中國社會與民間文化 [Modern Chinese society and folk culture], edited by Li Changli 張長莉 and Zuo Yuhe 左玉河, 88–106. Beijing: Shehuikexue wenxian chubanshe, 2007.

Zhao, Xudong 趙旭東. "Fei Xiaotong duiyu Zhongguo nongmin shenghuo de renshi yu wenhua zijue" 費孝通對於中國農民生活的認識與文化自覺 [Fei Xiaotong's understanding of peasants' lives and cultural consciousness]. *Journal of Social Sciences* [*Shehuikexue* 社會科學], no. 4 (2008): 54–60.

Zhao, Xudong 趙旭東. "Xiangcun chengwei wenti yu chengwei wenti de Zhongguo xiangcun yanjiu: Weirao 'Yan Yangchu moshi' de zhishi shehui xue fansi" 鄉村成為問題與成為問題的中國鄉村研究：圍繞"晏陽初"模式的知識社會學反思 [The rural area becoming a problem and the studies of rural China that has become a problem: An intellect revisit of James Yen's model]. *Social Science in China* [*Zhongguo shehui kexue* 中國社會科學], no. 3 (2008): 110–17.

Zheng, Dahua 鄭大華. *Minguo xiangcun jianshe yundong* 民國鄉村建設運動 [Rural construction movement in Republican China]. Beijing: Shehuikexue wenxian chubanshe, 2000.

Zhou, Yong 周勇, ed. *Xinan kangzhan shi* 西南抗戰史 [A history of the War of Resistance against Japanese in Southwest China]. Chongqing: Chongqing chubanshe, 2006.

Zhou, Yumin 周育民, and Shao Yong 邵雍. *Zhongguo banghui shi* 中國幫會史 [History of Chinese gangsters]. Shanghai: Shanghai renmin chubanshe, 1993.

Zhuang, Jifa 莊吉發. *Qingdai mimi huitang shi yanjiu* 清代秘密會黨史研究 [A history of secret society]. Taipei: Liberal Arts Press, 1994.

Part Four: The Legacies

10
Extracting the Essence of Sino-Western Interaction
Insights from the Educational Endeavors of Chinese Christian Colleges[1]

Ma Min

The term "Chinese Christian colleges" refers to the higher education institutions established by Western Christian churches in China since the late nineteenth century. Among them, thirteen colleges were set up by Protestant churches, while three of those were established by the Roman Catholic Church.[2] These Christian colleges were in the vanguard and significant components of modern Chinese higher education. They played an important role in disseminating knowledge of Western science and culture and facilitating Sino-Western cultural exchange and the modernization of China.

Given the important position of Christian colleges in Sino-Western cultural exchange, in the 1950s, Western historians began to research this topic. Since then, they have reaped fruitful results.[3] In Mainland of China, however, because of the

---

1. Earlier versions of this chapter were published in Chinese as "Zhong xi jiao rong, qu jing yong hong: Zhongguo jiaohui daxue banxue jingyan dui dangdai jiaoyu de qishi" 中西交融取精用宏—中國教會大學辦學經驗對當代教育的啟示, first published in *Huazhong shifan daxue xuebao (renwen shehui kexue ban)* 華中師範大學學報（人文社會科學版）60, 2 (2021): 112–20, and subsequently in Zhang Kaiyuan 章開沅, Ma Min 馬敏, and Elizabeth J. Perry, eds., *Huigu yu zhanwang: Zhongguo jiaohui daxue shi yanjiu sanshinian* 回顧與展望—中國教會大學史研究三十年 (Beijing: Zongjiao wenhua chubanshe, 2022), 13–29. Reused with permission.
2. Those thirteen Chinese Protestant colleges normally refer to Yenching University, University of Nanking, St. John's University, University of Shanghai, West China Union University, Shantung Christian University, Huachung University, Fukien Christian University, Hangchow University, Lingnan University, Ginling College, Hwa Nan College; the three Catholic universities are Aurora University, Fu Jen University of Peking, and Tsin Ku University.
3. The most prominent work among them is *China and the Christian Colleges, 1850–1950* written by Jessie G. Lutz (Ithaca & London: Cornell University Press, 1971). Its Chinese version was translated by Zeng Jusheng 曾鉅生 and published by Zhejiang Education Publishing House in 1988.

long-lasting influence of the leftist ideology, Chinese Christian colleges were simply considered the imperialist "weapons for invading China," "a fortress of reactionary ideologies," and a "cultural concession" in China. Consequently, very few scholars dared to touch this academic taboo. It was not until the early 1980s that, with the rise of "the new-generation emancipation movement," people got rid of the ideological shackles that were imposed on them and started to revisit and reassess the history of Chinese Christian colleges.

If we review Mainland of China's research progress on the history of Chinese Christian colleges over the past thirty years, we shall see that there has been a notable development in the field, and it keeps growing. Under the collaboration of scholars, both local and from abroad, especially the ones from the "three places across the Strait" (*liangan sandi* 兩岸三地), considerable academic achievement has been attained, and the study has become a new research branch. It is an anomaly in the academic history of China, since the "Reform and Opening-up" (*gaige kaifang* 改革開放). Zhang Kaiyuan 章開沅 described it this way: "In the late 1980s and early 1990s, despite the domestic and global upheavals, research on the history of Chinese Christian colleges was like a silently meandering stream. It was not tempestuous and spectacular. Yet, it continued to flow and unstoppably moved forward."[4]

However, compared with other areas of modern Chinese history, research on Chinese Christian colleges is still in its nascent stage. In-depth and comprehensive studies are still lacking. Although several quality scholarly works have been published since the 1990s, most of them are descriptive narratives of a college's history or case studies related to a particular period, institute, or individual. They lack a theoretical dimension and do not present a holistic understanding of that history. Frankly speaking, there is no academic work on par with the American scholar Jessie G. Lutz's *China and Christian Colleges* as comprehensive research on the Chinese Christian colleges. Other than that, historians, represented by Zhang Kaiyuan, remain the main group of scholars studying the history of Chinese Christian colleges. The involvement of scholars of education, sociology, and religious studies

---

There are other scholarly works such as the monographic series of the history of ten Protestant colleges (including Fukien Christian University, Ginling College, Hangchow University, St. John's University, Shantung Christian University, Hwa Nan College, Soochow University, Yenching University, Huachung University, and West China Union University) published by the United Board for Christian Higher Education in Asia in the 1950s; Charles H. Corbett's *Lingnan University: A Short History Based Primarily on the Records of the University's American Trustees* published in 1963; J. B. Hipps's *A History of The University of Shanghai* in 1964; Reuben Holden's *Yale-in-China: The Mainland 1901–1951* in 1964; Philip West's *Yenching University and Sino-Western Relations, 1916–1952* in 1976; and M.B. Bullock's *An American Transplant: The Rockefeller Foundation and Peking Union Medical College* in 1980.

4. Zhang Kaiyuan, "Xu" 序 [Preface], in *Zhongguo jiaohui daxueshi wenxian mulu* 中國教會大學文獻目錄 (Hong Kong: Chung Chi College, 1997).

is still limited. Until now, four book series on modern Chinese Christianity have been issued, but at the same time, only some twenty scholarly works directly related to Christian colleges were published. Compared with the rich historical value and myriad historical documents the Christian colleges possessed, the research is far from sufficient. It is a field that has not attracted enough attention from education studies, which should be considered a defect.

In short, thirty years have gone by, yet studies on the history of Chinese Christian colleges are still insufficient, and many aspects of the history have yet to be studied. Among all aspects, I think it is of paramount importance to remove the boundaries between contemporary and modern history. Reevaluating the experience of China's Christian colleges and the insights it gives to the country's current higher education development on talent cultivation is needed. By doing so, we can further propel the modernization of our higher education system. To achieve this aim, we must summarize the experience and characteristics of Chinese Christian colleges and make them applicable to our education reform and talent cultivation. As Zhang Kaiyuan said, "As this particular group of education institutions existed in China for more than half a century, scholars should pay extra attention to them and scrutinize their positive and negative social impacts as well as the historical lessons they give us. Otherwise, a comprehensive understanding of the history of modern Chinese education or even modern Chinese history can never be achieved."[5]

More specifically, scholars reckon the following features of Christian colleagues must be reflected on:

I. Distinctive and Quality Education

To accurately summarize the experience of Chinese Christian colleges, we must first determine their features in areas including educational aims, institution, organization, teaching staff, expenditure, curriculum, teaching methods, and regulations. A careful examination of these features is the only way to fairly and accurately judge the roles the Christian colleges played in the Sino-foreign cultural exchange and China's progress toward education modernization.

Compared to the public universities in the same period, the Christian colleges had fewer students and were smaller in scale. Nevertheless, thanks to the quality and characteristics of the education they offered, they were as competitive as the public universities. Again, Zhang Kaiyuan had an incisive argument: "Until 1949, there were only a dozen Christian colleges in China. Only 10 to 15 percent of college students studied there. However, it was the quality rather than the quantity that

---

5. Zhang Kaiyuan, "Xu" 序 [Preface], in *Zhongguo jiaohui daxueshi yanjiu congshu* 中國教會大學史研究叢書, ed. Zhang Kaiyuan and Ma Min (Zhuhai: Zhuhai chubanshe, 1999).

mattered. In that historical context, especially after the 1920s, the Christian colleges to a certain extent set up a model for education modernization in China. This was because these colleges more directly introduced the modern model of Western education [to China] in terms of institution, organization, planning, curriculum, teaching methods, and regulations, thus having a profound influence, both positively and negatively, on the realm of education and the society."[6]

Chinese Christian colleges possessed their own characteristics. They did not aim to have a large student population or a grand campus, or to cover every single subject. On the contrary; they valued uniqueness and innovativeness. For instance, major programs in agricultural economics and rural education were offered at the University of Nanking, journalism and social science at Yenching University, dentistry at West China Union University, library science in Boone Library College of Huachung University, comparative law in Soochow University, and business in St. John's University. These programs were highly reputed domestically and internationally at that time. Huachung University concluded its education characteristics as "small in scale," and "quality over quantity," and they paid particular emphasis to arts and humanities programs such as Chinese language and literature, history, English, economics, philosophy, religious study, and natural science programs such as biology, chemistry, and physics.

Chinese Christian colleges also played a significant role in contributing to the development of modern academic disciplines. Although they have disappeared for over fifty years, features of their academic discipline building (*xueke jianshe* 學科建設) still exist in Chinese universities that were restructured in the 1950s under the influence of discipline classification of Christian colleges, such as Peking University and Nanjing University, or those that inherited the campuses and institutions of Christian colleges like Central China Normal University.

Xiao Lang 肖朗 and Xiang Jianying 項建英 studied the education studies programs offered by Chinese Christian colleges, and they pointed out that the programs underwent a transformation process during which part-time pastor-teachers were replaced by professional lecturers, the courses became more and more practical and localized, and the teaching methods were more diversified and scientific.[7] Ying Fanggan 應方淦, on the other hand, thought that the Christian colleges in the late Qing period were not only a channel for introducing the Western academic degree system to China, but they also established a prototype for Chinese higher education

---

6. Zhang, "Xu," in *Zhongguo jiaohui daxueshi yanjiu congshu*.
7. Xiao Lang 肖朗 and Xiang Jianying 項建英, "Jindai jiaohui daxue jiaoyu xueke de jianli yu fazhan" 近代教會大學教育學科的建立與發展 [The establishment and development of education studies in modern Chinese Christian colleges], *Gaodeng jiaoyu yanjiu* 高等教育研究, no. 4 (2005): 84–89.

and propelled the development of the modern Chinese academic degree system.[8] In addition, according to Zhou Guping 周谷平 and Ying Fangang, the Christian colleges first introduced the Western academic degree system to China by registering with foreign governments or overseas universities so as to be entitled to confer degrees. As their teaching quality improved, they gradually expanded the variety and hierarchy of their degree programs. This facilitated the interaction between Sino-foreign higher education institutions and stimulated the birth and development of the academic degree system in China.[9] Wang Wei 王瑋 systematically elucidated the development process of science education in Chinese Christian colleges from 1901 to 1936. He considered that, influenced by the ideals of liberal education, the colleges adopted a scientific approach to education. The author divided the process into three periods: the period featuring single-discipline curricula, the period in which academic departments were established, and that in which faculties or professional schools were set up. He also discussed the engineering, medical, and agricultural education in Chinese Christian colleges in particular detail.[10]

Considered the best of all Chinese Christian colleges, Yenching University had the best development of its academic structure and the most profound academic influence. Therefore, most studies took Yenching University as the starting point to discuss the relationship between Chinese society and the Western academic disciplines that these colleges introduced to China. For instance, Tian Zhengping 田正平 and Liu Baoxiong 劉保兄 conducted a case study of the Sociology department of Yenching University, elucidating the department's transition process from an academic department with majority American teaching staff to one in which teaching staff were mostly Chinese. They proposed that those Chinese teaching staff had made a massive contribution to Sinicize sociology, as they were dedicated to developing Chinese sociological theories, training sociology scholars, and contributing to the development of Chinese society. The Chinese teaching staff also provided a valuable experience of academic discipline building.[11] Xiao Lang and Fei

---

8. Ying, Fanggan 應方淦 "Qingmo jiaohui daxue xuewei zhidu shuping" 清末教會大學學位制度述評 [An evaluation of the degree system of late Qing Christian colleges], *Gaodeng jiaoyu yanjiu*, no. 3 (2001): 94–96.
9. Zhou Guping 周谷平 and Ying Fanggan 應方淦, "Jindai Zhongguo jiaohui daxue de xuewei zhidu" 近代中國教會大學的學位制度 [The degree system of modern Chinese Christian colleges], *Journal of Zhejiang University (Humanities and Social Sciences)* 浙江大學學報（人文社會科學版）34, no.1 (2004): 13–21.
10. Wang Wei 王瑋, "Zhongguo jiaohui daxue kexue jiaoyu yanjiu (1901–1936)" 中國教會大學科學教育研究 (1901–1936) (PhD diss., Shanghai Jiao Tong University, 2008).
11. Tian Zhengping 田正平 and Liu Baoxiong 劉保兄, "Jiaohui daxue Zhongguo ji jiaoshi yu Zhongguo jindai daxue de xueke jianshe—yi Yanjing Daxue shehui xuexi wei gean" 教會大學中國籍教師與中國近代大學的學科建設——以燕京大學社會學系為個案, *Journal of Shaanxi Normal University (Philosophy and Social Sciences Edition)* 陝西師範大學學報（哲學社會科學版）36, no. 2 (2007): 99–103.

Yingxiao 費迎曉 thought that after Yenching University established the Department of Journalism in 1924, to adapt to the needs of society and self-development, the university transformed itself from producing "skillful and virtuous journalists" to nurturing "innovative leaders with the capability to reform." At the same time, corresponding adjustments in curriculum fostered a coordinated development of professional and liberal education.[12] By studying the cases of Soochow University, Yenching University, and Aurora University, Hou Qiang 侯強 pointed out that Christian colleges' legal education was independent of those in public and private universities in Republican China. During its birth and development, its distinctive characteristics were formed, which promoted the development of legal education in China.[13] Moreover, Zhang Yaguang 張亞光 and Li Yusha 李雨紗 systematically analyzed the classification and proportion of topics of Yenching University's undergraduate dissertations in economics written from 1924 to 1951 to illustrate the intellectual context of Yenching's economics.[14]

II. Internationalization and Sino-Western Integration

Internationalization was one of the most remarkable features of Chinese Christian colleges. Under the unsettling socio-political context of war-torn China, Christian colleges were able to stay energetic and maintain their academic growth. One important reason behind this is that they succeeded in establishing a multi-channel connection to the world, becoming a place where Chinese and Western cultures could meet and blend: "They formulated numerous open spaces within a relatively closed context. Moreover, compared to public universities, Chinese teachers and students in the Christian colleges had more opportunities to connect with Western culture and society. They also enjoyed more freedom, and they were more active in thought."[15]

---

12. Xiao Lang and Bi Yingxiao 費迎曉, "Yanjing Daxue xinwenxi rencai peiyang mubiao ji gaige shijian" 燕京大學新聞系人才培養目標及改革實踐 [The goals of talent cultivation and reform attempts of the Department of Journalism at Yenching University], *Gaodeng jiaoyu yanjiu*, no. 6 (2007): 92–97.
13. Hou Qiang 侯強, Minguo jiaohui daxue falu jiaoyu de shengzhang jiqi yingxiang—yi Dongwu Daxue, Yanjing Daxue he Zhendan Daxue wei zhongxin" 民國教會大學法律教育的生長及其影響—以東吳大學、燕京大學和震旦大學為中心 [The development and influence of Chinese Christian colleges' legal education in Republican China: A study of Soochow University, Yenching University, and Aurora University], *Ningxia Social Sciences* 寧夏社會科學 2012, no. 2 (2012): 14–17.
14. Zhang Yaguang 張亞光 and Li Yusha 李雨莎, "Yanjing Daxue de jingjixue jiaoyu yu yanjiu—yi xuewei lunwen wei wujian" 燕京大學的經濟學教育與研究—以學位論文為對象 (1924–1951) [The economics education and research in Yenching University: A study of undergraduate dissertations], *Economic Perspectives* 經濟學動態 no. 2 (2013): 148–53.
15. Zhang Kaiyuan, "Xu" 序 [Preface], in *Zhongxi wenhua yu jiaohui daxue* 中西文化與教會大學, ed. Zhang Kaiyuan and Arthur Waldron (Wuhan: Hubei Education Press, 1991), 1–4.

This openness, as opposed to cultural closedness, was the fundamental premise and the basis of internationalization. However, there was a process for creating such openness in every Christian college. Christian higher education in China in its nascent years aimed to train students for service in the missionary enterprise, and the denominational background of the colleges was apparent. Most of the students were second-generation Chinese Christians, and the openness and inclusiveness of the colleges was very limited. As the function of the Christian colleges shifted from evangelization-oriented to education-oriented in the 1920s, they became more secular and receptive. The trend of ecumenism and internationalization weakened their denominational slant. Take Huachung University in Wuhan as an example. During the early twentieth century, Boone University, one of its predecessors, could be considered a university privately run by the American Episcopal Church. More than 80 percent of its students were Christians, and they had a rigidly religious life. In the 1920s, Huachung University was established by uniting Boone University with other Christian colleges. The university had a multi-denominational background and was a truly internationalized higher education institution. The percentage of Christian students at Huachung University was lower than that of Boone University, and it was more open to students with different social backgrounds.[16] Huachung University had the following purpose: "to provide a college education of high standard, for the youth of China with a view to developing their character and intellectual capacity in its students, in order to that they may become loyal and useful citizens of China, and may be prepared to aid in building up and strengthening their respected communities along moral, intellectual and humanitarian lines," so as to fulfill "the general purposes had in mind" by its founders.[17]

The international characteristics of Chinese Christian colleges were shown not only in their "hard power," such as their board composition, financial sources, teaching staff, and use of English as their language of instruction, but also in their complementary, diverse, and open cultural atmosphere and educational environment arising from the "hard power." These multi-channel, multi-form international connections made the Christian colleges in China a melting pot of Chinese and Western cultures.

---

16. According to a survey conducted in 1950, the first batch of its post-liberation registered students amounted to 374. Around 220 of them were Christians, which accounted for 60 percent of this batch of registered students. It was the highest since the outbreak of the Second Sino-Japanese War. However, in the second half of 1950, the number dropped to 40 per cent. Meanwhile, there were thirty-six Christian teachers at the university, and they accounted for 58 per cent of the university's teaching staff.
17. "Constitution of the Board of Trustees, Known as the Board of Founders of Huachung College, Wuchang, China," Box 163, Folder 3053, United Board for Christian Higher Education in Asia Records (RG11), Special Collection, Yale Divinity School Library.

Before 1932, Chinese Christian colleges with different denominational backgrounds were only loosely connected. To better coordinate their educational goals, plans, and financial aid received from the West, in 1925 some Chinese Christian colleges set up the Permanent Committee for the Coordination and Promotion of the Christian Higher Education in China. However, it was not an active organization. In August 1927, representatives from churches in China met in Shanghai. In the meeting, John Leighton Stuart, president of Yenching University, suggested that a more formal coordinating body be established for Christian higher education in China. Thus, the Committee for Christian Colleges in China was founded in 1928. Although the committee's establishment facilitated cooperation among the Christian colleges, its membership did not include all Christian colleges in China, and it provided limited services to them. At the end of 1932, the Associated Boards for Christian Colleges in China, which was more representative and formally organized, was set up in New York. It had a permanent establishment and was made up of the boards of ten Christian colleges in China at its beginnings.[18] However, the Associated Boards was in nature a coordinating body with voluntary membership, and its influence and binding power over its member colleges was still very limited.

Around 1937, the Associated Boards proposed to set up a bigger and more united organization for Chinese Christian colleges. Therefore, the idea of a united board emerged. It was believed that the proposed "United Board" would have the following advantages: It could formulate a long-term procedure for effective correlation and unification of the Christian colleges in China, enable use of any disposable financial resources in the best interests of Christian higher education in China, enhance efficiency in administration and advocacy, reduce the number of meetings of board of trustees and committees to allow members to devote their time and energy to more important issues, and provide a sound basis for seeking broader cooperation and financial support.[19] On June 30, 1945, the Associated Boards held an annual meeting in New York and announced the establishment of the United Board for Christian Colleges in China (UBCCC).[20] It was a unified organization formed by thirteen Christian colleges in China and responsible for coordinating and directing the colleges' work. The United Board also provided the colleges with

---

18. They are Hangchow University, Fukien Christian University, Yenching University, Shantung Christian University, University of Nanking, Lingnan University, Huachung University, Soochow University, West China Union University and Ginling College.
19. *Zhongguo Jidujiao daxue xiaodong lianhehui huiyi beiwanglu* 中國基督教大學校董聯合會會議備忘錄 [Memorandum of Meeting of the Associated Boards for Christian Colleges in China], 1944, Archives of Central China Normal University.
20. The United Board for Christian Colleges in China was renamed the United Board for Christian Higher Education in Asia in 1955, and this name is still in use. For the history of the United Board, see William P. Fenn, *Ever New Horizons: The Story of the United Board for Christian Higher Education in Asia, 1922–1975* (North Newton: Mennonite Press, 1980).

recurrent financial support. To a certain extent, it could be regarded as the highest authority of the colleges. Its establishment marked the beginning of a new stage of organizational integration among the colleges.

Christian colleges in China also maintained close connections with some overseas universities. Their close relationship was exemplified by collaborations between Harvard University and Yenching University, Princeton University and Yenching University, Yale University and the Yale-in-China Association (now Yale-China Association), and Yale University and Huachung University. Some Chinese Christian colleges were even registered in foreign countries. Missionary educators generally modeled their Christian colleges in China on Western universities and adopted the standards of the latter to evaluate their own colleges. Therefore, the degrees awarded by these Christian colleges were usually recognized by foreign universities. According to the ratings of Chinese Christian colleges given by Yoshi Saburo Kuno of the University of California in 1928, the University of Nanking and the Yenching University after 1925 were given a class A or B rating. Their graduates might be permitted to enter graduate schools in the United States. Those receiving a class C rating were Huachung University, Ginling College, Lingnan University, University of Shanghai, St. John's University, and the College of Yale-in-China after 1926. Yenching University before 1925 and Shantung Christian University (Cheeloo University) were also categorized as class-C universities. Graduates of these class-C Christian colleges might be admitted to graduate schools in the United States, but they were required to take thirty extra undergraduate credits. Kuno thought that graduates of other unclassified Christian colleges in China could only be admitted as undergraduates in the United States. Some could be admitted as third- or fourth-year students and others as sophomores.[21]

The liberal educational goals and international connections of Christian colleges in China contributed to a unique cultural ambience. From the curriculum design, teaching methods, teacher-student relationship, campus cultures, and even library collections and extracurricular activities at these Christian colleges, we could see a cultural ambience different from that in their public and private counterparts.

The "reciprocal flow" of Chinese and Western cultures through Chinese Christian colleges is a focus of scholarly attention. It has been opined that the Christian colleges acted as a bridge between the two cultures; overall, the Sino-Western cultural integration as manifested by these colleges was not one-directional; it was a process of reciprocal and dynamic interactions. Chinese Christian colleges at first mainly learned from the experience of Western higher education institutions and adopted their modes of operation. However, after the Educational Rights Restoration Movement in the 1920s and 1930s, Chinese culture had a greater impact

---

21. Lutz, *China and the Christian Colleges, 1850–1950*, 202.

on these colleges, and thus the Sino-Western cultural integration in them intensified. Therefore, we should see not only the Western cultural influence on China but also the adaptation and accommodation of Western culture to Chinese culture.

While Chinese Christian colleges were vehicles of Christian culture and modern Western civilization, they were situated in a traditional Oriental cultural setting and ambience. Therefore, gradual localization and secularization were inevitable. Gao Shiliang 高時良 pointed out that Sino-Western cultural exchange in the colleges were intertwined with the infiltration of Christian doctrines, while Christianity was exploited as a tool of Western invasion of China in the past century. A specific, scientific analysis is needed to deal with this issue. The Christian culture brought to China by Western missionaries also went through a process of mutual infiltration with Chinese culture. The history of this socio-cultural phenomenon has shown that inclusiveness, which allowed both cultures to adopt the other's positive components while maintaining their own essence, could make Christian culture become part of China's traditional culture.[22]

A typical example of Sino-Western cultural integration in Chinese Christian colleges is that these colleges generally provided education in Sinology (*guoxue* 國學; "national studies") and conducted pertinent research. By doing so, a curriculum blending Chinese and Western learning was formed. This kind of curriculum included the following features:

- Chinese was the primary medium of instruction.
- Modern natural science in the West was the main content of the courses.
- Western social science and humanities were part of the curriculum.
- Confucian culture and traditional Chinese classical scholarship were also included.
- The curriculum made stronger connections between knowledge and real life, preparing students for the workplace.

Starting in the 1920s, to "better adapt to the situation of China and fulfill the local needs," Chinese Christian colleges expanded and reformed their Chinese departments. They also improved their Sinology courses. Some people even suggested that Chinese Christian colleges should "set up major programs in Chinese Philology, Philosophy, History and Sociology respectively."[23] All these changes

---

22. Gao Shiliang 高時良, "Quanmian pinggu Zhongguo jiaohui daxue de lishi zuoyong—jianlun ruhe duidai Jidujiao wenhua" 全面評估中國教會大學的歷史作用——兼論如何對待基督教文化 [A complete evaluation of the historical functions of Chinese Christian colleges, and a discussion on how to deal with Christian culture], in *Zhongxi wenhua yu jiaohui daxue*, 44–60.
23. Luo Bingsheng 羅炳生, "Jidujiao gaodeng jiaoyu zhi jinkuang ji dangqian de wenti" 基督教高等教育之近況及當前的問題 [The current situation of Christian higher education in China and its problems], *Zhonghua jidujiao jiaoyu jikan* 中華基督教教育季刊 2, no. 3 (1926): 21–31.

suggest that after the mid-1920s, Chinese Christian colleges generally valued Chinese intellectual thoughts, history, and culture.

In his study of the Harvard-Yenching Institute's role in Sino-American cultural exchange, Zhang Jiqian 張寄謙 pointed out that the institute made prominent contributions to the cultural exchange and became a model institution of Sino-Western cultural exchange. Under the sponsorship of the Harvard-Yenching Institute Fund, Yenching University recruited a group of scholars who had thorough knowledge of both China and the West. The university also nominated outstanding graduates to pursue doctoral study at Harvard University. After these students finished their doctoral studies, they would return to and teach at Yenching. As a result, Yenching's teaching staff would be strengthened. At the same time, the university fostered the studies of Chinese culture by publishing the semi-yearly *Yenching Journal of Chinese Studies* (*Yenching xuebao* 燕京學報), which published mainly scholarly articles in Chinese cultural studies. Meanwhile, Yenching University and the Harvard-Yenching Institute contributed considerably to Chinese cultural studies in America.[24] Some other scholars also looked into Sinology at Chinese Christian colleges. For example, Tao Feiya 陶飛亞 conducted research on the Sinological Institute of the Shantung Christian University.[25] In his study of Chen Yuan 陳垣 and Sinology at the Catholic University of Peking (Fujen University), He Jianming 何建明 held the opinion that education and research in Sinology featuring evidential scholarship (*kaozhengxue* 考證學) had been the university's educational focus since its establishment. Aimed at surpassing the achievements of overseas Sinologists, the university made remarkable achievements in its Sinological research and nurturing scholars of the field. It was one of the important research centers of Sinology in modern China.[26]

As Zhang Kaiyuan concluded, the "reciprocal cultural flow" in Chinese Christian colleges was also manifested by the fact that many long-serving Western teaching staff (including some missionaries) of Chinese Christian colleges were inevitably influenced by Chinese culture, absorbing its essence at different levels and bringing it back to their homelands. Therefore, to some Westerners, Chinese Christian colleges were a window to observe and understand Chinese culture and

---

24. Zhang Jiqian 張寄謙, "Hafo Yanjing Xueshe" 哈佛燕京學社 [The Harvard-Yenching Institute], in *Zhongxi wenhua yu jiaohui daxue*, ed. Zhang and Waldron, 138–63.
25. Tao Feiya 陶飛亞, "Qilu Guoxue Yanjiusuo he Hafo Yanjing Sueshe" 齊魯國學研究所和哈佛燕京學社 [The Sinological Institute of the Shantung Christian University and the Harvard-Yenching Institute] (paper presented at Shehui zhuanxing yu wenhua bianqian guoji xueshu yantaohui 社會轉型與文化變遷國際學術研討會, Central China Normal University, Wuhan, October 28–31, 1995).
26. He Jianming 何建明, "Tianzhujiao Furen Daxue zhi guoxue yu Chen Yuan" 天主教輔仁大學之國學與陳垣 [The Sinology and Chen Yuan in the Fu Jen Catholic University of Peking], in *Wenhua chuanbo yu jiaohui daxue* 文化傳播與教會大學, ed. Zhang Kaiyuan (Wuhan: Hubei Education Press, 1996), 233–65.

society. The reciprocal cultural flow between China and the West often went beyond political utility. For instance, missionary educators like Miner Searle Bates of the University of Nanking participated in the missionary and educational enterprises in China truly because of a passion for understanding Chinese culture and serving China. Thus, we should interpret this phenomenon of "reciprocal cultural flow" from the perspective of culturology.[27]

It is this kind of reciprocal cultural flow and the trend of "standing on the Chinese ground and keeping an eye on civilizations worldwide" that allowed Chinese Christian colleges to be energetic and demonstrate their vitality and momentum to develop.

III. High-Quality Teaching Staff and Talent Cultivation

In pursuit of quality in education, Chinese Christian colleges recruited high-quality teaching staff, so that talents could be nurtured there. High-quality teaching staff is key to a university's success. Chinese Christian colleges invested a lot in recruiting excellent teachers. Thus, their teaching staff often included top-notch Chinese and foreign scholars. These colleges had rigorous recruitment standards against which all candidates would be measured. A candidate's educational background, qualifications, personal conduct, teaching skills and academic standing were seriously considered. Careful consideration was also given to teaching staff members' duties, performance appraisal, and remuneration. These, together with institutionalized regulations, created good conditions for Chinese Christian colleges to attract high-quality teachers. Teaching staff at these colleges usually were better remunerated than those at the public universities.

Many foreign presidents and teachers in Chinese Christian colleges, such as John Leighton Stuart, Francis Pott, Joseph Beech, and Miner Searle Bates, were eminent figures. Living and positioning themselves where Chinese and Western cultures coexisted, they were often confused about their identities, being unclear about whether they were Americans, Britons, Canadians, or Chinese. They confronted cultural dissonance and challenges to self-identity. They experienced political turmoil and life crises. However, they had one thing in common: they were all dedicated to their work, loved their universities, and were passionate about Chinese culture. As missionaries and, at the same time, well-educated intellectuals and educators, they played a significant role in Sino-Western cultural exchange, contributed tremendously to the building of modern China, and became many students' unforgettable life and academic mentors.

---

27. Zhang, "Xu," in *Zhongxi wenhua yu jiaohui daxue.*

Many Chinese presidents and teachers at the Christian colleges were outstanding. Examples of eminent Chinese presidents of these colleges are Chen Yuan, Wu Yifang 吳貽芳, Zhong Rongguang 鍾榮光, Francis Wei (Wei Zhuomin 韋卓民), Lin Jingrun 林景潤, Yang Yongqing 楊永清, and Chen Yuguang 陳裕光. Distinguished Chinese scholars who taught at these colleges included Feng Youlan 馮友蘭, Gu Jiegang 顧頡剛, Yu Pingbo 俞平伯, Zhou Zuoren 周作人, Lao She 老舍, Zheng Zhenduo 鄭振鐸, and Zhang Dongsun 張東蓀. They were highly erudite, well-published scholars in their fields, and nurtured numerous outstanding students who made notable contributions to the development of science and culture in China.

To nurture outstanding students, in their nascent years, Chinese Christian colleges introduced ideals of humanities education that were often practiced in Western universities. Chinese Christian colleges valued a student's personal development and the formation of a student's reasonable knowledge structure. Thus, they designed a rather comprehensive curriculum. Yenching University, for instance, required students in social science to take at least one entry-level course in humanities and natural science each, and allowed them to take advanced courses in other disciplines as subsequent electives. Students in natural science were also required to take relevant courses in social science and humanities to expand the breadth of their knowledge. Well-known ideas of education nowadays such as "cross-fertilization between the arts and sciences" (*wenli shentou* 文理滲透), "cross-disciplinary studies of the arts and sciences" (*wenli jiaocha* 文理交叉), general education (*tongshi jiaoyu* 通識教育), and broad-based education (*dalei peiyang* 大類培養) were already practiced by the Christian colleges.

Chinese Christian colleges in general paid attention to an organic integration of teaching, research, and advocacy, as well as the cultivation of students' competence in social practice. Through such means as mock training, fieldwork, and social research, the colleges improved their students' practical skills and analytical abilities, nurtured their habits of making observations and analysis independently, and cultivated their creativity.

Thanks to their high-quality teaching staff and the aforementioned teaching practices, Chinese Christian colleges could nurture a large pool of talent actively engaged in different sectors of Chinese society. This is the greatest contribution the Christian colleges made to China's modernization.

If we say that education aims to nurture students, and students are "products" of universities, it is important to understand the growth and contributions of graduates from Chinese Christian colleges. However, a few individual cases do not speak for the whole picture. Only a large-scale quantitative analysis can provide objective evidence in this regard.

The Christian colleges nurtured a large pool of talent for modern China. By the time Japan launched its full-scale invasion of China in 1937, about 10,000 students had graduated from Chinese Christian colleges. Among them, more than 3,500 engaged in education, 500 in the medical field, almost 400 in agriculture and forestry, over 100 in engineering, and over 300 in the legal profession. Many graduates of the Christian colleges worked in the business and other social sectors. Over 1,100 graduates pursued further studies, while more than 300 of them chose to study abroad.[28] Well-known graduates of the Christian colleges like Bing Xin 冰心, Tao Xingzhi 陶行知, Wu Wenzao 吳文藻, Xu Dishan 許地山, Fei Xiaotong 費孝通, Huang Hua 黃華, Hou Renzhi 侯仁之, Yang Jiang 楊絳, Rong Yiren 榮毅仁, Qi Shounan 戚壽南, and Xie Jiasheng 謝家聲 were all prominent figures in their respective fields in modern China.

Tao Feiya and David Buck conducted quantitative analyses and surveys of the graduates of the medical college of Cheeloo University. They pointed out that around 700 students graduated from the college throughout its history. These students studied at the college because of the prospect of earning a living with a medical degree. However, from a social perspective, studying medicine reflected their desire to advocate for their country's development by alleviating people's suffering with the help of science. Although they received education in a Christian college, the revitalization of the Chinese nation weighed heavily in their decision to study there; religious factors, on the other hand, were rarely emphasized.[29]

Through a statistical analysis of graduates of Chinese Christian colleges, Li Xiangmin 李湘敏 and Xie Bizhen 謝必震 found that graduates of these colleges worked in church organizations, banks, post offices, hospitals, the commercial sector, and cultural and educational institutions, in which most of them served. Therefore, we can say that Chinese Christian colleges were an important source of talent for educational institutions and enriched the manpower in the education sector in modern China. Talent cultivation at the Christian colleges directly improved the quality of primary, secondary, tertiary, mass, and industrial education in China, as well as the impacts of education on the modernization of China.[30] Xu Yihua 徐以驊 agreed that the Christian colleges' graduates were brilliant and fast-growing. Except those who were "slaves of the West" embracing the Western world indiscriminately, most of the graduates aspired to serve their country. As the first enlightened ones,

---

28. Wang Zhongxin 王忠欣, *Jidujiao yu Zhongguo jindai jiaoyu* 基督教與中國近現代教育 [Christianity and modern education in China] (Wuhan: Hubei Education Press, 2000), 158.
29. David Buck and Tao Feiya, "Qilu Daxue yixueyuan biyesheng de lishi fenxi" 齊魯大學醫學院畢業生的歷史分析 [A historical analysis of graduates from Shantung Christian University, in *Zhongguo jiaohui daxueshi luncong* 中國教會大學史論叢, edited by Gu Kejia 顧學稼, Arthur Waldron and Wu Zonghua 伍宗華 (Chengdu: Chengdu keji daxue chubanshe), 250–67.
30. Li Xiangmin 李湘敏 and Xie Bizhen 謝必震, "Cong zhongguo jiaohui daxue de rencai peiyang kan qi lishi de keguan zuoyong" 從中國教會大學的人才培養看其歷史的客觀作用 [Looking into Chinese Christian colleges' historical functions through their talent cultivation], in *Zhongguo jiaohui daxueshi luncong*, ed. Gu, Waldron, and Wu, 120–31.

they had the spirit of "enlightening those who become enlightened later" (*xianjue juehou* 先覺覺後) promoted by Sun Yat-sen. These graduates are treasures of our country, past and present.[31]

How did the Christian colleges nurture so much brilliant talent? It is what we should reflect on by drawing on the educational experience delivered to students by the Christian colleges. Only by doing so can the so-called "Qian Xuesen's 錢學森 Question" be genuinely answered.

IV. Institutional Development and Building a Harmonious and Relaxed Campus Ambience

Chinese Christian colleges modeled themselves on Western universities. The Christian colleges attached importance to a modern management regime applicable to higher education institutions and established a highly efficient management regime. Their hierarchy consisted of various levels of organization such as faculties, academic departments, administrative units, committees, and councils. The hierarchy is clear, and every organization has its defined duties. The Christian colleges' administrative and teaching organizations were small but highly capable, operating in an efficient and orderly way and determined to avoid a situation in which they had too many staff members or operational obstructions. In terms of academic administration, the Christian colleges often adopted rigid grading and student management systems, having high drop-out rates. Take the University of Nanking as an example. About two hundred students were admitted every year. However, only about one hundred of them could graduate after four years of study. In other words, the drop-out rate there was 50 percent. The College of Medicine and Dentistry at West China Union University required that if pre-medical students failed any of the four compulsory subjects—chemistry, physics, biology, and English—they would be disqualified from studying medicine or dentistry. Hangchow University implemented a strict examination and grading system. If a student was absent from class for a certain number of hours, they were not allowed to take the examination of the course concerned and earn the credits. Also, the student's course grade was determined by the average marks of in-class assignments, the mid-term examination, and the final examination.[32] To guarantee the quality of its students, Huachung

---

31. Xu Yihua 徐以驊, "Jidujiao zaihua gaodeng jiaoyu chutan" 基督教在華高等教育初探 [A preliminary investigation of Christian higher education in China], *Fudan Journal (Social Sciences Edition)*, no. 5 (1986): 84–87.
32. Huang Xinxian 黃新憲, "Lun jiaohui daxue dui Zhongguo gaodeng jiaoyu zaoqi xiandaihua de cujin" 論教會大學對中國高等教育早期現代化的促進 [The facilitation of early educational modernization of China by the Christian colleges], in *Zhongguo jiaohui daxueshi luncong*, ed. Gu, Waldron, and Wu, 84–100.

University also implemented a strict examination system. In addition to rigorous entrance and exit examinations, students were required to sit rigorous examinations during their undergraduate studies. Before entering the third year of study, students were required to take an "intermediate examination" in general English, general Chinese, and two major subjects.[33] For instance, only 68 of the 153 students admitted between 1929 and 1932 passed the intermediate examination and were qualified to enter their third year. Twenty students repeated a year, while twenty-seven were knocked out. Also, thirty-eight dropped out of the university because they failed to take the make-up examination or for other reasons. In other words, only 44 percent of the students passed the intermediate examination, increasing to 57 percent if we include those who passed the examination after repeating a year.[34]

On the other hand, the Christian colleges adopted a liberal attitude toward religious beliefs, thoughts, and ideas, teacher-student relationships, and extracurricular activities. This attitude helped create a relaxed and harmonious campus ambience that fostered students' mental and intellectual development. Students in Chinese Christian colleges were usually actively engaged in extracurricular activities. For example, St. John's University had a Shakespeare society, military band, photography society, art society, singing club, and many other clubs and societies, as well as townsmen associations, to name a few. Furthermore, the Christian colleges attached importance to students' sports activities. Their sports teams were of high standing; some even won gold medals in local or overseas competitions, bringing glory to their Christian colleges.

The harmonious and relaxed ambience of the Christian colleges was also embodied in their tolerant and liberal approach to the relationship between education and politics. Zhang Kaiyuan mentioned more than once that compared to the teachers and students at public universities, those in the Christian colleges had more opportunities to have direct contact with Western culture and society; they had lively minds and enjoyed more freedom. At the same time, because they were more frequently exposed to political, religious, and racial prejudices held by foreigners, their nationalistic sentiments and revolutionary thoughts were more easily triggered. Therefore, not a few Christian college teachers and students actively participated in anti-imperialist, patriotic, and democratic revolutionary movements, and some Christian colleges even became important bastions of patriotic democratic movements.[35] Zhao Qing 趙清 also pointed out that some modern Chinese

---

33. Wei Chunguang 韋春光, *Wei Zhuomin jiaoyu sixiang yu shijian* 韋卓民教育思想與實踐 [The educational thoughts and practices of Francis Wei] (Wuhan: Central China University Press, 2014), 74.
34. Li Liangming 李良明, "Wei Zhuomin: jiechu jiaoyujia ji Kangde zhuanjia" 韋卓民：傑出教育家及康德專家 [Francis Wei: An outstanding educator and Kant scholar], *Jing bao* 晶報, September 30, 2008.
35. Zhang, "Xu," in *Zhongxi wenhua yu jiaohui daxue*.

intellectuals came from the Christian colleges. From the Western and New Learning disseminated by Western missionaries, these intellectuals learned the thoughts of the age of bourgeoisie revolutions; they called for a reform and a bourgeois revolution in China, where the Western path should be followed. Many of them became intellectual elites.[36]

The educational inclusiveness, freedom, and tolerance of Chinese Christian colleges were also revealed in their attitude to and practices of women's education. Many scholars noted that the Christian colleges were pioneers in women's tertiary education in modern China. Wang Qisheng 王奇生 thought that the Christian colleges initiated women's higher education in China. Whereas women's primary and secondary education offered by mission schools faded into insignificance owing to the rise of women's schools run by the Chinese, education at Christian women's colleges was still first-class of its kind, and these colleges continued to occupy a leading position in women's education in China, being an essential cradle of the first generation of Chinese women intellectuals. In the 1930s and '40s, the female students at the Christian colleges accounted for about 30 percent of female university students in China. They constituted a considerable proportion of advanced women intellectuals in China in an era where female graduates of Chinese universities were rare.[37] According to He Xiaoxia 何曉夏, the transformation of women's education in China from one governed by the traditional idea of "being a virtuous wife and good mother" to the modernized one was a profound social revolution. It was triggered by the social transformation of modern China, and Christian women's education greatly influenced it. With the emergence and development of Christian girls' primary schools, girls' high schools, and women's colleges, Chinese women threw off their family shackles and received school education. It was unprecedented in Chinese educational history and revolutionized traditional women's education. When women go to schools, they open a door to society.[38]

Most of the Christian colleges' buildings included both Chinese and Western architectural features. These buildings created a beautiful, harmonious education

---

36. Zhao Qing 趙清, "Cong fan 'kongjiao' yundong dao 'fei zongjiao da tongmeng' yundong—'wusi' qianhou zhishi fenzi fanzong jiaodao lu pouxi" 從反"孔教"運動到"非宗教大同盟"運動——"五四"前後知識份子反宗教道路剖析 [From the campaign opposing Confucianism as China's state religion to the campaign of the Great Anti-religion Alliance: an analysis of the anti-religion approaches of the intellectuals before and after the May Fourth Movement], in *Zhongxi wenhua yu jiaohui daxue*, 61–83.
37. Wang Qisheng 王奇生, "Jiaohui daxue yu Zhongguo zhishi nuxing de chengzhang" 教會大學與中國知識女性的成長 [The Christian colleges and the growth of Chinese women intellectuals], in *Wenhua chuanbo yu jiaohui daxue*, 175–280.
38. He Xiaoxia 何曉夏, "Jiaohui nuzi daxue yu Zhongguo nuzi jiaoyu de jindaihua" 教會女子大學與中國女子教育的近代化 [Christian women's colleges and the modernization of Chinese women's education], in *Zhongguo jiaohui daxueshi luncong*, 64–74.

environment where Chinese and Western cultures blended. According to Dong Li 董黎, who conducted an analysis of the architectural forms of some representative Christian college buildings, the Christian colleges were integral components of modern Sino-Western cultural exchange. They had a profound influence on modern Chinese education and a crucial role in the modernization of Chinese architecture. The formation of the architectural forms of the Christian colleges' buildings and the consequent revival of traditional and classical Chinese architecture constituted a unique example of the reciprocal flow between Chinese and Western cultures. Thanks to the architectural forms of Chinese Christian colleges, which broke through the long-standing idea of Chinese architecture that a building is constructed for practical use, for the first time, Chinese classical buildings were given a symbolic cultural meaning: they represented a national culture and an era. Regardless of the compliments to and criticism of the revival of traditional and classical Chinese architecture, buildings of Chinese Christian colleges, which featured a blend of Chinese and Western cultures and were scattered across China, remind us of the value and profound influence of the architectural forms of Chinese Christian colleges.[39]

Conclusion

Present-day Chinese higher education, which is now undergoing a difficult transition phase, can draw lessons from the educational endeavors of Chinese Christian colleges. It seems that to tackle the problems of the current Chinese higher education, such as favoring immediate benefits, lack of characteristics, serious bureaucratization, and low operation efficiency, as well as neglecting the importance of cultivating students' creativity and thus having difficulty nurturing outstanding innovative talents (i.e., Qian Xuesen's Question), we can somewhat find an answer or solution in the educational practices of the Christian colleges, which will thus enlighten us on how to implement a further educational reform in China, so that universities will operate according to fundamental academic values again and the country's tertiary education will be true to the essence of education.

It is true that the Christian colleges were not perfect. Throughout their history, to a certain extent, they had blind faith in the supremacy of Western culture and were gentrified. They also indulged in self-admiration and were detached from Chinese society. These issues were particularly obvious in their nascent years when

---

39. Dong Li 董黎, "Jiaohui daxue jianzhu—Zhongguo chuantong gudian jianzhu fuxing de qidian" 教會大學建築——中國傳統古典建築復興的起點 [Architecture of the Christian colleges—the starting point of the revival of traditional and classical Chinese architecture] in *Zhongguo jiaohui daxueshi luncong*, ed. Gu, Waldron, and Wu, 132–47.

they benefited from Western colonialism. We should have a clear understanding of them and look at them with a critical eye.

Nevertheless, as the old Chinese saying goes, "The stones of those hills may be made into grindstones." We must systematically summarize the merits and faults of the educational endeavors of Chinese Christian colleges, distinguishing the colleges' educational achievements, which was their primary function, from their religious and political functions, and also distinguishing the colleges' educational work from the invasion policies of Western colonialism in relation to China. In so doing, we will be able to evaluate Chinese Christian colleges' historical significance and functions on a more objective, scientific, and comprehensive ground. We must also learn from the essence of the educational endeavors of Chinese Christian colleges and their successful experience, applying them to the institution building of contemporary Chinese universities, so as to foster Chinese universities to move toward the goals of becoming "first-class universities" in the world and developing "first-class academic subjects."

Bibliography

Buck, David, and Tao Feiya 陶飛亞. "Qilu Daxue yixueyuan biyesheng de lishi fenxi" 齊魯大學醫學院畢業生的歷史分析 [A historical analysis of the graduates from Shantung Christian University]. In *Zhongguo jiaohui daxueshi luncong* 中國教會大學史論叢, edited by Gu Kejia 顧學稼, Arthur Waldron, and Wu Zonghua 伍宗華, 250–67. Chengdu: Chengdu keji daxue chubanshe, 1994.

Bullock, Mary Brown. *An American Transplant: The Rockefeller Foundation and Peking Union Medical College*. Berkeley: University of California, 1980.

Corbett, Hodge Charles. *Lingnan University: A Short History Based Primarily on the Records of the University's American Trustees*. New York: Trustees of Lingnan University, 1963.

Dong, Li 董黎. "Jiaohui daxue jianzhu—Zhongguo chuantong gudian jianzhu fuxing de qidian" 教會大學建築——中國傳統古典建築復興的起點 [Architecture of the Christian colleges—the starting point of the revival of traditional and classical Chinese architecture]. In *Zhongguo jiaohui daxueshi luncong*, edited by Gu Jiajie, Arthur Waldron, and Wu Zonghua, 132–47.

Fenn, William P. *Ever new horizons: the story of the United Board for Christian Higher Education in Asia, 1922–1975*. North Newton: Mennonite Press, 1980.

Gao, Shiliang 高時良. "Quanmian pinggu Zhongguo jiaohui daxue de lishi zuoyong—jianlun ruhe duidai jidujiao wenhua" 全面評估中國教會大學的歷史作用——兼論如何對待基督教文化 [A comprehensive evaluation of the historical functions of Chinese Christian colleges, and a discussion on how to deal with Christian culture]. In *Zhongxi wenhua yu jiaohui daxue* 中西文化與教會大學, edited by Zhang Kaiyuan 章開沅 and Arthur Waldron, 44–60. Wuhan: Hubei Education Press, 1991.

He, Jianming 何建明. "Tianzhujiao Furen Daxue zhi guoxue yu Chen Yuan" 天主教輔仁大學之國學與陳垣 [The Sinology and Chen Yuan in the Fu Jen Catholic University of

Peking]. In *Wenhua chuanbo yu jiaohui daxue* 文化傳播與教會大學, edited by Zhang Kaiyuan, 233–65. Wuhan: Hubei Education Press, 1996.

He, Xiaoxia 何曉夏. "Jiaohui nuzi daxue yu Zhongguo nuzi jiaoyu de jindaihua" 教會女子大學與中國女子教育的近代化 [Christian women's colleges and the modernization of Chinese women's education]. In *Zhongguo jiaohui daxueshi luncong*, edited by Gu Jiajie, Arthur Waldron, and Wu Zonghua, 64–74.

Hipps, John Burder. *A History of The University of Shanghai*. Shanghai: Board of Founders of the University of Shanghai, 1964.

Holden, Reuben. *Yale-in-China: The Mainland 1901–1951*. New Haven: The Yale in China Association, 1964.

Hou, Qiang 侯強. "Minguo jiaohui daxue falu jiaoyu de shengzhang jiqi yingxiang—yi Dongwu Daxue, Yanjing Daxue he Zhendan Daxue wei zhongxin" 民國教會大學法律教育的生長及其影響——以東吳大學、燕京大學和震旦大學為中心 [The development and influence of Chinese Christian colleges' legal education in Republican China: A study of Soochow University, Yenching University and Aurora University]. *Ningxia Social Sciences* 寧夏社會科學 2012, no. 2 (2012): 14–17.

Huang, Xinxian 黃新憲. "Lun jiaohui daxue dui Zhongguo gaodeng jiaoyu zaoqi xiandaihua de cujin" 論教會大學對中國高等教育早期現代化的促進 [The facilitation of early educational modernization of China by the Christian colleges]. In *Zhongguo jiaohui daxueshi luncong*, edited by Gu Jiajie, Arthur Waldron, and Wu Zonghua, 84–100.

Li, Liangming 李良明. "Wei Zhuomin: jiechu jiaoyujia ji Kangde zhuanjia" 韋卓民：傑出教育家及康德專家 [Francis Wei: An outstanding educator and Kant scholar]. *Jing bao* 晶報, September 30, 2008.

Li, Xiangmin 李湘敏, and Xie Bizhen 謝必震. "Cong Zhongguo jiaohui daxue de rencai peiyang kan qi lishi de keguan zuoyong" 從中國教會大學的人才培養看其歷史的客觀作用 [Looking into Chinese Christian colleges' objective historical functions through their talent cultivation]. In *Zhongguo jiaohui daxueshi luncong*, edited by Gu Jiajie, Arthur Waldron, and Wu Zonghua, 120–31.

Luo, Bingsheng 羅炳生 [Lobenstine, E. C.]. "Jidujiao gaodeng jiaoyu zhi jinkuang ji dangqian de wenti" 基督教高等教育之近況及當前的問題 [The current situation of Christian higher education in China and its problems]. *Zhonghua jidujiao jiaoyu jikan* 中華基督教教育季刊 2, no. 3 (1926): 21–31.

Lutz, Jessie G. *Zhongguo jiaohui daxueshi, 1850–1950* 中國教會大學史 1850–1950 [China and the Christian colleges, 1850–1950]. Translated by Zeng Jusheng 曾鉅生. Hangzhou: Zhejiang Education Publishing House, 1988.

Tao, Feiya. "Qilu Guoxue Yanjiusuo he Hafo Yanjing Xueshe" 齊魯國學研究所和哈佛燕京學社 [The Sinological Research Institute of Shantung Christian University and Harvard-Yenching Institute]. Paper presented at the Shehui zhuanxing yu wenhua bianqian guoji xueshu yantaohui 社會轉型與文化變遷國際學術研討會, Central China Normal University, Wuhan, October 28–31, 1995.

Tian, Zhengping 田正平, and Liu Baoxiong 劉保兄. "Jiaohui daxue Zhongguo ji jiaoshi yu Zhongguo jindai daxue de xueke jianshe – yi Yanjing Daxue shehui xuexi wei gean" 教會大學中國籍教師與中國近代大學的學科建設——以燕京大學社會學系為個案.

Journal of Shaanxi Normal University (Philosophy and Social Sciences Edition) 陝西師範大學學報（哲學社會科學版）36, no. 2 (2007): 99–103.

Wang, Qisheng 王奇生. "Jiaohui daxue yu Zhongguo zhishi nuxing de chengzhang" 教會大學與中國知識女性的成長 [The Christian colleges and the growth of Chinese women intellectuals]. In *Wenhua chuanbo yu jiaohui daxue*, edited by Zhang Kaiyuan, 175–280.

Wang, Wei 王瑋. "Zhongguo jiaohui daxue kexue jiaoyu yanjiu (1901–1936)" 中國教會大學科學教育研究 (1901–1936). PhD diss., Shanghai Jiao Tong University, 2008.

Wang, Zhongxin 王忠欣. *Jidujiao yu Zhongguo jindai jiaoyu* 基督教與中國近現代教育 [Christianity and modern education in China]. Wuhan: Hubei Education Press, 2000.

Wei, Chunguang 韋春光. *Wei Zhuomin jiaoyu sixiang yu shijian* 韋卓民教育思想與實踐 [The educational thoughts and practices of Francis Wei]. Wuhan: Central China University Press, 2014.

West, Philip. *Yenching University and Sino-Western Relations, 1916–1952*. Cambridge, MA, and London: Harvard University Press, 1976.

Xiao, Lang 肖朗, and Bi Yingxiao 費迎曉. "Yanjing Daxue xinwenxi rencai peiyang mubiao ji gaige shijian" 燕京大學新聞系人才培養目標及改革實踐 [The goals of talent cultivation and reform attempts of the Department of Journalism at Yenching University]. *Gaodeng jiaoyu yanjiu* 高等教育研究, no. 6 (2007): 92–97.

Xiao, Lang 肖朗, and Xiang Jianying 項建英. "Jindai jiaohui daxue jiaoyu xueke de jianli yu fazhan" 近代教會大學教育學科的建立與發展 [The establishment and development of education studies in modern Chinese Christian colleges], *Gaodeng jiaoyu yanjiu*, no. 4 (2005): 84–89.

Xu, Yihua 徐以驊. "Jidujiao zaihua gaodeng jiaoyu chutan" 基督教在華高等教育初探 [A preliminary investigation of Christian higher education in China]. *Fudan Journal (Social Sciences Edition)*, no. 5 (1986): 84–87.

Ying, Fanggan 應方淦. "Qingmo jiaohui daxue xuewei zhidu shuping" 清末教會大學學位制度述評 [An evaluation of the degree system of late Qing Christian colleges]. *Gaodeng jiaoyu yanjiu*, no. 3 (2001): 94–96.

Zhang, Jiqian 張寄謙. "Hafo Yanjing Xueshe" 哈佛燕京學社 [The Harvard-Yenching Institute]. In *Zhongxi wenhua yu jiaohui daxue*, edited by Zhang Kaiyuan and Arthur Waldron, 138–63.

Zhang, Kaiyuan 章開沅. "Xu" 序 [Preface]. In *Zhongguo jiaohui daxueshi wenxian mulu* 中國教會大學文獻目錄, edited by Ng Tze Ming [Wu Tszming 吳梓明] and Leung Yuen Sang [Liang Yuanseng 梁元生]. Hong Kong: Chung Chi College, 1997.

Zhang, Kaiyuan. "Xu" 序 [Preface]. In *Zhongguo jiaohui daxueshi yanjiu congshu* 中國教會大學史研究叢書, edited by Zhang Kaiyuan and Ma Min 馬敏. Zhuhai: Zhuhai chubanshe, 1999.

Zhang, Kaiyuan. "Xu" 序 [Preface]. In *Zhongxi wenhua yu jiaohui daxue*, edited by Zhang Kaiyuan and Arthur Waldron, 1–4.

Zhang, Yaguang 張亞光, and Li Yusha 李雨莎. "Yanjing Daxue de jingjixue jiaoyu yu yanjiu—yi xuewei lunwen wei wujian" 燕京大學的經濟學教育與研究—以學位論文為對象 (1924–1951) [The economics education and research in Yenching University:

A study of undergraduate dissertations (1924–1951)]. *Economic Perspectives* 經濟學動態 2013, no. 2 (2013): 148–53.

Zhao, Qing 趙清. "Cong fan 'kongjiao' yundong dao 'fei zongjiao da tongmeng' yundong – 'wusi' qianhou zhishi fenzi fanzong jiaodao lu pouxi" 從反"孔教"運動到"非宗教大同盟"運動——"五四"前後知識份子反宗教道路剖析 [From the campaign opposing Confucianism as China's state religion to the campaign of the Great Anti-religion Alliance: an analysis of the anti-religion approaches of the intellectuals before and after the May Fourth Movement]. In *Zhongxi wenhua yu jiaohui daxue*, 61–83.

Zhongguo jidujiao daxue xiaodong lianhehui huiyi beiwanglu 中國基督教大學校董聯合會會議備忘錄 [Memorandum of the Meeting of the United Board for Christian Colleges in China], 1944, Archives of Central China Normal University.

Zhou, Guping 周谷平 and Ying Fanggan 應方淦. "Jindai zhongguo jiaohui daxue de xuewei zhidu" 近代中國教會大學的學位制度 [The degree system of modern Chinese Christian colleges]. *Journal of Zhejiang University (Humanities and Social Sciences)* 浙江大學學報（人文社會科學版）34, no.1 (2004): 13–21.

11
A Competitive Advantage in Higher Education
The Practice and Realization of Whole-Person Education at Chung Yuan Christian University

Leah Yiya Lee

Background

> It was the best of times,
> it was the worst of times.
> —Charles Dickens, *A Tale of Two Cities*

For educators who hope to achieve the goal of whole-person education in Taiwan, there has been no better description of their situation than Charles Dickens's famous phrase in *A Tale of Two Cities*.

Backed by the government's calls to train more "high-tech talents," the number of universities in Taiwan has increased over the past 30 years by more than fourfold, from just over 30 to 160 in 2019.[1] Admission rates for college and university have been above 97 percent since 2008, and at one time even over 100 percent (more school openings than applicants). The Ministry of Education warned in 2017 that the number of college students is expected to drop by 40 percent between 2013 and 2028 because of Taiwan's low birth rate. No university in Taiwan can escape the impact of this crisis.[2] Then, how to maintain a sustainable higher education in Taiwan?

---

1. According to a website of the Ministry of Education, the total number of the higher education institutes in Taiwan up to October 15, 2019, is 160. See "A list of the higher education institutes in Taiwan," 111 Xueniandu dazhuan xiaoyuan yi lanbiao 111學年度大專院校一覽表, accessed March 29, 2020, https://ulist.moe.gov.tw/Browse/UniversityList.
2. According to statistics from the Ministry of the Interior's Department of Household Registration, there were 324,980, 227,447 and 166,473 babies born in 1997, 2003, and 2010 respectively. In

Every university in Taiwan strives to recruit students, strengthen its reputation, apply for more funding for teaching and research, and seek collaboration with business and industrial circles. Such strategies are quite common and popular. However, this chapter will examine another kind of university that promotes Christian values as an appeal to students and their parents. This chapter will discuss the case of Chung Yuan Christian University (hereafter CYCU), which has become one of the best private universities in Taiwan, surviving and gaining distinction, even in a world of secularization. It will also examine how CYCU arrived at its mission statement and educational philosophy and how it implements that mission statement through curriculum design, campus activities, and the Center for General Education.

The approach of this chapter is based on the concept of "contextualization," which originates in church studies and has been very popular among church scholars in the past several decades. Contextualization suggests a dynamic interaction between the message of the church and the context of a specific area.[3] In this chapter, we will see the interaction between CYCU's educational philosophy and strategies, which centered on whole-person education and the changing social context of Taiwan. The period this chapter covers is from the founding of the university in the mid-1950s to the early twenty-first century. Through a comparative and analytical examination of the CYCU's educational philosophy and strategies, we will not only be able to better understand the efforts and dedication of CYCU in modern Taiwan, but we can also reevaluate the strategy and direction of the holistic education for future higher education in Taiwan, as well as in other parts of the world.

CYCU Distinctions

Chung Yuan Christian University can be considered one of the best private universities in Taiwan. CYCU was awarded the largest funding available to private universities by the Ministry of Education from 2013 to 2019 and has received the largest funding granted from the Ministry of Education through its Teaching Excellence Project from 2014 to 2018. CYCU also ranked first among all of Taiwan's private

---

three years' time, many of the nation's colleges and universities will be facing a twelve-year-long "low birthrate cliff." Taiwan is now facing the impact of the first wave of declining birth rates. According to information from the Ministry of Education in 2017, more than 150 departments at Taiwanese universities have failed to recruit any students in the year of 2017. Even National Taiwan University could not escape from this problem. Seven graduate programs, including sociology, art history, ecology and evolutionary biology, registered no students in 2016.

3. According to a standard dictionary of theology, "Contextualization is a dynamic process of the church's reflection, in obedience to Christ and his mission in the world, on the interaction of the text as the word of God and the context as a specific human situation." See Sinclair B. Ferguson, David F. Wright, and J. I. Packer, eds., *New Dictionary of Theology* (Downers Grove, IL: InterVarsity Press, 1988), 164.

universities from 2011 to 2017 by the Center for World Universities Ranking. CYCU ranked first among all of Taiwan's private comprehensive universities when it comes to alumni earnings as indicated by 104 Job Bank in 2016, 2017, and 2018.[4] This shows that graduates of CYCU have been very competitive in the job market.

CYCU is not only one of the best private universities; it also outperforms many national universities. Generally speaking, national universities are in a good position to apply for funds from the government. Of around 160 universities in Taiwan, roughly 50 are national universities, and the rest are private universities. CYCU ranked first among private universities for government funding and ranked between eleventh to fifteenth among all national and private universities.

As stated before, more than 150 departments at Taiwanese universities failed to recruit any students in 2017. Despite being in such a difficult circumstance, the freshman registration at CYCU reached 97 percent of its enrollment goal that year. In the following year, the freshman enrollment climbed to 99.37 percent and came to 99.97 percent in 2019—both the highest enrollment in Taiwan.

In other words, no matter whether we evaluate the university based on its faculty, graduates, or campus, CYCU remains distinguished in Taiwan. This is related to its character as a Christian university famous for whole-person education.

The Changing Social Context of Taiwan

CYCU developed and defined its mission against a background of social and economic change. The story of CYCU starts with the outbreak of the Korean War and the growth of the Christian population in Taiwan. The outbreak of the Korean War on June 25, 1950, not only ushered the United States into a new relationship with Taiwan, but also brought about significant changes for the Christian churches in Taiwan. The United States' government first sent the Seventh Fleet to neutralize the conflict between the two sides of the Taiwan Strait, then resumed economic and military aid to the Nationalist government in 1951, and concluded the Mutual Defense Treaty between the United States and the Republic of China in December 1954.[5] Due to the security and stability of Taiwan, foreign missionaries, especially those from the United States, poured into Taiwan. Their arrival, their services, and their nurturance of local church people had a tremendous impact on every walk of Christian churches in Taiwan in the 1950s.

---

4. As for those figures, see "Incredible Enrollment Rate of the Chung Yuan Christian University 99.97%," Chung Yuan Christian University, accessed March 29, 2020, https://www1.cycu.edu.tw/news/detail?type=%e6%a0%a1%e5%9c%92%e8%8a%b1%e7%b5%ae&id=2285.
5. For a survey of Taiwan in this period, see Peter Wang Chen-main (Wang Chengmian 王成勉), "A Bastion Created, a Regime Reformed, an Economy Reengineered, 1949–1970," in *Taiwan: A New History*, ed. Murray A. Rubinstein (Armonk: M. E. Sharpe, 1999), 320–38.

The increase in the denominations in this period provides evidence to support this point. At the end of World War II, there were only four Churches in Taiwan—the Presbyterian Church, the True Jesus Church, the Taiwanese Holiness Church, and the Catholic Church.[6] Many other denominations hesitated to start their mission in Taiwan while the civil war was rampant in China. However, just a few years after the outbreak of the Korean War, the number of denominations soon reached thirty-three in 1954. "By 1968," according to a church scholar, "approximately 80 various missions and organizations were competing for space in Taiwan."[7] The number of foreign missionaries also increased from zero in 1945 to 300 in 1955, to close to 600 in 1960.[8]

Other factors also helped to draw missionaries to this field. First, when the door of evangelism was shut in China, mission boards and missionaries who were committed to preaching the Gospel to the Chinese found an island where thousands of Chinese people needed their service.[9] Most missionaries who came to Taiwan in the 1950s had had experience serving in China.[10]

The second factor for the influx of missionaries was that Taiwan at that time was an extremely understaffed mission field. In the year of 1948, there were only 51,000 Protestant-Catholic believers in a total population of 6,500,000.[11] Appeals for more missionaries were transmitted to the mission boards. Furthermore, more than a million mainlanders who retreated with the Nationalist government to Taiwan badly needed Mandarin-speaking missionaries. Requests to serve the mainlanders were especially appealing to those experienced missionaries who had a calling to serve the Chinese.

The third factor was the relatively harmonious relationship between the church and the state in Taiwan. In contrast to the religious persecution on the other side of the Taiwan Strait, Taiwan in the 1950s appeared to be a missionary heaven. In addition to Generalissimo and Madame Chiang Kai-shek, who professed their faith

---

6. Hollington K. Tong, *Christianity in Taiwan: A History* (Taipei: China Post, 1961), 84.
7. Allan J. Swanson, *Taiwan: Mainline versus Independent Church Growth: A Study in Contrasts* (Pasadena: William Carey Library, 1970), 88.
8. Tong, *Christianity in Taiwan*, 84.
9. Murray A. Rubinstein pointed out that many of those who went to Taiwan at this time belonged to politically conservative and anticommunist denominations. Murray A. Rubinstein, *The Protestant Community on Modern Taiwan: Mission, Seminary, and Church* (Armonk: M. E. Sharpe, 1991), 34.
10. At a missionary conference in Taiwan in July 1959, when "those who had previously labored in mainland China were asked to stand up, more than two-thirds of the 200 missionaries present rose." Tong, *Christianity in Taiwan*, 84.
11. Zha Shijie 查時傑, "Sishinianlai de Taiwan Jidujiaohui" 四十年來的台灣基督教會, In *Zhonghua mingguo shi zhuanti lunwenji* 中華民國史專題論文集, ed. Guoshiguan 國史館 (Taipei: Guoshiguan, 1992), 880 and 890.

in Christianity, quite a few high-ranking government officials were Christians.[12] Moreover, the Nationalist government adopted a favorable attitude toward missionaries in order to build friendships with and gain sympathy from the international community.[13]

The civil war in China (1945–1949) and the numerous upheavals in Taiwan, such as the tragic February 28 incident of 1947, gave people in Taiwan a feeling of uncertainty. Not only did more than a million mainlanders suffer from dislocation and uncertainty, but the people of Taiwan also faced disorienting changes. Thus, they became "fertile soil" for the Gospel because they needed help and guidance both materially and spiritually.

Under these favorable conditions, Christianity expanded quickly. In terms of both numbers of churches and believers, their growth in the 1950s was faster than at any other time. This phenomenon was true both for Protestants and Catholics. As pointed out by Allen J. Swanson, "Roman Catholics soared from 13,000 after World War II to 180,000 by 1960. The Protestant community shot up from about 37,000 after the war to over 200,000 in the same time period."[14] This church growth naturally included many Protestant denominations. For example, the Presbyterian churches jumped from 56,591 in 1952 to 86,064 in 1954 and to 179,916 in 1964.[15] As for the Southern Baptists in Taiwan, in 1949, there was only one Baptist church, and the total Chinese Baptist population stood at forty-six. In 1961, thirteen years later, church membership had increased many times over, and the total Baptist community was over 8,000, jumping from 2,195 in 1953, to 4,586 in 1956, to 8,165 in 1961.[16] The growth of the Taiwan Lutheran Church expanded from 791 members in 1953 to 1,884 in 1955, to 4,264 in 1959, and 4,952 in 1961.[17]

---

12. Yearbook Committee, *The Taiwan Christian Yearbook 1960: A Survey of the Christian Movement in Taiwan During 1959 With Special Attention to the Ten Years From 1949 to 1959* (Taipei: Taiwan Missionary Fellowship, 1960), 3.
13. Although quite a few Presbyterian leaders suffered during the February 28 Incident in 1947, the general secretary of the Presbyterian Church in Taiwan, Huang Wudong 黃武東, admitted that the church and the state had a rather harmonious relationship in the 1950s. Huang Wudong, *Huang Wudong huiyilu* 黃武東回憶錄 (Taipei: Qianwei chubanshe, 1988), 298.
14. Allan J. Swanson, *The Church in Taiwan: Profile 1980* (Pasadena: William Carey Library, 1981), 25.
15. The History Committee of the General Assembly of the Presbyterian Church in Taiwan, *Taiwan Jidu Zhanglao Jiaohui bainianshi* 台灣基督長老教會百年史 (Taipei: Presbyterian Church of Formosa Centennial Publications Committee, 1965), 351, 491–92.
16. Murray A. Rubinstein, 1983, "American Evangelicalism in the Chinese Environment: Southern Baptist Convention Missionaries in Taiwan, 1949–1981," *American Baptist Quarterly* 2, no. 3 (September 1983), 273–74.
17. Swanson, *Taiwan: Mainline versus Independent Church Growth*, 124. The Assemblies of God did not have similarly good results because of its strategy to start work simultaneously with Taiwanese, mainlanders, and mountain peoples. Their resources and strength were divided and thus they did not have the harvest other denominations did. See Swanson, *Taiwan: Mainline versus Independent Church Growth*, 115–21.

Before 1954, there were only four mid-size universities in Taiwan. Many high school graduates had no chance to pursue higher education. Christian circles and foreign missionaries were also aware of this situation and considered the vacancy would be a golden opportunity to launch Christian higher education in Taiwan. Three Christian universities were founded in 1954 and 1955, and CYCU was one of them.[18]

The Early Development of CYCU

CYCU was established in the 1950s, during the flourishing church growth and missionary activity in Taiwan. CYCU was a joint effort of three groups of people—foreign missionaries, Chinese Christians, and local gentries in Taoyuan 桃園. It seemed a perfect combination—foreign missionaries could help raise funds in the United States, Chinese Christians zealously offered their assistance ranging from paperwork to school administration, and the local gentry was happy to donate land because there was no university in such a broad area like Taoyuan.[19] As a result, Chung Yuan Christian College of Science and Engineering was born in 1955.

Sadly, conflicts arose once the college was founded. In the preparation period, the founders never contemplated how "Christian" the college would be, what kind of Christian education they would provide, and who had the final say in the administration if disagreements arose. They may have been too busy or too inexperienced to draft a mission statement and an educational philosophy for the college.

The first fight among the board of directors had to do with foreign missionaries' insistence on adopting a Bible college model with a compulsory Christian curriculum and Christian services. However, this practice conflicted with the government's regulations. Since the 1920s, the Nationalist government has set many educational rules and regulations. One of them was that religious courses and activities could not be compulsory. Therefore, Chinese Christians had to adopt an indirect approach to Christian education. However, Rev. James R. Graham, a co-founder of the college, deemed indirect evangelism unacceptable. He insisted that he could work something out for the college through his friendship with Chiang Kai-Shek and also through his powerful position with the American Military Advisory Group.[20]

---

18. These three Christian universities were Soochow University, Tunghai University, and Chung Yuan Christian University.
19. September 24, 1951, entry in the "Chang Ching-Yu Diaries," preserved in Chang Ching-Yu Memorial Library, Chung Yuan Christian University.
20. Li Yiya 李宜涯 (Leah Yiya Lee), "Kansi xunchang zui qijue, chengru rongyi que jianxin: Zhang Jingyu riji zhong youguan Zhongyuan Daxue chuangxiao shiliao de tantao" 看似尋常最奇崛，成如容易卻艱辛：張靜愚日記中有關中原大學創校史料的探討, in *Taiwan jiaohui shiliao lunji* 臺灣教會史料論集, ed. Peter Chen-main Wang (Taipei: Yuanliu, 2013), 280–81.

The second fight happened almost at the same time. According to the rules of the Ministry of Education, all faculty members must have a government-issued certificate. A faculty member's employment and promotion information must be submitted to the Ministry of Education by the college or university. Only then would the government issue a certificate to this faculty member. This procedure was considered quality control. However, Graham could not accept this certificate system and felt offended when his recommendation for someone's employment could not meet the standard of the government.

The relationship between Guo Keti 郭克悌, the Chinese president of the college, and Graham, the vice chairman of the board, went so badly that Graham told Chiang Kai-Shek that Guo was spreading communism on campus. Guo lost his job immediately. Then, Graham transferred the money he had raised in the United States to Taipei and founded Christ College in 1957, quitting his job with CYCU two years later.[21]

Since 1955, students from all four college departments had been crowded into one building. That building was everything to the college—classrooms, dorms, library, labs, chapel, restaurant, and kitchen. Perhaps the overcrowded space resulted in many staff and faculty members joining cliques and gossiping about each other. The withdrawal of the missionaries added a heavy blow to a college that was already in poor shape. Although the missionaries had never given any actual support, their promise to offer financial resources gave great hope to the impoverished college. Now the college found out what they had was only a false hope. Morale decreased, and the president's position stayed vacant for a year.

Turning Point

The turning point came when Han Wei 韓偉 (1928–1984) accepted the position of university president. Han was a tenured professor of physiology at the University of Pennsylvania. Through repeated contact and persuasion from the board, Han finally decided to become the college's president in 1970.[22] He dedicated himself to the college. One initiative he undertook was to repatriate Chinese scholars from the United States. The appeal to serve God as "missionary teachers" resonated with several accomplished scholars who were eager to collectively foster a Christian

---

21. Ruan Ruohe 阮若荷, *Zhongguo sin, xuanjiao qing: Jia Jiamei de yisheng* 中國心・宣教情：賈嘉美的一生 (Taipei: Christ College, 2001), 128.
22. Peter Chen-main Wang, "Taiwan Jidujiao daxue jiaoyu de jiantao—Yi Dongwu, Donghai, Zhongyuan sanxiao weili" 臺灣基督教大學教育的檢討――以東吳、東海、中原三校為例, *Fokuang Journal*, no. 1 (June 1996): 87.

campus.[23] Those scholars who responded to the call and relocated to Taiwan were not only exceptional professors but also became the cornerstone of the college. Their dedication, cooperation, and academic achievements eased the tension among faculty and staff. The college began to win academic recognition and achieved the university status in 1980.

Many of these scholars played important roles at the university and had been persistent in upholding the whole-person education on campus. For example, Han Wei served for four and a half years as the university president. Then, Ruan Danian 阮大年, another returned scholar, assumed the presidency when Han was assigned to establish a medical college by the government in 1975. Five years later, another team member of the missionary scholars, Yin Shihao 尹士豪, became the president when Ruan was appointed as the Vice Minister of Education. Xiong Shengan 熊慎幹 took a similar path when Yin was appointed to public service by the government. In this way, this group of dedicated scholars had been in the university presidency for more than twenty-five years. Together, they laid a solid foundation for the development of whole-person education at CYCU.

Another of their major contributions was to release a mission statement for CYCU in 1988. For many years, the majority of the faculty members did not share a common understanding of Christian education. It was not until 1987 that the administrators, under the presidency of Yin Shihao, made up their minds to form a ten-person committee to work out a mission statement and educational philosophy for CYCU.[24] The premise for the statement had to be clear, easy to understand, not filled with religious jargon, and in accordance with the basic values of the Christian faith. Furthermore, it must be connected with the local context.[25]

Through a year of effort, the committee finished the mission statement, as follows,

> Chung Yuan Christian University is founded on the spirit of Christian love for the world. With faith, hope, and love, we endeavor to promote higher education for the benefit of the Chinese people, aiming at the pursuit and advancement of genuine knowledge in order to maintain our cultural heritage and, thus, to serve humankind.[26]

---

23. Lin Zhiping 林治平, "Zhongyuan Daxue shishi quanren jiaoyu zhi linian yu shijian zhi yanjiu" 中原大學實施全人教育之理念與實踐之研究, in *Collected Essays on Chinese Christian Universities* 中國基督教大學論文集, ed. Lin Zhiping (Taipei: Cosmic Light, 1992), 356.
24. Wang Huangsan 王晃三, "Zhongyuan Daxue jiaoyu linian de zhiding, neihan yu shijian" 中原大學教育理念的制訂、內涵與實踐, in *Collected Essays on Chinese Christian Universities* 中國基督教大學論文集, ed. Lin Zhiping (Taipei: Cosmic Light, 1992), 260.
25. Wang, "Zhongyuan Daxue jiaoyu linian de zhiding, neihan yu shijian," 261.
26. Wang, "Zhongyuan Daxue jiaoyu linian de zhiding, neihan yu shijian," 264.

中原大學之建校，本基督愛世之忱，
以信、以望、以愛，致力於中國之高等教育，
旨在追求真知力行，以傳啟文化、服務人類。

This statement created a strong, vibrant identity for CYCU. The faculty now had a clear goal to pursue, while the students understood what kind of university and campus they had come to live and study.

Response to a New Challenge

Church growth around the 1950s was followed by a tide toward secularization. Benefiting from the protection of the mutual defense treaty with the United States and the Cold War confrontation, Taiwan concentrated on its domestic reforms and successfully transformed itself into an industrialized and modernized country in the two decades after 1960. Many socioeconomic symptoms of modern society appeared, and people in Taiwan did enjoy a much better life than before. Yet the Taiwan miracle, in one way or another, brought down the once-prosperous growth of the church.[27]

Because of its exceptional industrial infrastructure as well as the successful planning and execution of its export-oriented economic policy, Taiwan was touted as "the fastest-growing economy in the world" in the 1960s. According to a major handbook of Taiwan,

> Between 1960 and 1970, the average annual growth rate of gross national product (GNP) in Taiwan was 9.7 percent ... The growth of capital formation was more impressive. It rose from 20.1 percent of GNP in 1960 to 26.3 percent in 1970. The wealth of the people in Taiwan, as well as their confidence in their own economy, is also evident in the amount of domestic investment, of which 60 percent came from domestic savings in 1960 and 95 percent in 1970.[28]

The educational sector reflected the economic change. In 1950 there were 1,504 schools serving the needs of 1,054,927 students. By 1961, there were 3,095 schools and 2,540,665 students. The government expanded mandatory public education from six years to nine years in 1968, and school enrollment reached 4,130,671 students in 4,115 schools by 1971.[29] The proportion of primary school graduates who

---

27. Chen Liqin 陳麗琴, "Jidujiao Zhongyuan Daxue xiaoyuan fuyin shigong zhi yanjiu" 基督教中原大學校園福音事工之研究 (unpublished MA thesis, Chung Yuan University, 2003).
28. Wang, "A Bastion Created," 333.
29. Murray A. Rubinstein, "Taiwan's Socioeconomic Modernization, 1971–1996," in *Taiwan: A New History*, ed. Murry A. Rubinstein (Armonk: M. E. Sharpe, 1999), 377–78.

went on to junior high school jumped from 51 percent in 1961 to 80 percent in 1971.[30]

Many Christian schools lost their advantage when people had more choices in education. For example, when three Christian universities were established in 1954–1955, there were only four universities in Taiwan. However, Christian universities became not so popular when the number of higher education institutes reached twenty-five in 1976. With the swift growth in higher education in the 1990s, Christian values lost appeal among college students.

At that time in 1995, the economy of Taiwan had reached its peak, but higher education became secularized, and the concept of earning money dominated everything. Many college students (and probably also their parents) had a false belief of what was possible when they thought of college education. They wanted to acquire the most advanced and specialized knowledge so that they could find well-paying jobs and enjoy a good life. However, while their studies became more and more specialized, they lost a wider and deeper vision in life.

The administration of CYCU was alarmed by this trend and raised the ideal of "holistic education," which would help students cultivate "an integrated character." In response to cultural changes, CYCU reconsidered its mission statement and began to seek a new motto to define its distinctive educational philosophy. It eventually selected the phrase "Knowledge can be specialized, but life must be broad." This phase had its origin in the fortieth anniversary of the CYCU in 1995. And from that time on, CYCU began to use "holistic education" for its "whole-person education."

The guiding principle of this education is based on the "Four Balances." They are (1) the balance between specialty and general knowledge, (2) the balance between character-building and knowledge-building, (3) the balance between self and group, and (4) the balance between body, mind, and spirit.

Among the guiding principles of holistic education, the "balance between specialty and general knowledge" is particularly challenging. It seems to go against the common understanding of higher education, and few universities dare to do so. That is because most universities have blindly devoted all their energy to academic excellence at the expense of general knowledge, which shall be equally important for students and their future. However, CYCU is proud of reaching a balance on this point.

Holistic Education in the CYCU Curriculum

The key to CYCU's holistic education is to give a strong emphasis on General Education. The software of a Christian university is more important than its

---

30. Wang, "A Bastion Created," 333.

hardware—a phrase that is used quite often at CYCU. The Center for General Education plays an important role in offering a complete program to promote holistic education at CYCU. Each undergraduate is required to take thirty-four credits of General Education before graduation.

The Center for General Education is in charge of course design and its curriculum. This center currently offers 150 courses in 4 categories. Students need to take at least four to five courses in each category. These four categories are: *Tian* 天 (relationship between humankind and God), *Ren* 人 (relationship between humankind and society), *Wu* 物 (relationship between humankind and science), and *Wo* 我 (self-cultivation).[31]

The category of *Tian* tries to explore the meaning of life and the metaphysical thinking of value and judgment. It includes courses such as Philosophy of Religion, Philosophy of Life, Life and Faith, Seminar on Life and Death, and Seminar on the Mystery of Life.

The category of *Ren* tries to offer students an understanding of the interaction between humankind and society. Courses include Marriage and Family, Youth Voluntary Service and Social Participation, Investment Ethics, Industrial Engineer Ethics, Engineering and Law, and Leadership Theories and Skills.

The category of *Wu* emphasizes the relationship between humankind and science, and offers courses such as Psychology and You, Creative Thinking and Problem Solving, Science of Chinese Medicine, and Science and Environment.

The Category of *Wo* discusses an individual's life experience and gives courses such as Introduction to Art, Introduction to Music, Chinese Painting, Stress Management, Management and Life, and Health and Life.

To support so many courses, the Center for General Education has hired twenty full-time faculty members and more than eighty part-time teachers.[32] Furthermore, some faculty of other departments and institutes also reinforce this program with their related courses. With more than one hundred full-time and part-time professors, the Center for General Education is able to offer a great variety of courses for students to select at least four to five courses in each category above.

In addition to offering courses, the center has designed a series of cultural and artistic activities each semester to complement the curriculum. By doing so, students' passion will be aroused to explore the world so that they will not be limited

---

31. Li Yiya, "Tian Ren Wu Wo: Zhongyuan Daxue tongshi jiaoyu de linian yu shijian" 天人物我：中原大學通識教育的理念與實踐, in *Zhongyuan Daxue tongshi fengcai* 1 中原大學通識豐彩1, ed. Li Yiya (Zhongli: Zhongyuan daxue tongshi jiaoyu zhongxin, 2011), 7.
32. Peter Jen Der Pan (Pan Zhengde 潘正德), "Chung Yuan Christian University's Campus Ministry Model and Ministry Program: A Conceptualization and Implementation for Holistic Education," *Chung Yuan Journal* 29, no. 2 (2001): 175–81.

by certain academic professions or by local viewpoints. Music, drama, lectures, and other performances are sponsored on campus every week.

In order to facilitate the teaching and learning of these courses, there are many correlated programs offered by the Center for General Education. For example, in the category of *Tian*, the center offers three sets of board games for students to sharpen their thinking—(1) Independent thinking; (2) Morality and Law; (3) Human nature—Good or Bad? In the category of *Ren*, students can learn the inner feelings of human beings through the sharing of famous directors and players of opera and also through students playing different roles in drama (both traditional and modern). In the category of *Wu*, the most interesting programs are Tomorrow's Dinner Table and Repurposing Old Clothes. The former invites chefs to demonstrate how to turn "ugly" or excessive produce into delicious meals. Produce deemed ugly is usually discarded by grocery stores, and thus, food is wasted. Using those ingredients will not only be good for the earth but also give students an enjoyable and healthy meal. The other course (Repurposing Old Clothes) is to teach students to turn old clothes into various kinds of bags. The category of *Wo* has quite a few programs with guided tours to old buildings. The students will not only learn the local history through their observations, but also get training on how to rebuild and revitalize old buildings.[33]

The holistic education of CYCU is not bound by the campus; it connects Taiwan to the world. It can be illustrated by two examples of how students are encouraged to associate with society. The first one is Big Brothers and Sisters, and the second is Coastal Cleanup.

1. Big Brothers and Sisters. Campus bullying happens from time to time among students, especially in middle schools and high schools. To address this issue, student societies started anti-bullying campaigns by sending teams to local middle and high schools to teach the students how to protect themselves and how to deal with bullying activities.

2. Coastal Cleanup. Taiwan is an island embraced by a long seashore. Inevitably, coastal beaches have often been polluted by the garbage left by visitors or by marine debris washed up by waves. To cultivate a sense of caring for the ocean and environmental protection, CYCU has encouraged faculty and students for coastal cleanup activities. The seashore they have cleaned up starts from Guanyin 觀音 and Zhuwei 竹圍 of Taoyuan area to a small island (Xiaoliuqiu 小琉球 or Little Liuchiu) located

---

33. For the activities of the Center of General Education in these four categories in the academic year of 2019, see Tongshi jiaoyu zhongxin 通識教育中心, *Tongshi huodong xiangguan ziliao* 通識活動相關資料 (Zhongli: Zhongyuan daxue, 2019).

in the south-west of Taiwan.³⁴ In 2018, there were twenty-seven coastal cleanup operations from the CYCU.

The love and care of faculty and students is even extended to other countries, such as Cambodia, Burma, Vietnam, and the Solomon Islands. They have brought their knowledge in math, the English language, the use of computers, and others to the youth in remote villages in these countries. When they learned that students in a village in Cambodia did not even have raincoats for themselves and suffered a lot in long rainy seasons, the Department of Information Management of CYCU started a fundraising activity in 2018 for the purchase of raincoats for the village they served.³⁵ Another case was that a faculty member of the Department of Electrical Engineering of CYCU and his students helped install solar panels on the roof of a local library in El Salvador so that the library now has enough electric power to use at night.³⁶ When the students of CYCU returned from their service, they put in their reports that it was their most rewarding experience in college.

The college has been transformed and immersed in an atmosphere of arts and humanities, and students have plenty of opportunities to attend these events. The goal is that both the students and faculty will develop a more holistic nature and develop their understanding and appreciation for arts and humanities.³⁷ To quote a statement from the CYCU's educational philosophy,

> We believe that education has broader goals than merely exploring knowledge and improving technology. Education is also a process of building character and searching for the meaning of life and oneself.
> 我們認為教育不僅是探索知識與技能的途徑，也是塑造人格、追尋自我生命意義的過程。

With the courses and campus activities of the Center for General Education, CYCU hopes to cultivate students' interest in humanities and develop them into whole persons balanced in body, mind, and spirit.

---

34. A special report on their Coastal Cleanup at Xiaoliuqiu in 2017, see "CYCU students conducted public welfare activities during their holiday breaks" [Chinese], Chung Yuan Christian University, accessed March 29, 2020, https://www1.cycu.edu.tw/news/detail?type=%E6%A0%A1%E5%9C%92%E8%8A%B1%E7%B5%AE&id=270.
35. For their fundraising activity in 2018 for a village of Cambodia, see "Another Southbound—CYCU Sent Love to Cambodia" [Chinese], Chung Yuan Christian University, accessed March 29, 2020, https://www1.cycu.edu.tw/news/detail?type=%E6%A0%A1%E5%9C%92%E8%8A%B1%E7%B5%AE&id=1939.
36. For their activities in El Salvador, see "CYCU Students in El Salvador" [Chinese], Chung Yuan University, accessed March 29, 2020, https://wph.cycu.edu.tw/sl/woosa-woosa-%E8%96%A9%E4%B8%8Be%E5%9C%B0%E6%84%9B/ (site discontinued).
37. Li, "Tian Ren Wu Wo: Zhongyuan Daxue tongshi jiaoyu ti linian yu shijia," 7–8. See also Zhang Guangzheng 張光正, "Zhongyuan Daxue quanren jiaoyu ti linian yu naihan" 中原大學全人教育的理念與內涵", in *Zhongyuan Daxue tongshi fengcai 1*, 17–24; 27–32.

Concluding Remarks

In the time of the global village, competition between higher education institutes is no longer regional but international. To most, if not all, universities in Taiwan, the serious competition for incoming students has brought higher education into a dark season. Yet, looking from the bright side, universities with distinguished quality will be successful in attracting the attention and support of students and their parents. For CYCU, holistic education has become a key factor in its outstanding position in higher education in Taiwan.

Up to the twenty-first century, CYCU has successfully transformed itself to a modern university with due recognition from both Christian and secular circles. Its Christian principles are realized in the courses and activities of holistic education on campus. Both faculty and students share a consensus that CYCU is a place to offer a balanced education between character-building and knowledge-building. No wonder that CYCU was rated in 2017, 2018, and 2019 by the 1111 Job Bank as the most popular among all of Taiwan's private comprehensive universities in terms of alumni popularity among employers.[38]

Three points could be drawn from the experience of CYCU. First, contemporary higher education has been influenced by the secularization of modern society. Most universities are seen to blindly pursue academic excellence or to lead students to pursue a profitable career. But CYCU has succeeded based on a philosophy that education is to develop a balanced person—a whole person who keeps a balance between specialty and general knowledge. With this statement in mind, a strong, vibrant identity was created for CYCU's faculty and students.

Second, the human factor has played a crucial role in shaping the foundation of holistic education at CYCU. Dr. Han Wei's vision and persistence in the implementation of Christian education was the turning point for the stabilization of the university. Furthermore, his success in bringing a group of dedicated scholars who cherished the same ideals and collaborated with each other laid the foundation for a successful holistic education. Those faculty members were not only the mainstay of the university but also will carry on the mission in the future.

Third, the university endeavors to adopt a more flexible strategy in shaping a campus culture. The story of CYCU tells us that the Center for General Education

---

38. "2017 Qiye zuiai daxue diaocha" 2017企業最愛大學調查, 1111 Job Bank, downloaded on February 15, 2018, https://www.1111.com.tw/news/surveyns_con.asp?ano=100821; "2018 Guzhu zuimanyi daxue diaocha" 2018雇主最滿意大學調查, 1111 Job Bank, downloaded on July 23, 2019, https://hs.1111.com.tw/db/download/else/dfa62d62-0705-4034-8063-a0ea843f44c8.pdf. CYCU again won this title in the survey of 2019. See "2019 Qiye zuiai daxue diaocha" 2019 雇主最滿意大學調查, Chung Yuan University, accessed March 29, 2020, https://www1.cycu.edu.tw/news/detail?type=%e6%a0%a1%e5%9c%92%e8%8a%b1%e7%b5%ae&id=2285.

has a concerted plan for its course design and its curriculum. In addition to offering courses, the center has designed a series of cultural and artistic activities each semester to complement the curriculum. By doing so, both the students and faculty will develop a more holistic nature and cultivate their understanding and appreciation for arts and humanities.

These three points illustrated CYCU's efforts in whole-person education, which have helped it to gain a competitive advantage in higher education in Taiwan. The case of CYCU, though small, could serve as a reference for other universities that plan to realize their ideas of whole-person education in other regions. It also demonstrates that a university with whole-person education could not only survive in the modern world but keep its comparative advantage in the future.

Bibliography

"2017 Qiye zuiai daxue diaocha" 2017企業最愛大學調查. 1111 Job Bank, Downloaded on February 15, 2018. https://www.1111.com.tw/news/surveyns_con.asp?ano=100821.

"2018 Guzhu zuimanyi daxue diaocha" 2018雇主最滿意大學調查. 1111 Job Bank. Downloaded on July 23, 2019. https://hs.1111.com.tw/db/download/else/dfa62d62-0705-4034-8063-a0ea843f44c8.pdf.

"2019 Qiye zuiai daxue diaocha" 2019雇主最滿意大學調查. Chung Yuan University. Accessed March 29, 2020. https://www1.cycu.edu.tw/news/detail?type=%e6%a0%a1%e5%9c%92%e8%8a%b1%e7%b5%ae&id=2285.

"A list of the Higher Education Institutes in Taiwan." 111 Xueniandu dazhuan xiaoyuan yi lanbiao 111學年度大專院校一覽表. Accessed March 29, 2020. https://ulist.moe.gov.tw/Browse/UniversityList.

"Another Southbound—CYCU Sent Love to Cambodia." Chung Yuan Christian University. Accessed March 29, 2020. https://www1.cycu.edu.tw/news/detail?type=%E6%A0%A1%E5%9C%92%E8%8A%B1%E7%B5%AE&id=1939.

"Chang Ching-Yu riji 張靜愚日記." Preserved in Chang Ching-Yu Memorial Library, Chung Yuan Christian University.

Chen, Liqin 陳麗琴. "Jidujiao Zhongyuan daxue xiaoyuan fuyin shigong zhi yanjiu" 基督教中原大學校園福音事工之研究. Unpublished MA thesis, Chung Yuan University, 2003.

"CYCU Students Conducted Public Welfare Activities during Their Holiday Breaks." Chung Yuan Christian University. Accessed March 29, 2020. https://www1.cycu.edu.tw/news/detail?type=%E6%A0%A1%E5%9C%92%E8%8A%B1%E7%B5%AE&id=270

"CYCU Students in El Salvador." Chung Yuan University. Accessed March 29, 2020. https://wph.cycu.edu.tw/sl/woosa-woosa-%E8%96%A9%E4%B8%8Be%E5%9C%B0%E6%84%9B/ (site discontinued).

Ferguson, Sinclair B., David F. Wright and J. I. Packer, eds. *New Dictionary of Theology*. Downers Grove, IL: InterVarsity Press, 1988.

Huang, Wudong 黃武東. *Huang Wudong huiyilu* 黃武東回憶錄. Taipei: Qianwei chubanshe, 1988.

"Incredible Enrollment Rate of the Chung Yuan Christian University 99.97%." Chung Yuan Christian University. Accessed March 29, 2020. https://www1.cycu.edu.tw/news/detail?type=%e6%a0%a1%e5%9c%92%e8%8a%b1%e7%b5%ae&id=2285.

Li, Yiya 李宜涯 (Lee, Leah Yiya). "Kansi xunchang zui qijue, chengru rongyi que jianxin: Zhang Jingyu riji zhong youguan Zhongyuan Daxue chuangxiao shiliao de tantao" 看似尋常最奇崛，成如容易卻艱辛：張靜愚日記中有關中原大學創校史料的探討. In *Taiwan jiaohui shiliao lunji* 臺灣教會史料論集, edited by Peter Chen-main Wang, 265–89. Taipei: Yuanliu, 2013.

Li, Yiya 李宜涯 (Lee, Leah Yiya). "Tian Ren Wu Wo: Zhongyuan Daxue tongshi jiaoyu de linian yu shijian" 天人物我：中原大學通識教育的理念與實踐. In *Zhongyuan Daxue tongshi fengcai I* 中原大學通識豐彩1, edited by Li Yiya. Zhongli: Zhongyuan daxue tongshi jiaoyu zhongxin, 2011.

Lin, Zhiping 林治平. "Zhongyuan Daxue shishi quanren jiaoyu zhi linian yu shijian zhi yanjiu 中原大學實施全人教育之理念與實踐之研究." In *Collected Essays on Chinese Christian Universities* 中國基督教大學論文集, edited by Lin Zhiping. Taipei: Cosmic Light, 1992.

Pan, Peter Jen Der (Pan Zhengde 潘正德), "Chung Yuan Christian University's Campus Ministry Model and Ministry Program: A Conceptualization and Implementation for Holistic Education." *Chung Yuan Journal* 29, no. 2 (2001): 175–81.

Ruan, Ruohe 阮若荷. *Zhongguo sin, xuanjiao qing: Jia Jiamei de yisheng* 中國心‧宣教情：賈嘉美的一生. Taipei: Christ College, 2001.

Rubinstein, Murray A. "American Evangelicalism in the Chinese Environment: Southern Baptist Convention Missionaries in Taiwan, 1949–1981." *American Baptist Quarterly* 2, no. 3 (September 1983): 269–88.

Rubinstein, Murray A. "Taiwan's Socioeconomic Modernization, 1971–1996." In *Taiwan: A New History*, edited by Murray A. Rubinstein, 366–402. Armonk: M. E. Sharpe, 1999.

Rubinstein, Murray A. *The Protestant Community on Modern Taiwan: Mission, Seminary, and Church*. Armonk: M. E. Sharpe, 1991.

Swanson, Allen J. *Taiwan: Mainline versus Independent Church Growth: A Study in Contrasts*. Pasadena: William Carey Library, 1970.

Swanson, Allen J. *The Church in Taiwan: Profile 1980*. Pasadena: William Carey Library 1981.

The History Committee of The General Assembly of the Presbyterian Church in Taiwan. 1965. *Taiwan Jidu zhanglao jiaohui bainianshi* 台灣基督長老教會百年史. Taipei: Presbyterian Church of Formosa Centennial Publications Committee, 1965.

Tong, Hollington K. *Christianity in Taiwan: A History*. Taipei: China Post, 1961.

Tongshi jiaoyu zhongxin 通識教育中心. *Tongshi huodong xiangguan ziliao* 通識活動相關資料. Zhongli: Zhongyuan daxue, 2019.

Wang, Huangsan 王晃三. "Zhongyuan Daxue jiaoyu linian ti zhiding neihan yu shijian" 中原大學教育理念的制訂、內涵與實踐. In *Collected Essays on Chinese Christian Universities* 中國基督教大學論文集, edited by Lin Zhiping. Taipei: Cosmic Light, 1991.

Wang, Peter Chen-main (Wang Chenmain 王成勉). "A Bastion Created, A Regime Reformed, An Economy Reengineered, 1949–1970." In *Taiwan: A New History*, edited by Murray A. Rubinstein, 320–38. Armonk, NY: M. E. Sharpe, 1999.

Wang, Peter Chen-main (Wang Chenmain 王成勉). "Taiwan Jidujiao daxue jiaoyu de jiantao—Yi Dongwu, Donghai, Zhongyuan sanxiao weili" 臺灣基督教大學教育的檢討——以東吳、東海、中原三校為例. *Fokuang Journal*, no. 1 (June 1996): 79–86.

Yearbook Committee. *The Taiwan Christian Yearbook 1960: A Survey of the Christian Movement in Taiwan During 1959 With Special Attention to the Ten Years From 1949 to 1959*. Taipei: Taiwan Missionary Fellowship, 1960.

Zha, Shijie 查時傑. "Sishinianlai de Taiwan Jidujiaohui" 四十年來的台灣基督教會. In *Zhonghua mingguo shi zhuanti lunwenji* 中華民國史專題論文集, edited by Guoshiguan 國史館. Taipei: Guoshiguan, 1992.

Zhang, Guangzheng 張光正. "Zhongyuan Daxue quanren jiaoyu ti linian yu naihan" 中原大學全人教育的理念與內涵. In *Zhongyuan Daxue tongshi fengcai* 1 中原大學通識豐彩1, edited by Li Yiya. Zhongli: Zhongyuan daxue tongshi jiaoyu zhongxin, 2011.

12
Developing the Whole Person
Revisiting the History and Mission of Christian Higher Education in Asia

Wai Ching Angela Wong

Several missionary boards founded Christian colleges and universities in China since the late nineteenth century. In 1922, central coordination among the colleges was formalized, giving rise to the Associate Boards (1932) and the United Board for Christian Higher Education in China (1945).[1] When the United Board had to terminate its work in China in 1951, it left behind thirteen Christian colleges and universities in various Chinese cities. Today, the United Board, which has been renamed the United Board for Christian Higher Education in Asia, has expanded to work in sixteen countries/areas in Asia, reaching out to more than eighty higher education institutions. When the United Board adopted "Christian Presence" in its mission statement guiding its work through the 1990s and 2000s, it spelled out its commitment to the pursuit of "Christian values such as justice, reconciliation, and harmony between ethnic and religious communities, care for the environment, and civil society."[2] Considering the increasingly diverse Asian communities, the United Board decided to identify "whole person education" as an inclusive expression of the Christian values and heritage that have always underlined the United Board's work in the broader context. Since 2015, the United Board has adopted a new mission statement for its commitment "to education that develops the whole person—intellectually, spiritually and ethically."[3]

---

1. Cf. William P. Fenn, *Ever New Horizons: The Story of the United Board for Christian Higher Education in Asia, 1922–1975* (New York: The United Board for Christian Higher Education in Asia, 1980), 12–13.
2. United Board for Christian Higher Education in Asia, *Report of the United Board Christian Presence Task Force*, unpublished, 8.
3. See "Mission and Identity," United Board for Christian Higher Education in Asia, https://united-board.org/about-us/about-united-board/mission-vision/.

This sharpening of focus in the statement has happened over time. Earlier in 2011, institutional leaders met in the Asian University Leaders Program (AULP), one of the then United Board's flagship programs, for an intensive discussion on "Valuing Liberal Arts in Asian Higher Education." University and college heads gathered and reflected on the challenges facing higher education of the day and recommended actions to institutionalize whole-person education on campus. In 2012, the United Board supported an international conference on "General Education and University Curriculum Reform" held in Hong Kong. In-depth discussion took place around the need to broaden student learning from specialized studies to general education to cover cross-disciplinary learning, integrated studies, and critical and creative thinking. In the same year, the biennial conference of the Association of Christian Universities and Colleges in Asia (ACUCA) was held in Japan, taking up the theme of "Whole Person Education—Trends and Challenges." The United Board's staff and its institutional representatives attended the conference. They criticized, along with other university leaders, the trend of education going increasingly "specialized and compartmentalized, separating the head from heart, intelligence from spirituality, theory from practice, local knowledge from academic knowledge, skills from ethics."[4] They proposed that whole-person education, grounded in Christian values, would be the best way to ensure that students would learn and grow integrally.[5] A similar discussion was followed up by the Asian University Leaders Program (AULP) of 2013 on: "Whole Person Education: Practices, Challenges, and Prospects for Higher Education in Asia." This time a clear articulation of the relation between Christian presence and whole-person education was made:

> the concept of "Whole Person Education" captures the vision of the United Board to promote Christian presence in higher education in Asia. Christian presence in higher education is after all, about actualizing whole-person education—grounded in the belief that each person has been created in the image of God and deserves to grow as a whole person (physically, mentally, socially, and spiritually).[6]

Whole-person education has not only been seen as one of the best avenues to articulating Christian values but has also been regarded as the most thorough concept permeating and connecting all the program priorities and initiatives of the United Board.[7] The United Board's programs on peacebuilding, intercultural religious understanding, and gender equality have always been strong ambassadors of holistic education, bridging theories and action. The United Board's longstanding

---

4. United Board for Christian Higher Education in Asia, a concept paper for AULP 2013, unpublished, 1–2.
5. United Board, a concept paper, 2.
6. United Board, a concept paper, 1.
7. United Board, a concept paper, 1.

service-learning programs have emphasized precisely connecting the three Hs: head, heart, and hands. Through programs and grants, it supports higher education institutions to implement whole-person education through their leadership culture, faculty training, curriculum and pedagogy development, and campus community partnership projects to advance the United Board's mission of building a better society in Asia.

A. The Changing Context of Asia

Higher education in Asia has seen drastic changes over the past few decades. One of the most notable transformations has been the increasing departure from the "elitist" phase of higher education, in which less than 15 percent of the country's relevant age group is enrolled, to the "massification" phase enrolling 15–50 percent of a country's relevant age group. In some cases, such as South Korea, Japan, and Taiwan, they have either approached or reached the "universalization" phase by enrolling over 50 percent of their respective relevant age groups in higher education.[8] There is a significant improvement in education accessibility—at least in most of the urban cities of Asia.

1. Massification

Northeast Asia is one region that has experienced some of the most massive expansion in higher education. Over the past four decades, Korea's gross enrollment ratio for bachelor's programs alone has increased seven times, and Japan's and Hong Kong's have more than doubled. Although some institutions in Korea and Taiwan risk losing their revenue with the consistent decline in the population of the relevant age group, the Ministry of Education of China has recently announced its aim to raise the enrollment rate by 40 percent by the year 2020.[9] Inevitably, competitive demands between advancing research for ascendance in university ranking and investing resources for quality undergraduate education are a constant struggle in universities. In many cases, utilitarian purposes become the main driving force for institutional development.[10] The need for education for the whole person is more definitely felt than ever.

---

8. UNESCO Institute for Statistics, *Higher Education in Asia: Expanding Out, Expanding Up* (Montreal: UNESCO Institute for Statistics, 2014), 17–18.
9. UNESCO, *Higher Education in Asia*, 18.
10. Peach comments that the curricula are becoming more and more utilitarian and vocational, and appear highly influenced by market and consumerist ideologies. See S. J. Peach, "Understanding the Higher Education Curriculum in the 21st Century," *Critical Reflective Practice in Education* 3 (2012): 79–91.

Among many other cross-cutting issues, massification has demanded the most attention on the institutional level. Expansion of higher education implies escalating demand for instructional staff, resources for physical facilities, infrastructures, and sufficiently equipped classrooms, libraries, science, and computer labs, as well as the number and types of programs or courses for the much-diversified student body. In many countries, increased education access benefits are nearly offset by overstretching institutional capacities, low-quality maintenance, and sometimes mismatched talents and job markets. Diversification of educational models for the fast-changing economy, adaptability of graduates to an increasingly technological world, and standardization of quality assurance for the proliferation of tertiary institutions are just some of the urgent issues on the agenda.

In many developing countries, the expansion of higher education has primarily been made possible by the fast-growing number of private colleges and universities. In India, the number of higher education institutions increased to about 40,000 colleges and 600 universities in 2016.[11] Even though private institutions, aided and unaided, have taken up almost 70 percent of the total student enrollment, the government recently withdrew funding for private colleges.[12] In the Philippines, the Duterte government passed the Universal Access to Quality Tertiary Education Act (UAQTEA) for free education for government colleges and universities that began implemented in 2018.[13] Private colleges and universities, which accounted for 88 percent of all higher education institutions, enrolled about 46 percent of all tertiary students, and have been ranked on top in the country are left to compete for students with free state education.[14]

2. *Expansion versus quality*

As government investment increasingly concentrates on a handful of national universities, private universities and those lacking national fame face an even harsher

---

11. Numbers released in the Report of the Indian Ministry of Education in 2016.
12. Following the British model, higher education in India has incorporated the college system with the aided and unaided streams of autonomous and non-autonomous status. Each college is affiliated with a university for the award of undergraduate degrees. In 2017–2018, about 78 percent of them were private and yet enrolling together 67 percent of the total number of students. See Department of Human Resources Development, Government of India, *All India Survey on Higher Education 2017–18*, 2018, https://mhrd.gov.in/sites/upload_files/mhrd/files/statistics-new/AISHE201718.pdf.
13. See Ma. Teresa Montemayor, "Free College Education in Full Swing in 2018," *Philippine News Agency*, December 28, 2018, https://www.pna.gov.ph/articles/1057514, access date: September 15, 2019.
14. See Wilson Macha, Chris Mackie, and Jessica Magaziner, "Education in the Philippines," *World Education News + Reviews (WENR)*, March 6, 2018, https://wenr.wes.org/2018/03/education-in-the-philippines, access date: September 15, 2019.

battle. In 2017, the Indian government announced its plan to allocate $1.5 billion to make focus investments in ten public and ten private institutions over the next ten years. It means that the other over 650 tertiary institutions[15] in India could not expect any more support from the government and will have to survive on other means. The longstanding shortage of teaching staff due to insufficient facilities for postgraduate education and the lack of funding for staff replacement will hardly improve. Due to the general negligence of education development, India's quality of education has been adversely compromised by the domination of unregulated and profit-driven private colleges. It has contributed to an appallingly low rate of 30 percent employability among college graduates in 2014.[16] There are many universities in India. Still, scarcely twenty to thirty universities are considered to have faculty of high standing.[17]

Retaining high-quality leaders and faculty has become a challenge for Christian education institutions, which are primarily private. The quick turnover rate indicates a strong demand for new administrators and young faculty to be trained. The increasing pressure for institutions to become partially or fully self-financed has shifted the original focus of education on life to that of livelihood. An apparent gap exists between the knowledge that a faculty or leader ideally possesses and the actual knowledge they have. The leaders are generally uninformed about best practices in education management and governance. The faculty is mainly left on their own for trial-and-error in curriculum design, pedagogy, and skills in communicating with students.

Most central and state universities are supposed to be autonomous, but the government intervenes extensively in how they are run. Then comes the appointment of vice-chancellors, who are supposed to provide academic leadership and administrative skills. In one of its judgments, the Madras High Court stated that the heads of universities, the most visible symbols of the university system, are appointed not because they are distinguished academicians but because they have the right political connections in the Ministry of Human Resource Development. In the case of central universities or relevant political or caste affiliations in the concerned state—in many cases, they pay massive amounts of money with rates varying from one crore to three crores [INR10 million to INR30 million or US$140,000 to US$421,000] in some states."[18]

---

15. Listed on the website of the Department of Higher Education, Ministry of Human Resource Development, Government of India at http://mhrd.gov.in/university-and-higher-education, access date: April 10, 2018.
16. National Skills Report 2014, listed on the website of the Department of Higher Education above.
17. Mukhtar Ahmad, "What Is Wrong with the Indian Higher Education System?" *University World News*, February 8, 2019, https://www.universityworldnews.com/post.php?story=20190129125036113.
18. Ahmad, "What Is Wrong with the Indian Higher Education System?"

Moreover, an estimated 40 percent of college teachers work on a non-permanent, ad hoc basis and are designated variously as temporary, contractual, ad hoc, and guest faculty. It is a serious problem as people with a good academic record do not want to take such positions, which are less attractive than permanent positions. Even long-serving faculties are pressured to produce a certain number of papers to seek promotion, and thus they often publish papers in journals that may not be of high quality. It also means there is more emphasis on publishing papers than teaching.

Southeast Asia has twelve countries, ten of which are full-fledged members of the Association of Southeast Asian Nations (ASEAN).[19] The region reflects a wide range of diversity within and between the member countries in every aspect, from geography, politics, culture, and economy to language. The establishment of the ASEAN Community on December 31, 2015, aims to transform the ASEAN into an integrated region, triggering a host of reforms including education. The pressure to improve the quality of higher education has pushed the universities into a race for rankings. In Indonesia, the pressure has been worst for the arts and humanities since the government mandated that only new courses in the STEM (science, technology, engineering, and mathematics) fields will be introduced.[20] The Philippines had its share of pressure when it had to effect an educational reform requiring a shift from K–10 to K–12.[21] Of the four priorities in the ASEAN Work Plan on education, the United Board is well positioned to work on the following three: 1) raising the quality of education—performance standards; 2) lifelong learning and professional development; and 3) cross-border mobility and internationalization of education.

3. *The politicization of higher education*

The last two decades have seen some of the most intensive national investments in higher education in some Asian countries, generating both excellent and ambiguous results. Public investment has paid off in the multiplication of world-class universities in several Asian countries in a short time.[22] Yet it has also been translated into

---

19. They include five founding members from 1967: Indonesia, Malaysia, Philippines, Singapore, and Thailand and five later additions: Brunei, Vietnam, Laos, Myanmar, and Cambodia. Two countries, Papua New Guinea and Timor Leste, are on observer status.
20. Information shared in the keynote of BKPTKI 2017 by a representative of the Ministry of Education. BKPTKI is the Indonesian abbreviation for the Association of Christian Universities and Colleges in Indonesia.
21. Roger Chao Jr., "A Shift towards Good Quality Higher Education for All," *University World News*, February 9, 2018, http://www.universityworldnews.com/article.php?story=20180228175510534.
22. In 2015–2016, national funding to Tsinghua University and Peking University—two of the top five Asian universities—were nearly $3.6 billion and $2.5 billion respectively. Nanyang Technological University, established only in 1991, has emerged as a top university in Asia in a short time also

universities' tighter adherence to state agendas for research and education. In early April 2018, a member of the law faculty of the University of Hong Kong was ruthlessly attacked by the news media of mainland China and the Hong Kong establishment for a speech he delivered in Taiwan on the topic of Hong Kong's future. In it, he argued that if and when the autocratic rule in China eventually ends, independence might be an option for Hong Kong. This and several other incidents have challenged the capacity of the University of Hong Kong, one of the top-ranked universities in Asia, to weigh academic freedom against political reality. Unfortunately, this is not a single incident in Asia.

In 2019, academics from Singapore and worldwide expressed concern over Singapore's new bill against the internet "fake news." They were worried about the bill's impact on academic freedom and research in the country. Such a precedent could lead to "even wider restraints on global scholarly research and knowledge advancement and its public dissemination."[23] Curbs on academic freedom have escalated in Thailand as well. Andrew Johnson, assistant professor of anthropology at Princeton University, in the United States, was detained by the Thai immigration police, who informed him that he was one of thirty names on a "watch list" of academics and researchers on "society, culture, and politics" in Thailand.[24] In another case, a professor of sociology, who wished to remain anonymous, told the Thai Lawyers for Human Rights (TLHR) he was briefly detained fourteen times at immigration since September 2018, as he travels to Thailand regularly for his research. He was met by Special Branch Bureau officers inquiring whether he was an activist or wanted to know whom he planned to meet while in Thailand.[25]

Moreover, there are signs that the geopolitical rivalry between China and the United States has spilled over into scholarly exchanges and collaboration between US and Chinese institutions of higher learning. In 2018, the Chinese Ministry of Education canceled twenty-five partnerships with American colleges. In 2019,

---

because of government efforts. Anamika Srivastava, "Lessons from Asia on Road to World-Class Universities," *University World News*, February 16, 2018, http://www.universityworldnews.com/article.php?story=20180228175510534.

23. Stated in a letter from academics to Singapore's Education Minister Ong Ye Kung, sent on April 11 and signed by dozens of scholars involved in research on Singapore and Asia. Yojana Sharma, "Sweeping 'Fake News' Bill a Risk for Academic Freedom," *University World News*, April 15, 2019, https://www.universityworldnews.com/post.php?story=20190414195241201.

24. His treatment was likely linked to his signing of a petition related to a protest at the International Conference on Thai Studies (ICTS) held in July 2017. Those protesters were charged a month later for "holding an unlawful political gathering." One of the banners held up said, "An academic seminar is not a military base," in protest against the surveillance of the event by uniformed and plain-clothed officers. Suluck Lamubol, "Junta Steps Up Harassment of International Academics," *University World News*, March 1, 2019, https://www.universityworldnews.com/post.php?story=20190301083420506.

25. Lamubol, "Junta Steps up Harassment of International Academics."

hundreds of Chinese students and scholars studying and researching in the United States reported delays and cancelations in renewing their visas. Many have reported harassment by FBI agents.[26]

The lead article of *University World News* this past February identified a phenomenon that describes well the current state of higher education. It traces the developments in higher education back to the mid-1980s when the "quality" model first emerged in Japan's automobile industry and was applied to higher education. The author questions the dominance of this "orthodoxy" in higher education up to the present. He points out that exercises in quality assurance with standards and agencies measuring accountability and excellence have taken place in the context of public funding cuts and rising consumerism, blurring the goals and aims toward which these exercises are leading. Even more discouraging, the author shows that these exercises, complete with league tables and rankings, have borne "no tangible transformative or empowering benefit for academics or students and ... [no] positive effect on the quality of teaching and learning."[27]

The recent admissions scandal in some of the most highly ranked universities in the United States has made one thing clear: The supposedly best education systems, with the most influential financial positions and the largest pool of outstanding student applicants, may not have the solutions to meet the educational needs of the most deprived young people. Nor can they respond to the demand for fair and just administration of institutional wealth and societal resources for quality education. It is, therefore, not surprising to hear the piercing question: "Has the marketization of higher education reached its limits?"[28] It is an outcry to revisit the philosophy and practice of whole-person education today.

These concerns provide some immediate contexts for the United Board's mission to advocate for whole-person education. In a United Board position paper from 2008, the organization affirmed that the United Board aspires to support and advance "education that is not merely or narrowly market and vocationally driven, but *educates human beings for the fullness of life.*"[29] It is the education of the whole person, addressing the intellectual, ethical, and spiritual development of leaders, faculty, and students; it is about "justice, equality, reconciliation, tolerance, interreligious understanding, freedom, peace, and civil culture," values and imperatives

---

26. Marguerite Dennis, "Fewer Chinese Students in the US May Not Be a Bad Thing," *University World News*, May 11, 2019, https://www.universityworldnews.com/post.php?story=20190507111155578.
27. Juliette Torabian, "Has the Marketization of Higher Education Reached Its Limits?" *University World News*, February 22, 2019, https://www.universityworldnews.com/post.php?story=20190218123554751.
28. Torabian, "Has the Marketization of Higher Education Reached Its Limits?
29. "A Position Paper," *Report of the United Board Christian Presence Task Force*, 6. Italics added.

that concern humanity, society, and all of whole creation.[30] In a white paper on whole-person education that emerged from a consultation in 2017, the United Board further highlighted that "connection to a life purpose, connection to others and all creation, and committing to caring for them for the greater good" is the spiritual hallmark of whole-person education.[31] Whole-person education is a reminder of what Jesus says: "I came so that everyone would have life, and have it in its fullest" (John 10: 10).[32] From 2015, whole-person education has become the guiding post for the United Board's program conception and planning.

B. Whole Person Education in the United Board Programs

The United Board celebrated its centennial from 2022 to 2023. The organization has committed to addressing the needs of higher education in Asia. It will avail opportunities to strengthen the existing work and extend its reach to areas that have the potential to grow. The following goals guide the realignment of whole-person education with the United Board's program priorities:

Goals: Empowering Asian higher education institutions to face the challenges of the century by the following:

1) the development of quality and ethical leaders in senior management;
2) the development of a professional faculty for effective teaching and community-engaged research; and
3) cultivating a culture of care and spiritual nurturance in the learning community on campus.

The United Board approached these goals with grant-making and administered programs with the principles and philosophy of whole-person education firmly embedded in six key program areas: leadership development, faculty development, campus ministry, gender equality, integration of ethics and technology in teaching and learning, and service-learning. Significant programs in each of these areas will be outlined below for illustration.

---

30. "A Position Paper," 5.
31. United Board for Christian Higher Education, *Whole Person Education: The United Board's Perspective on Its Principles and Practice*, September 2019, https://unitedboard.org/wp-content/uploads/2020/10/Whole-Person-Education.The-United-Boards-Perspective-on-Its-Principles-and-Practice.pdf.
32. Contemporary English Version by American Bible Society, 1995.

1. Leadership development: Transformation and whole

In several articles referring to the leadership crisis in Asian universities, three major issues stand out. They include, first, a need for leaders with the stature to lead universities to greater heights;[33] second, a need for more transparency in the leadership selection process that has resulted in political collusion and nepotism; and third, a lack of systematic management training for leaders.[34] Some of these issues reflect precisely the macro structural problems faced by many Asian higher education institutions. On the micro-level, only a few university leaders come prepared for organizational management. These insufficiencies are no match to today's higher education challenges, as outlined above.

The connotation of leadership varies across contexts and cultures. The United Board seeks to empower individuals to make positive changes in higher education and believes there is a leader in every individual. Leadership theories have undergone considerable changes in the past half a century, and transformational leadership has been identified as the most relevant model in use today. According to B. J. Avolio and B. M. Bass, transformational leadership is distinguished from the earlier models for its focus on ethics. It is about authentic leaders who not only have high levels of self-knowledge but are also ethically virtuous.[35] They are leaders who are concerned primarily not for their self-interest but the interests of others. They have self-efficacy based on skill and experience. Most importantly, they care for the feedback from subordinates, peers, supervisors, mentors, family, and friends and therefore acquire good knowledge of the self.[36] Fundamentally, using the Aristotelian concept of *phronesis*, or practical wisdom, transformational leadership must be integrative and whole; it is multifaceted, combining mind, heart, body, and spirituality in the broadest sense.[37]

Since 2016, the program team has integrated whole-person education into the *United Board Fellows Program*. The program team identified transformational leadership as the key to changing institutional cultures toward holistic education. Besides a three-week Summer Institute supported by the Harvard Institutes for Higher Education (HIHE), there is an Asian Placement of one to four months in a university in Asia and a concluding five-day Leadership Seminar in about a year. In

---

33. Morshidi Sirat, Abdul Razak Ahmad, and Norzaini Azman, "University Leadership in Crisis: The Need for Effective Leadership Positioning in Malaysia," *Higher Education Policy* 25, no. 4 (December 2012): 511–29. See https://link.springer.com/article/10.1057/hep.2012.10.
34. Alya Mishra, "India: Crisis of Leadership in Higher Education," *University World News*, December 5, 2010, https://www.universityworldnews.com/post.php?story=20101203212653219.
35. Bernard McKenna and David Rooney, "Wise Leadership," in *The Cambridge Handbook of Wisdom*, ed. Robert J. Sternberg and Judith Gluck (Cambridge: Cambridge University Press, 2019), 653.
36. McKenna and Rooney, "Wise Leadership," 654.
37. McKenna and Rooney, "Wise Leadership," 660–61.

2018, the Summer Institute brought together a community of fourteen mid-career faculty-administrators, including faculty deans and department heads and six new college and university presidents, for in-depth reflection on team effectiveness, institutional collaboration, and the roles and meaning of academic leadership. Along with the managerial skills shared by experienced educational leaders in the program, the Fellows were particularly reminded of the need for personal and spiritual growth for transformation to take root.

For the Asian Placement to follow, each United Board Fellow designs their learning agenda while being encouraged to study topics in higher education management and whole-person education leadership, especially in the spiritual and ethical dimensions, at their host institutions. For the concluding Leadership Seminar, the United Board teamed up with the Ateneo de Manila University (AdMU) in 2018 and Singapore Management University in 2019 to showcase the practices of whole-person education in two different cultural and institutional contexts. The two seminars covered ethical leadership, leadership and faith, cross-cultural communication, and mindfulness exercises. The AdMU's framework of "leading the self, leading teams/organizations, and leading with a mission" has also been incorporated into the program. Sessions on psychometric assessment and emotional well-being for reflection on personal capabilities, strength, and room to grow are the most enlightening for the Fellows.

One author laments the shortage of Asian university "leaders—academics cum administrators—who are inspirational, visionary, respected for their scholarship, and progressive in their approach."[38] A former vice-chancellor of Delhi University appeals for leadership training beyond skills because a good leader also needs "vision, understanding of the university culture, and passion for developing the university further."[39] Whole-person education asks the leaders to refresh their aspiration to lead Asian colleges and universities for change. To lead change, they must first dig deep into themselves to admit their strength and blind spots in leadership and be able to change themselves. Effective leadership starts with a mission and vision for Asian higher education, for the institutions, and for the leaders themselves.

2. *Faculty development: Teachers teach who they are*

Faculty development is at the core of the United Board's work. In response to the need to move away from the utilitarian model of education in Northeast Asia, to bridge the knowledge gap identified by educators in South Asia, and to build on the ASEAN imperative to raise the quality of education in the region, the United

---

38. Sirat, Ahmad, and Azman, "University Leadership in Crisis," 511–29.
39. Mishra, "India: Crisis in Higher Education."

Board aims to provide quality regional faculty training programs, in alignment with its mission to promote whole-person education. Traditional teacher-centered teaching is challenged, and a new approach places importance on student-centered learning, focusing on student engagement, autonomy, critical thinking, creativity, and enhancement of their problem-solving skills. The United Board's goal is to help these educators increase the effectiveness of their teaching to guide students on journeys of inquiry and discovery and to ensure that students will grow holistically during their time at the institution.

Authenticity is again identified as an integral part of education. An authentic teacher understands that "all things are connected by an underlying life force or principle of being."[40] Reflecting on the ideas of Parker Palmer's *The Courage to Teach*, we are reminded that the core to good education is how teachers may "take heart again" to "give heart to others" because "teachers teach who they are."[41] "Good teachers possess a capacity for connectedness. They join self and subject and students in the fabric of life."[42] In a world of divided interests with people's general fear of losing control, higher education institutions' leadership and faculty can play a decisive role in either further instilling division and anxiety or connecting and holding up hope. To promote whole-person education, higher education must be a place to nurture connections for teachers and students to be themselves and what they do. They must escape the paralysis of fear and "enter a state of grace where encounters with otherness will not threaten us but will enrich our work and lives."[43]

In 2017, the United Board partnered with the Ateneo Teacher Center (ATC) and the Education Department of the AdMU to organize the *Whole Person Education Academy*. The idea was generated from two gaps observed in many Southeast Asian higher education institutions. First was the tension among teaching, research, and service, the supposedly three most essential functions of a university. Rather than an integrated approach, the three are often pitted against each other. Research is also known to be given more weight, especially in the universities' race for ranking worldwide. The second gap was the tension between educational content (theory) and methodology (pedagogy). Many teachings focus on transmitting theory or content from the teacher to the students, regardless of students' reception context and capabilities.

The Ateneo team addressed these gaps during the two-week intensive program. The main sessions are designed to inspire pedagogical shifts, from teacher-centered to student-centered learning, from classroom teaching to learning with the

---

40. C. Guignon, *On Being Authentic* (London: Routledge, 2004), 17.
41. Parker J. Palmer, *The Courage to Teach: Exploring the Inner Landscape of a Teacher's Life* (San Francisco: John Wiley & Sons, 2007), xv, 1.
42. Palmer, *The Courage to Teach*, 11–12.
43. Palmer, *The Courage to Teach*, 58.

community, and from explicit curriculum to implicit curriculum. The first shift considers the younger generations' way of knowing shaped by the digital age; the second addresses the need for students to work with the community to resolve real-world issues; the third emphasizes a well-rounded environment for whole-person education. Besides formal curriculum design, whole-person learning also involves how students, fellow teachers, and colleagues are treated or made to feel. At AdMU, the Ignatian motto of *cura personalis* (care for the whole person) permeates the university. Participants reported feeling inspired and empowered to be educators once again.

Moreover, in 2018 and 2019, the United Board organized two faculty training workshops on *Teaching about China in India* at Christ University, Bangalore, India. This program aimed to inculcate cross-cultural training for teaching and learning about China on Indian campuses. Rather than just an additional topic for class teaching, faculty are asked to be peacemakers and to cultivate intercultural sensitivity, critical thinking, broad understanding, and empathetic appreciation of differences—values that are critically required when living in a pluralistic Asia.

3. Campus ministries: A culture of care and spiritual nurturance

Spirituality is a broad concept that involves a search for purpose and meaning in life. Spiritual experience sustains one with a sacred, transcendent, or deep sense of aliveness and interconnectedness. Spiritual nurturance on campus is crucial for students going through critical moments of change. Students today are generally caught in the stress of studying not for their interests and the anxiety of rigorous competition among peers for jobs they may not be prepared for. Besides, the increased polarization of ideological and religious identification in society adds to their frustration and leads to widespread violence or misbehavior in the face of tension and conflicts. If appropriately delivered, spiritual support would serve as a source of social connection that facilitates the building of trusting relationships, in which an essential sense of belonging, identity, and security is provided and the nurturance of positive emotions toward tolerance, acceptance, and peace.

Asia has been a laboratory for pluralism, with many different cultures, religions, and languages living side by side for years. However, the policies of many governments have often instigated tension among religions and communities, aggravated the influence of fanaticism and communalism in the young generation. Rather than letting the student body be driven apart by religious radicalism and communal fervor, spiritual nurturance for students for broad-mindedness, mutual respect, and acceptance of differences is urgently called for. Rather than a narrow sense of spirituality or evangelism, efforts to cultivate a campus culture of compassion and care for others are more critical than ever.

In 2019, the United Board revived an Asia-wide campus ministry program. The *Asian Campus Ministry Forum (ACMF)* was created deliberately to extend our understanding of campus ministry beyond the traditional framework of a chaplaincy office. The program targets all—chaplains or not, ordained or lay, full-time campus ministers or regular faculty with additional responsibilities—who serve the university's core mission through caring for persons and cultivating a nurturing campus climate for holistic education beyond the classroom. For most Asian universities set in a pluralistic background with faculty and students from diverse religious traditions, campus ministry is expected to provide bridges for members of different cultures and traditions and inculcate mutual respect and social responsibility for the community.

While interreligious conflicts are frequent happenings in many Asian colleges and universities,[44] the first ACMF succeeded in bringing a Buddhist monk, a Muslim imam, and a Hindu, all faculty members in universities with strong religious identities, together to showcase the value and promise of open dialogue and cooperation for the respective communities. The many institutional efforts toward inter-faith collaboration on and off campus have reaffirmed and strengthened hope in building a campus of love and care. The forum also explored several crucial areas. They include character education, emerging student issues for care and support, religious resources for hospitality and spirituality, online counseling support for distressed students, and meditation and spiritual exercises for campus ministry staff to walk the journey with university administrators, faculty, and students.

4. Gender equality: Wholeness for all

Instead of being an independent area of programs, gender equality and women's leadership have been a longstanding concern of the United Board running through its various programs. For example, "Gender Equality and the Changing Face of Asian Higher Education" was the theme of the last AULP in 2016. Despite the fast-growing number of women graduates and high-sounding diversity policies, a recent study found that the proportion of women at every level of the corporate world has remained low,[45] and higher education is no exception. In a recent survey of Hong Kong universities, for example, women fell far behind men in academic leadership.[46]

---

44. Another act of violence took place in Pakistan in March. Cf. Ameen Amjad Khan, "Student Kills Professor on Campus over Alleged Blasphemy," *University World News*, March 21, 2019, https://www.universityworldnews.com/post.php?story=20190321130333998.
45. Cf. McKinsey & Company, *Women in the Workplace 2018*, https://wiw-report.s3.amazonaws.com/Women_in_the_Workplace_2018.pdf.
46. Sarah Jane Aiston, "Leading the Academy or Being Led? Hong Kong Women Academics," *Higher Education Research & Development* 33, no. 1 (2014): 59–72, http://dx.doi.org/10.1080/07294360.2013.864618.

The United Board must review the development of women's education and women's leadership with its robust network of women's colleges and universities in the face of ongoing changes.

Despite the impressive success reported for higher education in Asia, gender equality in leadership on the institutional level is still far from satisfactory. In the very well-established higher education of Hong Kong, for example, it was reported that despite a generally favorable ratio for women to men student enrollment, women in senior management (deans and above) accounted for only 22 percent and tenured women professors accounted for only about 24 percent in 2016. In one case, there was a continuous decline in the percentage of women in the institution's senior academic positions over the past five years.[47] Besides the question of parity, a recent review by UNESCO raised several questions about gender equity in education. They include the persistent low enrollment of women in STEM subjects, the everyday experiences of students on campus, and the broader gendered experiences in employment and family.[48]

The *Women's Leadership Forum* held in April 2019 achieved multiple purposes. It was both informational and transformational in allowing participants to share visions and aspirations for women's education in Asia and exchange new ideas of institutional strategies for leadership building for young women through digital learning, entrepreneurship, and curriculum reforms. A strong sense of mission and identity was renewed among the presidents of women's colleges and universities and the women presidents of a few of its network institutions. All women presidents felt empowered and agreed that there is still much more to do together to meet the challenges of gender equality and whole-person development for women in Asian societies. Women presidents of the same country were encouraged to strengthen their connections for continuous work in their respective countries.

5. Integration of ethics and technology in teaching and learning

Digital disruption for a better or worse future characterizes much of the current debate on the use of technology in education. Undoubtedly, Asia has become a significant player in digital learning.[49] Still, there is increasing concern about the

---

47. Peter Mathieson (former president of the University of Hong Kong), "Gender (In)Equality in Universities in Hong Kong" (Gender and the Changing Face of Higher Education in Asia Pacific, Asian University Leaders Program in Hong Kong, Education University of Hong Kong, October 27, 2016).
48. Vimala Ramachandran, *Gender Issues in Higher Education—Advocacy Brief* (Bangkok: UNESCO Asia and Pacific Regional Bureau for Education, 2020), http://unesdoc.unesco.org/images/0018/001898/189825E.pdf.
49. Asia has the largest number of adult online and distance learners in the world, with seventy open universities. There are currently 10 percent of university students engaging in online learning in

decline of ethical development in students in the physical absence of teachers, the involvement of society members (family, friends, and peer learners), or an ethically conducive institutional environment.[50] The advancement of technology and artificial intelligence is predicted to take over many jobs people are doing and put about 47 percent of them obsolete over the next twenty years in the States. Ironically, surveys show that the jobs that will not be easily replaced require soft skills such as creativity and social skills.[51]

Integrating whole-person education in the fast-growing technological world is the key to sustaining students' ethical development. Achieving the balance between skills acquisition and character/moral development has been the focus of the United Board's programs on digital learning of two consultations on technology-assisted teaching and learning (TATL) in 2017 and 2019. The speakers were given two tasks. They provided the assembled educators with an overview of how education has been impacted by the digital era and the means through which to develop innovative teaching and learning methods to meet the changing ways in which students are learning. At the same time, the United Board endeavored to provide educators with a sense of the ethical and moral challenges that have accompanied the rapid digitization of education as well as the United Board's perspective (as well as that of its partner institutions) on what it means to be a digitally adept whole-person educator. Both consultations were received with high commendations.

Information Communication Technology scholar and communications expert Colin Agur notes that "in the years to come, the question of who gets what technology will have a large effect on the educational and economic potential of citizens in developing countries."[52] It is commonly understood that deficiencies in educational accessibility have long-term and far-reaching effects. The United Board aims to bridge this divide by bringing together institutions working to integrate educational technology holistically and inclusively and supporting their efforts through innovation grants, faculty training, and the creation of regional TATL expertise hubs.

China, and 20 percent of tertiary students are enrolled in Indira Gandhi Open University in India. Cf. Rebecca Clothey, "Current Trends in Higher Education: Expanding Access in the Asia Pacific through Technology," *Journal of Comparative & International Higher Education* 2 (2010): 3–5, https://www.ojed.org/index.php/jcihe/article/view/792/560.

50. Abdul Hafeez Muhammad et al., "A Study to Investigate State of Ethical Development in E-Learning," *International Journal of Advanced Science and Applications* 7, 4 (2016): 284–90. See https://pdfs.semanticscholar.org/682e/9cde4924ed277d3a5c037de613585e9957af.pdf, access date: May 15, 2019.

51. See Carl Benedikt Frey and Michael A. Osbourne, *The Future of Employment*, Working Paper, Oxford Martin School, University of Oxford (Sep 2013), http://www.oxfordmartin.ox.ac.uk/publications/view/1314.

52. Collin Agur, "ICTs and Education in Developing Countries: The Case of India", in *Education and Social Media: Toward a Digital Future*, ed. Christine Greenhow, Julia Sonnevend, and Colin Agur (Cambridge, MA; London: MIT Press, 2016), 62.

As a whole, the United Board's strategy in this area involves leveraging its growing expertise in this area. More importantly, it works closely with its regional partners to develop contextualized and resource-provisioned solutions for TATL implementation in an ethical, educationally considerate, and holistically focused manner.

6. Service-learning programs

The next generation will undoubtedly face all kinds of new challenges that are feared to disrupt society. In some cases, the rapid expansion of higher education produces more graduates than the market demands and raises questions about employability and mismatched talents. The prevalent model of compartmentalization of knowledge and commercialization of education aimed at creating paper qualifications could not meet these changes. Instead, it is essential to develop holistic learning that can contribute to students' character formation and prepare them for the skills for problem-solving, knowledge application, lifelong learning, adaptability, and interpersonal skills to face the ever-evolving world.

Service-learning has been a key support item in the United Board's grant programs. Its contribution does not only confine itself to the nurturance of compassion and care for others but also inspires creativity, entrepreneurial spirit, and out-of-the-box thinking. It has become an essential component of holistic education, helping students integrate intellectual knowledge with personal growth through services to the community. It can cultivate the whole person by provoking students to ask questions about identity, values, and the meaning of life, and prepare them to be socially responsible citizens and qualified professionals in their own right.

Service-learning across cultures and countries has existed in some universities in Japan, Korea, Indonesia, and India since the turn of the century. In response to the catastrophic typhoon Yolanda in 2014,[53] the United Board organized for the first time the International Service Learning Program (ISLP) for the rebuilding of the much-shattered coastal communities of the Philippines. One hundred twenty staff and students gathered from June 28 to July 11, 2014, from twelve institutions from six countries[54] working side by side in ten remote villages of the Philippines for

---

53. Reported by *Philippines Associated Press* on November 9, 2013, typhoon Yolanda was portrayed as "one of the strongest typhoons on record struck the Philippines, forcing hundreds of thousands from their homes and knocking out power and communications in several provinces."
54. The program was co-hosted by Central Philippines University, University of St. La Salle and Silliman University and supported by Filamar Christian University and College of St. John Roxas. Other participating universities and organizations included South Christian College and the Trinity University of Asia in the Philippines, Amity Foundation from China, Christ University from India, Seoul Women's University from Korea, Dagon University from Myanmar, and Soegijapranata Catholic University from Indonesia.

two weeks.[55] This project involved concerted reconstruction efforts of institutional leaders, faculty, and students. It involved extensive community leaders, churches, local NGOs such as the YMCAs, and the municipal government who joined the local families in providing transportation and homestay for the different groups involved.[56] The two-week-long activities covered a wide range of services, including reconstruction of homes from building cement blocks and painting, clearing trash, conducting seminars on family planning and reproductive rights, feeding, and teaching children at the daycare centers. Feedback from the participants was not only about the knowledge they learned about disaster and reconstruction but also a life enrichment experience for faculty and students. Together the participants and the communities formed a strong bonding across countries, religions, education, and urban-rural boundaries that extended beyond the program.

Cross-regional exchange through service-learning can provide an immensely valuable opportunity for faculty and students of institutions from different cultures and social backgrounds to work and learn intensively together. When conducted right, cross-border/regional service-learning programs can nurture the best in-depth immersion experience to build the best form of heart-to-heart bonding across communities. Taking the opportunity of China's national initiatives on "one belt one road" and the strong desire for Northeast Asian universities to deepen their internationalization programs, further cultivation work can be done on peace and community building.

C. Conclusion

Aligning the United Board's program goals and implementation with whole-person education remains an ongoing challenge. One reason is that, to date, the United Board has yet to include specific measures to capture and evaluate whole-person education learning outcomes in its evaluation tools. Thus, while it regularly hears wonderful anecdotal comments about the content of its various programs and has always received demands for more of the same or advanced training, assessing participants' reception of its desired outcomes remains challenging. In 2018, the United Board began to test an assessment tool that would hopefully help it to accurately

---

55. Glenn Shive, *Site Visit Report and Reflection Program for the International Service Learning Project, Visayas, Philippines, June 26 to July 12, 2014*. Internal document of United Board for Christian Higher Education in Asia, unpublished.
56. Hope Antone, *Report on the International Service Learning Program, Panay and Negros Islands, Philippines, June 28 to July 11, 2014*. Internal document of United Board for Christian Higher Education in Asia, unpublished.

capture the development of whole-person education-related outcomes in its various programs. Based on this tool, the United Board shall also develop a longitudinal assessment of the personal growth of individual participants in programs for a more extended period.

The United Board has a highly mobile program team who is in touch with its network institutions all over Asia.[57] Over the years, it has built a network of dedicated leaders who aspired to improve higher education and faculty who engaged with students for active learning and service in the community. In projection to the future, the United Board may go miles further to identify and nurture local talents, build bridges among higher education stakeholders, and pull more considerable resources together to develop whole-person leaders for Asian societies today and in the future.

The author of the article on the marketization of higher education cited earlier argues that the time has come for change.[58] In essence, applying neoliberal, market-oriented higher education has exposed numerous problems. Firm steps must be taken to reverse this trend to enhance teaching and learning for future generations and society. Whole-person education is a vision and a tool for us to take these essential steps forward.

Bibliography

Agur, Colin. "ICTs and Education in Developing Countries: The Case of India." In *Education and Social Media: Toward a Digital Future*, edited by Christine Greenhow, Julia Sonnevend, and Colin Agur, 61–78. Cambridge, MA; London: MIT Press, 2016.

Ahmad, Mukhtar. "What Is Wrong with the Indian Higher Education System?" *University World News*, February 8, 2019. https://www.universityworldnews.com/post.php?story=20190129125036113.

Aiston, Sarah Jane. "Leading the Academy or Being Led? Hong Kong Women Academics." *Higher Education Research & Development* 33, no. 1 (2014): 59–72. http://dx.doi.org/10.1080/07294360.2013.864618.

Antone, Hope. *Report on the International Service Learning Program, Panay and Negros Islands, Philippines, June 28 to July 11, 2014*. United Board for Christian Higher Education in Asia. Unpublished, 2014.

Asia-Pacific Programme of Education for All. *UNESCO Bangkok, Advocacy Brief: Gender Issues in Higher Education*, http://unesdoc.unesco.org/images/0018/001898/189825E.pdf.

---

57. A special acknowledgment note to the United Board's former and present program team members, namely Hope Antone, Kevin Henderson, Maher Spurgeon, Vivica Xiong, and Cynthia Yuen, who contributed to formulating these programs and ideas from 2017 to 2019.
58. Cf. Note 22.

Chao, Roger Jr. "A Shift towards Good Quality Higher Education for All." *University World News*, February 9, 2018. http://www.universityworldnews.com/article.php?story=20180228175510534.

Clothey, Rebecca. "Current Trends in Higher Education: Expanding Access in the Asia Pacific through Technology," *Journal of Comparative & International Higher Education 2* (2010): 3–5, https://www.ojed.org/index.php/jcihe/article/view/792/560.

Dennis, Marguerite. "Fewer Chinese Students in the US May Not Be a Bad Thing." *University World News*, May 11, 2019. https://www.universityworldnews.com/post.php?story=20190507111155578.

Department of Human Resources Development, Government of India. *All India Survey on Higher Education 2017–18*, 2018. https://mhrd.gov.in/sites/upload_files/mhrd/files/statistics-new/AISHE201718.pdf.

Fenn, William P. *Ever New Horizons: The Story of the United Board for Christian Higher Education in Asia, 1922–1975*. New York: The United Board for Christian Higher Education in Asia, 1980.

Frey, Carl Benedikt, and Michael A. Osbourne. *The Future of Employment*, Working Paper, Oxford Martin School, University of Oxford (Sep 2013). http://www.oxfordmartin.ox.ac.uk/publications/view/1314.

Guignon, C. *On Being Authentic*. London: Routledge, 2014.

Khan, Ameen Amjad. "Student Kills Professor on Campus over Alleged Blasphemy," *University World News*, March 21, 2019. https://www.universityworldnews.com/post.php?story=20190321130333998.

Lamubol, Suluck. "Junta Steps Up Harassment of International Academics," *University World News*, March 1, 2019. https://www.universityworldnews.com/post.php?story=20190301083420506.

Macha, Wilson, Chris Mackie, and Jessica Magaziner. "Education in the Philippines," *World Education News + Reviews (WENR)*, March 6, 2018. https://wenr.wes.org/2018/03/education-in-the-philippines.

Mathieson, Peter. 2016. "Gender (In)Equality in Universities in Hong Kong." Presented at the Gender and the Changing Face of Higher Education in Asia Pacific, Asian University Leaders Program in Hong Kong, Education University of Hong Kong, October 27, 2016.

McKenna, Bernard, and David Rooney. "Wise Leadership." In *The Cambridge Handbook of Wisdom*, edited by Robert J. Sternberg and Judith Gluck, 649–75. Cambridge: Cambridge University Press, 2019.

McKinsey & Company. "Women in the Workplace 2018." *Report of McKinsey & Company*, 2018. https://www.mckinsey.com/featured-insights/gender-equality/women-in-the-workplace-2018.

Mishra, Alya. "India: Crisis of Leadership in Higher Education." *University World News*, December 5, 2010. https://www.universityworldnews.com/post.php?story=20101203212653219.

Montemayor, Ma. Teresa. "Free College Education in Full Swing in 2018," *Philippine News Agency*, December 28, 2018. https://www.pna.gov.ph/articles/1057514.

Muhammad, Abdul Hafeez, et al. "A Study to Investigate State of Ethical Development in E-Learning," *International Journal of Advanced Science and Applications* 7, 4 (2016): 284–90. https://pdfs.semanticscholar.org/682e/9cde4924ed277d3a5c037de613585e9957af.pdf.

Palmer, Parker J. *The Courage to Teach: Exploring the Inner Landscape of a Teacher's Life.* San Francisco: John Wiley & Sons, 2007.

Peach, S. J. "Understanding the Higher Education Curriculum in the 21st century," *Critical Reflective Practice in Education* 3, (2012): 79–91.

Ramachandran, Vimala. *Gender Issues in Higher Education—Advocacy Brief.* Bangkok: UNESCO Asia and Pacific Regional Bureau for Education, 2020. http://unesdoc.unesco.org/images/0018/001898/189825E.pdf.

Sharma, Yojana. "Sweeping 'Fake News' Bill a Risk for Academic Freedom," *University World News.* April 15, 2019. https://www.universityworldnews.com/post.php?story=20190414195241201.

Shive, Glenn. *Site Visit Report and Reflection Program for the International Service Learning Project, Visayas, Philippines, June 26 to July 12, 2014.* United Board for Christian Higher Education in Asia. Unpublished.

Sirat, Morshidi, Abdul Razak Ahmad, and Norzaini Azman. "University Leadership in Crisis: The Need for Effective Leadership Positioning in Malaysia." *Higher Education Policy* 25, no. 4 (December 2012): 511–29. https://link.springer.com/article/10.1057/hep.2012.10.

Srivastava, Anamika. "Lessons from Asia on Road to World-Class Universities." *University World News*, February 16, 2018. http://www.universityworldnews.com/article.php?story=20180228175510534.

Torabian, Juliette. "Has the Marketization of Higher Education reached Its Limits?" *University World News*, February 22, 2019. https://www.universityworldnews.com/post.php?story=20190218123554751.

UNESCO Institute for Statistics. *Higher Education in Asia: Expanding Out, Expanding Up.* Montreal: UNESCO Institute for Statistics, 2014.

United Board for Christian Higher Education in Asia. "A Position Paper." In *Report of the United Board Christian Presence Task Force,* 2007. Unpublished.

United Board for Christian Higher Education in Asia. "A Concept Paper for AULP," 2013. Unpublished.

United Board for Christian Higher Education. "Mission and Identity." https://unitedboard.org/about-us/about-united-board/mission-vision/.

United Board for Christian Higher Education. *Whole Person Education: The United Board's Perspective on Its Principles and Practice,* December 2019. https://unitedboard.org/wp-content/uploads/2020/10/Whole-Person-Education.The-United-Boards-Perspective-on-Its-Principles-and-Practice.pdf.

Contributors

CHEN Jianming holds a doctorate in history and is a council member of the Chinese Society of Religious Studies and a researcher of the Institute of Religious Studies at Sichuan University. He has studied the history of Christianity in China for more than thirty years, and his research areas include Christian literature, Christian charity, and Christianity and Chinese religions.

Wai Luen KWOK is professor of the Department of Religion and Philosophy, and associate director of the Centre for Sino-Christian Studies at Hong Kong Baptist University. He has written on the history of Chinese Christianity in the Republican period (1911–1949).

Thomas H. C. LEE holds a PhD degree from Yale and has taught at the Chinese University of Hong Kong and the City University of New York. He has also taught as a visiting chair professor at National Taiwan University, National Tsing Hua University, and, in China, Beijing Normal University. His *Education in Traditional China, a History*, which is available in a revised Chinese translation, is his most quoted work. The Chinese version was awarded Chinese National Library's *Wenjin* Prize in 2017. He is now retired at Wappingers Falls, New York.

Leah Yiya LEE received her PhD in Chinese literature from the Chinese Culture University. She began her teaching career at Chung Yuan Christian University in the late 1980s and held administrative posts as director of the Center for General Education and director of the University Library. She retired from Chung Yuan Christian University in 2020 and is currently serving as an adjunct professor in the Department of Business Administration, where she teaches courses affiliated with whole-person education. Her research interests include Chinese vernacular literature and Chinese Christian literature. She has authored several books, most recently *Creativity in front of the Holy Altar: A Study of Chinese Christian Literature in the 1920s* (《聖壇前的創作——20年代基督教文學研究》) (Taipei, 2010).

Jiafeng LIU received his PhD from Central China Normal University. He is professor at the School of History and Culture, Shandong University. He is the author of *Chinese Christian Colleges in the Sino-Japanese War* (2003), *Gospel and Plough: A Study on American Agricultural Missionaries* (2006), and *Christian Rural Reconstruction in Modern China: 1907–1950* (2008), and also the editor of *Alienation and Amalgamation: The Rising of Chinese Church* (2005).

MA Min is the Liberal Arts and Humanities Senior Professor at Central China Normal University. After having served as the vice president, president and chancellor of CCNU for many years, MA is now director of the Institute of Modern Chinese History, and chair of the University Academic Senate, CCNU. He is dedicated to modern Chinese history studies and has made pioneering contributions in many areas such as the China's Chamber of Commerce studies, modern Chinese exposition history studies, and the Christian College history studies in China.

George Kam Wah MAK, PhD (Cantab), FRAS, FRHistS, is associate professor in the Department of Religion and Philosophy and research fellow of the Centre for Sino-Christian Studies at Hong Kong Baptist University. He is also associate editor of *Ching Feng: A Journal on Christianity and Chinese Religion and Culture*. Among his academic interests are Bible translation, history of Christianity in modern China, and Sino-foreign cultural relations. He is the author of *Protestant Bible Translation and Mandarin as the National Language of China* (Brill, 2017), and he guest-edited a special issue of *the Journal of the Royal Asiatic Society* entitled "The Mandarin *Union Version*, a Classic Chinese Biblical Translation" (Cambridge University Press, 2020).

Brian STANLEY recently retired as professor of world Christianity at the University of Edinburgh, where he has taught since 2009. He is now professor emeritus of world Christianity. He is a historian of Christian missions and world Christianity. His many publications include *The World Missionary Conference, Edinburgh 1910* (Eerdmans, 2009), *Christianity in the Twentieth Century: A World History* (Princeton University Press, 2018), and he has edited for publication Andrew F. Walls's posthumous publication, *The Missionary Movement from the West: A Biography from Birth to Old Age* (Eerdmans, 2023).

Peter Chen-main WANG received his PhD from the University of Arizona in 1984. He retired from the post of the Distinguished Professor of Graduate Institute of History, National Central University, Taiwan, in 2018. He is now affiliated with the Graduate Institute of History at Fu Jen Catholic University as an adjunct professor. His fields of study include history of Christianity in China, US-China diplomatic history, and Ming-Qing transitional period. He has published six books and edited thirteen books, including the following: *The Life and Career of Hung Ch'eng-ch'ou (1593–1665): Public Service in a Time of Dynastic Change* (AAS monograph, 1999) and *Contextualization of Christianity in China: An Evaluation in Modern Perspective* (Monumenta Serica Institute, 2007). During his 40 years of teaching and research career, he has received a number of awards, grants, and honorary posts, such as the visiting research fellowship at Stanford; Fulbright scholarship; George C. Marshall/ Baruch Fellowship; The Fifth European Chair of Chinese Studies, IIAS (Leiden); and Distinguished Contributions to studies of Chinese Christianity (HK, 2015).

Di WANG (PhD in History, Johns Hopkins, 1999) is Distinguished Professor of History at the University of Macau. He is the author of *Street Culture in Chengdu: Public Space, Urban Commoners, and Local Politics, 1870–1930* (2003), *The Teahouse: Small Business, Everyday Culture, and Public Politics in Chengdu, 1900–1950* (2008), *The Teahouse under Socialism: The Decline and Renewal of Public Life in Chengdu, 1950–2000* (2018), and *Violence and Order on the Chengdu Plain: The Story of a Secret Brotherhood in Rural China, 1939–1949* (2018). He has won the Best Book Award (Non-North American) twice from the Urban History Association (2005, 2020). He is a recipient of the most prestigious research grants such as NEH, NHC, and Fulbright.

WONG Man Kong (FRHistS, FRAS, SFHEA) is professor in the Department of History and director of the Academy of Chinese, History, Religion and Philosophy at Hong Kong Baptist University. He is also an honorary research senior fellow in history at the University of Queensland, Australia. An author and editor of twenty-five books and over one hundred journal articles and book chapters in modern Chinese history and Hong Kong history, he is an editor of *Medical History: An International Journal for the History of Medicine and Related Sciences* (Cambridge University Press). His research interests include medical history, education history, Sino-British relations, Sino-Western cultural contacts, and Chinese Christianity.

Wai Ching Angela WONG, PhD in religious studies, University of Chicago, formerly senior advisor to the President and the Vice President for Programs of the United Board for Christian Higher Education in Asia. She is an honorary professor and formerly associate professor who taught at the Department of Cultural and Religious Studies and headed the Graduate Divisions of Cultural Studies and Gender Studies at the Chinese University of Hong Kong. Ecumenically, she was a United Board trustee (2002–2012), a Christian Conference of Asia president (2000–2005), and the World Student Christian Federation chairperson (1995–1999). Academically, she has published widely in Chinese and English on topics of religion, gender, and Asian culture.

Index

"A Brief History of Chinese Educational Thoughts" (Zhu). See "Zhongguo jiaoyu sixiang jianshi" 中國教育思想簡史

"A Rural Handicraft Family: A Report on the Du Family in Shiyangchang" (Yang). See "Yige nongcun shougongye de jiating: Shiyangchang Dujia shidi yanjiu baogao" 一個農村手工業的家庭：石羊場杜家實地研究報告

A Short Introduction to Elementary Civics. See *Gongmin changshi xiaojian* 公民常識小簡

Academia Sinica: Institute of Social Science (Shehui kexue yanjiusuo 社會科學研究所), 207

academic discipline building. See *xueke jianshe* 學科建設

academic freedom, 272

academies. See *shuyuan* 書院

ACMF. See Asian Campus Ministry Forum

AdMU. See Ateneo de Manila University

advanced people of the party-state. See *dangguo xianjin* 黨國先進

Agur, Colin, 281

Aim of Education in the Republic of China and Directions for Its Enforcement. See *Zhonghua Minguo jiaoyu zongzhi ji qi shishi fangzhen* 中華民國教育宗旨及其實施方針

Aishanlu shichao 愛山廬詩鈔 (*Selected Poems from Aishan Mansion*), 113n2, 135

Allen, Young John, 26

AMEM (North). See American Methodist Episcopal Mission (North)

American Bible Society, 180 table 8.1, 187, 187n82

American Board of Commissioners for Foreign Missions, 78, 181 table 8.1, 189

American Episcopal Church, 146, 147n6, 149, 149n17, 204n28, 233

American Methodist Episcopal Church: Publication Department of, 92, 99

American Methodist Episcopal Mission (North) [AMEM (North)], 173, 177, 179 table 8.1, 180 table 8.1, 189n90

American Methodist Episcopal Mission (South), 115

American Military Advisory Group, 254

American Presbyterian Mission (APM) (North), 92, 93, 93n8, 177, 179 table 8.1, 180 table 8.1

Amplified Instructions on the Sacred Edict. See *Shengyu guangxun* 聖諭廣訓

"An Appeal from Chengdu's Cultural Circle about the Current Political Situation," 205

Analects, 17

Anglo-Japanese Alliance, 80
Anti-Christian Federation, 37
Anti-Christian Movement, 9, 116, 162
Anti-Christian Student Federation, 37
Art Pictures for the Common People. See *Pingmin zihua ji* 平民字畫集
ASEAN. *See* Association of Southeast Asian Nations
Asian Campus Ministry Forum (ACMF), 279
Asian University Leaders Program (AULP), 267, 279
Assemblies of God, 253n17
Associated Boards for Christian Colleges in China, 234, 234n18. *See also* United Board for Christian Higher Education in Asia
Association for Democratic Youth in Chengdu. *See* Chengdu minzhu qingnian xiehui 成都民主青年協會
Association for the Study of the National Language. *See* Guoyu yanjiuhui 國語研究會
Association of Christian Universities and Colleges in Asia, 267
Association of Southeast Asian Nations (ASEAN), 271, 271n19, 276
Association Progress. See *Qingnian jinbu* 青年進步
Ateneo de Manila University (AdMU), 276, 277, 278
Au, Peter. *See* Ou Yingyu 區應毓
AULP. *See* Asian University Leaders Program
Aurora University, 36, 227n2, 232
Avolio, B. J., 275
Awakening Lion. See *Xingshi* 醒獅

Bacon, Francis, 125
Bai Limin 白莉民, 6
baihua 白話 (vernacular Chinese), 124. *See also* Mandarin
Bamber, Theo, 42

Baptist Missionary Society (BMS): Medical Auxiliary Fund, 83; Frederick Seguier Drake and, 53, 54, 66; Gordon King and, 9, 78–83, 79n8, 82n22; Harold Henry Rowley and, 39–45; its schools' registration in China, 41, 44, 66; Harriet M. Turner and circulation of her mission's *zhuyin zimu* hymnal, 188–89
Bass, B. J., 275
Bates, Miner Searle, 4, 238
Battle of Shanghai, 102
Bays, Daniel, 10, 76, 170, 176, 177; *China's Christian Colleges: Cross-cultural Connections, 1900–1950* co-edited with Ellen Widmer, 7
Beiping shehui diaochasuo 北平社會調查所 (Institute of Social Surveys in Peiping), 207
Beiyang 北洋 government, 172, 173, 174
Benefits to the Youth. See *Jiahui qingnian* 嘉惠青年
Bible, Frank W., 91–92
Bing Xin 冰心, 240
Bishop Boone Memorial School (Boone School), 146, 146n4, 147, 149, 150
Blackstone, J. H., 177, 179 table 8.1
Blodget, Henry, 189, 189n90
Blumenfeld, Samuel: *Is Public Education Necessary?*, 90
BMS. *See* Baptist Missionary Society
Boone School. *See* Bishop Boone Memorial School
Boone University, 204n28, 233
Bowen, Arthur J., 91n2
Boxer Rebellion, 131, 147, 147n5, 163
brainwashing, 36
bring relief to rural communities. See *jiuji xiangcun* 救濟鄉村
British Academy, 40
British and Foreign Bible Society, 177, 179 table 8.1, 187, 189
British Medical Council, 84, 85, 86

broad-based education. See *dalei peiyang* 大類培養
Brown, Robert E., 189n90
Buck, David, 240
Buck, John Lossing: *Chinese Farm Economy*, 206–7; *Land Utilization in China*, 207
Buddhism, 57, 60, 64, 67
Burgess, John Stewart, 208; *Peking, a Social Survey* co-authored with Sidney D. Gamble, 206
Burke Library, Union Theological Seminary, New York, 10, 170, 170n10
Burton, Ernest D., 116

C.L.S. Readers for Illiterates. See *Guangxue duben* 廣學讀本
Cable, A. Mildred, 179 table 8.1, 185
Cai Yuanpei 蔡元培 (Tsai Yuen Pei), 29, 113, 130, 153
Calvin, John, 90
Canadian Presbyterian Mission, 92
Catholic Church in Taiwan, 252, 253
Catholic University of Peking. See Fu Jen University
CCC. See China Continuation Committee
CCP. See Chinese Communist Party
Center for General Education of Chung Yuan Christian University, 250, 262–63; correlated programs, 260–61; curriculum design, 259–60. See also Chung Yuan Christian University (CYCU)
Central China Normal University, 11, 230
character building, 157, 158, 159, 161n67, 163
character saves the nation. See *renge jiuguo* 人格救國
Cheeloo Monthly. See *Qida yuekan* 齊大月刊
Cheeloo University. See Shantung Christian University
Chen Chun 陳淳, 20n7
Chen Enrong 陳恩榮 (Chen Zhefu 陳哲甫), 173, 175, 178 table 8.1

Chen Hansheng 陳翰笙, 207, 207n36
Chen, Janet Y.: *The Sounds of Mandarin*, 170
Chen Lifu 陳立夫, 84, 134
Chen Qitian 陳啟天, 116, 117
Chen Yuan 陳垣, 237, 239
Chen Yuguang 陳裕光, 239
Chen Zhefu 陳哲甫. See Chen Enrong 陳恩榮
Cheng Jingyi 誠靜怡 (Cheng, C. Y.), 177, 178 table 8.1, 178 table 8.1 note 2
Chengdu minzhu qingnian xiehui 成都民主青年協會 (Association for Democratic Youth in Chengdu), 203, 205
Chesterman, Clement, 82
Chiang Kai-shek, 125, 127, 132, 134, 205, 252, 254, 255; Madam Chiang (wife), 252
China Christian Advocate. See *Xinghua zhoukan* 興華週刊
China Christian Educational Association. See Zhongguo Jidujiao jiaoyuhui 中國基督教教育會
China Christian Independent Church Federation. See Zhongguo Yesujiao zilihui 中國耶穌教自立會
China Church Year Book. See *Zhonghua Jidujiaohui nianjian* 中華基督教會年鑑
China Civil War (1945–1949), 253
China College. See Zhongguo gongxue 中國公學
China Continuation Committee (CCC) (Zhonghua xuxing weibanhui 中華續行委辦會): adoption of *zhuyin zimu*, 174–75; Phonetic Promotion Committee (PPC) as a special committee of, 10, 168, 168n1, 169, 170, 177, 178–81 table 8.1, 178 table 8.1 note 2, 185, 191
China Inland Mission (CIM), 42, 91n2, 174, 177, 179 table 8.1, 180 table 8.1, 181 table 8.1, 183, 184, 185, 189

China Sunday School Union (CSSU), 177, 178 table 8.1, 179 table 8.1, 181 table 8.1, 186n73
China's Christian Colleges: Cross-cultural Connections, 1900–1950 (Bays and Widmer), 7
China's Modern Goliath and Her David, 188. *See also* Phonetic Promotion Committee
Chinese church leadership: training of, 55–56, 67
Chinese Communist Party (CCP), 36, 138, 203, 205; Central Committee of, 94
Chinese Educational and Cultural Foundation. *See* Zhonghua jiaoyu wenhua jijin dongshihui 中華教育文化基金董事會
Chinese Educational Mission in the United States. *See* Liu Mei xuesheng jianduchu 留美學生監督處
Chinese Exclusion Act (1882), 28n27
Chinese Farm Economy (Buck), 206–7
"Chinese learning as essence and Western learning as application," 24, 24n19, 30
Chinese National Association of the Mass Education Movement. *See* Zhonghua pingmin jiaoyu cujinhui 中華平民教育促進會
Chinese Recorder, 57, 60, 62, 153
Chinese Red Cross, 86
Chinese Students' Christian Association in North America, 149–50, 150n18
Chinese Youth Party. *See* Zhongguo qingnian dang 中國青年黨
Chongqing Negotiation, 205
Christ University (Bangalore), 278
"Christians and Patriotism" (Xie). *See* "Jidutu yu aiguo" 基督徒與愛國
Christian Colleges in China: academic discipline building and, 230–32; buildings of, 244; education model of, 229–30, 241–42; educational aim, 233; graduates, 239–41; inter-college cooperation, 234–35, 234n18; international connection, 232, 233, 235; list of, 227n2; list of Christian medical colleges in China, 77, 78n7; rating of, 235; research history of, 227–29, 227n3; Sino-Foreign cultural exchange and, 235–38, 244; staff and presidency, 237, 238, 239; students of, 229, 233, 233n16, 239, 241–43; women education and, 243
Christian Farmer. *See Tianjia banyuebao* 田家半月報
Christian Literature Society for China (CLSC) (Guangxue hui 廣學會), 9, 91, 92, 92n6, 93, 99, 101, 102, 103, 107, 189
Christian Missions in Many Lands, 180 table 8.1, 187
Christianity and Secondary Education in Modern China (Yin). *See Jidujiao yu Zhongguo jindai zhongdeng jiaoyu* 基督教與中國近代中等教育
Chu Heng-bi. *See* Zhu Hengbi 朱恆璧
Chu Hsi. *See* Zhu Xi 朱熹
Chu, King. *See* Zhu Jingnong 朱經農
Chuan, S. Peter. *See* Quan Shaowu 全紹武
Chung Hwa Book Company, 178 table 8.1, 181n48
Chung Yuan Christian University (CYCU), 11, 250–51, 262; Center for General Education, *see* Center for General Education of Chung Yuan Christian University; conflicts among the board of directors, 254–55; holistic education and, 258–61; mission statements of, 256–57, 258, 261; overseas activities, 261; presidency of, 255–56
civil service examination, 19, 25; abolition of, 25, 26, 150; system of, 17, 18, 24. *See also* imperial examination
CLSC. *See* Christian Literature Society for China
Cochrane, Thomas, 77

Coe, John L.: *Huachung University*, 4
Cole, G. H., 155
College of Yale-in-China, 235
Combe, George, 125
"Commemoration of the Double-Seventh Incident and the *Christian Farmer*" (Zhang). See "'Qiqi' jinian yu benbao" "七七" 紀念與本報
Commercial Press, 113, 122, 123, 128, 130, 134, 135, 138, 181, 185
Committee for Christian Colleges in China, 234. See also United Board for Christian Higher Education in Asia
commoners, 23, 24, 27, 102; definition of, 90, 91; education of, 19, 20, 21, 22, 26, 30; publications for, 99–102; Xie Songgao's impression of, 103, 106, 107
Communist Party of China (CPC). See Chinese Communist Party
community schools. See *shexue* 社學
compulsory education, 122, 134, 138, 172
Confucianism, 37, 57, 58, 60, 63, 64, 67, 68, 150; classics of, 17, 19, 24, 25, 60, 64, 124; Neo-Confucianism, 58, 67
Confucius, 17, 18, 19
contextualization, 250, 250n3
Correlated Program for Christian Higher Education in China, 115
Country Life in South China (Kulp), 206
Cressy, E. H., 135
critical theory (social anthropology), 213, 213n59, 214
cross-disciplinary studies of the arts and sciences. See *wenli jiaocha* 文理交叉
cross-fertilization between the arts and sciences. See *wenli shentou* 文理滲透
CSSU. See China Sunday School Union
Cui Derun 崔德潤, 98
Cunzhi 村治 (*Village Governance*), 200
Cunzhi yanjiuyuan 村治研究院 (Institution for Village Governance), 200
cura personalis, 278

CYCU. See Chung Yuan Christian University

Dadai Liji 大戴禮記, 24n19
Dagao 大誥 (*The Grand Pronouncements*), 22
Dahoufang 大後方 (Great Rear Area), 201
Daily Progress Society, 149
dalei peiyang 大類培養 (broad-based education), 239
dangguo xianjin 黨國先進 (advanced people of the party-state), 125, 127
danghua jiaoyu 黨化教育 (partified education), 123
dao: as principle, 20; as the Way, 64, 118; in *Daodejing* 道德經, 64
Daoism, 57, 60, 64, 67
Daoji huitang 道濟會堂 (To Tsai Church), 171
Daoyuan 道院 (Chinese folk religion). See Tao Yuan
Daozi zhuyin keben 道字注音課本 (*Workbook of Pronouncing Phonetic Symbols*) (Trench), 184
Darroch, John, 177, 179 table 8.1
Daxue 大學 (*The Great Learning*), 124
Daxueyuan 大學院. See Ministry of Education and Research (Nationalist government)
Day, Clarence Burton: *Hangchow University: A Brief History*, 4
Delhi University, 276
Democracy Daily. See *Minzhu bao* 民主報
Department of Sociology at Yenching University, 195, 196n3; and the distinction between sociology and anthropology in China, 196n5; departmental chairs' emphasis on social service, 202–3; establishment and development, 208–9; Shen Baoyuan and, 10, 196, 200, 205, 214. See also Yenching University
Dewey, John, 9, 112, 122, 126

Dickens, Charles: *A Tale of Two Cities*, 249
Ding Wenjiang 丁文江, 129
Dingxian shehui gaikuang diaocha 定縣社會概況調查 (*Investigation of the Social Conditions in Ding County*), 207, 207n37, 208n38
Dittmer, C. G., 206
Dong Li 董黎, 244
Donglin 東林 Academy, 20; activities of its members, 20–21, 21n8, 21n9, 23
"Dongsansheng zhi yinmin yu fanzui" 東三省之移民與犯罪 ("Migrants and Crime in Northeast China"), 209
Double-Seventh Incident, 105. *See also* Marco Polo Bridge Incident
Drake, Frederick Seguier, 8; biography, 53–54; education vision of, 69–70; enthusiasm for evangelism, 54–56; on functions of Chinese Christian Colleges, 65–68; "Problems Before Christian Education in China," 65; on understanding Christianity through Chinese culture and philosophy, 57–59, 61–65, 66, 67, 68, 69, 70; research on comparative religion, 59–60; Shantung Christian University (SCU) and, 53, 54, 59, 60–61
Drake, Samuel Bingham, 53
Duyin tongyi qicheng hui 讀音統一期成會 (Society for the Promotion of Zhuyin Zimu), 172, 173

Easy Chinese Lesson for the Illiterates (Zhu and Tao). *See Pingmin qianzike* 平民千字課 (Zhu and Tao)
education control. *See jiaoyu yongzhi* 教育統制
education of love, 120–21
Education: From the Nationalists' Point of View. *See Guojia zhuyi jiaoyu xue* 國家主義教育學
Education of Nationalism. *See Guojia zhuyi de jiaoyu* 國家主義的教育

Educational Thoughts (Zhu). *See Jiaoyu sixiang* 教育思想
Edwards, D. W., 208
Emergency Committee for the Conferment of Hong Kong Medical Degrees, 86
Emperor Guangxu 光緒, 28
Emperor Kangxi 康熙, 22
Emperor Taizu 太祖 of Ming 明. *See* Zhu Yuanzhang 朱元璋
Emperor Yongzheng 雍正, 22
encouraging learning (as a theme), 24n19
Encouraging Learning (Zhang). *See Quanxue pian* 勸學篇
Endeavour Monthly. *See Nuli yuebao* 努力月報
English Baptist Mission. *See* Baptist Missionary Society (BMS)
Erasmus, 35
Ertong jiaoyuxue 兒童教育學 (*Parenthood and Child Nurture*), 92, 107
European Renaissance, 35
evangelism, 42, 55, 56, 59, 102, 103, 151, 182, 184, 252, 254, 278
Examination Yuan. *See* Kaoshiyuan 考試院
Executive Yuan. *See* Xingzhengyuan 行政院

Fan, F. *See* Fan Yurong 范玉榮
Fan Shaozeng 范紹增, 198
Fan Yurong 范玉榮 (Fan, F.), 178 table 8.1, 178 table 8.1 note 4
Fangcao tianya 芳草天涯 (*Fragrant Grass at the Edges of the Sky*), 205, 211, 212n54
February 28 incident, 253, 253n13
Federation of International Famine Relief Commission, 206
Federation of Woman's Boards of Foreign Missions of North America, 183
Fei Xiaotong 費孝通, 207, 209, 209n42, 212, 240; and Wang Tonghui 王同惠 (wife), 215, 215n65; *Peasant Life in China*, 209
Fei Yingxiao 費迎曉, 231–32
Feng Youlan 馮友蘭, 239

Feng Yuxiang 馮玉祥, 162
Feng Zikai 豐子愷, 101
Fichte, Johann Gottlieb, 127
Fifteen Lectures in Elementary Civics. See *Gongmin changshi shiwu jiang* 公民常識十五講
Fifty Famous Stories Retold. See *Taixi mingren xiaoshuoji* 泰西名人小說集
First Plenum of the Chinese People's Political Consultative Conference, 94
First Sino-Japanese War (1894–1895), 171
First Steps in Teaching National Phonetic Script (Joyce and Griffith), 184
Fish-scale Land Registers. See *yü-lin ce* 魚鱗冊
Fitch Memorial Church. See Hongde Tang 鴻德堂
Fong Foo Sec. See Kuang Fuzhuo 鄺富灼
Forum on Democracy and Science. See Jiusan xueshe 九三學社 (Jiusan Society)
Fragrant Grass at the Edges of the Sky. See *Fangcao tianya* 芳草天涯
French, Evangeline, 184, 184n64, 185
French, Francesca, 184, 184n64
Fu, Daniel. See Fu Ruoyu 傅若愚
Fu Jen Academy. See Fu Jen University
Fu Jen University (Catholic University of Peking), 37, 35n5, 202, 227n2, 237
Fu Ruoyu 傅若愚 (Fu, Daniel), 160
fuji 扶乩 (planchette writing), 57
Fukuzawa Yukichi 福澤諭吉, 24n19
Fullerton, William Young, 39
fundamentalists, 26; versus modernists, 27
fuxing xiangcun 復興鄉村 (revive rural communities), 95

Gamble, Sidney D.: *Peking, a Social Survey* co-authored with John Stewart Burgess, 206
Gamewell, F. D., 154n38
Gandi xiaozhuan 甘地小傳 (*Mahatma Ghandi*), 92

Gao Shiliang 高時良, 236
Garland, S. J., 175, 179 table 8.1, 182, 183; the braille system of, 174, 174n31
Garnier, Albert J., 92
Gelaohui 哥老會, 197, 198. See also Paoge 袍哥
gender equality, 12, 267, 274, 279–80
General Assembly of the Church of Christ in China, 94
general education, 10, 146, 239. See also whole-person education
gentlemen. See *junzi* 君子
Gerrard, William I., 79
Ginling College, 227n2, 228n3, 234n18, 235
GMD. See Guomindang 國民黨
gongju 公局 (public bureaus), 23
Gongmin changshi shiwu jiang 公民常識十五講 (*Fifteen Lectures in Elementary Civics*), 105
Gongmin changshi xiaojian 公民常識小簡 (*A Short Introduction to Elementary Civics*), 105
"Good Ways to Popularize Literacy" (Zhang). See "Shi renren dou shizi de haofazi" 使人人都識字的好法子
"Good Ways to Teach Mothers to Read" (Zhang). See "Jiao muqin shizi de miaofa" 教母親識字的妙法
Gorky, Maxim, 205
Gotch-Robinson High School. See Shoushan Zhongxuexiao 守善中學校
Gowned Brothers. See Paoge 袍哥
Graham, James R., 254, 255
Gray, W. Parker, 44
Great Britain: expansion in Tibet, 148
Great Federation of Anti-Religionists, 37
Great Rear Area. See *Dahoufang* 大後方
Griffith, Mrs. J. C.: *First Steps in Teaching National Phonetic Script* co-produced with Mrs. F. C. Joyce, 184
Gu Jiegang 顧頡剛, 212n57, 239

Gu Weijun 顧維鈞 (Koo, Wellington), 162
Gu Xiancheng 顧憲成, 20
Gu Yanwu 顧炎武, 21
Guangwen zhongxue 廣文中學 (Guangwen Middle School), 93n8, 98, 99
Guangxue duben 廣學讀本 (*C.L.S. Readers for Illiterates*), 101
Guangxue hui 廣學會. *See* Christian Literature Society for China
Guanhua hesheng zimu 官話合聲字母 (Wang Zhao's Mandarin Syllabary), 172, 174, 175, 176
Guanghua Daxue 光華大學 (Kwanghua University), 113, 120, 130, 135
guanxi xushu 關係敘述 (narrative of relations), 213
Guo Keti 郭克悌, 255
Guojia zhuyi de jiaoyu 國家主義的教育 (*Education of Nationalism*), 116. See also *guojia zhuyi pai* 國家主義派
Guojia zhuyi jiaoyu xue 國家主義教育學 (*Education: From the Nationalists' Point of View*), 116. See also *guojia zhuyi pai* 國家主義派
guojia zhuyi pai 國家主義派 (Nationalist Group), 116, 117
Guomindang 國民黨 (GMD). *See* Nationalist Party
guoxue 國學 (Sinology), 53, 56, 236, 237
Guoyu yanjiuhui 國語研究會 (Association for the Study of the National Language), 172
Guoyuxue jiangyi 國語學講義 (*Chinese Phonetic System and Language*) (Li), 187; English translation of, 185

Haiyan jutuan 海燕劇團 (Petrel Troupe), 205
Hammond and Underwood typewriters, 186n73
Han Wei 韓偉, 255, 256, 262
Hangchow Christian College. *See* Hangchow University
Hangchow Presbyterian College. *See* Hangzhou Yuying Shuyuan 杭州育英書院
Hangchow University (Hangchow Christian College; Zhijiang Daxue 之江大學), 91, 227n2, 228n3, 234n18, 241. *See also* Hangzhou Yuying Shuyuan 杭州育英書院
Hangzhou Yuying Shuyuan 杭州育英書院 (Hangchow Presbyterian College), 91. *See also* Hangchow University
Hartford Seminary, 113, 135
Harvard Institutes for Higher Education (HIHE), 275
Harvard University, 10, 146, 149, 212, 235, 237
Harvard-Yenching Institute Fund, 237
He Jian 何健, 132, 133
He Jianming 何建明, 237
He Xiaoxia 何曉夏, 243
He Xinyin 何心隱, 20
higher education in Asia: academic freedom and, 271–73; inter-religious conflicts in colleges and universities, 279, 279n44; massification and, 268–71; nature of, 273; situation in India, 269, 269n12, 270; situation in Southeast Asia, 269, 271, 272
HKU. *See* University of Hong Kong
Hong Kong: academic freedom in, 272, gender equality in universities in, 279, 280, Gordon King and, 79–83, 85–87, Shen Baoyuan in, 205–6
Hong Kong Baptist University: Centre for Sino-Christian Studies, 7; Department of Religion and Philosophy, 7
Hong Kong Family Planning Association, 83
Hong Kong Refugee Relief Bureau, 84
Hongde Tang 鴻德堂 (Fitch Memorial Church), 102
Hongkong Eugenics, 83
Hope Township. *See* Wangzhen 望鎮

Horizontal Tablet. See *wobei* 臥碑
Hou Hsueh-fang. *See* Hou Xuefang 侯雪舫
Hou Qiang 侯強, 232
Hou Renzhi 侯仁之, 240
Hou Xuefang 侯雪舫 (Hou Hsueh-fang; Hou Yanshuang 侯延爽), 57
How to Teach Religion. See Zongjiao jiaoshou fa 宗教教授法
Hu Shi 胡適, 26n23, 118, 128, 131, 160, 162
Huabei Jidujiao nongcun shiye cujinhui 華北基督教農村事業促進會 (North China Christian Rural Service Union), 94, 95
Huachung University, 227n2, 228n3, 230, 233; Boone Library College, 230; collaboration with Yale University, 235; examination systems, 241–42; rating of, 235; student admission, 233
Huamei 華美 Girls' Middle School, 212, 212n57
Huang Fu 黃郛, 129, 130
Huang Hua 黃華, 240
Huang Zongxi 黃宗羲, 21
huidang 會黨 (Rebel Bandit Clique), 198
Hunan Provincial Government (Nationalist government), 113, 115, 124, 132, 133, 135; Education Bureau of, 136; Experiment District of Compulsory Education (Yiwu jiaoyu shiyan qu 義務教育實驗區), 138; Mass Training Guidance Office (Minzhong xunlian zhidao chu 民眾訓練指導處), 138
Huxley, Aldous, 125

imperial examination, 19, 24, 26, 28, 65, 66. *See also* civil service examination
Imperial University, 23, 27, 28
India: state universities versus private colleges, 269, 269n12, 270
indoctrination, 8, 24, 36, 37, 39, 45
Ingle, Laurence M., 80, 81

Institute of Social Surveys in Peiping. *See* Beiping shehui diaochasuo 北平社會調查所
Institution for Village Governance. *See* Cunzhi yanjiuyuan 村治研究院
International Service Learning Program (ISLP), 282, 282n54, 283
Introduction to Religious Education. See Zongjiao jiaoyu gailun 宗教教育概論
intuitive knowledge. See *liangzhi* 良知
Investigation of the Social Conditions in Ding County. See Dingxian shehui gaikuang diaocha 定縣社會概況調查

January 28 Incident, 101
Japanese: invasion into and occupation of Hong Kong, 9, 83; invasion into Shandong, 79; Kwantung Army, 79
Jen Pang-che. *See* Ren Bangzhe 任邦哲
Jesuits, 21n8, 36
Jesus Christ, 41, 64, 65, 68, 105, 106, 158; patriotism and, 107; spirit of, 69, 70
Jiahui qingnian 嘉惠青年 (*Benefits to the Youth*), 157
Jiang Menglin 蔣夢麟, 121, 122, 131
Jiangsu Provincial Education Association, 155
"Jiangyan wei shehui jiaoyu zhi liqi" 講演為社會教育之利器 ("Lecture is a Useful and Effective Instrument of Social Education") (Yu), 156
"Jiao muqin shizi de miaofa" 教母親識字的妙法 ("Good Ways to Teach Mothers to Read") (Zhang), 98
Jiaoyu sixiang 教育思想 (*Educational Thoughts*) (Zhu), 119, 120, 121
jiaoyu tongzhi 教育統制 (education control), 128
Jiating de yanjiu 家庭的研究 (*The Family: Its History and Problems*), 92
Jidujiao tichang zhuyin zimu weiyuanhui 基督教提倡注音字母委員會. *See* Phonetic Promotion Committee

Jidujiao yu Zhongguo jindai zhongdeng jiaoyu 基督教與中國近代中等教育 (*Christianity and Secondary Education in Modern China*) (Yin), 6
"Jidutu yu aiguo" 基督徒與愛國 ("Christians and Patriotism") (Xie), 107
jinbu xuesheng 進步學生 (progressive students), 203
Jindai jiaoyu sichao qijiang 近代教育思潮七講 (*Seven Lectures on Modern Educational Thoughts*) (Zhu), 121, 123–28
Jindai xuandaoxue dagang 近代宣道學大綱 (*Principles of Modern Preaching*), 92, 106
jisuan fangfa 計算方法. *See* Operational Method (social anthropology)
jiu wang tu cun 救亡圖存 (save the nation from extinction and strive for its survival), 25, 25n21, 29, 30
jiuji xiangcun 救濟鄉村 (bring relief to rural communities), 95
Jiusan xueshe 九三學社 (Jiusan Society), 93
Jize 濟澤. *See* Xie Songgao 謝頌羔
John Hopkins University School of Medicine, 78
Johnson, Andrew, 272, 272n24
Joyce, Mrs. F. S.: *First Steps in Teaching National Phonetic Script* co-produced with Mrs. J. C. Griffith, 184
junzi 君子 (gentlemen), 18, 19

Kang Youwei 康有為, 28, 28n26
Kangzhan jianguo gangling 抗戰建國綱領 (*Program of the War of Resistance and National Construction*), 125, 127
Kaoshiyuan 考試院 (Examination Yuan), 131
Kexue de Jiduhua sixiang 科學的基督化思想 (*Scientific Christian Thinking for Young People*), 92

"Kexue yu zongjiao" 科學與宗教 ("Science and Religion") (Zhu), 118–19
Key, Ellen, 125
King, Gordon, 8, 9, 75, 76; as a visiting professor at the National Shanghai Medical College, 84, 85 figure 4.1; BMS and, 78, 79, 79n8, 80, 81, 82, 82n22, 83; contributions to HKU's medical training during WWII, 84–86, 87, 88; early life in England, 78; meaning of his Chinese name (Wang Guodong 王國棟), 75; medical services in Hong Kong, 83, 86; Ong Guan Bee's comment on, 86, 87; services in SCU, 79; transfer to HKU from SCU, 79–83, 87
Kong Xiangxi 孔祥熙 (Kung, H. H.), 131, 132
Koo, Wellington. *See* Gu Weijun 顧維鈞
Korean War, 251, 252
Kowloon Hospital, 86
Kuang Fuzhuo 鄺富灼 (Fong Foo Sec), 177, 177n46, 178 table 8.1, 181, 187
Kulp, Daniel H.: *Country Life in South China*, 206
Kung, H. H. *See* Kong Xiangxi 孔祥熙
Kuno, Yoshi Saburo, 235
Kuzuoğlu, Uluğ, 169–70, 175, 175n36, 175n38
Kwanghua University. *See* Guanghua Daxue 光華大學

L'Institut des Hautes Études Industrielles et Commerciales, 36
Lacy, George Carleton, 180 table 8.1, 187n82
Land Utilization in China (Buck), 207
Lao She 老舍, 239
"Lecture is a Useful and Effective Instrument of Social Education" (Yu). *See* "Jiangyan wei shehui jiaoyu zhi liqi" 講演為社會教育之利器

Lei Mingyuan, 195, 202, 214, 216; as Paoge leader, 195, 198–99; Shuying (daughter), 211, 212; Woman Lei (wife), 210, 211
Lei, Sean Hsiang-lin, 77
Li Anzhai 李安宅, 202, 202n24, 209
Li Huang 李璜, 116
Li Jinghan 李景漢, 207
Li Jinxi 黎錦熙, 185, 186; *Guoyuxue jiangyi* 國語學講義 (*Chinese Phonetic System and Language*), 187
Li Tianlu 李天祿 (Li T'ien Lu), 41, 43, 68, 69
Li Xiangmin 李湘敏, 240
Li Yuanhong 黎元洪, 150, 156
Li Yusha 李雨紗, 232
Liang Shuming 梁漱溟, 99, 200, 200n19, 201
liangzhi 良知 (intuitive knowledge), 119
Liao Ping 廖平, 25
Liao Taichu 廖泰初 (Liao T'ai-ch'u), 196, 196n4, 198, 204, 209
Lim Kho-Seng. *See* Lin Kesheng 林可勝
Lim, Robert. *See* Lin Kesheng 林可勝
Lin Jingrun 林景潤, 239
Lin Kesheng 林可勝 (Lim Kho-Seng; Lim, Robert), 86
Lin Yaohua 林耀華, 196, 202, 202n24, 204, 209, 212, 213, 213n59, 214, 215; *Shehui renleixue jiangyi* 社會人類學講義 (*Teaching Notes on Social Anthropology*), 214
Lin Zhiping 林治平, 5
Ling Daoyang 凌道揚, 154n39, 155, 155 table 7.1
Lingnan University, 78n7, 84, 227n2, 234n18, 235
literacy education, 95, 96, 98, 105, 169, 171, 181, 184, 185, 186, 188, 190, 191
Liu Baoxiong 劉保兄, 231
Liu Guangjing 劉廣京 (Liu, K. C.), 2, 5, 6
Liu, Herman C. E. *See* Liu Zhanen 劉湛恩
Liu, James T. C. *See* Liu Zijian 劉子健

Liu Jiafeng 劉家峰, 4, 9
Liu Jing'an 劉靜庵, 149
Liu, K. C. *See* Liu Guangjing 劉廣京
Liu Mei xuesheng jianduchu 留美學生監督處 (Chinese Educational Mission in the United States), 112
Liu Qiongyin 劉瓊英, 149
Liu Shouqi 劉壽祺, 138
Liu Zhanen 劉湛恩 (Liu, Herman C. E.), 161, 190
Liu Zijian 劉子健 (Liu, James T. C.), 3
Lixiang zhong ren 理想中人 (*My Ideal People*) (Xie), 92, 107
LMS. *See* London Missionary Society
Lobenstine, Edwin C., 177, 180 table 8.1, 180 table 8.1 note 5
London Missionary Society (LMS), 78, 171, 172, 172n20, 176, 180 table 8.1
Longheu Girls' School (Qianzhen Nuxiao 虔貞女校), 6
Lu Jiuyuan 陸九淵, 26, 26n23
Lu Yuanding 陸元鼎, 102
Lu Zuofu 盧作孚, 200–201, 201n20; "Sichuan Jialingjiang Sanxia de xiangcun jianshe yungdong" ("The Rural Reconstruction Movement in Jialing and the Three Gorges Areas"), 201
Luo Dajing 羅大經, 20n6
Luo Rufang 羅汝芳, 20
Luo Yunyan 羅運炎, 99
Lushi Chunqiu 呂氏春秋, 24n19
Lutz, Jessie G., 2–3, 6, 38; *China and the Christian College 1850–1950*, 3, 227n3, 228; "The Role of the Christian Colleges in Modern China before 1928" (PhD thesis), 2–3
Lyon, D. W., 151, 154n36, 180 table 8.1

Ma Min 馬敏, 4
Mackenzie, A. R., 180 table 8.1; English translator of *Guoyuxue jiangyi* (*Chinese Phonetic System and Language*), 185

Mackenzie, John Kenneth, 77
Madras High Court (India), 270
Mahatma Ghandi. See *Gandi xiaozhuan* 甘地小傳
Malone, C. B., 206; *The Study of Chinese Rural Economy* co-authored with J. B. Tagler, 206
Manchurian Plague, 77
Mandarin, 170, 171, 173, 184, 190; Bibles printed in, 172, 186, 187–88; standardization of pronunciation, 169, 172, 190; *Union Version*, 187. See also *baihua* 白話 (vernacular Chinese)
Mao Zedong 毛澤東, 205
Marco Polo Bridge Incident, 79. See also Double-Seventh Incident
Martin, William Alexander, 26, 29n29
mass education movement, 9, 90–91, 146, 157, 159, 161, 169
mass illiteracy: in late Qing and early Republican China, 170–71
Mateer, Calvin Wilson, 4
May Fourth Movement, 28, 76, 157
May Thirtieth Incident, 41, 162. See also Shanghai Massacre
Medhurst, Walter Henry, 26
Metaphysician School. See *xuanxue pai* 玄學派
Meyer, F. B., 39
"Migrants and Crime in Northeast China." See "Dongsansheng zhi yinmin yu fanzui" 東三省之移民與犯罪
Milne, William, 24n17, 26
Milton Stewart Evangelistic Fund, 177, 182–83
mind-heart. See *xin* 心
Miner, Luella, 131
Mingdeng 明燈 (*Shining Light*), 92
Minguo zhuyin zimu zhengce shilun 民國注音字母政策史論 (Yu), 169
Ministry of Education (People's Republic of China), 268, 272

Ministry of Education (Republic of China), 46, 113, 130, 131, 134, 135, 138, 202, 249, 249n1, 250, 250n2, 255; Commission on the Unification of Pronunciation (Duyin tongyihui 讀音統一會), 172, 173, 190; development and promulgation of *zhuyin zimu*, 172, 173, 190; Education Investigation Committee (Jiaoyu diaocha weiyuanhui 教育調查委員會), 121; Preparatory Commission on the Unification of the National Language (Guoyu tongyi choubei hui 國語統一籌備會), 185
Ministry of Education and Research (Daxueyuan 大學院) (Nationalist government), 113, 123, 130. See also Ministry of Education (Republic of China)
Ministry of Human Resource Development (India), 270
Minzhu bao 民主報 (*Democracy Daily*), 112
Mission Book Company, 107
Missionary Herald, 55, 58
missionary medicine, 77
Modern Education in China and Its Impacts: A Historical and Philosophical Investigation (conference held in 2018), 7
Mongols, 19, 205
Mott, John R., 151, 163
mutian mushan 募田募山 (raising funds from fields and hills), 133
My Ideal People (Xie). See *Lixiang zhong ren* 理想中人
"My Religious Views" (Xie). See "Wo de zongjiaoguan" 我的宗教觀

Nanjing Massacre, 4
Nanking Theological Seminary, 92, 93–94
narrative of relations. See *guanxi xushu* 關係敘述
nation-building, 7, 10, 105, 170, 191

National Central University, 113, 131, 134, 138
National Christian Conference, 177, 189
National Christian Council of China (Zhonghua quanguo Judujiao xiejinhui 中華全國基督教協進會), 94, 95, 168n1, 169, 169n4, 177; How Should Christianity Contribute to Rural Construction? (conference held in 1933), 95
National Constituent Assembly, 113
National Hsiang Ya Medical College, 84
National Origins Acts (1924), 28n27
National Phonetic Alphabet. See *zhuyin zimu* 注音字母
National Phonetic Script. See *zhuyin zimu* 注音字母
national salvation through scholarship. See *xueshu jiuguo* 學術救國
National Shanghai Medical College, 84, 85 figure 4.1
national sovereignty, 38
nationalism, 3, 4, 10, 45, 75, 117, 127, 146, 158. See also nation-building
Nationalist government, 39, 130, 136, 201, 202, 205, 251, 252, 253; against students' compulsory attendance at Christian services, 8, 38, 41, 254; establishment of the Ministry of Education and Research, 130; SCU's registration with, 41, 54, 131; Zhu Jingnong on the implementation of educational regulations of, 124–25, 128; Zhu Jingnong's services in, 113, 128. See also Nationalist Party; Ministry of Education (Republic of China)
Nationalist Group. See *guojia zhuyi pai* 國家主義派
Nationalist Party (Guomindang 國民黨) (GMD), 36, 39, 45, 46, 123, 127, 128, 129, 130, 131, 134, 135, 136, 138, 199, 205; Central Club Clique, 134;

dangguo xianjin, 125, 127. See also Nationalist government
New Culture Movement, 122
Ng, Peter Tze Ming. See Wu Ziming 吳梓明
Nie Shaojing 聶紹經 (Nieh, Elijah S.), 189
nongcun gongzuo dui 農村工作隊 (rural work teams), 203
nongcun gongzuo zhe 農村工作者 (rural activists), 196
Nongcun shehuixue 農村社會學 (*Rural Sociology*) (Yang), 208
Nongmin qianzike 農民千字課 (*Thousand Character Primer for Peasants*), 97
North China Christian Rural Service Union. See Huabei Jidujiao nongcun shiye cujinhui 華北基督教農村事業促進會
Nu xing 女星 (*Woman's Star*), 101
Nu xing yu pingmin jiating yuekan 女星與平民家庭月刊 (*Woman's Star and The People's Family Magazine*), 101
Nuli yuebao 努力月報 (*Endeavour Monthly*), 118

Ong Guan Bee. See Wang Yuanmei 王源美
Operational Method (social anthropology) (*jisuan fangfa* 計算方法), 213
Ou Yingyu 區應毓 (Au, Peter): *Jiaoyu linian yu Jidujiao jiaoyuguan* 教育理念與基督教教育觀 (*The Ideas of Education Concept and the View on Christian Education*), 106
"Outline of County Organization at All Levels." See "Xian geji zuzhi gangyao" 縣各級組織綱要

Pacific War, 54, 202
Palmer, Parker: *The Courage to Teach*, 277
Pan Gongzhan 潘公展, 130, 137
Pan Shu 潘菽, 94
Pan Zifang 潘子放 (Pan, T. F.), 189
Paoge 袍哥 (Gowned Brothers), 10, 215, 216; Lei Mingyuan and, 195, 198;

overview and nature, 197–98, 198n14, 199. *See also* Shen Baoyuan's thesis on Lei Mingyuan's family and Paoge
Parenthood and Child Nurture. See Ertong jiaoyuxue 兒童教育學
Park, Robert Ezra, 208, 208n41, 212
Parker, Peter, 77
Parsons, Talcott, 212
partified education. *See danghua jiaoyu* 黨化教育
patriotism: PPC and, 182; of Christian college teachers and students, 41, 242; of Jesus, 107; of Xie Songgao and Zhang Xueyan, 107–8; of Yu Rizhang, 148–49, 156, 158; YMCA in China and, 158; Zhu Jingnong on, 127
peacebuilding, 12, 267
Peasant Life in China (Fei), 209
Peill brothers: and their modified version of Wang Zhao's Mandarin Syllabary, 172, 172n18. *See also* Peill, Ernest J; Peill, Sidney G.
Peill, Ernest J., 171, 180 table 8.1
Peill, Sidney G., 171, 172n18, 177, 180 table 8.1; attitude towards *zhuyin zimu*, 175, 175n38, 176
Peking Gazette, 150
Peking Union Medical College (PUMC), 77, 78, 78n7, 79, 79n8, 84, 86
Peking University, 29, 113, 128, 196n5, 230, 271n22
Peking, a Social Survey (Gamble and Burgess), 206
People's 1,000 Character Primer (Yan). *See Pingmin qianzike* 平民千字課 (Yan)
Permanent Committee for the Coordination and Promotion of the Christian Higher Education in China, 234
Peter, W. W., 155, 155n40
Petrel Troupe. *See Haiyan jutuan* 海燕劇團
Philippines: free education in, 269

Phonetic Promotion Committee (PPC) (Zhonghua xuxing weibanhui zhuyin zimu teweihui 中華續行委辦會注音字母特委會; Jidujiao tichang zhuyin zimu weiyuanhui 基督教提倡注音字母委員會): activities to promote *zhuyin zimu*, 184–89; as a Sino-Foreign Protestant Establishment (SFPE) organization, 170, 176, 177, 178–81 table 8.1, 182, 190, 191; CCC's establishment of, 168, 174; financial support to, 182–83; historical overview, 168–69, 169n4, 169n5; membership and chairmanship, 175, 176, 177, 178–81 table 8.1, 181, 182; nature of, 169, 182, 190; research history of, 169–70, 183; results of its work, 189–90; stance on *zhuyin zimu*, 176
Phonetic Spelling Book, with Easy Sentences. See Zimu pinyin keben 字母拼音課本
pictorial central scrolls. *See zhongtang* 中堂
Pingmin gushi duben 平民故事讀本 (*The Story Readers for the Common People*), 101
Pingmin qianzike 平民千字課 (*People's 1,000 Character Primer*) (Yan), 99
Pingmin qianzike 平民千字課 (*Easy Chinese Lesson for the Illiterates*) (Zhu and Tao), 122
Pingmin yuekan 平民月刊 (*The People's Magazine*), 92, 99, 101; "Benkan de xinnian shiming" 本刊的新年使命 ("The New Year's Mission Statement of *The People's Magazine*"), 100; example of its literary style, 100–101; format and contents of, 100; purpose and mission, 100
Pingmin zihua ji 平民字畫集 (*Art Pictures for the Common People*), 101
pinyin zipu 拼音字譜 (Wang), 171
planchette writing. *See fuji* 扶乩
Pott, Francis Lister Hawks, 154n38

PPC. *See* Phonetic Promotion Committee
Presbyterian Church in Canada, 184
Presbyterian Church in Taiwan, 252, 253, 253n13
"Problems Before Christian Education in China" (Drake), 65
Price, Harry, 180 table 8.1, 187
Price, Philip B., 80, 81
Principles of Modern Preaching. *See Jindai xuandaoxue dagang* 近代宣道學大綱
Program of the War of Resistance and National Construction. *See Kangzhan jianguo gangling* 抗戰建國綱領
progressive students. *See jinbu xuesheng* 進步學生
Prophecy and Religion in Ancient China and Israel (Rowley), 47
proselytism, 37, 45
proselytization, 26
Protestantism, 90, 115
Provisional Constitution for the Period of Political Tutelage. *See Xunzheng shiqi yuefa* 訓政時期約法
public bureaus. *See gongju* 公局
PUMC. *See* Peking Union Medical College

Qi Shounan 戚壽南, 240
Qian Xuesen's 錢學森 Question, 241, 244
Qianzhen Nuxiao 虔貞女校. *See* Longheu Girls' School
Qida yuekan 齊大月刊 (*Cheeloo Monthly*), 123, 126, 126 table 6.1. *See also* Shantung Christian University
Qingnian jinbu 青年進步 (*Association Progress*), 158
Qingnian you 青年友 (*Young People's Friend*), 92
"'Qiqi' jinian yu benbao" "七七"紀念與本報 ("Commemoration of the Double-Seventh Incident and the Christian Farmer") (Zhang), 105
Quan Shaowu 全紹武 (Chuan, S. Peter), 178 table 8.1, 178 table 8.1 note 3

Quanxue pian 勸學篇 (*Encouraging Learning*) (Zhang), 24–25, 25n20
Queen Mary Hospital, 83

Radcliffe-Brown, Alfred Reginald, 208, 208n41, 212
raising funds from fields and hills. *See mutian mushan* 募田募山
Rawlinson, F., 185
Rebel Bandit Clique. *See huidang* 會黨
Reformation, 90
religious education, 8; compulsory Christian service in Chinese Christian colleges as, 36, 66; Xie Songgao on, 106–7; Zhu Jingnong on, 115–21
Religious Tract Society (RTS), 177, 189
Ren Bangzhe 任邦哲 (Jen Pang-che), 85 figure 4.1
renge jiuguo 人格救國 (character saves the nation), 158
Restore Educational Rights Movement, 37–38, 39, 116, 235
revive rural communities. *See fuxing xiangcun* 復興鄉村
Richard, Timothy, 26
Robertson, Clarence H., 151, 152, 152n27, 153, 154, 155, 155 table 7.1
Rockefeller Foundation, 78
Romanization (simplified writing system), 174, 176
Rong Yiren 榮毅仁, 240
Roots, Logan H., 149, 149n17, 180 table 8.1, 180 table 8.1 note 6
Rousseau, Jean-Jacques, 125
Rowley, Harold Henry, 39, 40, 40 figure 2.1, 47; BMS and, 39–45; feelings on SCU students' patriotism, 41; *Prophecy and Religion in Ancient China and Israel*, 47; *Submission in Suffering and Other Essays in Eastern Thought*, 47; resistance to SCU's registration with the Nationalist government, 42–44, 46
RTS. *See* Religious Tract Society

Ruan Danian 阮大年, 256
rural activists. See *nongcun gongzuo zhe* 農村工作者
rural construction movement, 95
rural education, 200, 201; Rural Education Movement, 10, 196, 200, 215
rural reconstruction, 200, 201; Rural Reconstruction Movement, 10, 196, 200n18, 201, 215
Rural Research Reconstruction Institution, 200; *Cunzhi* (*Village Governance*), 200
Rural Sociology (Yang). See *Nongcun shehuixue* 農村社會學
rural work teams. See *nongcun gongzuo dui* 農村工作隊
Russo-Japanese War, 148

Sacred Edict. See *Shengyu* 聖諭
salvation, 59, 69
Salvation Army, 149
san min zhuyin 三民主義 (Three Principles of the People), 8, 9, 42, 45, 114, 123, 124, 125, 126 table 6.1, 127, 128
save the nation from extinction and strive for its survival. See *jiu wang tu cun* 救亡圖存
"Science and Religion" (Zhu). See "*Kexue yu zongjiao*" 科學與宗教
Scientific Christian Thinking for Young People. See *Kexue de Jiduhua sixiang* 科學的基督化思想
Scottish Enlightenment, 35
SCU. See Shantung Christian University
secret societies, 195, 196, 197, 197n6, 206
Selected Poems from Aishan Mansion. See *Aishanlu shichao* 愛山廬詩鈔
Seven Lectures on Modern Educational Thoughts (Zhu). See *Jindai jiaoyu sichao qijiang* 近代教育思潮七講
Seymour, Horace, 84
SFPE. See Sino-Foreign Protestant Establishment

Shangdi 上帝, 62, 120
Shanghai Baptist College. *See* University of Shanghai
Shanghai Massacre, 113. *See also* May Thirtieth Incident
Shanghai Party Purification Committee (Shanghai shi qingdang weiyuanhui 上海市清黨委員會), 130
Shanghai Students' Union (Shanghai xuesheng lianhehui 上海學生聯合會), 130
Shantung Baptist Union, 44
Shantung Christian University (SCU), 53, 68; Frederick Seguier Drake and, 53, 54, 55, 59, 60–61; Gordon King at, 79–82, 84, 87; Harold Henry Rowley at, 39–44, 40 figure 2.1; medical college of, 78n7, 79, 79n10, 84, 240; presidency, 41, 68, 131–33; *Qida yuekan* (*Cheeloo Monthly*), 123, 126, 126 table 6.1; rating of, 235; registration with the government, 41–44, 131; Sino-Foreign cultural exchange and, 237; Zhu Jingnong at, 113, 115, 123, 131–33, 135, 138
shehui 社會 (society) (Shen Baoyuan's usage of), 210
Shehui kexue yanjiusuo 社會科學研究所. *See* Academia Sinica
Shehui renleixue jiangyi 社會人類學講義 (*Teaching Notes on Social Anthropology*) (Lin), 214
Shen Baoyuan 沈寶媛, 10; analysis and criticism of Paoge, 198, 199; communist ideology and, 203, 205, 209; family background, 204–5, 204n28; impression on rural life, 203; interactions with Lei's family, 202, 210–12, 215; Operational Method and, 213–14; teachers' influence on, 203, 204, 212–14. *See also* Shen Baoyuan's thesis on Lei Mingyuan's family and Paoge

Shen Baoyuan's thesis on Lei Mingyuan's family and Paoge, 195, 214, 215, 216; format and structure, 195n2; historical backgrounds of, 200–203; methodologies, 210–14; motive, 215; supervisors of, 196, 196n4
Shen Bin 沈彬 (Sund, Marcus W.), 178 table 8.1, 181n48
Shen Enfu 沈恩孚, 121, 122
Shen Zurong 沈祖榮, 204, 204n28
Shengyu 聖諭 (*Sacred Edict*), 22, 22n13, 22n17
Shengyu guangxun 聖諭廣訓 (*Amplified Instructions on the Sacred Edict*), 22
Shengyu shiliu tiao 聖諭十六條 (*Sixteen Maxims*), 22
shetuan 社團 (social organization) (Shen Baoyuan's usage of), 198, 210
shexue 社學 (community schools), 19, 20, 20n6, 22
Shi Jinghuan 史靜寰, 4
"Shi renren dou shizi de haofazi" 使人人都識字的好法子 ("Good Ways to Popularize Literacy") (Zhang), 98
Shining Light. See *Mingdeng* 明燈
Shoushan Zhongxuexiao 守善中學校 (Gotch-Robinson High School), 54
shuyuan 書院 (academies), 18, 19, 22, 26; Zhu Xi and, 19
"Sichuan Jianglingjiang Sanxia de xiangcun jianshe yungdong" 四川嘉陵江三峽的鄉村建設運動 ("The Rural Reconstruction Movement in Jialing and the Three Gorges Areas") (Lu), 201
Singapore Management University, 276
Sino-Foreign Protestant Establishment (SFPE), 29n30, 76, 78; definition of, 176–77; leadership, 177; PPC as an organization of, 10, 170, 177, 182, 190, 191
Sinology. See *guoxue* 國學

Sixteen Maxims. See *Shengyu shiliu tiao* 聖諭十六條
social anthropology, 209, 213
social education, 9, 10, 145, 146, 146n3, 163; definition of, 145, 145n1, 145n2; Yu Rizhang's ideas of and YMCA's programs of, 156, 157–62
social organization (Shen Baoyuan's usage of). See *shetuan* 社團
society (Shen Baoyuan's usage of). See *shehui* 社會
Society for the Promotion of Zhuyin Zimu. See Duyin tongyi qicheng hui 讀音統一期成會
Soochow University, 91, 92, 230, 232, 234n18
Soochow University (Taiwan), 254n18
Southern Baptist Convention, 46, 253
Spencer, Herbert, 125
Spurgeon, C. H., 39
St. Hilda's School for Girls, 149
St. John's University, 4, 26n24, 78n7, 146, 147, 147n6, 227n2, 228n3, 230, 235, 242; *St. John's Echo*, 147
Stanley, C. A., 61
STEM education, 271, 280
Stimson, Henry, 162
structural functionalism, 208, 208n41, 212, 213
Stuart, John Leighton, 4, 234, 238
student movements, 28, 28n27, 28n28
Submission in Suffering and Other Essays in Eastern Thought (Rowley), 47
Sun Ensan 孫恩三, 94, 95–96
Sun Yat-sen (Sun Yixian 孫逸仙), 9; as *dangguo xianjin*, 125, 127; bequeathed teachings of (*Zhongli yijiao* 總理遺教), 127; Three Principles of the People, 8, 42, 45, 125, 127
Sund, Marcus W. See Shen Bin 沈彬
Swanson, Allen J., 253

Tagler, J. B., 206; *The Study of Chinese Rural Economy* co-authored with C. B. Malone, 206
Taiwan: Christianity in, 252, 252n9, 252n10, 253, 257; higher education in, 249–50, 249n1, 249n2, 254, 254n18, 257–58; relationship with the United States, 251, 251n4
Taiwan Lutheran Church, 253
Taiwanese Holiness Church, 252
Taixi mingren xiaoshuoji 泰西名人小説集 (*Fifty Famous Stories Retold*), 92
Tang Shaoyi 唐紹儀 (Tang Shao Yi), 153
Tao Feiya 陶飛亞, 237
Tao Menghe 陶孟和, 207
Tao Xingzhi 陶行知, 90, 91, 104, 114, 118, 160, 240; *Pingmin qianzike* (*Easy Chinese Lesson for the Illiterates*) complied with Zhu Jingnong, 122
Tao Yuan (*Daoyuan* 道院) (Chinese folk religion), 56, 57, 60
Taoism. *See* Daoism
Teaching Notes on Social Anthropology (Lin). *See Shehui renleixue jiangyi* 社會人類學講義
technology-assisted teaching and learning (TATL), 281–82
Terry, M. E., 93
Tewksbury, Elwood G., 181 table 8.1, 186, 186n73
Thai Lawyers for Human Rights (TLHR), 272
The China Mission Year Book, 182, 189
The Courage to Teach (Palmer), 277
The Doctrine of the Mean. *See Zhongyong* 中庸
The Family: Its History and Problems. *See Jiating de yanjiu* 家庭的研究
The Grand Pronouncements. *See Dagao* 大誥
The Great Learning. *See Daxue* 大學
The Ideas of Education Concept and the View on Christian Education (Ou). *See Jiaoyu linian yu Jidujiao jiaoyuguan* 教育理念與基督教教育觀
"The Life of Jesus" (Zhang). *See* "Yesu shengping" 耶穌生平
The New Education. *See Xin jiaoyu* 新教育
The People's Magazine. *See Pingmin yuekan* 平民月刊
"The Rural Reconstruction Movement in Jialing and the Three Gorges Areas" (Lu). *See* "Sichuan Jialingjiang Sanxia de xiangcun jianshe yungdong" 四川嘉陵江三峽的鄉村建設運動
The Song of Upright Spirit. *See Zhengqi ge* 正氣歌
The Sounds of Mandarin (Chen), 170
The Story Readers for the Common People. *See Pingmin gushi duben* 平民故事讀本
The Study of Chinese Rural Economy (Malone and Tagler), 206
Thousand Character Primer for Peasants. *See Nongmin qianzike* 農民千字課
Three Principles of the People. *See san min zhuyin* 三民主義
Tian Zhengping 田正平, 231
Tianjia banyuebao 田家半月報 (*Christian Farmer*), 9, 91, 93, 94, 99, 105, 107, 108; circulation and number of subscriptions, 96–97, 96n17; establishment of, 95–96; format and contents of, 96; purpose and mission, 96, 97, 106; Office of (Tianjia she 田家社), 94, 99; readers' responses, 98; the summer camp held in Yuhetou, 98–99
Tianjia zhanwang 田家瞻望 (Zhang), 96
Tin Ka Ping Foundation, 7
TLHR. *See* Thai Lawyers for Human Rights
To Tsai Church. *See Daoji huitang* 道濟會堂
Tolstoy, Leo, 125
Tongzhi Restoration, 24
transformational leadership, 275

308 Index

Trench, E. O.: *Daozi zhuyin keben* (*Workbook of Pronouncing Phonetic Symbols*), 184
True Jesus Church. *See* Zhen Yesu jiaohui 真耶穌教會
Tsai Yuen Pei. *See* Cai Yuanpei 蔡元培
Tsan Yuk Hospital, 83
Turner, Harriet M., 188

UBCCC. *See* United Board for Christian Colleges in China
UNESCO (United Nations Educational, Scientific and Cultural Organization), 113, 128, 135, 280
United Board for Christian Colleges in China (UBCCC), 6, 234, 234n20, 235; histories of individual Protestant colleges published by, 2, 2n3. *See also* United Board for Christian Higher Education in Asia
United Board for Christian Higher Education in Asia, 2, 11, 12; ASEAN Work Plan and, 271; assessment of program outcomes, 283–84; campus spirituality development programs of, 278–79; digital literacy training programs of, 280–82; educational goals, 274, 277, 281; establishment and development before 1951, 234–35, 234n18, 234n20, 266; faculty development programs of, 276–78; gender equality promotion programs of, 279–80; leadership development programs of, 275–76, 280; mission statement, 266; service learning programs of, 282–83; understanding of whole-person education, 266–68, 273–74, 276
United Christian Publishers, 92–93
United Free Church of Scotland, 185
Universal Access to Quality Tertiary Education Act (UAQTEA), 269
Université l'Aurore. *See* Aurora University

University of George Washington, 112
University of Hong Kong (HKU), 9; academic freedom and, 272; continuation of medical students' training during WWII, 84; established the scholarship named after Gordon King, 86–87; F. S. Drake and, 54; Gordon King's transfer to, 79–83; recognition of students' medical degrees, 85–86
University of Nanking, 4, 91n2, 206, 227n2, 230, 234n18, 235, 238
University of Shanghai, 113, 115, 190, 206, 227n2, 235
University of Shanghai for Science and Technology, 46
upright spirit. *See zhengqi* 正氣

vernacular Chinese. *See baihua* 白話
village compacts. *See xiangyue* 鄉約
Village Governance. See Cunzhi 村治

Waldron, Arthur: *Zhong xi wenhua yu jiaohui daxue* (*Christian Universities and Chinese-Western Cultures*) co-edited with Zhang Kaiyuan, 3–4
Wang Bingyao 王炳耀. *See* Wang Yuchu 王煜初
Wang Chengmian 王成勉 (Wang, Peter Chen-main), 5, 6
Wang Chonghui 王寵惠 (Wang Chung Hui), 153
Wang Fansen 王汎森, 23n16
Wang Gen 王艮, 20, 20n7, 30
Wang Guodong 王國棟. *See* King, Gordon
Wang Hengtong 王亨統, 6
Wang Jingwei 汪精衛, 132
Wang, Peter Chen-main. *See* Wang Chengmian 王成勉
Wang Pu 王璞, 173, 175, 179 table 8.1
Wang Qisheng 王奇生, 243
Wang Shouren 王守仁 (Wang Yangming 王陽明), 20, 22, 30, 119, 120
Wang Wei 王瑋, 231

Wang Yangming 王陽明. See Wang Shouren 王守仁
Wang Youqi 黃有琪 (Wang Yu-chi), 85 figure 4.1
Wang Yuanmei 王源美 (Ong Guan Bee), 86, 87
Wang Yuchu 王煜初 (Wang Bingyao 王炳耀): *Pinyin zipu*, 171
Wang Yunwu 王雲五, 113, 114, 130, 134, 136, 137
Wang Zhao 王照, 173; Guanhua hesheng zimu (Wang Zhao's Mandarin Syllabary), 172, 172n20, 174, 175, 175n38, 176
Wang Zhengting 王正廷, 150, 154, 157n46, 162
Wangzhen 望鎮 (Hope Township), 195, 198, 199, 201, 204, 205, 209, 210, 211, 212, 212n57, 215
War of Resistance against Japan, 92, 96, 99, 105, 107, 113, 119, 120, 121, 125, 128, 134, 198, 201, 212n56, 239
Warnshuis, A. L., 181 table 8.1, 181 table 8.1 note 7
Washington Conference, 161
Wei Zhuomin 韋卓民 (Wei, Francis), 239
Wells, Ralph C., 93
Weltanschauung, 25, 27
Wen Tianxiang 文天祥, 119, 120
Weng Wenhao 翁文灝, 129
Wenhua Shuyuan 文華書院, 93, 93n8
wenli jiaocha 文理交叉 (cross-disciplinary studies of the arts and sciences), 239
wenli shentou 文理滲透 (cross-fertilization between the arts and sciences), 239
West China Union University, 227n2, 228n3, 230, 234n18, 241
whole-person education: as guiding principle of the United Board, 266–68, 273–74; CYCU and, 11, 250, 256, 258, 263; programs organized by the United Board to promote, 11, 275–83
Whole Person Education Academy, 277

Widmer, Ellen: *China's Christian Colleges: Cross-cultural Connections, 1900–1950* co-edited with Daniel Bays, 7
Williams, George, 151
Wilson, Charles Edward, 41, 42, 43, 44, 54, 61, 68, 82, 82n22
"Wo de zongjiaoguan" 我的宗教觀 ("My Religious Views") (Xie), 106
wobei 臥碑 (Horizontal Tablet), 23
Woman's Star. See *Nu xing* 女星
Woman's Star and The People's Family Magazine. See *Nu xing yu pingmin jiating yuekan* 女星與平民家庭月刊
women education, 243, 280
Women's Leadership Forum, 280
Workbook of Pronouncing Phonetic Symbols (Trench). See *Daozi zhuyin keben* 道字注音課本
World War I, 45, 157, 159
World War II, 27, 252, 253
Wright, H. K., 92
Wu Liande 伍連德 (Wu Lien-teh), 77
Wu Wenzao 吳文藻, 207, 208, 208n38, 209, 212, 240
Wu Yifang 吳貽芳, 239
Wu Zhihui 吳稚暉, 129, 131
Wu Zhixiong 吳志雄, 101
Wu Ziming 吳梓明 (Ng, Peter Tze Ming), 4, 5

Xia Yan 夏衍, 205, 211n54
"Xian geji zuzhi gangyao" 縣各級組織綱要 ("Outline of County Organization at All Levels"), 201
Xiang Jianying 項建英, 230
xiangyue 鄉約 (village compacts), 22
Xiao Lang 肖朗, 230
Xiaozhang 蕭張, 172
Xie Bizhen 謝必震, 240
Xie Jiasheng 謝家聲, 240
Xie Songgao 謝頌羔 (Z. K. Zia), 9, 91, 99, 101, 102, 103, 105, 108; biography, 91–93, 92n5; impression of

commoners, 103, 106, 107; "Jidutu yu aiguo" ("Christians and Patriotism"), 107; *Lixiang zhong ren* (*My Ideal People*), 92, 107; patriotism of, 107; thoughts on mass education, 104–5; thoughts on religious education, 106; translation work examples, 92, 106–7; "Wo de zongjiaoguan" ("My Religious Views"), 106

xin 心 (mind-heart), 26, 26n23

Xin jiaoyu 新教育 (*The New Education*), 116, 122

Xinghua zhoukan 興華週刊 (*China Christian Advocate*), 115

Xingshi 醒獅 (*Awakening Lion*), 116. See also *guojia zhuyi pai* 國家主義派

Xingzhengyuan 行政院 (Executive Yuan), 132

Xiong Shengan 熊慎幹, 256

Xiong Xiling 熊希齡, 122

Xu Baoan 徐保安, 129

Xu Deheng 許德珩, 94

Xu Dishan 許地山, 240

Xu Yihua 徐以驊, 4, 240

Xu Yongshun 徐雍舜, 196, 209

Xu Zuotong 許佐同, 99

xuanxue pai 玄學派 (Metaphysician School), 118, 119

xueke jianshe 學科建設 (academic discipline building), 230–32

xueshu jiuguo 學術救國 (national salvation through scholarship), 129

Xunzheng shiqi yuefa 訓政時期約法 (*Provisional Constitution for the Period of Political Tutelage*), 125

Yale-in-China Association, 235

Yan Fu 嚴復, 29n29

Yan Yangchu 晏陽初 (Yen, James; Yen, Y. C. James), 90, 91, 91n2, 104, 114, 118, 122, 160, 169, 169n7, 200, 201, 207

Yang Jiang 楊絳, 240

Yang Kaidao 楊開道, 207, 207n38; *Nongcun shehuixue* (*Rural Sociology*), 208

Yang Shuyin 楊樹因: "Yige nongcun shougongye de jiating: Shiyangchang Dujia shidi yanjiu baogao" 一個農村手工業的家庭：石羊場杜家實地研究報告 ("A Rural Handicraft Family: A Report on the Du Family in Shiyangchang"), 214

Yang Xingfo 楊杏佛, 129

Yang Yongqing 楊永清, 239

Yen, James. *See* Yan Yangchu 晏陽初

Yen, Y. C. James. *See* Yan Yangchu 晏陽初

Yenching School of Chinese Studies, 78

Yenching University, 3, 3n8, 94, 227n2, 230, 234n18; academic discipline building of, 231–32; Chengdu campus of, 202, 212, 212n56; CCP and, 203, 205; collaborations with overseas universities, 235, 237; curriculum, 239; Department of Sociology, *see* Department of Sociology at Yenching University; Lei Mingyuan's family and, 210–11; rating of, 235; rural survey of the staff, 204, 206, 209; summer school in Hope Township organized by, 201–2, 210

"Yesu shengping" 耶穌生平 ("The Life of Jesus") (Zhang), 94

"Yige nongcun shougongye de jiating: Shiyangchang Dujia shidi yanjiu baogao" 一個農村手工業的家庭：石羊場杜家實地研究報告 ("A Rural Handicraft Family: A Report on the Du Family in Shiyangchang") (Yang), 214

Yin Shihao 尹士豪, 256

Yin Wenjuan 尹文涓: *Jidujiao yu Zhongguo jindai zhongdeng jiaoyu* 基督教與中國近代中等教育 (*Christianity and Secondary Education in Modern China*) edited by, 6

Ying Fanggan 應方淦, 230

YMCA. *See* Young Men's Christian Association; Young Men's Christian Association in China; Young Men's Christian Association in North America
Young China Association, 37
Young Men's Christian Association, 98
Young Men's Christian Association in China: 145, 146, 163, 177, 181, 178 table 8.1, 180–81 table 8.1; "character-building" as the motto of, 158–59; citizenship education movements, 161–62, 161n67, 163; Clarence H. Robertson and, 151–55, 152n27; establishment of, 151; lecture programs of, 151–57, 152n30; mass education programs of, 159–60
Young Men's Christian Association in North America, 151, 159
Young People's Friend. See *Qingnian you* 青年友
Young Women's Christian Association (YWCA), 178–79 table 8.1, 205–6
Yu Jiaju 余家菊, 116
Yu Jinen 于錦恩: *Minguo zhuyin zimu zhengce shilun* 民國注音字母政策史論, 169
Yu Ke 俞可, 129
Yu Pingbo 俞平伯, 239
Yu Rizhang 余日章 (Yui, David Z. T.), 9, 10, 145, 146, 150, 150n20, 155 table 7.1; as general secretary of the YMCA in China, 157n46, 159–63; as head of the Lecture Department of the YMCA in China, 154–57; citizenship education and, 161–62, 163; education and training of, 146–48, 149, 149n17; educational career, 149, 150; "Jiangyan wei shehui jiaoyu zhi liqi" ("Lecture is a Useful and Effective Instrument of Social Education"), 156; mass education project by, 159–60; patriotism of, 148–49, 156, 158

Yu Wenqing 余文卿, 146
Yu Xianli 余先礪, 133, 136
Yuan Shikai 袁世凱, 156, 157
Yui, David Z. T. *See* Yu Rizhang 余日章
yü-lin ce 魚鱗冊 (Fish-scale Land Registers), 27, 28n25
YWCA. *See* Young Women's Christian Association

Zhang Boling 張伯苓, 154n38
Zhang Dongsun 張東蓀, 239
Zhang Guandao 張貫道, 93
Zhang Jiqian 張寄謙, 237
Zhang Junmai 張君勱, 118
Zhang Kaiyuan 章開沅, 3, 4, 228, 229, 237, 242; *Zhong xi wenhua yu jiaohui daxue* (*Christian Universities and Chinese-Western Cultures*) co-edited with Arthur Waldron, 3–4
Zhang Xueyan 張雪岩, 9, 91, 98, 102, 104, 105, 106, 108; biography, 93–95; *Christian Farmer* and, 95–98, 99; elected as member of the Drafting Committee of the Common Program, 94; impression of farmers, 103–4; "Jiao muqin shizi de miaofa" ("Good Ways to Teach Mothers to Read"), 98; patriotism of, 107–8; "'Qiqi' jinian yu benbao" ("Commemoration of the Double-Seventh Incident and the *Christian Farmer*"), 105; "Shi renren dou shizi de haofazi" ("Good Ways to Popularize Literacy"), 98; *Tianjia zhanwang*, 96; "Yesu shengping" ("The Life of Jesus"), 94
Zhang Yaguang 張亞光, 232
Zhang Zhidong 張之洞, 24, 24n19, 25, 30, 149; *Quanxue pian* 勸學篇 (*Encouraging Learning*), 24–25, 25n20
Zhang Zuolin 張作霖, 93
Zhen Yesu jiaohui 真耶穌教會 (True Jesus Church), 182, 252
Zheng Linzhuang 鄭林莊, 196, 209

Zheng Zhenduo 鄭振鐸, 239
zhengqi 正氣 (upright spirit), 120
Zhengqi ge 正氣歌 (*The Song of Upright Spirit*), 120
Zhijiang Daxue 之江大學. *See* Hangchow University
Zhong Rongguang 鍾榮光, 239
Zhong xi wenhua yu jiaohui daxue 中西文化與教會大學 (*Christian Universities and Chinese-Western Cultures*) (Zhang and Waldron), 3–4
Zhongguo gongxue 中國公學 (China College), 112, 113, 131
Zhongguo jiaohui daxue shi yanjiu 中國教會大學史研究 (*Studies in the History of Christian Universities in China*) (book series), 4
"Zhongguo jiaoyu sixiang jianshi" 中國教育思想簡史 ("A Brief History of Chinese Educational Thoughts") (Zhu), 137
Zhongguo Jidujiao jiaoyuhui 中國基督教教育會 (China Christian Educational Association), 115, 135, 187
Zhongguo qingnian dang 中國青年黨 (Chinese Youth Party), 116
Zhongguo Yesujiao zilihui 中國耶穌教自立會 (China Christian Independent Church Federation), 182
Zhonghua jiaoyu wenhua jijin dongshihui 中華教育文化基金董事會 (Chinese Educational and Cultural Foundation), 207
Zhonghua Jidujiaohui nianjian 中華基督教會年鑑 (*China Church Year Book*), 156, 173
Zhonghua Minguo jiaoyu zongzhi ji qi shishi fangzhen 中國民國教育宗旨及其實施方針 (*Aim of Education in the Republic of China and Directions for Its Enforcement*), 123
Zhonghua pingmin jiaoyu cujinhui 中華平民教育促進會 (Chinese National Association of the Mass Education Movement), 90, 122, 160, 200, 201
Zhonghua quanguo Judujiao xiejinhui 中華全國基督教協進會. *See* National Christian Council of China
Zhonghua xuxing weibanhui 中華續行委辦會. *See* China Continuation Committee
Zhonghua xuxing weibanhui zhuyin zimu teweihui 中華續行委辦會注音字母特委會. *See* Phonetic Promotion Committee
zhongtang 中堂 (pictorial central scrolls), 188
Zhongyong 中庸 (*The Doctrine of the Mean*), 64
Zhou Guping 周谷平, 231
Zhou Yichun 周詒春, 154n38
Zhou Zuoren 周作人, 239
Zhu Hengbi 朱恆璧 (Chu, Heng-bi), 84, 85 figure 4.1
Zhu Jingnong 朱經農 (Chu, King), 9, 113, 114, 118, 121, 122, 123, 128, 129, 136, 137, 138, 160; Anti-Christian Movement and, 116–17; biography, 112–13, 113n2; conversion to Protestantism, 115, 116; education and political careers, 129–36; "education of love," 120–21; *Jiaoyu sixiang* (*Educational Thoughts*), 119, 120, 121; *Jindai jiaoyu sichao qijiang* (*Seven Lectures on Modern Educational Thoughts*), 121, 123–28; "Kexue yu zongjiao" ("Science and Religion"), 118–19; on patriotism, 127; on religious education, 117–18; on restoration of education rights, 117; personal education aim, 122; *Pingmin qianzike* (*Easy Chinese Lesson for the Illiterates*) complied with Tao Xingzhi, 122; Three Principles of the People and, 123; "Zhongguo jiaoyu sixiang

jianshi" ("A Brief History of Chinese Educational Thoughts"), 137
Zhu Qihui 朱其慧, 122
Zhu Wenchang 朱文長, 115
Zhu Xi 朱熹 (Chu Hsi), 19, 20, 20n6, 20n7, 58, 64, 65
Zhu Yuanzhang 朱元璋, 20, 22, 23
Zhuo Kangcheng 卓康成, 154n38
zhuyin zimu 注音字母 (National Phonetic Alphabet; National Phonetic Script), 9, 10, 168, 169, 177; CCC's adoption of, 174–75, 176; Chinese Protestants' attitudes towards, 173, 175; circulation of printed materials in, 189–90; development of, 172–73; functions of, 172, 173, 182, 190; patriotism and, 182; pedagogy of, 184–85; PPC and government's communications and collaborations about, 185–87; PPC's efforts to promote, 183–89; previous research on, 169–70; other Christian publications printed in, 188–89, 189n90; Sidney G. Peill's attitude towards, 175–76, 175n38; textbook examples of, 184, 185; training of teachers of, 185; type and typewriters of, 181, 187n73; the Protestant Bible and, 169, 186, 187–88, 189
Zia, Z. K. *See* Xie Songgao 謝頌羔
Zimu pinyin keben 字母拼音課本 (*Phonetic Spelling Book, with Easy Sentences*), 184, 184n64, 184n65
Zongjiao jiaoshou fa 宗教教授法 (*How to Teach Religion*), 106
Zongjiao jiaoyu gailun 宗教教育概論 (*Introduction to Religious Education*), 92, 106–7